"Violence against women is a major health problem for American women. More than 2.5 million women are victims of violence each year. "

- The Office of Women's Health,
U.S. Department of Health and Human Services.

"A total of 22%of women in the United States, a projected 30 million, say that they have been abused by their husbands or partners."

- Gallop Poll Analysis of October 25, 1997
The Gallop Poll survey reports, "53% of the total sample of Americans say that they personally know of such a situation."

"Nearly 1 in 3 adult women experiences at least one physical assault by a partner during adulthood."

-Bureau of Justice Statistics Special Report: Violence Against Women: Estimates from the Redesigned Survey (NCJ- 154348) August 1995, p. 3.

"One out of every four American women report that they have been physically abused by a husband or boyfriend at some point in their lives. Thirty percent (30%) of Americans say they know a woman who has been physically abused by her husband or boyfriend in the past year. "

-Lieberman Research Inc., " Tracking Survey Conducted for the Advertising Council and the Family Violence Prevention Fund," July - October, 1996.

"Nearly one-third of American women (31 percent) report being physically or sexually abused by a husband or boyfriend at some point in their lives."

– Commonwealth Fund survey, 1998

"Nearly one quarter of women in the US, that's more than 12 million women, will be abused by a current or former partner some time during their lives."

-American Medical Association, Chicago, IL Diagnostic and Treatment Guidelines on Domestic Violence

*A Back Pocket Book
From Dreamers Tapestry*

Just

Keep

Dancing

by Susan Brauer

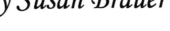

Dreamers Tapestry, Inc.
www.dreamerstapestry.com
Bringing women's creative works into public view
for the enjoyment and benefit of all.

Just Keep Dancing
Published by Dreamers Tapestry, Inc.
PO Box 207
Palos Park, IL 60464
Copyright © 2005 by Susan Brauer

Library of Congress Control Number: 2005905065

ISBN: 0-9745878-0-X

Printed in the United States of America

Back Pocket Books are published by
Dreamers Tapestry, Inc. May 2005.

For Dean, Eric, Warren, Keith, Matthew, Joseph,
and as always Arthur.

A special thanks to Warren and Joyce, who without
their help this book would not be possible.

For those who, in the midst of tragedy and despair, ask, *"How did I get here?"* And also for the others who ask, *"Why does she put up with that?"* Was there ever a choice?

PART 1

"THE ATTIC"

I

Time to go up to the attic and hang my laundry. Ever since I was a child the attic has given me an odd feeling. As a little girl I avoided it unless I had the uninterrupted company of my grandmother. At best it seemed like an uninviting place. Even the steps leading to the attic seemed to pose a barrier, guarding the entrance to a place one should enter with extreme caution or maybe not at all. The width of the steps was very narrow and the angle of the ascent was steep, due to the nine-foot ceilings of the apartment below. The stairs themselves were wood and their edges were worn round from the countless numbers of feet, from before the turn of the century until now, that had trudged up and down them. Attics seem to have been, and are, the best place to hang laundry amongst the crowded conditions of big city tenement life.

The top of the staircase as viewed from the attic level was just a hole in the attic floor. There was no guardrail around it, nothing to grab to steady yourself on ascent or descent. It was as if even that small token of safety was denied in this surrealistic realm of uneasy feelings. Surely the appearance of a railing would break the attic's spell.

The floor of the attic was made of overly worn, wide wood planks, which did not reach to the corners where the roof and floor joists met. This left a perimeter of studs and fragile plaster exposed to any mishap that may occur. Visions were conjured up in my brain of absent-mindedly stepping back, off the wood flooring, and falling through the ceiling to the room below. Even the floor itself had gaps between the planks and areas where the boards bowed and gave under a person's weight. These facts lead to the uneasy feeling that not even the floor could be trusted to keep you safe and sound, that at any given moment your concept of reality could be turned upside down, and you would go crashing into the world below.

The air in the attic had a cedar chest aroma with an underlying musty smell. It was very comforting in a way, and reminded me of trips down the block to the neighborhood grocery store when I was a child. The sweet woodsy smell permeated that place too. With dreams of the sugar confections that I could trade for the quarter clutched in my hand, I would enter the shop and hear the bell tinkle above my head. Sometimes, if Jean, the owner of the store, was busy in her apartment in the back, there would be a few moments of peaceful silence. In those moments I could stand suspended in time, drawing the sweet aroma into my soul, and casually observing tiny pieces of dust turned into gold in the beams of sunlight that streamed through the window and spilled onto the wooden floor of the shop.

The attic could provide the same feelings of complete peace and contentment. However, there were rules. Only after a cautious investigation of creaking boards beneath your feet could you find a place to sit where you would be assured of your safety. And there, watching the dust dancing in the sunlight a feeling of peace and contentment would wash over you. However, these inspired feelings of security only lasted as long as you did not venture out to a new section of the attic floor, opening yourself up to some undefined danger.

Dragging my wicker laundry basket up the steep steps with my wet laundry inside was quite a physical accomplishment. By the time I was at the top step, I was breathing heavily and my heart was pounding in my chest. Taking care to stay as close to the middle of the floor as possible, I made my way to the clothes lines that were strung towards the front of the attic near a tiny window. I'd always wondered what the window was for. It and the one just like it on the opposite side of the house were the only sources of daylight in the attic. Opening them produced next to no breeze and even on hot summer days, they provided very little relief. They were both so tiny that not even a child could squeeze through them. As I stood there laundry in hand, I could visualize the horror of being trapped in the attic with a fire raging in the apartment below, unable to escape and desperately trying to force my body through the opening.

"Oh God, Susan. Get a hold of yourself! "I whispered, and shaking the eerie thoughts off, I proceeded to the task that I'd ventured up here to perform. As the wooden clothespins slid down on the corners of a cold damp work shirt draped over the clothesline, I glanced over at the stacks of boxes stored in the dim corner. A warm feeling of satisfaction filled me as I absentmindedly gazed in the direction of the boxes and remembered that I knew what was in them.

One rainy afternoon, a few months ago, shortly after Jake and I had moved into the downstairs, second story flat that had once belonged to my grandparents, I'd slowly and quietly climbed up the steep attic steps. I'd been full of anticipation like a child about to secretly open a Christmas present, when she knew it was forbidden. The stillness had hung heavy around me as I'd stood at the top of the staircase. Holding my breath, I could hear the sound of my own blood rushing in my ears. Goose bumps had formed on the skin of my arms and the hair on them had stood straight up as I'd shivered.

Rubbing my arms to ward off the sudden chill, I'd slowly scanned the dimly lit recesses of the attic and spotted what I'd been looking for. Tucked neatly under the eaves at the edge of the attic floor were several old boxes and a large gray trunk, all of which I had remembered from the times I'd spent in the attic as a child.

After creeping over to the boxes, I'd sat down beside them on the worn wooden floor becoming aware of the excitement welling up inside of me. Finally, I would satisfy the childhood curiosity that had gnawed at me each time my eyes had fallen on those beckoning boxes of mysteries, and other people's secret things.

Running my fingers over the edges of the nearest cardboard box, I'd carefully lifted the fitted cover. Crumpled pieces of old newspapers, turned brown and discolored with age, momentarily had come to life, slowly spreading open like the petals of a flower, as they had been released from the constraints of the closed box. The dates on the papers were from the thirties and I had stopped my poking and prodding for a moment, to chuckle over a few of the advertisements. When I'd glanced back into the box I'd caught a glimpse of a delicately cut crystal goblet, peeking out of the remaining papers. I'd known in an instant that it had belonged to my Auntie Tillie along with the set of fine bone china dishes and exquisite silverware, each wrapped neatly and hidden away in their own separate box.

Auntie Tillie had been my grandfather's sister, my godmother, and she'd owned some of the most beautiful things that I'd ever seen.

As a child, the quarter that had bought me a bag full of scrumptiously delicious penny candy, from Jean's candy counter, had come from her. Weekly visits to my grandmother's had always included a trip down the steps to the basement flat where my aunt lived, to insure that most precious gift, the silver coin that had been my entry fee to Jean's confectionery paradise. I would enter her apartment where the strong scent of pine filled the air. And while she was off looking for her brown leather change purse, fascinating, unique and beautiful things would catch my attention.

Her front room furniture had been a set of woven white wicker chairs and a sofa, with colorful floral print cushions. An ornately hand carved wood player piano had sat opposite the furniture against one of the living room walls. Sometimes just for fun, she would play the piano for me. She would slip a roll of music into a compartment, hidden by small sliding doors in the front of the piano, pump the pedals, and share the magic with me of a piano that could move its keys and play lovely music all by itself. I would marvel at the music flowing unbidden out of the instrument. At times, I would envision a ghostly presence sitting in her lap, caressing the keys, and imagine it to be the real source of the piano's melodic tones.

On a shelf, high up, not far from the piano, had been an intricately etched, large crystal flower basket. Even in the meager daylight that had filtered through the basement windows, it had seemed to shimmer and glow. Inside it, arranged in a perfect bouquet, had been twelve gaily-colored glass tulips. The reds, pinks, and yellows brightly contrasted the green glass tube stems and perfectly formed green glass leaves. From the front room I'd been able to see a large, Tiffany type, leaded glass lamp made of variegated shades of green milk glass that had been centered on her dining room table. It had been that crystal basket and leaded glass lamp which had initiated my longing and passion for beautiful things made of glass.

Auntie Tillie had been married for almost thirty years to my Uncle Nick and then had been widowed almost that long. He'd died before I was born, of some exotic sounding disease called Dropsy, and though I'd never known him, my head had been filled with stories about him from as far back as I could remember. It had been told to me that he'd been very good to my aunt and had kept her in fine style, and she'd adored him. He'd been a collection man for Al Capone, a dubious occupation at best, however, my aunt could believe no wrong when it came to her Nick. Even many years later when I knew her, she would always speak of him with love and deep respect. They'd never had any children, and after his death, she had never remarried.

Suddenly, an ugly memory brought me back from the past. Standing there with a wet shirt in my hand and the sound of rain pelting the tiny attic window, sadness and anger flashed like lighting inside of me. It was so awful and so unfair! I was fourteen when it had happened. I remembered sitting in study hall, in the early afternoon…

SUSAN BRAUER

❧ II ❧

Lifting my drowsy eyes from my geometry book I noticed a slip of paper being handed to the class monitor. Sister read the note, glanced up at me and met my stare. With a small gesture of her hand she motioned me up to the front of the room. Quietly she whispered that the principal wanted to speak to me immediately. Fear shot through me leaving a feeling of tingling in my fingertips and toes.

"Have I done something wrong?" I asked myself. Frantically I searched my mind as my footsteps echoed down the empty hallway to the principal's office. I couldn't think of anything.

The self-assurance of my complete innocence made me feel a little better, however, an underlying feeling of fear and apprehension still remained. Entering the reception area of the principal's office, the principal's assistant invited me to sit down while she went to tell Sister Dominci that I'd arrived. She returned in an instant and as she bade me to follow her, the look of concern on her face rekindled my fear.

"What's going on?" I nervously thought, as I entered the principal's office, the inner sanctum of catholic school discipline.

By her very presence, Sister Dominici, commanded a young woman's respect and attention. She was firm yet kind in her dealings with the students and she was one of the strongest and most self-assured women I have ever known. She ran the all girl school that I attended with an iron fist and a golden heart and I liked her. Immediately on entering the room I sensed sister's air of concern, compassion, and something else that I couldn't identify. Instinctively I sensed that something bad had happened to someone close to me, and the thought raced through my mind, "Please God, don't let it be my mother!"

With total control, Sister calmly walked over to me and putting a firm hand on my shoulder said softly and gently, "Susan, I have some sad news for you. Your Auntie Tillie has passed away and your mother is coming to school to pick you up in a few minutes. I would like you to go to your locker and get your things. I'll take care of informing the teachers of your afternoon classes that you won't be in attendance. Don't worry about homework for the next few days. You can make that up when you return. Come straight back to the office with your things and wait for your mother here. Don't stop to chat with anyone on the way. You wouldn't want to keep your mother waiting, would you?"

With that, she took my hand and gently patted it, and with genuine concern, tried to console me saying, "You know that you have my deepest sympathy for your loss." Mixed emotions of relief, sadness, and curiosity whirled inside of me.

"How did she die? Was it a heart attack?" I asked.

"I don't know the details but I'm sure your mother will explain everything to you when she gets here. Now go and get your things from your locker and hurry back." Something in her demeanor suggested that she wasn't being fully honest with me. She was holding something back.

Sister kindly but firmly led me to the door, indicating that there would be no more discussion and it was time to do what I'd been told.

Rushing through the hallway to my locker I thought, "Poor Auntie Tillie, it probably was a heart attack like her brother, Uncle Pete. That's a quick way to go. At least she hadn't been sick before she died."

I'd known what that was like. Just a few short years before, I'd watched my grandparents, both of whom I'd loved very much, slowly die. It was hard for us all, especially for my mother. The nightmare had started with Grandma. At one of our bi-monthly family get-togethers at my grand-parents flat, Momma had noticed that my grandmother was slurring her speech and slightly dragging her left foot. Then followed the slow but certain devastation of a strong-willed woman, by a parade of small but potentially deadly strokes, which left her speechless and an invalid.

During Grandma's last days, she and Grandpa had lived at our house and my mother had tried to take care of them as best as she could. However, the responsibility of two parents and a full time job had been tough to juggle. Then the inevitable had happened, a massive stroke. As the emergency technicians prepared to wheel my grandma out of our house on a gurney, while Momma was saying goodbye, I'd looked into my grandmother's eyes and had seen such enormous sadness there, that it left a permanent ache in my heart. My mother had stroked her head while my grandma cried as the gurney rolled out of the front door and into the waiting ambulance. In less than a week she'd died.

And without my grandmother, his life long friend, my grandfather had given up on life and followed his wife less than six months later. It seemed as if he had willed himself to waste away both mentally and physically and it had broken my heart to have helplessly watched it happen.

"At least Auntie Tillie was spared that." I thought as I tried to shake the remembered pain away. She was seventy-six years old and still worked hard everyday. She was a scrubwoman and every night washed the floors in a high-rise office building downtown. She said that she loved her job, but somehow, I could never imagine why. Incredibly punctual, she even caught the same CTA bus to and from work, which was a real feat considering that a different bus passed the same city corner every one and a half minutes.

The feeling that something wasn't quite right again poked into my thoughts, and again I pushed it aside. "Susan, sometimes you think too much!" I chided myself.

I turned my attention to getting to my locker and back to the principal's office as fast as I could, so that I would be ready for my mother when she came to pick me up. Arriving back at the office, I sat down and waited for her. After a few minutes of looking out of the window, I could see the bronze painted '60 Chevy pulling up to the glass front doors of the school. I gathered my purse, coat, and a few schoolbooks together, told the assistant principal that my mother was here, and bounded down the hallway, out the doors, and into the front seat of my mother's car. Leaning over I gave Momma a hello kiss on her cheek. God, how I loved her! She was my mother and she was my friend.

I was the baby of the family. There were three daughters and I was separated by six years from my sister Claudette, and eight years from my sister Carole.

From the age of eleven it was as if I were an only child. Both of my sisters were married by then, and since, I've had the house and my mother, all to myself, and we've spent many a quiet night together.

My dad was non-existent during the weekdays of my life. The bar was his first stop after work and the only time that I saw him was on weekends when he did his chores and puttered around the house. In the evenings he liked to sit on a barstool at the neighborhood tavern, preferring the company of drunks to the company of his wife and daughters. Sometimes late in the evening, when he came home, he would plant a sloppy, drunken kiss on my cheek to say goodnight. It was a well-intended act of affection, but the thought of it turned my stomach.

Drunk or sober my dad was always very kind to me when I was sick, holding my hand and checking my forehead for signs of a fever. However, I'd learned early not to expect that you ever came first in his life. One of my earliest memories was of my mother sitting at the kitchen window in the old apartment that we used to live in, staring at the bar just a short distance across the street. Tears streaming down her face, she would wait for hours for my father to walk out of the tavern door and come home to her. But he never came. At least, not until after we were all fast asleep.

He used to tell the three of us how beautiful we were and how he loved us. But I can still remember the way I felt when I had called the tavern one night, hoping to entice him to come home, and I'd heard his voice in the background, like some trite country western song, say, "Tell them I'm not here." After more than thirty years, my mother had long since given up on any hope of things getting better between them. And now, as a teenager just starting to date, I swore that I would never marry a man who drank like my father.

So, I had my mother all to myself. She worked in a factory that made band-aids, gauze pads and other medicinal products, and when she came home from standing on a concrete floor all day, she was sometimes too tired to cook. When that was the case, we would order food from the neighborhood pizza parlor. They had the greatest cheeseburgers and homemade fries, and they would deliver them right to our door. In the evening, we would sit in front of the television, savoring each delicious morsel like cheeseburger connoisseurs, and watching "Secret Agent", "The Prisoner", "Star Trek", and many other alluring mysteries and flights of fancy. And sometimes, my mother would talk to me, not like a mother to a teenage daughter, but like one woman to another. Friends. Those were the moments that I treasured most of all.

"Hi Momma! What happened to Auntie Tillie? Did she have a heart attack or something?" I blurted out, as I reached over and tossed my books onto the back seat of the Chevy. Settling down in the front seat beside her, I turned and caught a look of apprehension on her face. Then I noticed that her normally crystal clear, deep-set, green eyes were red and puffy as if she had been crying hard for a long time.

"Gee", I thought to myself, "I didn't know that she and Auntie Tillie were so close."

She hesitated as she looked off into the distance, as if searching for just the right words to answer my question.

"You haven't heard anything from your friends at school about it? Nothing from the radio?" She softly asked. Confused by her inquiries, I slowly shook my head.

"Good, I'd hoped that I could reach you before you heard anything. It would have been terrible for you to have learned what had happened like that." A quick look of relief passed across her face but almost instantly it was replaced by a look of great sadness, then revulsion and pain.

"Momma, what's wrong?" A cold feeling of fear chilled me like a gust of winter wind. Tears began to show in my mother's eyes, a sight that frightened me further. My mother prided herself in being a strong woman and emphasized the fact by seeing to it that tears were rarely shed in her life. Now, as the tears slowly and silently began to run, first one than another, down the cheeks of her face, she cleared her throat and began.

"Two policemen knocked on your sister, Claudette's, door this morning about ten o'clock. They started to ask her a lot of questions about Auntie Tillie. When did Claudette see her last? Had she seen or heard her come home from work last night? Was she at home now? Since Claudette and

Mick live in the flat upstairs from Auntie Tillie they figured that she might be able to answer their questions.

Claudette answered, that she'd seen Auntie Tillie yesterday, sometime in the early afternoon before she'd left for work. Claudette hadn't heard her come in after work last night. She very rarely did. She supposed that Auntie Tillie was at home downstairs, as she usually was, at that time of the morning. Then one of the policemen said that no one was answering the door of the downstairs flat. He asked Claudette if she had a key so they could check and see if her aunt was inside and possibly needed some help.

Your sister got frightened and asked what the questions were all about. The other policeman told her that an old woman had been found dead early this morning, a few houses up the block. One of the neighbors who'd been at the scene had suggested to the police that from the clothing on the body and the style of the old woman's hair, it might be Tillie Kramer. And she showed the police the way to Auntie Tillie's flat."

Up to this point in her story, my mother had to pause every few sentences, to sigh and to keep as controlled as possible, wiping away her tears with a tattered tissue as soon as they began to pool in her eyes. But now, as she began again, the tears started to flow hard and the sighs changed to small sobs during which, at times, she could hardly speak.

"Upset with what the policemen said, Claudette asked why the neighbor hadn't told them whether the dead woman was her aunt or not? 'Surely, after fifty years of living in the neighborhood anyone would know who she was.' She'd told them. Then, hesitating and looking slightly uncomfortable, one of the cops had asked Claudette if she would like to sit down. He must've figured that she would get upset, and he didn't want a very pregnant woman passing out in shock. After she sat down on the sofa, he gave a short, blunt, summary of the horrible details. It seems that the woman, whose body had been found a few houses away, had been beaten beyond recognition. Her attacker had used something heavy, probably a lead pipe, so it was important for Claudette to help the police determine if the murder victim was her aunt or not.

Well, that piece of information shook your sister up! She told the police that she didn't have a key to the down stairs flat. Only Aunt Lollie had that, and they would have to call her for it. And then, do you know what happened? Those two cops asked your pregnant sister if she would go downtown to the morgue to view the body for identification! Can you believe that? Thank God she had the presence of mind to call her doctor who'd said 'No way'!"

My mother's anger and outrage with the police and their blatant disregard for my sister's condition and the possible ramifications of their request, was apparent.

"God knows what a shock like that could do to her and the baby!" After a few seconds of silence, Momma took a breath and continued.

"So they got in touch with Loretta for both the key and the trip to the morgue." My Aunt Lollie was my mother's sister, who at times Momma referred to by her real name, Loretta, however, most of the time she was Aunt Lollie to all of us. It was a loving nickname given to her by my oldest sister when she first began to talk, and it had stuck to my aunt ever since.

As the story unfolded, it was as if I didn't understand the full weight of what was being said. The whole situation was far beyond the experience of a fourteen-year-old child. My mother, who seemed to have recovered most of her composure, went on.

"Loretta came with the key, unlocked the door to the apartment, and let the police inside. Auntie Tillie was not in her flat and we can't locate her anywhere, so it's very possible that she may be the older woman that was found this morning. Aunt Lollie got in touch with me at the factory to tell me what was going on, and then she went downtown to the city morgue to identify the old woman's body. I figured that I'd better pick you up from school as soon as possible. If it is your aunt, the minute that Loretta makes the identification it will be all over the news. I wanted you to hear it from me first, not from the radio or the TV."

Feeling that she had given me enough details for the time being, Momma said, "Let's go home and wait for Loretta's call." and started the Chevy up. I stared at her and nodded my head absentmindedly in agreement. It was all too impossible for me to grasp.

"It's not going to be her," I thought.

"No one would murder an old woman like her. We're going to find out it's all a big mistake, and then all this fuss will have been for nothing." I reassured myself as we both sat silently while we drove home, each in our own thoughts, both secretly hoping that all this would turn out to be some kind of misunderstanding, and nothing more.

Arriving at the house with my mother in the early afternoon on a weekday added to my feelings of unreality about the situation. She never stayed home from work, not even when she was sick, and it seemed strange to be walking up the steps to the front door with her beside me at that time of day. It seemed to reinforce the idea that all that was happening was somehow unreal, and that everything would turn out to be all right in the end. The every day act of driving the car had temporarily drawn my mother's thoughts away from the pain of the present situation. The ride had produced a calming effect on both of us. My mother's tears had stopped and she appeared to have regained her composure as we entered the front door. Quietly, we walked through the front room, the hallway, and into the kitchen. I silently sat down at the kitchen table to keep my mother company as she busied herself with daily tasks, and to wait.

I sat in the kitchen, watching my mother go through the reassuring ritual of preparing dinner even though it wasn't even 2 o'clock. The familiarity of the task seemed to give us some comfort and momentary relief from the fear, anxiety, and impatience to know the truth, which ebbed and flowed like waves inside of each of us. The conversation between my mother and me was devoted to small talk, the kind that we had almost everyday. Comments about her job and my school day passed between us, however, unlike other days, today they sounded forced and contrived.

Suddenly, the front door bell rang. I sat frozen, motionless in my chair, not wanting to answer the door, knowing that it was my Aunt Lollie and reluctant to face the possibility of bad news. My mother sensed my apprehension and without a word, went to answer the door herself.

My Aunt was a "tough cookie". She never had a problem telling anyone exactly the way she felt about any situation, and Momma said that she had been the same when she was a child. As young girls, even though my mother was the older of the two, when they were out and about in the city together, Loretta was the one who interfaced with the outside world, asking a stranger for directions or a bus driver when their street was coming up. Self-expression was her forte, and she gave the impression that she was as strong as steel, tough as nails. I never saw a tear fall from her eye. A seventeen-year bad marriage to a husband who didn't hold a job for long, and went on prolonged alcoholic binges, seemed to have toughened her up even more.

Even when one of his binges had culminated in some woman sprawled out, in a drunken stupor, on my aunt's front door step at 6:00 o'clock in the morning, she didn't cave in. With the woman loudly calling out my uncle's name, just in time for the entertainment of the neighbors on their way to work, she held her head up high, hardened her heart, and resolved to be rid of him. This she did after secretly and painstakingly saving every dime she could. And in the end, when the divorce was final, she had the police forcibly remove him from their home when he inexplicably refused to budge from the living room sofa.

She was tough! So the sight of her, as she walked with my mother into our kitchen where I still sat, was a shock. Her eyes were red and swollen, but eerily dry. Not uttering a sound, she slowly walked over to the kitchen table and wearily sank down into the kitchen chair. She immediately lit a cigarette while my mother got her a soda from the refrigerator. She inhaled deeply and then blew the smoke out in one long breath, the kind that comes when you are trying to relax yourself before you have to face something extremely unpleasant. I knew before she even got the words out that the old woman found this morning beaten to death, was my aunt. There was white-hot lightning in the pit of my stomach when the implications of what that meant started to flash in my mind.

"It's her Dorothy!" As she spoke those words I could hear her breathing becoming raspy and labored. Her emotions were rising up in her chest and then into her throat, not allowing the air to pass, strangling her as she fought to get my mother's name out. Still the tears did not flow. She slowly took a few breaths trying to relax the constriction in her throat so that the words could come out less painfully.

A little bit more under control she started again, but she breathed slowly and deliberately as she talked, her breath sometimes whistling in her chest. It sounded as if she was breathing under a great weight.

"It's been over fifteen years since I've cried. I

even thought that I had lost the ability, it's been so long, but I found out how wrong I was. I stood in the morgue. The dead body lay in front of me on a gurney, covered with a sheet. Trying to prepare myself for what I was going to see, I was telling myself that it might be bad but with what I've seen in my life, I could handle it. The coroner had tried to lessen the shock by telling me ahead of time that the blows to the woman's face had been so vicious that it might be difficult to make an identification. But it wasn't enough. Nothing he could've said could've ever been enough!"

The last few words got stuck in her throat, and she forced them out, determined to finish the sentence. She took another long pause, breathing in gasps until the air passed more easily through her throat. Then she began again.

"The homicide detective was standing next to me when the coroner pulled the sheet back, exposing the body from the shoulders up. Now that I think back, he must have been there just in case I got woozy."

"Oh my God, Dorothy, you should've seen what that animal did to her!" Slowly and with great emotional effort, she described, as best she could, the horror of what she'd seen just a few hours before.

All the bones in the woman's face had been completely shattered, and in places, the skin of her face looked as if it had exploded under the force of the heavy blows, leaving the underlying meat and muscle exposed. The flesh that was left was deeply discolored with such dark bruising that the blue had mostly turned to black. Her cheeks and the bridge of her nose were crushed and sunken in, and her top lip had been partially ripped away, the remnants of which was left dangling over jagged broken teeth, all a testimony to the savagery of the beating.

Aunt Lollie said that as she stood there, revulsion shooting up from her stomach into her mouth, her eyes riveted to the corpse's face, now and for eternity frozen in a ghastly grimace, she had thought "So this is what it means to be beaten beyond recognition!"

In self-defense against the horror that lay before her, her eyes were drawn to a wisp of waved hair lying softly at the woman's temple, and just below it, a small section of the side of the woman's face that had somehow escaped the carnage. As her eyes ran over its shape and texture, it whispered familiarity into my aunt's mind, and in an instant she knew that the sad, lifeless bundle of abused flesh on the table in front of her was my Auntie Tillie. And the tears began to flow.

"I knew it. I just knew it was her! And then every tear that I haven't cried for all of these years came rushing out of me and I couldn't stop them! The detective tried to comfort me while he led me out of that place and into a small room with a few chairs and a soft light. He kindly asked me if I would like a cup of coffee and then left me alone with my grief for awhile."

My mother and I sat quietly, not interrupting her, intuitively identifying her need to tell her story from beginning to end, every detail, no matter how painful. Perhaps she felt that the very telling of the story, sharing it with those she loved, would help to lighten the load and ease her pain.

She continued telling us that when the detective came back into the room he'd explained that he needed to ask a few questions before she left and maybe something she would know might help the police to find the killer.

"During the questioning, I told the detective that I'd been worried about Auntie Tillie's safety for quite awhile. She walked from the bus stop about 12:30 every night, on her way home after work. She and I had many conversations about how concerned I was, a woman alone on the dark city street going passed the park and all. I'd begged her to let me pick her up when she got off the bus, but she wouldn't hear of it! Auntie Tillie had told me that she knew how to take care of herself. She would walk down the middle of the street, staying away from the shadows and the bushes. If some strange man were to follow her home, she would walk quickly to the nearest house and say, 'Don't bother me, I live here!' and then walk down the gangway between the houses, and out of his sight. When it was safe, she would continue down the gangway to the alley in back of the houses, and walk to her own house as fast as she could.

'Besides', she would say, 'who would want to bother an old lady like me, anyway.' And she would laugh. I should've never let her convince me that she would be all right, never! When I'd heard where the body was found I knew that she'd done exactly what she had said she would do if someone followed her. But this animal knew that she didn't live in the house, of the gangway that she walked into. He followed her and killed her! But, why?

Why an old woman who never hurt a soul? She never carried large amounts of money, only her change purse and that was still in her pocket!"

With a strange detachment, I noticed that there were still no tears in my Aunt Lollie's eyes, even though her face showed the misery she was in.

"You know, between the tears that I cried at the morgue and the time that I cried on my way here, I'm all cried out. No more tears left, only this awful weight on my chest that won't let me breathe. Every time I close my eyes I see her as she was on that slab, and no matter how hard I try I can't stop seeing her that way." Letting out a heart-wrenching sigh, she proceeded to tell us the rest.

"The detective said that her assailant might be someone from the neighborhood. The police knew that the murderer was a white, dark haired man about 35 to 40 years old. They knew this from the skin found under her fingernails. He probably had grabbed her from behind as she hurried along the walkway beside the garage, to get to the alley to get home safely. She had tried to fight her attacker off, because her fingernails were cracked, ragged and bleeding. Two of them had been completely torn off during the struggle. She must have left scratches all over him. But the murderer stopped her from struggling when he beat her in the face with a pipe." My aunt paused for a second and then went on.

"What a horrible way for her to die! She was left, by the killer, on the ground next to the garage, lying on her back. Her blood was splattered across the side of the garage from the force of the blows, and she wasn't dead when he was done! He left her to drown in her own blood!

What sickens me most is that her skirt and slip were pulled up over her waist and her undergarments were pulled down. He probably sexually assaulted her or was in the process when he was scared away. She was a seventy-six year old woman who had been widowed for forty years, for God's sakes! For that to have been the last thing for her to have gone through as she lay dying is unbearable to think of!"

❧ III ❧

Suddenly, a deafening clap of thunder jolted me back into the present, and the lightning flashed brightly through the little attic window. Startled, with my heart racing, I regained my bearings and took a few slow deep breaths and tried to calm down. The rain was pelting the roof making a low soft drumming sound and I laughed awkwardly, partly from nerves and partly from relief. I was alone in the house and the frightening memories made me feel uneasy. I fought to keep my imagination from running away with me. I saw the laundry basket on the wooden floor in front of me and I remembered what I had been doing when I'd gotten lost in old and scary memories. With a shaking hand, I reached down into the basket for another of Jake's work shirts to hang on the line, when the phrase, "…the killer was probably some one in the neighborhood…" flitted through my mind. Now that I lived in the apartment above the flat that used to be my Auntie Tillie's, that phrase at times really terrified me. It was only four and a half years since her death and they had never caught the killer. He was still out there somewhere, a crazy man who would probably kill again. I guess it was good in some ways that Jake would never allow me to go out of the house without him. He was overly jealous it was true, and we did fight about it a lot. But in this case, it did provide me with some degree of safety.

In this old, city neighborhood there was

certainly no shortage of odd, eccentric, and sometimes scary people. A middle-aged man named John lived just two houses down and across the street from me. As a young man, he had lived in the flat with his mother until the authorities had taken her away to the county psychiatric facility from which she had never returned. My grandmother had said that the woman used to roam the streets of the neighborhood with several house bricks in a cloth shopping sack. She had been trying to hide and protect herself from fictitious gypsies in a big long black car, who she thought wanted to do her harm. After several loud and threatening encounters with passersby, who she swore were really the gypsies in disguise, she was reported as a public nuisance and taken away.

After that, John had remained a recluse in the second floor apartment, and since I'd recently moved into the neighborhood, I'd seen first hand, that he ran a close second to his mother's insanity. Looking out my front door and just a little up and to the left, I could see John's front room windows. The blinds were always closed tight against the outside world. And when gazing at his windowpanes, I could make out the outlines of several light gray cardboard blotches taped to the inside of his windows. These were images of people that he'd cut out from the front of cereal and soap detergent boxes and hung in the windows much the same as people place pictures of ghosts and goblins in their windows for Halloween. With one exception, the faces of these two dimensional people were turned in so that they could stare into his apartment, not out for the amusement of the rest of the world. Every so often, I would see him pull open a tiny space between the blinds as if he was taking small peeks out at the cardboard people who were looking in at him. And then in a split second the blinds would snap shut, only to be followed a little later by another quick peek. Once, while I was buying a loaf of bread from the neighborhood store, Jean the shopkeeper had remarked to me that John was harmless but at times a real nuisance. He would sometimes wander into the store and engage in a lengthy conversation with the woman ironing her laundry on the Tide box or with the eye on the Maybelline eyeliner package. Once engaged, it was very difficult to get him to leave the store, and as you can imagine his behavior was not exactly conducive for business.

Just last week, Jean had mentioned that John had been in the shop and became so engrossed in a conversation with the Maybelline eye, that the only way she was able to convince him to leave the store was to cut out the eye from the label of the makeup package and give it to him. Ecstatic, he had lovingly took it into his cupped hand and delicately placed it in the pocket of his sweater, taking it back out every few steps to chat with as he left the store. Sad but scary.

John was known to everyone in the neighborhood, so once my aunt's body was found it didn't take long for the police to pay him a visit. He was held for questioning at police headquarters for several days, but then he was released back to his apartment and the neighborhood, to the dismay of the neighbors who were sure that he was the killer. However, no evidence had ever surfaced that warranted his arrest and to this day he still lived in the same apartment that he grew up in, just across the street.

The thought of him sitting, at this very moment, in his apartment lost in his conjured up dream world while I hung laundry in the attic less than two hundred feet from his door, was really creepy.

Growing up in an old Chicago neighborhood tends to make a person cautious and fearful of strangers. As far back as I can remember, Momma impressed into our minds the little girls golden rule of city life, "Never talk to strangers!" As children, there were rules for my sisters and me, when playing outside or walking down the street to the store or a friend's house. Momma would tell us "You should never walk close to bushes along the sidewalk or cars that are parked near the curb. Someone could grab you if you aren't careful. Don't be fooled by strangers in cars asking for directions, often it's just a ploy to lure you close to the car so that they can pull you into it. Be careful when you are outside playing, and don't trust strangers!"

These were the laws of survival and I followed them to a tee. Even as an adult, I followed those rules so that I would be safe when I was out and about in the neighborhood. Auntie Tillie's fate had certainly put my mother's rules and warnings from my childhood, in a very serious light. She had not been careful enough.

Despite warnings and horror stories from parents who love them, children sometimes just don't listen. My two sisters came close to falling prey to some sick bastard in a car when they were little children, playing just down the block from where I was now hanging my wet laundry.

Claudette was five and Carole was seven. My grandmother was watching them while my mother worked, and they had been playing down the street from the house, just at the end of the block by the old Methodist Church. Thinking about it now, as I hung another pair of pants on the line, it seemed so strange. They had been playing just a short distance from where my Auntie Tillie would violently lose her life fifteen years later. Maybe some places tend to have bad things happen in or around them.

Carole had looked up from the game that she and Claudette were playing and noticed a man sitting in a car near the curb a few yards from the two of them. The man had called to the both of them and gestured for the girls to come over to the car. When they wouldn't budge, he'd gotten out of the car and started to place nickels on the curb leading to the car, trying to entice them to move closer to the open car door. Claudette had been just outside of Carole's reach and being the younger and therefore the less apprehensive of the two, the sight of the nickels had easily drawn her towards the open car door. As Claudette slowly moved closer to the nickels and to the car, Carole had called for her to come back, but she didn't seem to listen. Being older and wiser, Carole had wanted to run up and grab Claudette but she was afraid that if she did, she would be close enough for the stranger to grab them both. Just as Claudette had been a hair's breadth from within the man's reach, my grandfather had appeared out of nowhere, shouting their names and loudly ordering them to get away from the car. With that the man had slammed the car door shut, and peeled away from the curb. If my grandfather had started looking for them one minute later than he did, God knows what would have happened to them. It's funny, when you think of it. Just sixty seconds, a very small piece of time, spent one way or another, can be the pivotal moment of a person's life.

As soon as I'd been able to understand, the story about my two sisters and the stranger in the car was told to me in a very ominous tone with explicit detail. It was meant to frighten me and it did. Especially in light of what had happened to the Grimes sisters... They had been two little girls who lived not far from our flat, and had disappeared one afternoon when they were on their way to the movies. Several weeks later, their bodies had been found in the forest preserve on the outskirts of the city, chopped up in little pieces. As small as I was at the time, I was not spared the details, for my own good. It was thought that the knowledge of so wicked an event might protect me from someday suffering a similar fate.

Standing here, smelling the freshness of the wet clothes filling the air of the attic, I wondered just how many strange people and associated strange stories there were in my childhood. Was the number more than most?

"I can't be that much different from the average woman out there. Surely everyone grows up with nonsense such as that to put up with."

Then I started to recount to myself all the so-called "weirdoes" who had been part of my growing up. Occupying my mind as I continued with the tedious task of laundry hanging, several names and faces whirled in my memory.

"Maybe I should start in chronological order so I don't miss one crazy person. I mean, I would like to do justice to each "nut" that I have had the dubious pleasure of meeting up with in my short, young life." I joked and laughed to myself, "I wouldn't want to leave anyone out! Let's see, I think that Eagan is the first to come to mind …"

❧ IV ❧

Before I was five, my sisters and I had lived with our parents in a three bedroom flat on the third floor of an apartment building not far from my grandmother's place. The landlord, an old woman named Mrs. Bronsell, lived in the basement apartment with her son, Eagan. He was in his early thirties and a veteran of World War II. My sisters and I had thought that he acted very strangely and were afraid of him. My father used to assure us that Eagan was harmless and would tell us that his strange behavior was due to being "shell shocked" from the war. The expression didn't mean much to me at the time, but I knew that it somehow meant that we should give him some sympathy and understanding. However, "shell shocked" or not, the man was down right creepy.

Outside the back door of each apartment was a rickety wooden porch that was partially enclosed, to provide shelter from the winter's snow and ice, and to keep you dry when it rained during the rest of the year. A large wooden staircase zigzagged down the back of the old brick building from the third floor porch to the second, and then down to a small enclosed cemented walkway just outside the basement flat. It was on the back porch that Eagan used to creep around at night, trying to situate himself in just the right position, to see into our windows through whatever slight slit that might happen to exist between our shades and the window sills of our bedrooms. When my father or mother used to catch him peeping in at us they would chase him away, complain to his mother, and dismiss it by telling us that he was harmless. This mode of behavior never seemed to discourage him, and so it was with much reluctance, that my sisters and I would spend any time in our rooms at night. And when it became necessary to do so, it was always with the frightening knowledge that he would probably be watching every move we made. We weren't even safe from his spying eye in our kitchen, which was where the front entrance to the apartment was. He would sneak into the hallway, crouch down just outside the door, and look through the keyhole. Once I'd gotten an eerie feeling that I was being watched, and when I'd walked over and looked into the keyhole, his eye had been looking back at me. That had scared the hell out of me, and I'd told my mother, but I don't remember that it made any difference.

Having him around was quite an emotional burden for three small girls, and being a peeping Tom wasn't his only perverted pastime. We used the back stairs most of the time, whether we were coming home from school, in from play, or going to and from the corner grocery store to get my mother some milk. Eagan liked to stand very quietly in the corner of the enclosed portion of the first and second floor porches, as deep in the shadows as possible, and silently watch us go by him as we ran up the next set of steps. The enclosures were very narrow and you would have to pass within a foot of him, which was definitely within his reach if he'd wanted to lean forward and grab you as you went by. He never actually touched any of us but the shock of looking up and suddenly seeing him in the shadows, a few inches away towering above you, was very frightening especially at night.

Momma sent us on errands to the store pretty often, and sometimes she would send my two older sisters to get some small thing that she'd forgotten and needed for supper, even in the winter when it was dark early in the evening.

I'd always wondered why she'd done that. Despite all the turbulence of emotion that Eagan caused within us, she would still send us out knowing that we had to come back up those steps. I know that in her heart she'd thought that he was harmless, and maybe she'd thought that we'd exaggerated things because we were children. And she, being a child of the great depression and having recently lived through a world war, might have thought the whole affair worrisome, but insignificant as far as real problems go.

Whatever the reason, her sending us out to face Eagan, time and time again, made it seem like our feelings weren't important and that we were powerless to keep that man out of our innermost fears, and therefore our souls. So we endured him as best we could.

Eagan was the first strange man in my life, but the more I thought about it, the more I realized that strange men were commonplace in my childhood. Several additional peeping Toms have slithered next to our pulled down shades to spy on what was going on inside my family's private places. Even, when we went out to my grandparents' summer cottage in Indiana, we were not free from prying eyes. Not far from the cottage, down an unpaved dirt road, in an old ramshackle house, lived a single middle-aged man named Robert. His right arm and leg were deformed and his speech was slurred and very difficult to understand. He would drag his leg as he walked and his hand was curled, twisted, and held tightly to his chest by an arm that was permanently at a ninety-degree angle. In addition to his physical deformities, his mental competency was questionable. He liked my grandmother and demonstrated it by appearing in front of a screen door or window in the evening, as it got dark. He would stand there staring in at us, not saying a word. This behavior disturbed my grandmother, and when she would notice him out there silently watching us, she would call to him and tell him to go home, that it was late. This gentler tone didn't always work and sometimes she would have to raise her voice and literally chase him away. One summer he'd stopped coming and we were all relieved but curious as to why. Later, a neighbor had told my grandmother that Robert's condition had deteriorated to such a point, he no longer could take care of himself properly, so his sister had taken him to a convalescent home in the city. I didn't feel very much sympathy for him. I only felt relief and peace. At last we could relax at the cottage when night started to fall.

Even when we moved to a new neighborhood disturbing and unpleasant things still happened. We moved just after my fifth birthday. We had a raised ranch built in the Midway Airport neighborhood. It was a new and less dense part of the city, but it didn't lessen the caution that my sisters and I needed in order to stay safe as young women going about their lives in the city.

After I started first grade, warnings about strangers hanging around the school trying to entice little girls into their cars were common occurrences, and continued throughout my elementary education. And despite the move, my sisters and I still had to put up with a neighborhood peeping Tom. Only this one was just the teenage boy who lived next door. Pretty boring, after the caliber of peepers that we'd been used to dealing with.

My sisters were older, thirteen and eleven, and because of the public transportation available, were very autonomous for young teenage girls. Traveling on the bus opened up a completely new set of rules for survival. Especially after what had happened to Roberta, our neighbor's daughter from two houses down. She had a harrowing experience after getting off of the bus one evening. The news of the incident had spread through the neighborhood like wildfire. My mother had said it was best that as many neighbors learned of what had happened as possible, so the women and young girls in the neighborhood would be warned of the danger and be prepared on what to do if the same scenario played itself out again on a new potential victim.

Roberta's terrifying experience began while she was riding home on the city bus after school. She had noticed a man sitting across the aisle staring at her. As the minutes went by, observing his constant stare out of the corner of her eye, she became increasingly uncomfortable. When her stop neared, she was glad to get up and work her way to the front of the bus and away from his prying eyes.

She stood in the front of the bus looking out of the door, getting ready to exit as her street came up. She noticed that it was already dark outside. During the winter months the darkness always came so early. She was relieved as she stepped off the bus and left the man behind.

While the bus pulled away, and the roar and the wind that belonged to it diminished, she became aware of a presence behind her. Casually she looked over her shoulder and not more that ten feet from her stood the man from the bus. He must have gotten off using the bus's rear door! He stood staring, watching her every move. Nervously she turned and hurriedly crossed the street. At first he did not follow, he just stood watching, giving her a brief moment of relief. But then slowly he began to walk in her direction. She had only two and a half blocks to walk before she got to her house, and she thought that if she hurried she could keep well ahead of him. But after half a block, she glanced back and realized that his pace had picked up, closing the gap between them. She sped up every so often breaking into a slow trot when her panic would grow.

Crossing the next street, she started to race down the second block, passed several houses of people that she didn't know. Hearing his footsteps coming up behind her, she turned and took one last look, and saw that he was within a few feet of her. As he passed under the streetlight she could clearly see that he'd pulled down his zipper and exposed himself. Terrified she broke into a full run. Knowing that there was no way that she could reach the safety of her home before she would be within his grasp she bolted up the first set of steps that she came to. Not caring what the people inside would say or do, only seeking a safe place to get away from HIM, she violently banged on the front door of the house screaming, "Let me in! Please, please, let me in!" In less that a second the door flew open and a man, bewildered, disheveled, and in his underwear, stood in the doorway. Seeing her panic, he quickly let her in to the safety of his home. The police were called, but the man who had tormented her had gotten away and disappeared into the night.

Shortly before the incident, the word had gone around the block that there was a "black and white team" working the neighborhood. This sick con game was described as a black man chasing a white woman after she'd gotten off the bus. As she ran down the street, away from her would be attacker, a white man in a car would screech to a stop, open his car door, and tell her to get inside. Without hesitation, she would rush into the car, feeling that she was safe, only to be followed in by the black man as he jumped into the car after her. Then the both of them raped her. My mother had said that, "It goes to show you that you can't trust anyone, not anyone!" The more I think about it the more I believe she was right.

Roberta's assailant had been white, so the police knew that he probably wasn't part of the team. That meant that there were possibly three "crazies" in and around our neighborhood, and my sisters and I had been instructed to be more careful than ever.

Now as a young married woman standing in

what used to be my grandmother's attic, hanging my husband's shirts, I wondered what it would be like to be born a male and not have to worry about such things. What would it be like to walk outside after dark and not always be searching the shadows for some sudden movement or a glimpse of a silhouette lurking there? Not to have to plan your errands for specific times of the day, or have to figure out the safest route on which to walk from the bus stop to your home. Those routes never included paths that led passed parks, bushes, or the local weirdo on the block. It seemed so stifling, but it was necessary. Still, I couldn't help wondering what it would be like to be free from that constant undertone of caution and fear.

Come to think of it, it was kind of ironic that with all the warnings and carefully crafted rules handed down to me as I grew up, none had protected me from the damage that would be caused by an enemy from within. The memory of it still caused me pain and overwhelming embarrassment. I guess since I am listing all the sexual perverts in my life, I'd better list my brother-in-law Mick, too.

❧ V ❧

Mick, more than any other weirdo that I have brought out of the recesses of my childhood to take a look at on such a rainy afternoon, had and still has, the most negative impact on my psyche.

There was a time, while Mick and my older sister Claudette were dating and during the first few years of their marriage, when I viewed him as the brother I never had. He'd started dating my sister when I was nine and he was always very kind to me and seemed so cool in a tough guy kind of way. They would take me to the drive-in movies. And while on the way, driving in his Studebaker through the warm, breezy summer twilight, my sister would sit very close to him and shift the gears of the car as he drove, and I would sit in the back seat feeling very important and special to be going on their date with them.

Later, as a frightened teenager, Mick was the person that I had called on the phone for help when the one and only violent argument that I'd ever witnessed between my mother and father, had abruptly erupted. I'd been in my bedroom with my door shut, doing homework, when I'd heard shouting through the door. All at once, I recognized my father's voice screaming words that I didn't understand and Momma's cries.

"Irv don't! Stop it!"

I opened my bedroom door and was horrified by the sight of my father throwing my mother into the upright piano in the front room, just across from the doorway where I stood. I could hear a jangle of notes from the piano wire that vibrated inside the instrument as my mother was slammed into it. Daddy was in a drunken rage and Momma was whimpering in shock and fear. Again he roughly grabbed her and threw her against the chair by the draped picture window.

This was incomprehensible to me! How could this be happening? My father had never been a violent man; he had never even spanked us. He had recently been very quiet when he came home from the tavern, and any comments that he had made as he sat and ate his supper had been bitter, almost venomous. His nasty attitude had caused me to stay clear of him when he had come home at night, but I never dreamed he would do something like this!

Terribly frightened, I had closed the bedroom door and locked it. Shaking, I called Claudette and Mick's house and frantically begged Mick to come over and stop all the insanity. He came as soon as he could, but in the time it took him to arrive the argument had stopped, and the house was eerily silent. My father had packed a suitcase and was sitting on the back porch drunk and sobbing. My mother, who often said, that she would never put up with a man who pushed her around, had thrown him out of the house. Although she didn't stop him when he came sullenly and silently back into it in the early morning light, my mother punished him in her own way. She didn't speak to him or even acknowledge his existence for a full six months, a feat that never has ceased to amaze me. When she did start talking to him again, you could tell that something was missing, something had died and it would never be the same between them again.

When Mick had come in through the front door that night, I had felt safe. I knew that my father wouldn't dare start anything with him there, and that everything would be all right. In my eyes, he had become my knight in shining armor, my brother and trusted defender. Shortly after that things changed.

I'd started dating Jake when I was fifteen years old. He was sixteen and he didn't get to use his mother's Corvair very often. Because he didn't have a car of his own, we used to take turns going to each other's houses to watch TV. Jake lived in an older part of the city, and it wasn't very safe for a young girl to take the bus alone through that part of town. My mom was having a family get together at our house and Jake had called and asked if I would come over for the evening. I asked my mother if she could drive me over to Jake's. Mick overheard, and volunteered. He said that he'd wanted to finish his beer first and then he would gladly give me a ride.

Mick drank a lot. I never saw him really drunk, but generally, by the time whatever celebration we were celebrating had come to an end, he was always feeling pretty good. It bothered me as we got into the car that he might have had too much to drink and drive, but I figured that Momma wouldn't let me go with him if she felt that there was any danger. So I got into the car and away I went. Lost in my own thoughts as I looked out the window, it took me awhile before I realized that we were going the wrong way. We were not on our way to Jake's house. Instead of heading toward the older, more densely populated part of the city, we were going out of the city, towards the prairies, trees and the seclusion of the forest preserves.

"Hey Mick, I think that we are going the wrong way. I don't think this is the way to Jake's." I said.

"Yeah," he replied. "I know. It's a round about way of getting there but I like this way better. It's prettier. Let's just take our time." And he patted my shoulder.

There was something odd about his manner that made me feel uncomfortable. I turned away from him, looked out the window and became aware of how isolated the road we were on was. No other cars had passed us for awhile. The trees and brush pushed up tightly against the roadside, and the blue sky was blocked from my view as the branches of the trees reached up and over the road, choking out the sunlight. And then I thought to myself, as I shivered.

"This is the place where young girls are brought to be molested or raped, and sometimes killed. Their bodies are dumped in the thick undergrowth, like those two little girls who disappeared in the city when I was a kid." Mick interrupted my thoughts.

"You know", he cooed, "I have always been very fond of you." As those words fell on my ears, the hair on the back of my neck started to rise up. I sat silent and still, my eyes riveted to the view out of the car window, trying to push down the feeling that something was very wrong.

"I feel that we have gotten very, very close, as close as if we were brother and sister. And I think that we should act as if we were brother and sister. Don't you think? See, just like brother and sister." He cooed again. He spoke the words slowly, and his breathing had become heavy.

It was clear that he wanted some response from me, for me to turn around and comment on the things that he just said. Yes, we were like brother and sister, but there was a certain underlying tone in his voice that made me feel very uncomfortable. Confused and uncertain of what I was going to say, awkwardly I turned toward him. Any response, that I might have been about to express, stuck in my throat. Shock and disgust were my reactions to what had fallen into my field of vision. There, in the driver's seat next to me, sat my brother-in-law, with his pants unzipped, exposing his fully erect penis, and definitely enjoying it! I could hear him quietly repeating, "Just like brother and sister…"

Trying not to skip a beat, and not looking at his face, I swiftly turned my gaze back out the window. Inside I was screaming, "Oh God, don't let this be happening!" Outwardly, I spoke as unemotionally as possible, trying to act as if nothing had happened.

"Yeah Mick, it's nice you think of me as your little sister, but it's getting late and Jake is going to wonder where I am." It was a completely unrealistic reaction to an insane situation. As I gazed out the window at the trees and shrubbery silently passing by, the impact of how truly alone we were hit me. I tried to keep my hands from shaking as fear of what my brother-in-law might do next started to take hold of me. His silence seemed like an eternity. We'd passed a few deserted roads and I prayed.

"God, please don't let him pull off the road! Please!"

"Yeah, you're right." He suddenly said. "We'd better get you there." It was as if nothing had happened, but I knew it did, and so did he. I sat there staring out the window and wondering.

"What am I going to do now? Do I tell Claudette? Do I tell Momma? Claudette is pregnant and the stress that this might cause her could make her lose the baby! God, what do I do?"

Thirty minutes later, we were pulling up to Jake's house. From the forest preserve to Jake's front door, I hadn't said a word and I got out of the car without once looking Mick in the face. I just couldn't do it, the embarrassment seemed overwhelming. His Studebaker pulled away from the curb and I ran up to the house where Jake was standing, waiting behind the front screen door. With just one look he knew that something was wrong. I entered his house and the two of us passed quickly by his mother who was drinking a beer in the front room and watching TV. Concentrating on the tube she absent-mindedly said a hello and I returned the greeting, grateful for the opportunity to pass by her without being noticed. I wanted to keep things as much to myself as I could. I needed to figure out what to do.

Jake had the whole upstairs of his parents' house to himself. It had been a separate apartment with a back entrance when Jake's paternal grandmother had lived with them. Jake and his sister were small children then. His mother and grandmother had never gotten along. Jake's father was the only son, a momma's boy, and strong willed Momma did not want to let go. Since she had died Jake's dad had opened up the stairwell inside the house that lead up to the second floor, and Jake was allowed to use the upper floor as his own private place.

"You won't believe what just happened!" I blurted out as soon as we reached the top of the stairs. Then I quickly walked over to Jake's couch and sat down. Embarrassed, I sat for a second with a nervous smile on my face, a curse of mine that rears its ugly head whenever I'm in the midst of a very uncomfortable situation. I searched for the words, and a place to start, as I averted my eyes from Jake's curious stare.

"You have to promise me that you won't get angry and do something stupid. I want to tell you what happened but I don't want you to make a big scene." I said. My hands shook as I spoke these words, and Jake looked more irritated than concerned.

"Tell me what's going on, you're pissing me off!" he said.

Reluctantly, I started from the beginning and outlined the whole disgusting story, rubbing my hands together as I went along, trying to get them warm again and stop them from shaking. It was no use, my whole body was trembling by the time I was finished, and nausea loomed in the pit of my gut as unsummoned images of Mick acting like a "brother" pushed into my thoughts. Jake's reaction was pure anger.

"How could he do that? And you! You don't

seem to be very upset by this. You seem to think it's funny or something!" For the six months that Jake and I had been dating, he'd gotten to know Mick pretty well and considered him his friend. I guess he was taking the whole ugly incident personally and my feelings were getting lost in the shuffle.

"Jake, that's not fair! You know that when I'm really upset about something, I smile. How could you say that? I don't know what I'm going to do! Can't you help me figure it out?" I stared at him waiting for a reply, a comforting word, something.

"You know this whole thing is partially your fault!" he suddenly snapped at me. "You are always running around in front of him in a robe and pajamas, you shouldn't be doing that! Maybe you gave him the wrong idea!"

I couldn't believe my ears. "How could an old chenille bathrobe that went to the floor and flannel pajamas give anybody ideas? It's not my fault and you should know that!"

As I screamed the words at him, the tears began to flow. Intellectually I knew that what I had said in my defense was true, but somewhere deep inside he'd struck a nerve. Part of me was afraid that somehow, without knowing it, I had done something to encourage this thing to happen, but the rest of me knew that it was crap.

He was acting like I was the sexual aggressor in this situation. This is not the reaction that I had expected. Where were the comfort, kindness and understanding that I envisioned receiving once I arrived at Jake's house, as I had stiffly stared out my brother-in-laws car window? This was no safe harbor. This was the Inquisition! Feeling betrayed by this person who supposedly loved me, my anger flared.

"How could you say such a thing?" I hissed in a low seething voice, my eyes riveted to his.

His reaction was as if I'd thrown a bucket of cold water on him. The realization of what his words had implied seemed to momentarily pierce through his self absorbed train of thought. He forcibly pulled me to him, but I was in no mood to feel him close to me in light of his behavior, and the questions it was raising about the person that I thought he was, and the relationship that existed between us. I pushed against him as he tried to bring me closer to him. When he felt my resistance he jerked me to him and held me tightly to his chest, my arms pinned down at my side.

"Wait a minute, wait a minute," he said into my ear as I struggled and tried to break his grasp. "I don't know what I was thinking. You don't have to worry about anything. I'll take care of it all. Come on give me a kiss, and we'll talk about what we have to do to make things right again." He started to kiss my cheek and the doubts that had emerged in my mind, began to fade away.

"He just has some growing up to do." I said to myself. "In time, as he gets older, he will change."

Jake kissed me and sat me back down on the couch, and then orchestrated the plan for how the "situation" would be handled. Jake said that there was no need to tell my mother about the incident, and that he would spare my sister the heartache of finding out the truth about Mick's dastardly deed. That was if and only if, Mick would admit what he had done to Jake and apologize to me, face to face.

"Fuck! He probably was drunk when he did it and is regretting the whole thing right now." Jake said. "I'll get Tom to drive us over to their flat, and we'll settle it tonight!" Tom was Jake's friend since childhood and would do anything for Jake at the drop of a hat. So when Jake called him and explained things, he didn't hesitate to become part of the grand plan.

For me, the thought of facing Mick so soon after the incident was extremely painful. I imagined that the embarrassment would be unbearable, something akin to the dreams that I have had of suddenly being naked in the school parking lot during recess, and then running all the way home trying to cover up my nakedness as I ran.

"Oh God, this is going to be terrible!" I thought to myself.

"Jake, I really don't want to see him right now. Can't we do this another time?" I said as I nervously rolled a shredding piece of Kleenex between the palms of my hands. My hands had started to sweat, and I began feeling queasy just at the thought of the encounter.

"Fuck no, we can't wait!" Jake shouted at me. "You'll have to see him again, sometime, and it might as well be tonight. And besides, he needs to know that he can't pull this shit ever again or next time the whole world will know! And he needs to know that right now!"

Jake was so forceful about it, and so insistent, that I pushed my feelings aside, reluctantly agreed and went along with him and Tom in the car to my sister's apartment. When we got there, I stayed in the car hiding in the back seat, feeling frantic about seeing my brother-in-law again. Mick opened the door to let Jake in, and then, a few long agonizing minutes later, I heard several footsteps shuffling down the buildings wooden front steps.

"Oh God, here they come!" I whispered to myself. Softly, I talked to myself again, "Hold on Susan! You don't have to look him in the face just listen to what he has to say, accept his apology, and it will all be over quickly."

And that is just what I did, as I rolled down the window of the car and he bent down to look in at me sitting there. He delivered a stiff apology entwined with excuses about too much to drink, followed by an oath that it would never happen again. I accepted his apology with a flat dull sounding "OK", and off he walked back up his stairs and into my sister's home. I sat there, feeling as if my world from this day forward would never be the same, and in some ways, I was right.

Jake strutted around the front of the car like the winning rooster after some cockfight, and he and Tom got into the car congratulating each other on a job well done. Sitting in the back seat alone, Jake called back to me, telling me that everything had gone just as planned. My sister hadn't a clue about what was going on, everything had been taken care of and no one else would ever need to know. I could carry on as if nothing had ever happened, and he was sure after his conversation with Mick, that nothing like this would ever happen again. Jake was wrong.

As I continued to hang my laundry on the attic clothesline, the phrase, "just like brother and sister", echoed in my head. I had always wondered about exactly what that had meant. Mick's family was far from what you would call "normal", but was it that far from normal?

Mick's father was a short, fat, bald, quiet man who had seemed nice enough. He had died from a cerebral hemorrhage within the first year or so after Claudette and Mick's marriage. His mother however was a different story. She was an extremely unattractive middle-aged woman, with dyed, greasy jet-black hair. Jaggedly cut short to mid ear, it looked as if she had taken a pair of kitchen shears to it. Her straight chopped hair was combed to the side, and then back behind her ears into a DA (duck's ass), like the popular style that young teenage boys wore. Her face was puffy from way to much alcohol and cigarettes, and her eyebrows were shaved off and replaced by two thick black semicircles, which gave her face the look of some demented drunken clown.

Her wardrobe was entirely male, and consisted of a man's white tee shirt, pair of jeans and shoes. She smoked incessantly, and literally drank beer nonstop from morning 'till night. I could not recall one time that I had ever seen the woman sober. She was a sloppy, disgusting drunk.

Weird stories about her had trickled down to me through my sister. In confidence, she had told me about his mother being some kind of sexual deviate, the knowledge of which shocked us both considering the always socially acceptable, and asexual behavior of our own mother. Mick's mother was supposed to have been a very loose woman while Mick was growing up. On several occasions, her husband and her children had walked in on her at home, while she was drunk and having sex with some strange man she had picked up that day in a bar. That really boggled my mind. A parent's blatant infidelity was unthinkable to me.

Mick had a younger brother and sister, which made the comparison of him exposing himself to me, to that of an act that would be part of an intimate brother-sister relationship, a strange testimony to his passed home life with his own sister.

"Is that what he thinks is normal?" I still wondered. Well, it was definitely not normal in my home!

Mick robbed me of something that day, a subtle type of innocence. Until that car ride, I had looked at the men that were close to me in my family, as non-sexual human beings. My father was very modest around the house. There was not one time that I can recall, that I ever saw him walking through the house bare-chested, or that I got a quick glimpse of him making a run for it from his room to the bathroom in his boxer shorts. Hugs and kisses were only those that were appropriate between fathers and daughters, the kind that expressed love and mutual respect. The thought would have never occurred to me that my father would ever look at me in any other way than a parent looks at their child. However, after my experience with Mick, any alone time with my dad was no longer relaxing and enjoyable. I found that I couldn't sit alone in the same room with my father, much less any other male relative, without feelings of discomfort and embarrassment engulfing me. Sometimes it got so intolerable that I would make some excuse to quickly get up and leave the room. Even as the years went by, some ugly thing was always there, hammered down and wedged between my father and me by my sister's husband. Quiet times between the two of us, were never the same.

At the first family get together after the "incident", it was really hard to face Mick. But as time went by and the holidays came and went, things got easier. After close to a year had passed, it almost seemed as if nothing had ever happened, as if it were all some horrible dream. Then my mother asked Mick to paint the basement of the house at Midway, and Mick's odyssey of sexual perversion began again, but this time with a vengeance.

Momma had gotten Mick a job as a painter at the same factory where she worked. He often did side jobs to get some extra cash. Claudette was pregnant with their third child and they were saving to buy a house, so they needed all the money that they could get.

Even though my mother and Mick worked at the same place, Mick started earlier, and got off from work one hour earlier than my mom did. The plan was that he would come to our house straight from work and get a couple of hours of painting in every night until the job was done. Mick would get to our house about ten minutes before I came home from school, change into his painting clothes, and start to paint. I was a little apprehensive about being home alone with him even though it would only be for a short time until my mother arrived. The first day wasn't too bad and I chided myself for worrying about the situation. Then I came home from school on the next day to quite a surprise.

Running up the concrete front porch steps, I flung open the screen door, and juggling my pile of books, I walked through the living room into my bedroom. I dropped my books on my bed like a pile of bricks and noticed that across the hall the bathroom door was shut. "Mick must be changing into his painting stuff." I thought to myself. I shut my door and hurriedly changed my school uniform, putting on a pair of jeans and an old sweater. I wanted to get the dinner dishes done before Momma got home from work. It was my job and I had gone to bed without doing them last night. My mother hadn't said anything about it this morning but I knew she was giving me a break, and I didn't want to disappoint her when she came home from work.

When I opened up the bedroom door, I barely noticed Mick sitting on my mother's couch drinking a beer. As I rushed back though the living room, towards the front door and the mail slot, my mind was preoccupied with getting the day's mail. On the way back through the living room and into the kitchen, I glanced up briefly from sorting through the mail, at Mick sitting, sipping his beer, and then it registered. In his lap, strutting out stiff and hard from among the folds of his painter's pants, was his dick.

"Oh my God! He's doing it again!" The thought screamed in my head. Then, in an instant, trying to give the appearance that my attention was solely focused on the various letters, bills, and magazines in my hands, I made an about face and hurriedly went out the front door without uttering a word.

As I sat down on the cool concrete of the front porch, I started to shake. Mixed feelings of fear and anger filled me. Shame was also there in the dark snarled mess of emotion because I didn't have the guts to go back into the house and yell into his face, "What the hell are you doing to me, you pig!" I just sat there on the porch, afraid to go back into my own home, and I waited. I sat and wondered what to do this time. I sat and waited for my mother to come home.

When Momma came home, we went inside. Mick was down in the basement painting, and outwardly acting as if his day had gone on in the usual fashion. I stayed up stairs, and started the dishes right away, making excuses to my mother followed by an apology for why they hadn't gotten done. As my hands slid over the dishes in the soapy warm water, I tried to make some sense of what was happening, and what I should do. If I told Jake, he would go on a rampage. I had enough to handle, I didn't need to put up with his ranting too.

"Do I tell Momma?" I thought to myself. If I did, it was almost a certainty that Claudette would find out, and I knew how painful the knowledge of something like this would be to her. I could just imagine it.

"Pardon me Claudette, I just thought that you'd like to know that the man that you have chosen to be with for the rest of your life, and to be the father of your children, is a PERVERT! He likes to impress your baby sister by leaving his barn door open with his winkie hanging out!"

"Oh God, Susan" I sadly said to myself as I leaned against the sink and closed my eyes. "What am I going to do?" I tried to take some comfort from the warmth of the sudsy water, and to concentrate on the mindless task, hoping going through the motions would allow my mind some relief from the confusion in my head over the decision that I knew I must make.

Every few seconds, I would stop what I was doing and listen nervously to see if Mick was coming up the back stairs from the basement. I was praying he would stay down there at least until I could finish the dishes and then I could seek the refuge of my room. He did just that, and I spent the rest of the evening in my bedroom under the pretense that I had stacks of homework due the next day. When I fell asleep in my bed that night, I was fully clothed, and face down in a book. I awoke in the morning, heartsick and without a plan as what to do.

All the next day at school I was preoccupied. It had occurred to me, that not only did I have to worry about whether or not to tell my sister, but I also had to worry about Mick "greeting" me when I walked through our front door this afternoon.

When I got on the bus to go home, I still hadn't decided what the right course of action should be. Different scenarios danced dizzily in my head until it ached. I didn't want to face telling my sister, and the ramifications that would surely follow her enlightenment about the situation. My agitation was growing as the bus followed its daily afternoon route, with each passing stop getting closer and closer to my house and to Mick. Suddenly, looking out the bus window, my rising panic was headed off by the realization that the final decision could wait.

"Such an important, life altering decision should be given as much thought as possible!" I told myself. "And I don't need to face Mick today at all. It was a beautiful day, and I can sit on the porch, doing my homework, until Momma comes home from work. That will give me some more time to think and look at all the possibilities."

And that's exactly what I did for the next few days, until the phone call came. My luck had held out. The weather had been warm and balmy, so my mother didn't ask any questions when she drove up and saw me sitting outside on the front porch for the next day or two. I'd escaped facing Mick too. By the time I went inside, he was already painting in the basement, and I was in my room when he left for home, a few hours later.

That Thursday night my cousin Harry's wife, Tina, had called me. She and Harry were living downstairs from Claudette and Mick, in Auntie Tillie's old flat. As a matter of fact, they were living there now, while Jake and I were in the apartment above. At the time of the Mick incident, Tina was about sixteen. She and Harry had gotten married the year before when it became very apparent that she was "with child". Harry had reluctantly married her under duress from my Aunt Lollie, so the union was bad from the start.

Tina was bubbly and bright but very young, and Harry was a nineteen-year-old man with a boatload of problems inherited from his mother, Aunt Lollie, and father's disastrous marriage. And now that we lived above them it didn't surprise me much, when at times on quiet afternoons, I could hear violent arguing emanating from the apartment below. Often, the yelling culminated in a loud slap, silence, and then Tina's heart wrenching sobs. God, Harry was such a jerk!

Anyway, when the phone call came two years ago, I can still remember the odd tone in her voice as she said my name.

"Susan," she said. Then momentarily hesitating, she went on. "I don't know how to tell you... I mean, I just don't know how to say this...I'm having this problem with Mick..." In that instant I knew, he was doing the same thing to her that he was doing to me!

"He's flashing you!" I said with astonishment.

"How did you know that?" she replied. "I haven't told anybody about it, not even Harry, and I don't know what to do!"

"Brace yourself Tina. I have a ton of things to tell you about Mick!" Taking a deep breath, I started at the beginning of my story, recounting all the sordid details to her, one by one, relieved to finally share the burden of the knowledge that I had been carrying for what seemed like an eternity, with a friend. Every so often, on the other end of the line, Tina would utter an "Oh my God!" followed by a silence as the story unfolded and the weight of what I was telling her hit home.

When I was done she blurted out, "That sounds like what he's doing to me, only he hasn't been doing it for as long. It started about a month ago. He sits on the back steps in the evening smoking a cigarette. When I take out the garbage, I can see him there in the dim light, the tip if his cigarette glowing bright red. The very first time it happened,

Harry had already gone to work for the night. I'd placed the garbage in the trashcan in the alley and was on my way back to the apartment when he called me over. He was just making small talk when he asked me what time it was. I said that I didn't know and he said that he forgot that his watch was in his pocket. He stretched out his legs to get his hand in his pocket in order to take out his pocket watch and BAM! There it was! I was dumbfounded, and abruptly turned and walked away.

When I thought about it later, I figured that it must have been an accident. Maybe he had been peeing in the backyard or something right before he saw me and forgot to zip up. You know how the guys are, when they're drinking beer, and Mick is always drinking beer. So I decided to forget about it and just pretend it didn't happen. For awhile everything was OK, but then it happened again. After borrowing some sugar from your sister, I closed her back door and started down the steps when I saw Mick sitting three quarters of the way down them. As I passed him, I said hello and at a glance I could tell that he was hanging out! Without a word I quickly walked to my back door and entered my flat, locking and bolting the door behind me.

You know that he did it this time with your sister just a few feet away! I just couldn't believe it! I knew then that he was doing it on purpose, and with Harry working nights I'm just terrified. If he is crazy enough to do stuff like this right under Claudette's nose what will he do when she's gone? I didn't know what to do so I called you."

"This is out of control!" I said, "It's got to stop

right now. If he's doing this to women that he knows what is he doing to strangers? My mom is home right now, and it's time to tell her what's going on. She'll know what to do. Don't worry Tina. I'll take care of this. Enough is enough!"

And that's exactly what I did. It surprised me that something I'd thought was going to be so hard turned out to be so easy. That night we sat at the kitchen table, my mother and I, and she listened quietly and patiently to me as the locked gate slowly opened and a torrent of words came tumbling out. Her reaction was one of surprise and then concern tempered with a worldly matter-of-factness that comforted me and made me feel safe.

When I had told Momma everything there was to tell, she leaned close to me and with an odd smile said, "Why didn't you say, 'Mick, put that thing back in your pants!' the first time he did it?" Her words fell heavy on my heart. I felt that I was somehow incriminated in a foul, dark deed that I had no part in. Shame again reared it's ugly head for not being strong enough to stand up for myself by confronting Mick in the first place, and confusion as to whether my mother thought that I was some how at fault in this filthy situation began to take it's toll.

"Momma, I just couldn't say that! The whole thing is so disgusting!" I said and tears came to my eyes. My mother immediately grabbed me and hugged me.

"Sorry baby. That was my feeble attempt at a joke to make you laugh. Not so good, huh? It's OK. It's not your fault. None of this is your fault!" While she was still hugging me, rocking slightly, she suddenly stopped.

"Oh, my God!" she said. "Now I understand what's been going on!" The astonished look that I saw on her face was quickly replaced by an odd smile and then a throaty laugh with an accompanied slow shaking of her head from side to side.

"I guess Mick isn't only trying to impress you and Tina, it seems that he is playing games with me as well! Every afternoon since he's started painting the basement, the minute I get home, I've been going down there to say hello and see how he's doing. The first day when I came down, he was standing on a ladder painting the top portion of the basement wall. As I stood next to him I looked up and noticed that he was peeking out of a hole in the bottom of his painter's pants! Oh, he wasn't at full attention like he was when he was saying hello to you, just kind of hanging limply out of the hole in his pants."

"What? What are you saying? You mean that Mick…." I think that flabbergasted might be the word that described my reaction, as the sentence just drifted off while my mouth hung slightly open. Momma laughed a little at my reaction, and then we both nervously chuckled like two schoolgirls who had just found out that the school principal was having an affair.

"What did you do?" I asked.

"The same thing that you did, I said nothing. I assumed that it was a very embarrassing accident. So that night after he went home, I found his painter's pants hanging on the back of the bathroom door where he was keeping them for the next day. I looked for and found the hole in the crotch of his pants and promptly sewed it up. I supposed that would take care of the situation."

"But it didn't." She sighed and continued. "The next day when I came down the steps, he was on the ladder and hanging out again! Stunned, I thought a minute, and then surmised that the bulkiness of his painter's pants probably caused them to be difficult to put on. In the rush to get them on so that he could quickly begin painting, he probably just ripped them in the weakest spot, the place that I'd just sewn. Then, I thought, that was probably how the hole had gotten there in the first place."

"So he continued to rip, and I continued to sew everyday this week!" And then with a troubled look of sadness, she stared intently into my eyes and softly said, "Susan, now what do we do?"

❧ VI ☙

"Crack!" a flash of lightning followed by a large "Boom!" shook me and I was back in the attic again.

"Boy! That must have been close!" I spoke out loud, my voice breaking the heavy silence of the attic. I noticed that as my words echoed in my ears, they sounded strange, foreign to me. Standing motionless, I could still hear the continuous drumming of the rain on the shingled roof, but now it seemed to be even louder than before. As I looked through the old rippled glass of the tiny attic window, sheets of rain swept passed. The street and cars below were barely visible.

"God, it's really pouring out there. Good thing it's still November and not a month from now. This could be one heck of a snow storm." Refocusing my attention back to my wet laundry, I noticed that the wicker basket was empty. Carefully, I turned and walked slowly down the center of the attic's worn wood floor, being watchful not to misstep onto a board that might not hold my weight. Muffled sounds of creaking, wood on wood, emanated from beneath my feet as the boards slightly gave under the strain and I made my way to the staircase. I knew that everyone said that the floor was sturdy and there was no need to be so careful, but still…

The steep descent of the narrow wooden steps necessitated a one step at a time approach, so it always took some time to get to my apartment below. Half way down I could hear the muffled words of a song faintly playing in the background. "I must have left the radio on in the parlor." I mumbled to myself as the voice of Peggy March belted out the words, "I love him. I love him. I love him, and where he goes I'll follow. I'll follow. I'll follow. He'll always be my true love, my true love, my true love, for now and 'till forever, forever, forever!"

The song was kind of sappy, but I liked it. It was a couple of years old so the disc jockey must be playing it as "A blast from the past". Listening to the music while I continued the journey down, I finally reached the bottom of the steps, where I started to relax. "Well, I made it down one more time without my often envisioned tumble and subsequent broken limbs." Walking over to the last load of wet laundry to be hung in the attic, I glanced around the small lime green, linoleum floored room. It had been our toy room at Grandma's when we were children and was full of wonderful memories of wooden blocks, tinker toys, jacks, and soft gray, green, yellow and red clay. Being in the room was still comforting to me, even though now, all it held was a refrigerator and a small portable wringer-wash machine.

"I will follow him. Follow him wherever he may go. There isn't an ocean too deep, a mountain so high it can keep, keep me away...away from my love!" Peggy sang her heart out as she ended her song, and "He's a Rebel" by the Crystals took its place. "Wow, two oldies in a row, and both my favorites!" I thought as I started to sing to the music. While loading the wicker laundry basket up one last time, I thought about how nice it was to be totally dedicated to a human being, like I was to Jake. We were bonded together, childhood sweethearts. Even the melody we chose for "our song" depicted how we felt about each other. It was called "You're my Soul and my Inspiration" by the Righteous Brothers. I loved it! The words said things like, "Baby, I can't make it without you! And I'm telling you honey, you're my reason for laughing, crying, living and for dying!" It was so romantic!

"Just because he doesn't do what everybody else does, that's no reason why we can't share a love! He's always good to me, and good to him I'll try to be, 'cause he's not a rebel …No, no, no…He's not a rebel…No, no, no…To me-eee!" Reaching the finale the Crystals and I sang, shouting enthusiastically and soulfully in a fashion that I imagined would be very much apropos for a revival meeting.

Jake was a rebel in some respects and he certainly didn't do what other people did. He had dropped out of high school when he was fifteen, but that was over a year before I met him. I'd gone out with him for several months before he'd told me the truth about his short-lived academic accomplishments. Until that time he would recount to me, with vivid detail, the events of his day at school during our daily phone calls. Details that I later found out were very imaginative untruths. He had also told me that he was a Catholic, and for someone who unbeknown to me had never stepped foot in a Catholic Church, was very informed about the mass schedule of the parish in his neighborhood. He'd made a point never to call me on a Sunday morning. Not until he, as he'd said, "got home from church". Even though he'd lied very well, I must confess, at times, small wisps of doubt had floated through my mind. They'd lightly tugged at my reason only to be brushed aside because I'd wanted everything that he'd said to be true.

Finally, only after a few cryptic remarks thrown out by my cousin, Harry, about Jake's school grades and church habits did I face the truth. Confronting him with what I'd learned, Jake did fess up to the lies and begged for my forgiveness. And I'd done just that. I had to. He had reluctantly and with much embarrassment, admitted to me the reason for his dishonesty. It was because he hadn't thought that he'd been good enough for me that I wouldn't want to go out with him if I'd known the truth. So he just had to lie to me, in order to win my heart. God, he needed me! And I in turn needed him.

He was my first and only lover, and that fact, good Catholic girl that I am, sealed our bond forever. That fact had also haunted me the few times that we'd broken up during our "going steady" days. After all, what man would want you after you had given yourself to someone else? "Soiled goods" that's what you would be if you didn't marry the first man you went to bed with. Somehow, knowing that I was going to marry him had made it seem all right. Thank God, I never had to worry about that again. We were married and that was that!

We had gotten married last June in the year of our Lord nineteen hundred and sixty-six. Just six days after my eighteenth birthday, twenty days after my high school graduation, and ninety days before Jake's nineteenth birthday. We were young. It was true. And I had heard or read somewhere that the statistics for lasting marital bliss among couples that were childhood sweethearts were pretty dismal, but we were different. My sister Carole had talked to me a few months before the wedding.

"The person that you marry at eighteen may not be the same person that you would like to marry at twenty-five. People change as they grow." Carole had said, emphasizing one of the potential pitfalls of a marriage between two people who were too young.

She may have been right about other people, but not Jake and me. She didn't know how much we loved each other. She had wanted me to wait awhile, to put the wedding date off. That just seemed like such a waste of time. Married was what I wanted to be, what I was meant to be. It was time for me to get on with my destiny.

"God, I'm a poet and don't know it. But my feet sure show it. They're long fellows!" I recited, laughing at myself…

"Bong! Bong!" The dining room wall clock chimed.

"Two o'clock. Wow, time flies when you're having fun. I better get this last load of work uniforms hung and get supper started before Jake gets home. One knows how testy he gets when his supper isn't ready the minute he walks through the door. Good thing I picked up around the house before I started the laundry. The dusting can wait 'til tomorrow. Gee, I probably shouldn't have talked on the telephone to Peggy so long this morning." A pang of guilt and a slight feeling of apprehension nibbled at me.

"Oh well, up we go!" I lifted the now heavy wicker basket, crossed the room, and started the steep ascent up the narrow wooden staircase to the attic. Slowly and laboriously I climbed the worn steps, while Carole's premarital advice surfaced again in my thoughts. She had been wrong about Jake and me.

Oh, it was true that we did fight a lot. We always did, even from the beginning. Jake was so damned jealous! It was very flattering in a way to have someone who was so crazy about you, but it did have its price. I had been a loner in school, so friends from that realm never were a threat to Jake and our time together. But the horse stables were. When I was thirteen, my sister Claudette reluctantly gave her prize possession to me, a fine boned palomino quarter horse mare named "Peanuts". As a young teenager my sister had scrimped and saved every penny she earned from her part time, waitressing job to purchase her childhood dream, a horse. Peanuts was a soft, tan and white bundle of equine energy that, as a married woman, my sister could no longer afford. Both money and her time were at a premium. She had been married to Mick just over a year and a new baby was on the way. So I'd been the grateful recipient of a most precious gift.

Riding through the forest preserves on eighteen hundred pounds of power and pride, through luscious green valleys full of brilliantly colored wild flowers, across sparkling bubbling brooks, and over winding dirt and cinder trails, was heaven. I'd found unbounded beauty, and also friendship. Deb was the first real friend that I'd ever had. She owned a horse too, a striking black and white Appaloosa gelding named "Snowflake". We would ride together for hour after hour through the woods, telling each other our innermost secret thoughts and feelings, things that we did not want to tell any other human being. And it still ached inside of me to know that everything we had enjoyed together was gone forever. Jake had seen to that.

Once Jake and I had started going steady, he became extremely possessive of my time. Most of our fights had boiled down to my time spent with friends. He didn't want me to have any. Initially, I'd stood my ground. I'd refused to curtail my riding and my friendships, but the constant bickering over any other interests besides those that included him, wore me down. Every battle had become a proof of love, and little by little, the ground slipped out from under me. My riding had become infrequent, stolen bits of time that I'd seemed always to be apologizing for, and Deb's deep friendship had become a memory. She had found someone too, and he'd also seemed not to be fond of the friendship that she and I shared, discouraging it as often as possible.

Since my wedding, less than six months ago, my mother had been taking care of Peanuts for me, and Claudette was trying to find time to ride again. I hadn't seen Deb in over a year. She hadn't been able to come to my wedding; she and Ted couldn't make it. Something had come up at the last minute.

Well, I guess that was the way things were supposed to be. My new friends were his friends, and my old friends were no more.

We were married now, and we were married for keeps. We had just had our fourth month wedding anniversary and were already trying to get me pregnant. With Vietnam hanging heavy over our heads, we needed to get that done as quickly as possible. The demand for more and more soldiers grew larger every day. So many young men were being killed in the war, that it had become necessary for the government not only to draft single men but also married men without children. Oh, a guy could get out of serving completely if he went to college, or at least until he graduated. If he drug his feet about getting a degree he could probably put it off for a long time, by then maybe the war would be over. But that didn't help Jake and me, Jake wasn't going to college and he never would be. That was for other people.

Our best bet to keep him from being drafted was for me to get pregnant. Since the day that we had gotten married, we had been trying but so far, nothing had happened. If it did happen, it would be tough financially, but we would make it. After we had gotten engaged and Jake had turned eighteen, Momma had gotten him a job at the factory where she worked. He was a material handler, which meant that he hauled material to the gauze pad and bandage machines for the operators to use when their machines ran out. There were better jobs in the plant but getting one of those would take time, and at least this had been a start.

The most important thing was for Jake not to

have to go to 'Nam. Everything else would fall into place. I already knew that a baby wasn't going to be this month. "God, let it happen next month!" The alternative was unthinkable.

"Please God, let it happen!" I prayed out loud as I stopped several steps from the top of the staircase. The attic floor was waist high and I swung the heavy basket onto the old wooden floor beside me so that I wouldn't have to carry it up the last few steep steps.

One last batch of wet laundry to hang and then I would be done. After pulling the cloth clothespin bag along the line towards me, I took out two wooden clothespins, placed them in my mouth and got a pair of Jake's wet work pants out of the basket. Shaking and snapping them out in front of me to get rid of some of the wrinkles, stirred up the attic air. As it gently swirled around me, the faint fresh smell of newly washed laundry enveloped me. I closed my eyes, and for an instant I was back in time in my mother's backyard. I saw myself as a child standing between two brightly flowered billowing sheets, breathing all the moist sweet smelling air that danced on the wind deep into me.

I breathed in, opened my eyes, peacefully took a clothespin out of my mouth and slowly slid it over the inside waistband of Jake's pants. My attention began to drift again...

✎ VII ✎

My mother had always been pretty lenient with me as I grew up. I don't remember any spankings as a child, and she never shouted. She used to say that just a firm "No!" accompanied by a stern look was punishment enough for me.

Growing up I was my own rule maker. I was expected to act in a proper manner, and I did. As a teenager, there was no set time for me to return home from a date. I was expected to come in at a decent hour, usually twelve, and if something came up I was expected to call. Momma very rarely stayed up until I got home, at least it appeared that way, and I don't recall ever disappointing her. She trusted me completely.

I never knew if she had put two and two together, and figured out that Jake and I were having sex for quite a long time before we were married. That was the only thing that had caused me to lie to her in my whole life, and I always had felt guilty about it. Maybe premarital sex is one of life's experiences that a person is expected to lie to their parent about.

One day, out of the clear blue sky she had said, "You know, Susan, it would be a shame if you and Jake wound up having to get married. I hope that you are being careful." And that was that. Without an accusation, she had made a statement, the meaning of which was very clear. "It's your life, but be careful!"

I remember one night Jake and I had a flat tire

coming home from his house. The neighborhood was run-down, "on the wrong side of the tracks", and it was not a place for two teenagers to be broken down in the middle of the night. It took us several frightening hours to wait for and then flag down a passing squad car, fix the flat, and drive me home. When I walked in the door at four in the morning, my mother was sitting in the front room quietly waiting for me.

"Susan, are you all right?" was all she'd said. Full of relief to be home and safe, I gladly recounted every scary detail of our horrific ordeal, to my mother, my friend. Without question, she had believed me. Jake's mother didn't believe us then, and probably still doesn't believe us now.

"Boy, his mother is really a strange lady," I thought to myself, "and she really does drink a lot." Well, that was probably an understatement. She drank like a fish! She was a tiny woman, five feet tall or so, with short medium brown hair, and she weighed about one hundred and five pounds. She chain-smoked, and between her oily hair and the pungent smell of cigarette smoke that permeated her clothing, one always got the impression when seeing her that she hadn't recently taken a bath. I couldn't understand why Jake's dad stayed with her. He was an attractive man with a strong resemblance to Errol Flynn, the 30's Hollywood leading man, and he probably could easily find someone else. I was amazed to learn that they still had sex. A fact that Jake's mom had brought to my attention one day while showing me a large bruise on her upper arm. She had said with a little snicker, "Dad had gotten a little rough last night. He gets like that with too much Seagram's." She'd laughed, "You should have heard him howling like a wolf as he chased me around the house. When he gets like that he's great in the sack!"

"God, what a disgusting thought!" had been my only reaction as I'd stood and looked at her in disbelief.

When I'd first met Jake, she had been a bit of a shock. Drinking women were not what I was accustomed to. Things were quite to the contrary in my family. My mother drank very little, and women who did were considered not to be very high class. I'd also been very surprised to find out that she rarely cooked for the family. Even with Momma working, she always made, or made arrangements for a meal for my father and me. Jake's mom was usually too busy getting drunk to prepare a meal. Most evenings, Jake would cook for himself or his older sister Marie would wearily take over the responsibility when she got home from a long day at work.

Our house wasn't spotless with Momma working and all, but their home was filthy. It seemed that she didn't clean either. When I visited, I couldn't help but notice how dirty Jake's upstairs bathroom was. Jake used to make designs with his finger in the built up body scum on the inside of the tub when he took a bath. I could see the little rubbed clean circles inside the tub, as I passed the bathroom door. The tub was so dirty, I couldn't figure out how he got into it in the first place. Jake and his mother had slept on sheetless mattresses like homeless people. Later I'd found out that it was because she would often wet the bed when she drank. So I guess she'd figured, "Why waste the energy?" No wonder he was such a stickler, almost compulsive, on our apartment being immaculate.

My heart went out to Jake, Marie, and Jake's dad. What an awful thing to come home to. My dad was revolting enough when he drank, but at least I only saw him like that late at night, or at family doings. Jake's mom was in some degree of drunkenness twenty-four hours a day.

But her drunkenness, sloppy housekeeping, and lack of culinary artistry weren't her worst flaws. She was weird.

During the evenings that I would spend at Jake's house, she would sometimes corner me for some late night chitchat. She would confide in me and tell, and retell, dark and twisted tales that when hearing them for the first time, extremely disturbed me. I would reluctantly sit at her sticky kitchen table, politely and obediently listening. In whispers she had told me that as a child, her father had sexually molested her. Then when still very young, her father and mother had divorced and he had moved far away. Her hatred for him and for what he had done to her had boiled and seethed inside her, as she grew, vengeance a constant thought in her child's mind. When she'd turned fourteen she took the chance to finally give him what she had felt that he deserved. She hitchhiked her way across the United States to California, the state that he had made his new home, for one purpose. That purpose was to kill him. But when she'd gotten there, she had said to me dryly laughing in a low raspy voice, made horse from too many cigarettes, "The bastard was already dead!"

Sometimes her stories were even darker, more twisted, and more unbelievable. In a low quiet voice, she had told me that she knew, even though he had always denied it, that Jake's dad had molested their daughter when she was a little girl, a disturbing story that Marie denies to this day. She had even confided in me that when Jake was five years old, he had, little sex pervert that he was, tried to have sex with her! She'd also alluded to some bizarre idea that she had, about a mother being, as she thought she should be, the source of her little boy baby's first sexual experiences. YUCK! How twisted can you get!

She adored Jake. He was the light of her life, but her alcohol-scrambled mind had tainted that too. Every chance she got, she would try to show him affection by sitting on his lap and kissing him full on the mouth forcing her tongue between his lips. An occurrence that disgusted him so, he would literally push her off of him with such force, that she would fall to the floor with a thump, resulting in a sick mewing, pleading sound of rejection, emanating out of her mouth.

After all the late night shock stories, and witnessing her odd and truly bizarre behavior, I not only had concluded that Jake's mother was a drunk, I had also concluded that she was as close to insane as anybody I'd ever met. Just thinking about her would give me an eerie, uneasy feeling. Even now, as I stood in the attic I could feel the spasms in my stomach start to stir. Slowly bending down for another pair of wet uniform pants in the basket I shivered, becoming aware of a slight damp chill in the attic air that I hadn't noticed before.

"The temperature outside must be dropping. Probably need to turn on the gas heater when I get downstairs to take the chill out." Standing up straight, I wrapped my arms around myself in a big hug, and began rubbing my upper arms through my sweater with my hands, attempting to ward off the cold for a few more minutes until I was finished. Standing silently, thoughts of last nights curious thumping popped into my head.

An unwelcome need to go to the bathroom had interrupted a peaceful sleep. My fear of the dark had been overwhelming as a child, and even though I was now an adult, it had not diminished. So when I returned, being proud of myself that I had braved the jet-black expanse between my bed and the bathroom without turning on a light, I began to settle back down beneath the bed covers. Safe and warm, sleep softly engulfed me.

I had started to drift off... And then I heard it, that familiar sound. I'd heard it several times over the last six months. It was a muffled thumping sound, much like, what I imagined the footsteps of a man would sound like who was trying carefully and quietly to sneak across the attic floor above me. Jake had heard it also, and when we had mentioned the eerie pitter-patter to my sister, the previous resident of my grandmother's flat, she whispered with her eyes widening, "So, you've heard it too? The ghost in the attic! Have you ever gone upstairs and looked for it when it happened? No? Well, Mick and I did, and nothing is ever there! At first we thought it was some squirrels that had gotten into the attic for the winter, but there was no sign of them. No sign of anything, ever! Eventually we just got used to our 'Ghost in the attic'." She finished with a small dry smile.

And we had gotten used to him too. But now, it felt kind of unsettling to be standing in the same spot where our nightly visitor romped and frolicked. The mood of the attic could change quickly from light to dark, and maybe that was why a trip to the attic, rain or shine, was always tinged with an underlying feeling of fear causing me to feel slightly unsure about climbing the steep steps when the need arose.

"C'mon Susan, let's get this finished. Jake will be home before you know it. You certainly don't want to get into another little tiff with him when he walks in the door!"

"Little tiff..." I retorted to myself as I thought about what I'd just said. "It certainly could be more than a little tiff." Occasionally, in the past, some of our average everyday disagreements had turned into pretty scary battles. I had never experienced arguments of that level of emotional brutality before. So for me, our fights were extremely frustrating and sometimes very frightening. Once drawn in, I couldn't stop. Much like scratching an intensely itchy mosquito bite until it bleeds.

It always seemed that Jake instinctively knew just which one of my buttons to push to send me off the deep end. He could whip me up into a frenzy of frustration and anger, an emotional state of being that I was completely unaccustomed to, and unprepared for.

Early on in our relationship, during one of our really overheated disagreements, worked up to the point of desperation, I'd slapped him in the face, only to learn you don't do that to Jake. The impact of his return blow had rocked me back on my heels.

"Well, I guess I deserved it! That's what you get for losing your temper and wanting to hurt someone!" That was something I had never done before, and had never done again. The whole incident still made me feel terribly ashamed.

I had often wondered how he could get me so angry. Maybe it was the frustration of not being able to sense any feelings behind his steel blue eyes. He could be coaxing me into bed or calling me a bitch, and not change the expression on his boyish face. Lengthy conversations between us were rare, and he, next to never said that he loved me. Sometimes I felt that his frequent periods of silence were suffocating. At times I felt lonely, really lonely, even though he was living in the same house with me. But I knew that as he got older he would change, warm up and mellow. I could wait.

Still, Jake had an emotional point, passed which you didn't want to make him go, and that well learned fact disturbed me a little. It seemed like he didn't possess the same barriers that kept other people and their actions within the realm of normalcy. It wasn't just having the last angry word, tickling me too long, playing too rough with the dog to continually impress on her who was boss, or any other kind of childish one-upmanship. It was dragging me by my arm to a nearby mailbox on a starry summer night. Forcibly shoving my tightly closed fist into the mail slot and violently shaking my arm, in order to cause me to release the precious object that was held in it. This violent vignette was orchestrated by my decision to break our engagement and give him back his ring. It was another lesson learned. Jake was willing to go places that I would never be willing to go. Thinking about it now, he was the only person that I knew who was like that. Unsettling, yes but...

"Just because he doesn't do what every body else does..." I sang out loud as the Crystals' tune echoed in my head. But as the words drifted off, other memories of Jake's odd behavior started to float into my free flowing thoughts. Sometimes, deep inside, he did seem to be like a jigsaw puzzle with a piece missing.

My cheeks flushed as an old memory of Jake surfaced, one that struck a loud deeply embedded chord of shame and embarrassment. Without my knowledge, Jake had secretly audio taped an evening of lovemaking during our courtship. Not for his own amusement, but for what he thought was to be the amusement of our friends. He began to play the surprise tape at a get-together one evening at his apartment. The astonished and shocked look on my face as well as that of our friends, seemed after a long and agonizing moment, to relay something to him that he should have already known, but hadn't.

Looking at me, first laughing, then with puzzlement, and finally with understanding, he had moved his hand quickly to the button on the tape recorder, switching the horrid thing off. Watching the emotions pass over his face, the idea had dawned on me that he initially hadn't had a clue about how unacceptable his behavior had been. He seemed genuinely surprised and perplexed by my reaction, and the reaction of those around us. There was no doubt that he had gotten the message loud and clear that he shouldn't have done it. But sometimes when I think about it, I believe that he still doesn't quite know why.

The last five months since our wedding had been bitter sweet. We'd spent our one-week honeymoon at his mom and dad's house in Michigan, which was only a half of a mile from the beach. It was beautiful. And an unexpected display of warm affection on that sunny sandy honeymoon beach had provided me with the proof that I had been hoping for, supporting my belief that he was growing and changing. On that day, as he rubbed suntan lotion over my shoulders, back, and arms, he warmly looked into my eyes and told me how he loved me and how wonderful it was that I was his wife. Since then, I have held that small moment in time, close to me, like a precious stone, taking it out to look at anytime I needed some assurance of what was going to be.

Yes, it would happen. He would grow and all of the ugly things would fade away into oblivion. I would work on improving myself too. Working on removing any causes for our fights had become my main priority. I was becoming an immaculate housekeeper, my cooking was improving, and I was learning to cultivate a heartier sexual appetite. In the beginning it was tough. Finally, unconstrained by the restrictions of living our single lives under the microscopic view of our parents, Jake became insatiable. If I warmly received his sexual advances four times a day he would push for five.

Sometimes it seemed no matter how many

times a day we made love, he wasn't satisfied until I pushed him away and the inevitable fight would ensue, along with his accusation that I didn't love him enough. When I had broached the subject with my mother during one of our alone times, she had said cryptically, "Don't complain, Susan. One day you'll go to the pump and it'll be dry! So do what you can to work things out." And I was doing just that.

Bending over and reaching down in the basket for the last article of clothing, a piece of my long black hair fell into view. I still wasn't used to it. My own chestnut brown hair had been so beautiful, but Jake liked this much better. The day that we had returned from out honeymoon he had declared, "Blonde or black, make up your mind. The brown is just too plain!" So black it was and so it would stay. It was his wish and I was trying to be what he wanted me to be. After all, he was my husband.

As my mother had said, "You made your bed and now you have to lie in it." Well, I guess she didn't say those exact words, but it was pretty close to it.

We had been home from our honeymoon about two weeks when it had started. Jake had gotten home from work and after a hello kiss at the door I took his lunch pale from him and went into the kitchen to check on supper. When I went back into the living room he was already sitting wordlessly in his chair, looking over the TV guide to see what was on the tube. Jake was not much of a talker when he came home from work, and getting him to say more than two words about any subject was a task. Starving for another human being's company, after being cooped up alone in the apartment, I had begun to make small talk about my day.

"Crazy John was in Jean's store again today. Boy, he really makes me feel uncomfortable when I'm around him. I know that Jean says that he's harmless, but..." At that point he snapped to, his disinterest and overt bored expression instantly changed. His eyes became riveted to mine.

With a fierce, intent stare he hissed, "What do you mean, 'in Jean's store'? You were in Jean's store? You went out alone today?"

"Well, I...I... yes I did. I was out of butter, and it's just a few houses down, and I didn't think that you would mind..."

"What do you mean, 'I wouldn't mind'? You know that I told you that you can't go out of this house without me! YOU FUCKING KNOW THAT!" As he said each word, his voice got louder and louder, until the last sentence boomed out of his mouth.

The walls of the old apartment building seemed to vibrate with his bellowing, and a small tingling of fear from the anticipation of what was possibly to come, moved through the muscles of my body. "Oh no, not this again", I'd thought to myself.

"But I really needed that butter for dinner Jake, and it only took a couple of minutes." I'd explained, as I started twisting the ring on my finger in some kind of nervous, knee jerk reaction to the situation.

Fueled by what Jake thought to be an inadequate explanation, he continued to shout.

"What have you been fucking doing all day, you lazy bitch? Look at this fucking place! It's a fucking pigsty!"

I quickly glanced around the room and it appeared to be spotless. Seeing the look on my face, Jake walked over to the molding around the doorways and reaching up, brushed his fingertips across the tiny ledge of the wood molding at the top of the doorway. Dust sprinkled down on the carpet like little pieces of dirty snow.

Shoving his dirty fingers in my face, he shouted, "Do you fucking see this, bitch? It's fucking dirt. I want this house FUCKING SPOTLESS! IT'S YOUR FUCKING JOB! YOU FUCKING DIDN'T HAVE TIME BETWEEN WALKING THE FUCKING STREETS AND FUCKING BABBLING ON THE FUCKING PHONE WITH YOUR FUCKING FRIENDS!"

As he screamed these last few words, his face scarlet with rage, small pieces of spittle sprayed out of his mouth, and a few of the larger droplets landed on my cheek. Wiping away the disgusting liquid, my fear began to give way to indignation.

"I was not walking the streets! It is just a few hundred yards from our door and I needed that butter for YOUR supper!"

Then, trying to calm myself and the situation down a bit, I'd said in an appeasing tone, "C'mon Jake. You know that if I'd gone to beauty school and had a job, I'd have to walk to the bus everyday. People do it all the time."

"Let's not fucking start that crap again! I fucking told you a thousand times. I don't want you to go to fucking beauty school. I don't want you to get a fucking job. I want you to fucking stay at home. Besides you're too fucking STUPID to keep a job. YOU'RE FUCKING STAYING HOME,

AND YOU WILL NOT LEAVE THIS FUCKING APARTMENT WITHOUT ME! DO YOU FUCKING UNDERSTAND THAT, YOU STUPID FUCKING CUNT?"

Now it was my turn. My rage exploded and I screamed.

"I have had it! That's enough! I'm getting out of here. This was a mistake!" Yelling, I'd stomped through the front room into the dining room towards the dark wooden desk and the heavy black telephone that sat on it. I could hear Jake's footsteps pounding across the floor right behind me. As my arm reached out for the receiver Jake roughly grabbed me from behind. He pinned my arms at my sides as he forcibly held me in a big bear hug, squeezing me tight and lifting me off my feet as I'd struggled to get free.

"Let me go! I'm leaving! I want to call my mother so that I can get out of here!" Suddenly he let me go and I lunged for the phone again. Taking the handset off the hook, I'd started to dial Momma's phone number, when Jake yanked the phone out of my hands and held it out of my reach.

"Give me that!" I screamed as I jumped towards him, and began grappling with him over possession of the phone. With one large burst of energy he had pushed me away from him, and into the wall behind me. The jarring blow had stunned me for a second, and then in shock and surprise, I saw Jake rip the phone cord out of the wall. He screamed back at me, his voice bellowing.

"Now, fucking try and call your mother, bitch!" With an ugly laugh he'd thrown the useless phone into the nearest corner where it had landed with a loud clatter, the impact musically accented by the tinkling of its bells. Then, without an additional word, he'd made an about face and stomped off into the bedroom, loudly slamming the door behind him.

Leaning against the dining room wall, I'd begun to sob. I allowed my body to slowly slip down the smooth light green painted plasterboard and settled down like a bundle of rags on the floor. I'd cried there for almost an hour, reviewing my life with Jake. It had been a mistake. I needed to leave him and go home. A range of emotions came and went, from anger to frustration to disappointment and fear.

How I wished that I could drive. At sixteen I had flunked my "on the road" driver's test twice. The instructor had said that I was just too nervous, and I needed to learn to calm down. Authority figures scared the hell out of me, and having him sitting right next to me, scrutinizing my every move, was just too nerve racking. Fearful and ashamed to fail again, I'd put the test on the back burner, and consequently, never returned.

"And now because you are such a coward, you have to sit here like a baby and try to figure out how to get in touch with your mother so that she can come and get you, instead of walking out the door, putting the key in the ignition, and driving away. Maybe Jake is right, maybe I am just too goddamn stupid for anything!"

Exhausted from both the mental and physical exertion, I'd coaxed my weary bones over to the royal blue sofa in the living room, and cried myself to sleep.

When I woke up in the morning, the phone was connected to the wall and Jake was outside in the alley washing his car. Quickly I went to the phone and dialed Momma's number. "Momma, I need to come home. Jake and I had an awful fight. I think that I made a mistake. I need to come home!" Then I briefly recounted the argument to her, carefully and purposefully playing down the violence of the whole situation. I didn't want to fully expose Jake's behavior. Once such things were said, the damage would be done, and her opinion of him would be changed forever.

Undeniably compassionate yet firm, my mother told me, "Susan, this was your choice and now you must stay and work it out. Believe me when I say that it is the best thing for you."

"Momma, just let me come home for awhile and think things out." I pleaded.

"Susan, you are home."

"Momma please, can't I come home?"

After a long silence I heard her very sad voice say, "No Susan, you can't." And with that I hung up knowing that I had made my bed.

❧ VIII ❧

Well, things were better now. And if I wanted to have everything run smoothly today I'd better get my keister in gear and get downstairs. The last wooden clothespin slipped down over the wet corner of the last piece of laundry from the wicker basket at my feet, with a soft little "squeak". I felt it through my fingertips more than I heard it

"Done" I said, as I hurried down the center of the attic to the hole in the wooden floor.

"Done, done, done." I chanted all the way down the steep steps. Entering the old toy room the tantalizingly delicious smell of cooking pot roast caused my mouth to water slightly. "I guess I must be hungrier than I thought." Placing the laundry basket on the toy room floor, next to the washing machine, I turned and walked into the kitchen.

"Bong! Bong! Bong!"

"Three o'clock! Only an hour and a half before Jake gets home. Better turn the oven temperature for the pot roast down. I want it to cook nice and slow so it gets really tender and the potatoes and carrots get golden brown." I loved cooking pot roast. It was so cheap and easy, and turned out so well. Besides, I needed to cook a meal today that was low maintenance, and wouldn't get ruined if I added a few extra minutes on to the cooking time.

Today I was going to surprise Jake when he came in the door. I had gotten the idea from one of those woman's TV talk shows that I'd been watching yesterday afternoon. I was going to meet him at the front door in my tan trench coat, with nothing on underneath.

"That will give him a shock! One thing that he won't be able to accuse me of is being boring." I would make sure of that. I liked sex and I was open to his suggestions of where, how, and what to do. A few months ago after taking some "sexy" pictures of me in his favorite white sweater dress and a pair of high heels next to our new car, he'd suggested that we take a few pictures with his Polaroid camera, the one that I'd given him as a present last September, for his nineteenth birthday. These pictures, he said, were to be his "private collection". At first I was reluctant, but with a little coaxing from him I caved in. Between husband and wife, I guess it's silly to be shy.

Peggy had mentioned on the phone today, that Jake had been showing some pictures of me around work last week. Buddy, Peggy's husband, has a rock and roll band, and one of the guys, Ralph, who plays guitar in it, also, by coincidence, works with Jake at the factory. Ralph had told Buddy about the pictures, and how he thought that showing them was tacky.

In the past, Jake had confided in me, that he'd thought that Ralph was jealous of how happy the two of us were together.

"Maybe, he's just trying to get a little friction going between Jake and me." I thought to myself as I walked from the kitchen into the bathroom.

"Anyhow, I'm going to have to mention it to Jake. I really don't feel comfortable with a casual acquaintance looking at pictures of me posing next to our brand new Chevelle, like some bad caricature of Marilyn Monroe in a white sweater dress and heels. Jake may think that I look great, but I don't!" Reaching down in the tub, I started to run the water for my shower.

The next hour or so passed rather quickly as I prepared for my husband's arrival. While I showered, combed my hair, and put on my makeup, I occupied my mind with visions of how surprised and pleased Jake would be when I opened my coat up as he walked through the front door.

Once finished with my pre-lovemaking rituals, I slipped on the trench coat that was hanging in the front closet and I went into the bedroom to look at myself in the mirror.

"How do I look?" I asked myself as I pulled the heavy wooden bedroom door toward me. It swung slightly shut to just the right angle so that I could see a complete view of myself from head to toe in the full-length mirror that was fastened to the back of the door. I pursed my rose colored lips creating what I surmised was a provocative, little girl pouting look, in the mirror.

"Not bad! Even if I do say so, myself." Pleased, I further scrutinized what I saw in the mirror. My makeup was a work of art. Eyebrow pencil, green eye shadow, eyeliner, blush, and long false eyelashes, all blended together to create a look. A look, I decided, that could rival any model, posing on the cover of the magazines displayed at the checkout counter of Jean's grocery store. I looked great in makeup, and I saw to it that Jake never saw me without it. Jake liked the look so much that we never had sex without it. Sometimes that bothered me a little, but I had to agree that my natural skin tones made me look plain and almost sickly.

My long black hair was swept up and mounded high on my head. It was held together by a large wide rubber band which was neatly hidden by a number of cascading thick black curls, the bottoms of which were fixed tightly to my head with long hairpins made of thin black wire. Out of the top of the cluster of curls hung a cascading ribbon of long black hair that shimmered in the dim light from the tall thin bedroom window, which faced the brick wall of the next-door apartment. Every hair was neatly in place, and would remain that way thanks to a generous dose of "super hold" hair spray.

A light tan trench coat was cinched tightly around my naked waist making it look tinier than it really was. I was down to 121 pounds, thin for my 5'6" frame, and my waist was still larger than I liked. It kept me from squeezing into anything less than a size 10, no matter how much weight I lost.

My wardrobe was topped off by a festive pair of sparkling sequined high heels. I loved those shoes. I had bought them for my sophomore school dance, the only dance that Jake and I had ever attended. He hated dances and never danced, probably because he couldn't. Too bad too, because as far back as I could remember, I'd always loved to dance. My sister Claudette had taught me to jitterbug when I was six years old and I was pretty good at it, even then. Oh well. The shoes had remained barely broken in over the last three years, so the gold, silver, red and green, microscopic pieces of glitter that covered the material of the shoes still sparkled like tiny diamonds.

I heard our dog, Honey, begin to bark as I looked at myself one more time in the mirror. Honey was a full-blooded, silver haired, green eyed, Weimaraner that we had bought from a veterinary clinic when we were on our honeymoon. The Michigan vet had assumed that she had run away from her master and gotten lost, or someone had abandoned her along a forested Michigan roadside. Either misfortune resulted in our gain. She was a great watchdog and we treated her like our baby. We spoiled her and allowed her free reign of the apartment, including sleeping privileges on the living room sofa and in our bed. The furniture was just a few months old and had been bought with the money that we had received as gifts for our wedding, but we still allowed her full use of it.

"Who's out there, girl?" I said to the dog as I hurriedly made my way from the bedroom to the front room windows. Once in front of the window, I peered through the slits between the old aluminum blinds. I could see the "Super Sport" parked in the street, in front of the house, and then immediately heard Jake's footsteps rhythmically pounding up the wooden front steps, and ending at the porch landing, just outside the front door.

Through the thick wooden door I could barely hear the muffled sound of a metal on metal creak. It had emanated from the rusty wrought iron hinges of the silver painted metal mailbox mounted on the front of the house, just next to the front door. The creak was followed by a hollow sounding clank, as the lid of the mailbox was slammed shut.

"He must be getting the mail." I said to myself

as I quietly waited for him to open the front door. I took the opportunity to take one more, quick look around the apartment to make sure that everything was neat and in its place. Satisfied that all was as it should be, I repositioned myself in front of the door and waited.

I stood listening and waiting for, at any instant, the door knob to turn, and the door to open wide with an accompanying whoosh of chilly damp air swirling in from the outside. But nothing happened. I waited for what seemed like an eternity, and still nothing.

"What's he doing?" Impatiently, I spoke out loud, my warm glow of anticipation quickly turning to slight irritation. "It's raining cats and dogs out there. Fine time to decide to look at the mail!"

And then without any warning, the door flung open and Jake stepped inside followed instantly by the loud angry bang of the storm door, as the gusting wind caught it and slammed it shut behind him. The sound, piercing my ears like a gunshot, had startled me, causing my whole body to involuntarily flinch and my eyes to snap tightly shut.

Opening my eyes, I saw Jake standing like a statue in front of me. The rain had soaked into his cloth coat and work pants, and droplets of water were dripping from his sleeves, forming tiny pools of liquid on the linoleum floor of the foyer. As I looked up at his face, my attention was drawn to one tiny raindrop precariously hanging on the end of a strand of greased blonde hair. It momentarily hung onto the curl in the middle of his forehead, growing larger and larger until it almost comically dripped down, onto the tip of his nose.

The giggle forming in my throat was immediately choked off as my gaze met his, and I looked into his eyes. There, in those inexpressive, cold blue eyes, was something I had never seen in them before, pure unadulterated fear. The color had completely drained from his face and the muscles in his jaw jumped as he ground his teeth together. It seemed to me that every muscle in his body was stiff, almost rigid, as if he were bracing himself to withstand some impending, immense blow.

Slowly, and with what looked like great effort, he raised his hand to bring into my view something that I had not seen before, and now noticed was clutched tightly in his hand. It was a piece of paper, a letter, wet and dripping. The ink was smeared, but the U.S. Department of the Army heading at the top of it was still barely legible. Just under the heading was typed the one word that we both knew in that instant of time, would change the course of our lives forever. Such power, yet so simple, the salutation read:

"Greetings"

PART 2

"VIRGINIA"

IX

Beautiful! God, Virginia was beautiful in the spring! It seemed like every plant, bush, or tree that was planted here had one necessary requirement, and that was it had to blossom in the spring. I could just picture what the trees and bushes looked like back in Chicago. It was early March, and I'd bet that at home, the winter wind and some frosty flakes of snow whirled around gray dead looking branches. But here, here it was like a fairyland of colorful blossoms and sixty-degree days. Light pink, white, fuchsia, yellow, and bright red flowers covered the branches of the trees and filled the world with a kaleidoscope of brilliant colors, the view of which was striking against the crystal blue sky. And the only snow, like pieces of flotsam and jetsam that filled the air, were the tiny soft petals of blossoms that lazily drifted down from the trees, slowly swirling on the warm southerly spring breeze and settling in soft multicolored velvet drifts, like pillows that muted the harsh lines of the outside world and lent a fairyland appearance to reality.

The sweet fragrance of cherry blossoms was overpowering as I walked down the street on my way home from the grocery store. I had arrived here about a month ago, just before the blossoms had opened, and I had been more than pleasantly surprised at how intense the various flowers and blossoms smelled on the first warm spring day. I was amazed at the scent of real southern honeysuckle. There was a "viney" bush of it growing on the old rusty heating oil tank next to the back of the house that we had rented. For some reason that I don't understand, what was called honeysuckle in Chicago had never smelled like that.

The colors and smells of Petersburg were new wonderful experiences. However, there were other less pleasant experiences about living here too. During my first bus ride in the city it became very evident that the residents of Petersburg cared passionately about something that had next to never crossed my mind except in a classroom, the Civil War. From the moment that I had climbed the steps of a city bus, and smiling, asked the extremely overweight driver how much the fare was, I sensed a curious, unfamiliar chill in the man's demeanor. The change was immediate and puzzling to me. It seemed, for some strange reason, as if the man had taken an instant dislike to me the minute that I had opened my mouth. This distinctly odd behavior, I would come to find out, would become a familiar occurrence, as I was a "Yankee" living in the lap of Virginian, southern hospitality.

"Twenty-five cents", the driver replied to my initial inquiry about the fare, in a thick syrupy southern drawl. This was followed by a slow, scrutinizing "Y'all ain't from around here, are ya'?"

"No," I said politely, "I'm from Chicago."

"Oh... Shee-caw-go..." he retorted, mumbling to himself as he slowly shook his head in an affirming nod, as if to say, "Now it all makes sense."

He continued on. "Well, why don't cha just sit yourself ri'ch down there," he motioned to the seat directly across from him, "and I'll tell y'all the fine and glorious history of this here town!"

So, for the next thirty minutes, as the bus slowly zigzagged back and forth, meandering its way through the city streets, I obediently sat and listened to the bus driver's twenty-five cent tour of Petersburg, VA, and its place in civil war history. It seemed that every small clearing along the route had been the scene of a battle between the Stars and Stripes and the Union Jack. Polished granite stones erected to commemorate each battle stood close to the street, and the driver would stop the bus and read out loud the inscriptions carved into their mirror-like surfaces, in a somber reverent voice.

One of the highlights of the tour, at least for the bus driver, was Crater Park. Hardly able to contain his amusement, the driver gleefully recounted the story of several hundred Union soldiers, who, jackasses that they were, without any help from the Confederacy, accidentally blew themselves up. The park was a Southern monument and daily reminder to the North's stupidity.

The finale came as the bus passed General Lee's Headquarters, with it's one out of the only two surviving cucumber trees in the whole world, majestically standing in front of the white brightly painted wooden building.

Petersburg had the dubious distinction of being

the city that had provided me with my first personal experience as the target of irrational, purposeful prejudice. It also was the only place that I had witnessed unbridled bigotry flaunted on its streets. It was common place on a warm breezy Sunday afternoon to see a Ku Klux Klansman, complete with white robes and hood, standing in the middle of a four lane country highway, enthusiastically waving any white skinned passersby into a field for a Klan rally, like it was some kind of family picnic. It was my experience that at least the bigots in the North had the common sense to hide their feelings, but here, these people wore their hate like a badge, with a sense of pride for all the world to see. There definitely was ugliness under the bright Easter egg colored blossoms of the city. For me it was a foreign and disturbing place to live, but let's face it, there wasn't any choice.

Jake had been drafted into the Army. Twenty-one days after receiving his draft notice, at 4:30 on the morning of December 12, 1966, he reported for duty at a downtown Chicago induction center, just two weeks shy of our six-month wedding anniversary. The speed, at which our lives had completely changed, had left our heads spinning and made the whole process seem like a bad dream.

The three weeks between his draft notice and his report date were filled with investigations and formulations of plans for making Jake a less desirable candidate for the military. Punctured eardrums, missing fingers, and dislocated shoulders all were considered sufficient reasons to flunk the Army physical. But neither of us had the guts or the stupidity to perform the necessary physical abuse that would result in crippling Jake just enough to keep him out of harm's way. So he went to report as a perfect 1-A. His parents and I had watched in the early morning darkness, as the sleet lightly tapped against our car window, while he walked through a dimly lit doorway and into an uncertain and frightening future.

Jake went through the mental and physical torture of boot camp at Fort Campbell, Kentucky, including a nasty bout with double pneumonia and a resulting ten-day stay in the base hospital. As for me, after a few nights alone in our apartment, I locked the front door and moved back into my mother and father's house, back into my old room. It was almost as if I'd never left.

Christmas was spent apart. The Army had not allowed him to come home for the holidays so the first time that I'd seen him after we had parted on that dark, cold December morning, was at his graduation from boot camp. His father and mother had driven me to Kentucky for the event. The drive had been nerve-racking. It had started to snow from the minute that we had gotten into the car, and the storm did not let up until we crossed the Kentucky border. Jake's father had been drinking while he was driving, something that had made me very uneasy. However, the almost head-on collision with a semi-truck that resulted from an out of control skid, across four lanes of desolate highway, had sobered him up for the rest of the trip. God, I hated going anywhere with his family!

After an all too short two-week leave, Jake went to Fort Lee Virginia for his MOS (military

occupational specialty) training. Jake had re-upped
in boot camp when he had learned that a 3 year, RA
(Regular Army) soldier, had a better chance of not
being sent to 'Nam, than a 2 year, US draftee. As a
matter of fact, the recruiter had promised him that
his first duty station would be in the States and that
he would probably wind up with a tour in
Germany instead of 'Nam. So far, the Army had
come through. He had been sent to Virginia, to be
trained in heavy equipment repair instead of to Fort
Leonard Wood for jungle training as a foot soldier.

As soon as Jake found out that wives were
allowed to live off base with their soldier husbands,
I had packed up a suitcase with two plates, two
cups, corresponding cutlery, clothing, and a set of
bed sheets. And apprehensive but ecstatic, I went to
Virginia, on a Greyhound bus.

Jake had become friendly with another soldier
in his MOS training class, whose wife was also
coming to Virginia so we wound up sharing a place
to live with them. We shared a first floor, two-
bedroom apartment. The building had originally
been slaves' quarters and the land it was on had
been a large plantation, which had subsequently
been turned into a small estate in the better part of
suburban Petersburg.

So many soldiers were being killed in Vietnam
that it had become necessary to run the military
training school twenty-four hours a day. Jake and
Jim had the third shift. They went to class from
eleven p.m. to seven a.m. while Darlene and I were
home together alone during the night.

The two-story wood framed building where we
lived was situated several hundred yards off the

main road and nestled among trees and bushes. Over ten acres of land lay between our building and the luxurious estate house of the landlord. All of that didn't mean the apartment was pleasant to live in. It wasn't. The house was set directly on a cement slab. The floor was damp, cold, and covered with old maroon and tan streaked asphalt tiles, whose finish had long since been worn down to a scuffed, rough surface. There were no doors on the bedrooms, only shabby cloth curtains hung on rods placed across the tops of the doorways. Mold grew in the damp wallboard corners of every room causing an under lying mildew odor to be ever present.

And the place had bugs! Large black hard-shelled bugs with long antennae sticking out of their heads. God! They were disgusting! I had never lived with bugs before and I was shocked to learn that the ugly black beetles were cockroaches! The sight of one scurrying across the floor made my skin crawl. The landlord didn't seem too concerned and said, when we complained, that we should get used to it because "The south is full of bugs and such."

The shower had a cement floor and cinder block wall, both of which had been painted numerous times. Peeling paint produced multicolored globs of residue on the floor, which felt like slime under your feet when you showered. There was a small metal framed, rectangular frosted window in the shower located about five feet up from the floor. We used to partially tilt it open at the top, just enough to allow the steam to escape from the damp, foggy bathroom, into the moist warm night.

We couldn't do that anymore. One night last week, after walking out to the road at about midnight to place a letter to Momma in the mailbox, I'd turned to walk back. And in the faint moonlight, standing along the side of our building, I saw something. The silhouette of a tall white man in what appeared to be Army fatigues, looking in our small bathroom window while Darlene was taking a shower.

"A peeping Tom!" I'd silently whispered to myself as I stood staring, my eyes fearfully frozen to the figure. Then, suddenly, as if he had heard me shout those words out loud, he had looked directly at me, sending a shot of fear through me. For a split second the two of us stood perfectly still just staring at each other and then in an instant he'd bolted through the bushes and was gone.

The police had been called and it was almost funny at how certain they were that he must have been some big black guy, instead of the tall lean white soldier that I had seen, so they really were no help at all. Talking about it later, Darlene and I figured that he must have been from the base and somehow knew that Jake and Jim had wives that were alone at night. When the police had gone the two of us went around to the side of the house and looked at the place in the bushes and weeds, outside the shower window, where the peeper had been standing. From the way that the greenery had been trampled into the wet earth, we could tell that he must have been coming to see the nightly show for quite awhile.

"Maybe my catching him in the act, and the

police showing up and all, scared him and he won't be coming back." I thought to myself, as I walked down the sidewalk and underneath the cherry blossoms on this wonderfully warm and sunny morning. It had been over a week since I'd caught the peeper, and Darlene and I still hadn't been able to sleep very well at night, even with every light on in the apartment. Between that incident and the bugs, I didn't think that Darlene and I had gotten a decent night's sleep since we'd moved in. Jake and Jim were certain the peeper had been permanently frightened away but what else could they choose to believe? Uncle Sam doesn't change your schedule just because some loony likes to look at your wife when she's naked!

A puff of warm wind brought my attention back to the present, and I realized that I was almost home. Stepping up the pace, I rounded a turn in the street and the trees and bushes that marked the beginning of the grounds of the estate came into view.

"Jake should be awake soon. When I get home I'll start cooking his eggs." Today was Friday and because he had been in school until seven this morning, he would be off the rest of the day and tomorrow. And back in class late Sunday night.

Things had changed a lot since we'd come here. Jake had started to realize, as he'd gotten to know other Army guys who were married, that some of the "dos" and "don'ts" that he had set down for me were not the norm. Going out of the apartment without him was no longer a taboo as long as it was to do necessary things. Trips to the store or to the Laundromat were done during the day while he slept, and going out alone gave me a feeling of freedom that I hadn't experienced since our marriage.

Living with Darlene and Jim had not worked out so well. Their concept of what was too dirty to live in and ours were miles apart. Her housekeeping was non-existent and neither picked up after themselves. At first we tried to buy groceries together but they always ate more than their share. Now we bought our food separately, labeled it, and stored it in different sides of the refrigerator and pantry. We rarely talked anymore and when we did the dialogue included only what needed to be said. The only good point to the arrangement, other than the fact that they split the rent, was that at least she was a body in the house at night, which was some comfort when she and I were alone.

I walked several yards passed the front row of yellow flowering forsythia bushes that bordered the property, and turned down the sandy dirt driveway towards the house. The warm breeze kicked up a little and softly blew my hair around my face. This was the first really warm day since we had arrived and all the blossoms were out in force. The grounds certainly were lovely. Too bad the house was so yucky.

Walking through the side door I looked into the kitchen and saw that Jake was sitting at the table having a cigarette.

"Where have you been? I've been up for almost a fucking hour and I'm hungry!" he said. I could tell that he was pissed.

"Just walked up to the store to get a few things

that we were out of so I could cook you some breakfast when you got up." I said in the most cheery tone I could muster, and went over to him and gave him a kiss on the cheek. That seemed to calm him down a bit, and he got up, looked into the fridge and got a beer out.

"Jake, you haven't had anything to eat yet. Do you have to?" That was the one thing about him being in the service that I hated. Even though he was only nineteen, he could buy all the beer that he wanted. Nobody cared if a soldier drank beer. After all, let's get real. He could be blown away in some Vietnamese jungle by his next birthday.

"Hey, get off my fucking back! It's passed noon, and as long as ya' don't fucking drink before noon, you're not an alcoholic." And then he kind of laughed to himself. I stood there and watched him grind his Camel out in the glass ashtray, open the can and take a sip.

"Get those fucking eggs going, I got things that I want to do!" That was another thing I didn't like about the service. Every other word out of his mouth was fuck. He said it more often than I had liked before he went into the Army, especially when he was mad. But now it was a non-stop articulation.

Suddenly, without a warning, I heard Darlene let out a blood-curdling scream from the front room where she and Jim were sitting when I came in the door.

"EEEEE... Oh my God! Look at them! What do we do? Oh my God!"

Jake and I bolted into the front room and stopped dead in our tracks, overwhelmed by the sight in front of our eyes. BUGS! Hundreds of BUGS! BUGS pouring like a black river out of the two twelve inch square gratings in the floor that were located on either side of the room. I thought that a few roaches were bad, but this was beyond belief!

"Do we have bug spray?" I shouted above her screams. Everyone shook their heads. And the bugs kept coming. I didn't want them to get out of the front room so I ran and got the broom out of the kitchen. Returning, broom in hand, I started to sweep the torrent of big black water bugs, back into the front room.

Darlene looked comical in a bizarre kind of way, as she frantically hopped from one leg to the other while the black beetles started to swarm around her feet. She hopped back and forth her arms clenched tightly against her body, each movement emphasized with a short piercing scream. Her movements became very quick and jerky and her hopping ended in loud stamps as she tried to keep the beetles from climbing up her legs.

Instinctively, almost in unison, we all started to stamp on the big black bugs trying to crush as many of them as we could beneath our feet. It was truly revolting! As I stomped the tile floor I could feel what seemed like hundreds of the bugs' shelled bodies popping under my feet.

Finally, after about fifteen minutes of foot pounding and smashing, the four of us stood still and surveyed the carnage. What looked like thousands of smashed beetles covered the front room tile floor. It had become littered with insect corpses. Their shells were flattened and cracked open with yellow ooze leaking out of them and it was smeared all over the tiles. Clumps of bug parts had stuck to the soles of our shoes and we all went running out the door and began rubbing the remnants of the disgusting things off the bottoms of our shoes on the fresh, clean, green grass.

"Jesus H. Christ!" Jim half laughed half shouted in a shaking voice, still rubbing his shoes over and over in the soft grass as if he would never get them clean, no matter how much he tried.

"I've never seen anything like that before!" Darlene said as she stood next to Jim trembling, her voice tinged with tones of hysteria.

"Well, whatever it was we have to get back in and clean it up. There are a bunch of guys coming over tonight for a party." Then as an afterthought I mumbled, "God, where did they come from?"

"Who the fuck knows?" Jake said with irritation. "Fuck! That lousy bug shit is all over my boots. I just shined 'em, and I'm going to have to fucking do it again!" Then without another word, he made an about face, stomped back in through the doorway, made an abrupt right turn, turning away from the bugs and the slime, and disappeared in the direction of our bedroom.

The three of us stood looking after him for a moment and then Jim turned to Darlene and me.

"I'll walk across the yard, over to the main house and tell the landlord about the bugs." he said. "You guys should start cleaning up the mess ASAP." With that he turned and began to walk towards the landlord's place.

"Some help the both of them are!" I said, but then after a few seconds of thought, I continued.

"God, I hate to say it, but I guess Jim's right. No use putting it off. Come on let's get going."

Darlene and I reluctantly entered the front door, as we anticipated the job that we had to do. I was surprised to learn, when that many bugs get smashed in one place, there actually is a sickening sweet smell. It made me gag a little because I was unprepared for it. I picked up the broom that I'd dropped when the bug stomping frenzy had started.

"Hey, Darlene, go get the dust pan. I think that the first thing we need to do is sweep this shit up."

Several hours later, I stood in the archway looking into the front room. "Bugs! God, I hate them!" I said, as I sniffed the air. "Well, at least the yucky smell is gone." I had used almost every drop of pine cleaner that we had in the apartment to get the maroon asphalt tile clean. All of the smashed bug bodies were in a paper grocery bag in the garbage can out back. I was amazed at the number. They filled the bag almost three quarters full!

The landlord hadn't been too concerned about the whole disgusting episode. His comment to Jim when Jim had told him about the bug invasion had been, "One expects bugs this time of year around here. No big deal." And promptly shut the door in his face. Jim, made speechless by the comment, turned and slowly walked down the cement stairs of the mansion's front porch. It was obvious that he was not going to be any help. Boy, the people in the south were strange!

With one more look around the room I walked into the kitchen and started getting the onion dip out of the refrigerator. As the sun was setting, the small room had surprisingly taken on a warm homey atmosphere. The last rays of sunlight filtered through the dingy old kitchen window, filling the kitchen with a peachy-orange glow, softening the usual harsh naked look of the room.

Bang! The kitchen screen door had flown open, slamming against the wall with a loud noise. I jumped a little, as Jake and his best buddy, Paul, rushed through the kitchen screen door. They each had two cases of beer in their arms and were hurrying to put the heavy load down quickly on the floor. Looking at the four cases of beer stacked near the wall made me feel uneasy.

"Oohh baby! Are we going to do some serious drinking tonight!" Paul exclaimed as he surveyed the mountain of beer in front of him.

"Fucking A!" Jake shouted as the two of them slapped hands in some kind of ritualistic Army handshake.

"Shit!" I thought to myself. "Here we go again!"

$\wp$ X $\wp$

Parties! Their definition had changed since Jake had gone into the Army. Instead of being a pleasant get together of friends with a few drinks and copious hors d'oeuvres, they had turned into boozing marathons with each guy trying to out drink the other.

I guess you could say that I was a non-drinker. I didn't care for it much. My only experience with the stuff had been five double shots of Duffy's, "150 proof", Bourbon. Supplied to me by Jake, and pinched by the same, from an old dusty case of bottles hidden in his father's basement. It was the same potent stuff that, several months later, had caused Jake to collapse and fall down a flight of steps clutching his chest from lack of breath, after downing half a bottle.

I was fifteen and naive enough at the time to think that inebriation was a state of the mind. Jake had lined up five double shots of the brown liquid fire to prove a point and I had downed every one of them in defiance, one right after the other. For a short time afterwards, nothing seemed to happen. Jake was amazed. Then in one movement I found out how wrong I'd been. I stood up, and instantly I went from sober to totally creamed! To this day, I barely remember bits and pieces of the rest of the night, and the hangover the next morning had been a doozy!

Now, sitting here on the old bumpy armchair, I surveyed the crowd. The party had been going on for hours and I was getting really tired of it all. That episode, up in Jake's "apartment", was my one and only experience with alcohol and it had been enough. Not so, it seemed, for the soldiers who were attending our party this evening. Not knowing if one was going to be alive in a year or dead in some jungle or rice patty, seemed to emphasize to each of them the importance of getting drunk as often as was feasibly possible. You know the old adage, "Party today, for tomorrow you may die!"

The small apartment was packed with young soldiers, Jake's friends and acquaintances from Fort Lee. Each one was in some stage of drunkenness. The worst of which was the guy sitting upside down, and playing the guitar in the raggedy dirt brown, simulated leather chair in the corner across from me. The calves of his legs were leaning on the headrest of the chair, and his ankles were folded one over the other, with his feet sticking straight up into the air. His short bristly ash brown hair lightly brushed the maroon asphalt linoleum, the previous scene of the untold bug and guts carnage of a few hours before.

"If he only knew!" I chuckled a bit. A well-worn acoustic guitar lay precariously across his chest, his hands still in position and his fingers on the strings. He looked as if he was floating upside down, defying gravity. The strumming had stopped. With his eyes closed and a slight boyish smile on his face, the soldier looked serene. Then without warning it happened. Vomit spewed out of the guy's nostrils spreading quickly into a large slimy pool on the tile. What was weird about it was that he didn't seem to be making a sound while the putrid liquid streamed out his nose and onto the floor.

As the disgusting stuff splashed, two other soldiers who had been sitting along the sides of the chair, quickly jumped to their feet, picked him up still upside down with guitar in hand, and swiftly carried him towards the kitchen door. The jostling motion must have cleared his airway and allowed him a breath or two, because as they carried him out the door into the side yard, dumping him onto the grass, his retching could be heard above the hoots and roars of male laughter.

I really failed to see the humor in the situation! I had just gotten done a few hours ago cleaning a bunch of bug guts and now this shit! Yeah, I knew that some of these guys may not make it to their next birthday, but that story gets old after a few piles of puke. Getting a bucket from under the kitchen sink and filling it with dish soap and water, I hurried back into the front room. Just as I had thought, in the time it took me to get the bucket, some drunken idiot not watching where he was going, had slipped and almost fell in the stuff and succeeded in tracking it all over the front room floor.

Disgusted, I yelled over the racket, "OK everyone, give me a brake! Move away from the crap until I get it wiped up!" With dull eyes, about ten guys slowly reacted, stepping a couple feet back, and then blankly watched me as I started to clean up. Someone in the background was still laughing. "Some guys have a great sense of humor." I murmured to myself as I dunked and swished the slimy rag through the hot sudsy water.

Fifteen minutes later, the job was finished. Carrying the bucket through our bedroom to the bathroom to dump it down the toilet, I noticed that the bathroom door was closed. I hadn't seen Jake since before the guitar guy threw up and I wondered where he'd gone. Maybe he was in the bathroom, so I knocked on the door and called his name. Silence. I knocked again, and still nothing. I put the bucket down and tried the door. It was unlocked but it only opened a sliver of the way. Through the slit I could see the cuff of a pants leg belonging to someone curled up around the base of the toilet bowl. I tried to push against the door to open it wider but it wouldn't budge.

"Damn, if that's Jake, I am going to be so pissed! Maybe I can still find Paul and he can help me get the door open." Turning around to go back through the bedroom and into the kitchen, I caught a glimpse of a bare foot sticking out from under the covers of my bed.

"So that's where you are!" I said disgusted, as I carefully pulled back the bed cover. He was passed out again, laying face down, fully clothed (except for his socks and shoes and God knows where they were!), and spread eagle across our bed. I flipped the cover back over him. Obviously, in his condition, he wasn't going to be any help.

I wondered who it could be laying on my bathroom floor, hugging my toilet. Irritated, I walked quickly through the curtained bedroom doorway and into the short hallway that led to the kitchen, loudly calling Paul's name. In a second or two, Paul came bounding through the screened back door amazingly sober and willing to help out in any way.

Paul was a nice guy. He seemed to be older and wiser than his nineteen years, and I'd often thought how lucky his wife was to be able to depend on him and always trust that he would do the right thing. He was that kind of a guy. He and his wife had decided that she wouldn't join him at MOS training. She needed to keep working and save some money so that she could afford to join him at his first duty station, wherever that might be. Paul had been drafted like Jake, and he also had chosen to re-up for the extra year to make the odds better that he might not go to 'Nam. He and Jake made kind of an odd pair. He seemed so together and Jake had such a long way to go.

"I guess that opposites do attract." I thought to myself as I looked at Paul while he was asking me why I had called him.

"Hey, what's up?" Paul said with a smile.

"Some guy is passed out on the bathroom floor and he seems to have wedged himself between the toilet and the door. Jake is no help. He's unconscious. I can only get the door open an inch and no matter how hard I push, it won't budge! I'd hate to see all these guys start relieving themselves in the backyard. I'm sure the landlord would love that!" I nervously started to laugh a little. God I hated "parties"!

Calmly he said, "Don't worry. I'll take care of it. I'll get the joker out of the john. It shouldn't take too long." And that's exactly what he did.

"Thank God for small favors" I thought to myself.

An hour or so later, the last soldier had stumbled out of the apartment. Darlene and Jim had gone to the movies and then stayed in their bedroom all evening. It was Jake's party and neither of them had wanted anything to do with the drinking bash. Exhausted, I plopped down on the nearest kitchen chair like a sack of potatoes. Paul came into the kitchen and flopped down in the chair a few feet away. We both had surveyed the damage in the apartment and the place was a mess! Ashtrays with cigarettes over flowing and partially drank or spilled bottles of beer littered every room. The place smelled like a cheap bar. The bathroom floor had pee puddles all over the linoleum around the toilet and it smelled like a dirty urinal. Even the backyard was full of empty beer bottles and I also found a few piles of puke strategically placed next to the honeysuckle by the back fence. God, it was such a mess!

"Hey, don't look so down. I'll help you clean it up and we'll be done before you know it." Paul reached over and patted my shoulder.

By four in the morning, the place was cleaned up. I said goodnight to Paul who was sleeping over on the front room sofa, and made my way back to my bedroom. Untying the rope that held back the cheap dingy flowered curtain, I pulled it across the doorway affording myself a small shred of privacy. My body ached from all the floor scrubbing and my hands were red and sore from the hot soapy water that they'd been in, on and off, all day. Rubbing them together I was wishing that I had some lotion to put on them. Too tired to change I took off my shirt and pants, and stood in my underwear at the side of the bed evaluating the situation.

Jake was still facedown and sprawled entirely across the bed in the same position that he was in a few hours before. I felt a slight tinge of panic as I wondered if he was still breathing. But looking closely I could see the sides of his chest moving slowly in and out. Quietly I sat down on the corner of the bed and tried to figure out how I was going to fit. After moving around for a second or two, I softly, tried nudging Jake's arm and shoulder out of the way, but it didn't do any good.

"Jake. Jake, could you move a little so that I could lie down and go to sleep?" I whispered, as I tried nudging his shoulder again. There still was no response. So I nudged him a little harder and said a little louder, "Jake come on. Please move over so I can lie down." Again there was no response. I was starting to get irritated about the whole thing. God, the least he could do, was move his ass over so I could get some sleep!

"Jake!" I said loudly, "Move over!" And as I said "move", I pushed his shoulder as hard as I could, trying to roll him over on his side so that there would be enough room for me to lie beside him.

Before I knew what had happened his full weight was sitting on top of me! Both of his hands were around my neck, squeezing so tight that I couldn't make a sound, and choking my air completely off! I tried to move but my body was pinned under him as he straddled my waist and pushed down harder on my throat. He squeezed tighter and tighter and my head buzzed as I tried to pry his hands off of my neck by peeling his fingers from my throat. For what seemed like an eternity I laid there soundlessly, mouth wide open, pulling at his hands, shock giving way to fear as I looked into his eyes. His face loomed over me but there was no expression on it. There was no anger or rage, only a blank stare. It was as if he was looking at me but didn't see me or know who I was. It was like nobody was home behind his eyes.

My head was swimming from lack of oxygen, and then for some unknown reason, he loosened his grip for a second. That was just enough time for me to croak out "Jake! What are you doing?" before his hands tightened their grip around my throat again. As I struggled, trying to gasp for air, I saw a flicker of recognition pass over his blank stare, and he again loosened his hands a little.

"Jake… Stop…" I croaked, and this time he did not retighten his grip. I started to make choking gagging sounds and with that he let go.

As abruptly as it had started, it had ended. With a sudden thump, he collapsed on top of me, limp like a dead man. Hoarsely sobbing and coughing, I managed to roll him off of me and onto the far side of the bed. Cowering, I scurried to the top portion of the mattress and leaned against the cracked dirty wall. My breath was coming in short, raspy spurts, a result of the throttling, the panic, and being on the edge of hysterical tears.

"What the hell was that?" I said with tears finally flowing down my beet red cheeks. "Oh my God! What the hell was that?" I croaked again, as I began to quietly rock back and forth. Bewildered and in shock I began to sob. I cried until dawn, still in total disbelief, not knowing what one does next in a situation like this. Finally, I fell asleep curled up on the corner of the bed.

When I woke up later that morning, I could hear Jake and Paul's voices in the kitchen. My face felt like it had five pounds of water pumped into it. My eyes were so swollen from the previous night's tears, that I could hardly open them. I went to the bathroom and looked into the old spotted mirror that hung above the chipped, discolored sink, and was disturbed by what I saw.

After gazing at my puffed up face and eyes, I carefully inspected the long thin red raspberry marks that had appeared on my neck. They reminded me of the marks I used to get on my arms as a child when my cousin Harry got carried away giving me an "Indian burn". You know, taking a persons forearm in both hands and twisting them, and the skin between, in opposite directions.

I was surprised to see that there weren't any deep dark bruises. Last night's episode had certainly felt like there should be bruises. My neck and throat were still sore, and the action of clearing my throat was painful.

If I didn't know last night what I should do, I woke up in the morning understanding the next step completely. My mother had always said that being hit by a man was the one thing that a woman should never tolerate. It was true that she and my father still lived in the same house since the incident that I had witnessed in the front room, but I knew that night had sealed his fate. She had recently told me that she had made arrangements with a lawyer to start divorce proceedings. Now that I was married it was her turn to live life, and she didn't have to wait to enjoy it any longer. Oh, there was one more thing. There was someone else, someone that she loved, an older widower named John whom she had met at work. He adored her and she adored him and I was glad for her. She deserved to finally have some happiness.

Well, I knew what I would have to do. It would be difficult but I would have to leave him. Being pushed around by a man was not an option for a woman. I knew that.

"So much time invested and wasted!" I silently thought.

I got my clothes on and walked out of the bedroom, through the hallway, and into the kitchen where Paul and Jake were sitting at the kitchen table, both with a cup of coffee in hand. Soft morning light was filtering through the thread worn kitchen curtains and I could hear some kind of bird singing just out side the window.

"What the fuck happened to you?" Jake asked in a truly concerned tone, the expression on his face mirroring the worry and concern in his voice.

Dumbfounded, with my mouth hanging slightly open, I silently stared back at Jake in disbelief.

"I said, what the fuck happened to you?" He paused, waiting for a response. The concern in his voice was starting to wane and irritation was taking its place.

I didn't respond.

Impatiently he started to raise his voice, "What the hell is wrong with you?" Then he loudly ordered, "Answer me!"

Breaking my silence, my first few words were

forced out almost in a whisper, and then the rest followed quickly, tumbling out of my mouth. My voice raised in intensity as I spoke each word, the last of which was uttered in a high-pitched screech.

"Are you telling me that you don't remember what happened last night...What... you did to me?"

"What the fuck, are you talking about?" Jake seemed genuinely confused and extremely irritated by my questions.

"This is bullshit!" I screamed. "You choked me for no reason, until I was almost unconscious and then passed out on top of me, and all you can say is that you don't know what I'm talking about? I'm going to have to leave you! Everything we've gone through, our life together is over! Wasted! And all you can say is that you don't know what I am talking about?"

"Your fucking crazy, you bitch!" he roared. "I never touched you last night! Why the fuck are you making this up? You're fucking crazy!" As the last sentence boomed out of his mouth, his beet red face grossly contorted in anger, he started to stomp towards me, knocking over the gray plastic upholstered kitchen chair, it's pitted chrome legs "pinging" as it hit the asphalt tiled floor.

"Hold on a minute!" Paul shouted, jumping up from his seat and getting between Jake and me. Forcefully, he placed his hand in the middle of Jake's chest attempting to hold him back.

Jake roughly pushed his hand away and yelled into his face, "Paul! Stay the fuck out of this! It's none of your fucking business!"

Firmly, and with complete control, Paul placed his hand back on Jake's chest and replied, "It is my business, buddy! I was here last night. Remember? And I heard the whole thing!"

Jake looked as if Paul had just hauled off and slapped him square in the face. He stopped dead in his tracks and stared straight into Paul's eyes, desperately looking for some sign, some flicker of untruth in them.

"It's true!" Paul said keeping his eyes riveted to Jake's. And then in a soft tone laced with compassion, he placed his other hand on Jake's shoulder and said, "It's all true, buddy. Everything that she said is true. I heard it all. It got so bad that I was just about to go into your bedroom and pull you off of her when I heard her start to cry. When I didn't hear anything else I figured it was all over. Nothing for me to do, but leave it alone." The conflicting feelings of sadness and guilt in Paul's voice were evident as he finished the last few words.

"You're fucking crazy!" Jake shouted as he jerked his shoulder away from Paul's touch. "You're both fucking crazy." This time he said it with a little less conviction, a look of confusion growing in his eyes. "Fuck! I can't remember anything like that happening! I can't... I, fuck..."

As Jake's words dropped off, Paul firmly said again, "You did it, Jake. You did what she said."

Confused and bewildered, Jake placed his fingertips on his temples and began to rub. His eyes darted back and forth, first to me then to Paul and back again.

"Why can't I...remember? I...," his voice falling off as his mind overloaded, trying to comprehend something that was incomprehensible. For a moment we all stood silently, a light gentle breeze softly blew the tattered kitchen curtains in a slow rhythmic dance.

"Shit, Jake!" Paul's words shattered the silence. "Just too much booze, buddy! Way too much! I'll bet you drank more than a case of beer along with the shots that you and Pete were doin'! It messed with your mind, man. Just way too much..." The last sentence was said in a quiet comforting tone, accented by Paul laying his hand back on Jake's shoulder.

Jake flopped onto one of the kitchen chairs, the air escaping out of the gray plastic covered stuffed seat making a sound like a trickster's whoopee cushion. Sitting in the chair, he began to massage his head again as he stared blankly at the floor. Slowly, he raised his face to me, expressionless except for a solitary tear track that ran down his right cheek.

"Fuck! I'm sorry! I...I don't know what else to say. I just don't remember!" I believed him. I just knew deep in my gut that he was telling the truth.

"Well, where do we go from here?" I softly said, more to myself than to him. It's like the old joke about being a little pregnant. There's no such thing. You can't take something like this back. Either you're a virgin or you're not. He crossed the line. He pushed you around and now you HAVE TO leave him! No smart self respecting woman stays with a man who pushes her around! That's the rules!

"I just won't fucking drink that much anymore! I think that's what did it. I just drank too fucking much!" He said this with such conviction as he stared back down at the cracked asphalt tile floor, that I felt a glimmer of hope. Maybe he was right! Whatever happened had been beyond his control. He didn't mean it. Since he had gotten to Virginia, he'd been drinking more than he ever had in his whole life. In this inexperience, he'd probably passed over into a realm that he didn't understand or know how to control. He had never done anything like this before. He hadn't actually hauled off and hit me, and I knew, if he hadn't drank so much it wouldn't have happened.

So maybe he was right! Maybe all he needed to do was not to get that drunk again. A feeling of relief washed over me.

"That's the solution!" I thought to myself. No more wasted life, no more broken dreams. It could be like it was just yesterday, before this ugly thing had happened.

And so it was.

❧ XI ❧

"Big Burgers" were absolutely delicious! Besides cherry blossoms, they were the only other things that Virginia had introduced me to that knocked my socks off. Jake and I took a walk to get "Big Burgers" for supper as often as we could afford to. They were the only six-inch wide hamburgers that I had ever seen. They were almost twice as big as the competition and twice as good. The hamburger meat was pressed thin and covered the large bun all the way to its edges. Fried onions and chopped lettuce smothered the top of the patty and melted cheese oozed out from the bottom of the meat. Some kind of mayo secret sauce mixture was spread on the inside of both the bottom and top buns, and the whole thing was placed in a large flat brownish gray cardboard box.

Sitting on a brown wooden picnic table outside of the "Big Burger" hamburger stand, Jake and I were soaking up the last few rays from a bright orange-pink setting sun. The early spring days had turned to gentle warm summer days, even though the calendar still said early May. A few weeks longer and we would be on our way to Ft. Hood Texas, Jake's first duty station. He was almost done with school and the Army had kept its word. His next stop was state side, not Vietnam.

"Hurry up and fucking finish!" I was finishing up my last bit of "Big Burger" when Jake had interrupted my thoughts. "You know we still have about a half a mile to walk before we get to the fucking phone booth. I don't want to have you talking to your mother all fucking night! I'd like to take a fucking nap before the guys come over."

Every other week Jake and I would take turns calling our parents to tell them that we were OK and to check to see how things were going back home. Today was an exception to the rule. We had heard on the news that a tornado had done a lot of damage to homes and businesses in Oak Lawn, a middle class suburban community a few miles south of the Chicago city limits. It was a place where, as teenagers, we'd spent a lot of time cruising the streets, and stopping at a local drive-in for hamburgers. A tornado touching down that close to the city was unheard of, and having it happen in our childhood stomping grounds made it all feel kind of personal. Jake had thought that maybe the news programs were blowing the whole thing out of proportion, so we were anxious to get the real story.

Fifteen minutes later I was standing in the phone booth dialing my home phone number. I missed my mother a lot. I missed just hearing her voice. The bi-monthly phone calls helped my homesickness a little. She had a really painful kidney infection lately, and I was mildly worried about her. Bladder and kidney infections were no big deal in a woman's life, but this one was taking a long time to get rid of. The pain in her lower back never seemed to go completely away. She never complained about aches and pains, but I could tell from her letters that the stubbornness of this bug was getting her down. After a couple of faraway sounding rings, the ever so wonderfully familiar, "Hello" came over the wires and into my heart.

"Hi Momma! How are you doing?" I could hear the sounds of little children playing in the background. Before she could answer I followed up with, "Are Claudette and the kids over?"

"Well, I guess you could say that. Since Mick is in jail for thirty days, Claudette decided to come and stay with us."

Mick in jail? What did he do? Could we have been wrong? I remembered that after I had told Momma about Mick and his affinity for flashing, way back when, just after the Tina incident, Momma had called my brother-in-law John for help. After all, he was my sister Carole's husband and a doctor. Momma felt that if anyone could give her good advice on what to do next in this situation, it would be John.

John had gotten in touch with one of his old friends from medical school who had become a shrink, and asked his opinion. His friend said guys that expose themselves, rarely, if ever, do much of anything else. They don't progress to rape or anything like that, they are virtually harmless. He suggested that we tell his wife (Claudette) about the situation, and get him some psychiatric help, if he'd accept it.

After that bit of advice, Momma had a heart to heart with Mick and told him that she knew the whole disgusting story about what he had been up to with Tina and me. She told him about John and his psychiatrist friend, and said that she intended to tell Claudette about the whole mess as soon as possible. Momma told me later, that Mick had tearfully admitted his transgressions, blaming booze for all the episodes of perversion. He begged her to let him explain things to Claudette and feeling compassion for the sobbing asshole in front of her, she had agreed.

That day had been painful for all of us. On the following Saturday, Mick had made arrangements for he and my sister to drop the kids off at our house. He told Claudette that he needed some time alone with her to talk about something important. I can remember my sister smiling, standing in the front room unbuttoning one of the girls' sweaters, getting ready to leave the children with Momma and me. She appeared to be looking forward to some time alone with her husband, not suspecting what unpleasantness lay in store for her. Mick had stayed in the car, and I had felt terribly guilty standing there holding the baby and returning her smile as she hurried out the door.

"God!" I thought to myself, "This was going to crush her! How would she be able to stay with him after what she was about to find out?"

But she did.

Several hours later, she had returned to the house. Her eyes were red and swollen. The front room was eerily silent as Momma and I helped to get the kids together for their ride home. Not one word was spoken between us and I figured that there was no reason to ask her how she was feeling. It was obvious. I remember hoping that she didn't hate me because of what had happened, but after that day she acted as if nothing had. That's something that I still couldn't figure out. Neither of us had ever brought up the issue for discussion, no question about how or why, no details were asked or given, nothing. So I reasoned, if that was the way she'd wanted it, I would respect that, and not talk about it again.

There had been two cases of his weirdness since then, and her reaction to them both still kind of puzzled me. Both episodes had happened in the month or so before my wedding. Claudette, being my matron of honor, was going to hold my bridal shower at her house, so it was necessary for me to spend several evenings planning the event with her in her kitchen. On one of those evenings Mick had been sleeping on the couch downstairs in their recreation room. Unknown to both of us, he had evidently been sleeping naked, wrapped up in a large thick comforter. As my sister and I started down the steps to look at some of the decorations that she had stored there, Mick had sleepily gotten up from the sofa and started for the stairs with the blanket still wrapped around him. Just as my sister passed him at the bottom of the steps, Mick appearing to be half-asleep rearranged the blanket around himself, and when he did, he flashed me a full view of his naked body! Claudette looked back and caught a glimpse of the look on my face.

"Mick! Be careful! Remember, Susan is here!" Then, embarrassed, she nervously laughed and said, "Sorry, he's so tired lately, he didn't realize." To that remark I remembered thinking, "Boy, who is she kidding?"

Shortly after that, he'd struck again. The evening of my shower, after everyone had gone home, Claudette and I were sitting on the couch in her front room, looking at all the cards and gifts that I'd received. Suddenly, I got a strange feeling, a feeling as if someone was staring at me. I looked up from the cards in my lap, up towards the staircase directly across the room from the both of us, up to where the bedrooms were. Something odd caught my eye. At first, I couldn't make sense out of what I was seeing, and then recognition kicked in. It was a disembodied dick sticking out of one of the bedroom doorways! Immediately I knew that Mick was up to his old tricks again. This time I'd made the decision not to ignore what was happening, to call my sister's attention to it immediately. She had also been looking at a card in her lap, when I gave her shoulder a nudge. I saw her follow my gaze up the steps to her husband's penis sticking out of the doorway, approximately three feet or so from the ground. It took only a second. She shot up off the couch and bounded up the stairs. A few short minutes later, she came back down, making apologies for the embarrassing episode.

"Sorry about that. Mick sleeps in the nude and you know how men get when they've been sleeping and have to go to the bathroom. Well, Mick was trying to make a quick run for it, and he didn't realize he was, shall we say, sticking out into our view."

I pretended to accept her rationalization, but considering the past, was bewildered as to why she even acted like she'd believed it. I'd figured that instead of admitting to me that her husband was still a pervert, she would rather keep up the facade that it wasn't so. She was in denial, and who was I to point out reality to her. After all, I wasn't the one with a sexual deviate for a husband. How could I judge? I knew that she was handling things as best as she could, but I still couldn't figure out how she could live with him, knowing the truth. And that had been my view on things until now.

"What has he done now?" I reluctantly asked Momma, heartsick by the fact that my deranged brother-in-law was causing my sister to live in hell.

"Oh Susan, I am sorry! I haven't had a chance to tell you what's been happening. It's been such a nightmare. He's out done himself this time!" Momma really sounded upset.

"That's OK. I know that things can get overwhelming, especially when you're not feeling so good. So what happened?" I asked again.

"There's been so much going on I don't know where to start. I think that it was about a month or so ago. According to Mick's lawyer, the police had initially gotten Mick's license plate number from an old woman who had been riding home on a city bus a couple of weeks before. She'd been looking out the window when she had noticed a man in a car riding along side the bus. To her shock and dismay, he was exposing himself. She reported that he had rode along side the bus in that state for quite awhile, speeding up and slowing down, attempting to give everybody in the bus a good look. Even though she was shook up, she had the presence of mind to copy down his license plate number and reported the incident to the police as soon as she got off the bus and could reach a phone.

The police had called Mick at home and said that his license plate number had been reported in a minor hit and run accident and he needed to come down to the station and get things straightened out. Knowing that he hadn't been involved in any such thing, and anxious to prove his innocence, he hurried to the station. When faced with the accusation, Mick denied the whole thing. The police couldn't do much with the charges because, believe it or not, the old lady was the only one on the bus to report it! Plus, she hadn't seen the driver's face, so she couldn't positively identify him. So Mick was released, and Claudette never did find out the real reason why Mick had been called down to the police station.

And then, according to the police report, the second incident happened. Two elderly women had been sitting in their kitchen next to a large picture window that faced the alley in back of their house. They had just finished dinner and were relaxing and chatting over a cup of coffee at the kitchen table, when one of them noticed a man climbing onto the garbage cans in the alley. She quietly called the attention of her companion to the strange goings on. Then, without a word, she got up from the table and slowly and calmly left the room to call the police, pretending that she hadn't noticed anything peculiar. The other woman sat and casually looked around the kitchen while she waited for her friend to return and the police to show up to investigate. Every so often, she would try to nonchalantly turn his way and catch a glimpse of what he was doing. At first, it was hard to figure out and she couldn't stare. She didn't want to frighten him away before the police got there. It was dark and he was about twenty feet from where she sat. He was silhouetted against the light shining from the street lamp in the alley as he stood on top of the garbage cans. He was turned slightly towards the light and she noticed his hands were fumbling below his waist. He was rhythmically rubbing something, and in the sudden flash of light that illuminated and poured over him when the police arrived on the scene, no doubt was left in her mind, what he was rubbing. I guess you could say that he got caught red-handed!"

I gave out an agonized groan at Momma's attempt at humor.

"Mick was arrested and put into a lineup where he was positively identified by the two elderly women as the man who exposed himself to them!"

"Oh my God! I knew that he was sick but I never dreamed anything like this would happen!" I said. Momma then continued.

"Daddy and I had gotten a late night phone call from Claudette telling us that Mick was in jail and needed to be bailed out. She was upset and wasn't very clear about the reason for Mick being behind bars. In between her sobs, she had spoken some gibberish about mistaken identity and hitting a bus or something, so your father went to the police station thinking that Mick probably had gotten into some kind of trouble because he'd been drunk. We all know that he drinks too much, but your father was in no way prepared for what turned out to be the real story.

Daddy was really shocked and disgusted by the whole thing. He was mortified when he found out what the charges were when he went to bail Mick out." Momma gave a wry laugh.

"When Mick went to court, his flimsy defense was that he was coming home from bowling where he had a couple of beers, and had to pee so he pulled into the closest alley. The judge didn't believe him. After all, he never could explain why he needed to climb on a garbage can to empty his bladder. He got thirty days in Cook County and was instructed by the court that he had to attend therapy sessions for six months after that. Maybe, he'll finally get some help."

"How's Claudette taking it?" I asked concerned about how my sister was holding up under all this.

"All right I guess. She sure can't deny that he has a problem now. She was too upset to stay alone in their house and she didn't want to answer any prying questions from the neighbors, so she's staying here. It's kind of nice to have the kids here for a little while, and Daddy and I are trying to make things easier for her."

The conversation ended shortly after that. We talked for a few minutes about the tornado, which had been as bad as the radio had said it was, but after the thing with Mick it didn't seem quite so shocking. While saying goodbye, I thought about Mick. He still gave me the creeps. When I had gotten to know the neighbors at the old apartment, they had told me things, things that I'd kept to myself because they had seemed too unbelievable, too bizarre. Pat from across the street had told me that the neighborhood women were afraid of him because of his strange behavior.

She, as well as half the block, had watched him in the evenings in the dark shadows, "riding the rail on the front porch". And as she so descriptively had put it, "Rubbing himself all over it, and playing with himself too!" Whispering, she had also confided in me, "We all think that he's the one that killed Tillie, not crazy John, but him!" She was a character herself, loudmouthed and smelling from beer most of the day, and what she had been telling me was so fantastic it was easy to dismiss it as the ravings of a wacky boozer. But now, after this, the thought haunted my mind, "Could all of it have been true?"

Jake, who had been sitting on a wooden bench a few feet from the phone booth and having a cigarette, got up and came over to me as I stepped out of the booth.

"So what's new?" He asked as he ground his non-filtered cigarette into the dirt with his foot, and I told him. Walking home in the warm gentle breeze, I detailed the whole ugly thing. His reaction was not what I'd expected. He thought that the whole thing was pretty funny!

"What a fucking asshole!" he commented and laughed out loud. "He's a fucking stupid idiot! Fuck! He never could hold his fucking booze!" Puzzled at his reaction, I also mentioned the things that Pat had told me several months before and he just laughed louder.

"You don't believe that fucking fat bitch do you? She's a fucking crazy drunken cunt!" Still laughing, he looked at me as if I was some naive fool.

"Fuck! Susan, by the look on your face you would think that something really fucking horrible happened!" he said.

"Hey, what did your mother say about the fucking tornado?"

❧ XII ❧

Finally, everything was quiet. Everyone had either passed out somewhere in the apartment or had gone home. I certainly would be glad when we left Virginia. Maybe things would be different in Texas. Maybe the partying would slow down a bit. Lying in bed, I could hear Jake bumping into the walls in the bathroom just a few feet away. The sound of his pee hitting the water came and went, in time with the thumping sound of his body against the wall.

"Shit! I bet he's missing the bowl half of the time. I'll have to wipe it up once he's asleep."

Bam! The bathroom door across from the bed flew open and smacked the edge of the dresser. I jumped a little bit at the sound. Since the night Jake choked me, I began to keep an eye on the amount of booze that he consumed at our fun filled drinking extravaganzas. Fear would grow as the evening wore on, matching the growing number of empty beer cans that I would count as he threw them in the garbage.

He had stopped mixing his drinks, no more shots just beer, and I was trying to be as pleasant as I could be at the end of the evening's festivities. After all, thinking over what had happened that night, I'd realized that I could have set him off by shouting at him and giving him that very large nudge to get him to move over on the bed. Maybe I had started some kind of weird chain reaction inside of him. So, no more hard liquor on his part and no more attitude on mine, seemed to be doing the trick.

Watching Jake swaying as he took his jockey shorts off by the foot of the bed, I knew I was in for it. If he had just plopped on the bed I would have been all right. He would lie where he fell all night and I could get some sleep. But shorts off meant he wanted some action, and in his condition I was not about to give him "no" for an answer.

Virginia had been an education in many respects. One of the things that I'd learned was that when men drink to oblivion they are lousy lovers. Jake would assume the position and start to pump and then, nothing. He could and would, pump for what seemed like hours, and still nothing. The massive amount of alcohol in his system would keep him from being able to come, but he would continue to shoot for it no matter how long it would take.

On my part, this flavor of fucking (it sure as hell wasn't lovemaking!) was torture. Physically it made me raw, and the next morning, urinating felt like I had been set on fire. Emotionally, it was the pits. Disgusting isn't strong enough of a word for how it feels to lay in bed for hours with a grunting drunk pumping between your legs, trying to get off.

When it first started happening, I'd tried to get into it, be responsive, sexy, hoping that I could speed things along. But I quickly found out that nothing I did mattered. He still took forever. Part of me got the feeling that the more unresponsive I was the better he liked it, but that was crazy.

The whole thing always ended one of two ways, either he finally would get a little squirt out, or more often than not, he would pass out on top of me. Either ending was fine with me as long as it was over.

"Great," I thought to myself, "here we go again. Maybe if I lay still he'll forget about it." I slowly turned on my side, and closed my eyes. In less than a second, I felt Jake yank the covers off the bed. The words "bumbling idiot" came to mind as he crawled onto the mattress towards me, falling forward on his face once, like a drunken spider. A bubble of laughter started to form in my throat but was snuffed out when I felt his hand pulling on my shoulder to roll me off of my side and onto my back. Fumbling, he tried to pull down my underpants, but when he couldn't manage it, he started to yank and pull with instant frustration and anger.

"Hold on, Jake. I'll help." And with that he let go and I slipped them off.

Well, it was inevitable.

"Brace yourself Susan! Here comes the ride!" I opened up my legs and he roughly started to push himself inside me. I wasn't ready so the first few strokes hurt like hell!

"Jake, take it easy. You're hurting me!" But saying this didn't slow things down, it sped things up. He pushed harder and faster, and I tried to move around a little, rearranging things so that it wouldn't be so uncomfortable. After a few more strokes, my body started to respond, making things easier. Now started the pumping marathon.

Time passed, maybe minutes, maybe hours, his rhythmic movement never stopping. It was like fingernails on a blackboard that went on and on.

I tried to think of other things to take my mind

off what was happening. I opened my eyes and took a look at Jake looming above me. I wondered what he was thinking, feeling. His eyes were closed and except for his mouth hanging slightly open, his face was expressionless. Every so often, his eyes would open and he would look straight at me, but I could tell, like that night when he grabbed my throat, nobody was home. A small rivulet of fear flitted through my body but quickly vanished as the reality of how sore I was getting pushed into my thoughts.

"C'mon Jake! Hurry up!" I thought to myself. "Get this over with!"

As if he heard the shouting in my head, he stopped for a second, blinked, and then closed his eyes and continued on. A few more thrusts and then in mid stroke, vomit spewed out of his mouth and splattered on to the floor beside the bed. With that "piece de resistance" he flopped on top of me unconscious and pinning me under him, one arm dangling over the edge of the bed and precariously swinging above the pile of puke.

"Thank God, that's over with!" I mumbled under my breath. Now all I needed was to get him off of me without waking him up and I was home free!

I decided not to try to roll him over, remembering what happened the last time I had nudged him too hard. We were both laying almost on the edge of the bed, so I decided to try and slip out from under him. It was some trick maneuvering myself so that I could slide out and drop down on to the floor without falling directly into Jake's partially digested supper. But I did it, and only wound up with a little slime on the bottom of my feet and hands.

Free! Even the prospect of having to clean up the mess didn't dampen my spirits. Relieved that Jake was asleep, I got the bucket from the bathroom and started to clean up. Jake had eaten peas and carrots for supper before the party had started, and now they were laying in a large glob on the green flowered linoleum floor beside the bed. The floor covering was really old and it was worn and cracked in several places. One section of it had a piece missing and some one had stuffed newspapers between the linoleum and the sub floor to fill the hole. My luck, some of Jake's regurgitated vegetables had landed on the paper, and liquid slime was soaking into it. I would need to replace the paper or the smell would never go away.

I was getting pretty good at being able to clean up disgusting stuff. It just took a little detachment from what you were doing and before you knew it everything was done. I got down on the floor and started to work, scooping up peas and carrots with my hands and ripping out pieces of disintegrating newspaper. My sister Claudette had told me that one time Mick had gotten sick and threw up in the bathroom sink. He filled the sink to the top and the chunks had plugged the drain. She had to put her whole hand in it passed her wrist to get the sink to start draining. That had cured her, after that she could clean up anything. I understood what she had meant. Virginia had been my training ground. After all, someone's got to clean things up.

❧ XIII ❧

Jake was still asleep. I'd gotten up about ten this morning to start cleaning the apartment. All of the sleeping stragglers to the party last night had left by the time I woke up. Jake and I had tons of things to do before my dad got here tomorrow night. He was coming in the Chevy "Super Sport" to help us drive through the mountains and back to Chicago. It was time to go home. Jake had two whole weeks before he had to report in at Fort Hood and we were both anxious to spend every minute we could with family and friends. Momma couldn't come. She had to work and her back was still giving her some problems. The long ride home would probably make it worse.

Jim and Darlene had already left. Jim was a two-year guy who had not re-upped and had wound up with a tour in Vietnam for his first duty station. He was already on his way home for a month's leave. After that it was on to 'Nam to fix trucks and tanks in some rice paddy. The odds were that he wouldn't be right on the frontline, fighting in hand-to-hand combat. Mechanics were usually away from the fighting so we speculated that he had a pretty good chance, that he'd be OK.

It was nice to be alone this morning, and it was peaceful and quiet in the kitchen. I had already started a pot of Sloppy Joes on the stove for lunch. I needed to use up the last bit of food in the refrigerator before we cleaned it out and this would be enough to feed us until Daddy came and we were on our way. While the hamburger and ketchup mixture slowly boiled and bubbled away, I started to clean up the kitchen so that it would be spotless when the landlord came for the walk through tomorrow.

And then I saw it. It had squeezed out of the crack between the wall and the counter top next to the stove. At first it was cautious, moving slowly, its antennae swaying high above its head in large graceful circles, smelling the air, trying to sense any possible danger. Then, when it felt safe, it started to scurry across my counter top, racing to get to the other side. I was standing like a statue, a large spoon still in my hand from stirring the simmering pot, as it ran directly in front of me.

Wham! With one swift movement I had got the bastard! I'd hit it with my spoon and the force of the blow had caused the hard-shelled bug to fly up into the air and... into the Sloppy Joes! I looked intently at the large cockroach carcass in the middle of my lunch and evaluated the situation.

Calmly, and without a hesitation, I scooped around the insect and plopped the spoonful of mixture, bug and all, in the garbage.

"No use wasting all that food." I said aloud to myself.

My own words fell on my ears and caused me to reflect on what I had just done. I remembered how I'd lay awake all night, my skin crawling with phantom bugs, after the first time I'd realized that the place was infested with little multi-legged creatures.

"Wow, some difference, huh?" I chuckled to myself. "Well, with enough time, I guess a person can get used to anything!"

PART 3

"HIATUS"

XIV

People don't always act the way you would think that they would. I'd bet that if you lined up one hundred people and outlined for them a particular circumstance and asked them what they thought their reaction or someone else's reaction to it would be, when it came right down to the real event, all one hundred would be wrong.

I acquired this unique bit of knowledge after living in Texas for less than a week. Jake had arrived first, reporting for duty and taking care of all the necessary things that a soldier needs to take care of, before he can make arrangements for his wife to join him. He had rented a room by the week for us to stay in until we could find an apartment. Off base housing was pretty scarce. Fort Hood was being over crowded with soldiers to supply the growing need for more and more men to be sent to Vietnam. The word was out that soldiers were getting wounded or killed by the droves and Army bases such as Fort Hood operated like enormous revolving doors, feeding the war machine's insatiable appetite. It was possible to find something better to live in than our weekly accommodations, but we would have to be quick and lucky.

And that's just how we found the little house on the corner, at 510 West Sprigg, Killeen, Texas. I had arrived from Chicago on a Wednesday and by Saturday we were moving into the one bedroom frame house. We had found out about the possible vacant house on late Friday afternoon. We were in a neighborhood not far from the entrance to the base, randomly walking and looking for "For Rent" signs and their associated phone numbers. An old woman sprinkling her front yard noticed us and asked if by chance we were looking for a place to rent. She believed that a house might be immediately available just up the road. With a warm smile she gave us the name and number of a person to call, and said that considering how many soldiers and their wives needed a place to stay, we would have to be quick or it would be gone. I thought that the whole thing was kind of weird and was reluctant to follow up but Jake thought that we had nothing to lose and anywhere would be better than the room where we were presently staying.

He was right about that. The woman who had rented us the room had five kids, a filthy house, and there were two old broken down cars in the backyard. Between the two of us, Jake and I referred to the place as our little piece of hillbilly heaven.

Jake and I had found a cute kitten on the dirt road in front of the woman's house, the second day that we had stayed there. The poor little thing was half-dead, and the landlady was not crazy about us keeping it in "her" room. This made no sense to me.

Once we gave little JuJu a bath (Jake named the kitten and said that it was a voodoo term that meant "strong magic") the cat was certainly cleaner than any one of her own dirty little gremlins. By Friday, we all were getting anxious for Jake and me to find another place to live.

We found a phone at the gas station about a half a mile from the old woman's house and Jake called the number that she'd given us. The next morning at 8:00 am we were standing in front of a small cottage. We had paid the landlord his money and moved our suitcases in. The place was completely furnished and it was clean! I couldn't believe that we had gotten such a deal! It had one large bedroom, a front room, a cozy little kitchen with room enough for a small table and three chairs, and a bathroom. There were old lace curtained windows and linoleum throughout the whole place and they gave the house a cool, open feeling.

The house was situated on a large corner lot, and the closest neighbor on one side of us was about a half a block away. On the other side, the neighbor's house was situated around the corner facing the adjacent street, and was set at a ninety-degree angle to ours. The two wooden back porches were fairly close and the neighbor's back door was about fifty feet from ours. There was a large lot on the other side of their house so the two houses were somewhat isolated from the rest of the neighborhood. We had an enormous common area behind the two houses and as it turned out, it was easily shared with Ray and Donna, the young Army couple who lived next door.

Texas was hot! Even though it was early June, the one hundred and five degree days had already turned the grass into short brown hay. The only green grass was above the septic tank, which I later found out was a bad thing. There also was no air conditioning in the tiny cottage and when the sun went down the darkness gave very little relief from the heat. When Jake and I went to bed that first night, we shut off all the lights and pulled the curtains back to catch the breeze through the large wooden windows. For the same purpose we had left the front and back doors open with just the screen doors hooked and locked.

I had put the clean sheets and pillowcases that I'd brought with me in my suitcase, on the aged mattress and feather pillows of our double bed. Jake and I stripped naked. Sweaty and exhausted we flopped face down on the mattress, arms and legs stretched out, being careful not to touch each other's sticky bodies. I lay there for awhile drifting, listening to the sounds of the Texas night and Jake's rhythmic breathing. The crickets were softly singing and despite the heat their peaceful chanting lulled me to sleep.

Sometime after I had fallen asleep, wisps of consciousness had come and gone, interrupting and bending my dreams. The loud conversation of soldiers, the idle of a car engine close but far away, the calling of someone's name, all faded in and out of my sleeping, dreaming mind.

"Reeowww!" I heard JuJu scream. It took me a second to compute what that meant in a fuzzy, sluggish half-awake state.

"It sounds like someone stepped on the cat. How could that be? Is the cat outside?" I thought to myself. A loud blunt thud brought me back to my senses.

"No! JuJu's inside and that's the sound of a boot landing on my front room floor! Someone's inside the house!" And before I could react, heavy footsteps shook the floorboards in the room next to me, crossing the front room quickly and assuredly from the front door to the doorway of my bedroom, and then, suddenly stopped.

I sensed the presence of a large man standing in the doorway a few feet over from the foot of my bed. I lay frozen, not moving a muscle, stark naked and calmly thinking "Gee, I'm glad I fell asleep face down!" when a deep slightly hushed southern voice broke the eerie silence.

"Jolene, is that you?"

"That was the name in my dream!" I thought to myself. Or was it a dream?

The guy seemed uncertain, hesitant and possibly confused. One thing was for certain, he had been partying. I could smell the booze as a small swirl of air created by his rushed entrance, flowed over my naked body.

And then what did I do? Did I jump up? Did I scream or yell for help? Did I shout at him, "Get the hell out of here!"? No, I did what I would never have imagined that I would do in a million years.

Still laying flat on my stomach, legs spread eagle, I lifted my head up and turned slightly toward my night visitor, and calmly but firmly said, "My name is not Jolene! And further more, I don't even know who she is! So if you would please leave so that my husband and I could go back to sleep, it would be most appreciated."

With that the man, who by now I had figured to be a young drunken soldier wanting his lady love to come out and play, began to mumble an embarrassed, drunken apology.

"Sorry Ma'am, I uh...guess I got the wrong house or somthin'. Sorry that I uh...woke you up and all. Excuse me. Sorry, uh...good night." And with that I heard his footsteps shuffle on the floor as he turned and thumped out through the front room, kitchen, and out my back screen door!

I rolled over on my back and stared up towards the ceiling in the dark for a few seconds in amazement. In the distance, I could hear a car door slam, an engine start and tires squeal.

"How nice of him to have his chauffeur waiting!" I said out loud, starting to tremble.

Then booming, "Jake! What the hell happened to you?"

"Whaat...?" he said still slightly dopey. "What do you mean? Did that just really happen?" I could hear the genuine shock and amazement in his voice.

"I uh, thought it was a dream. I thought that you were taking it all too easy for it to be really happening. Fuck! I figured that it was one hell of a vivid fucking dream!"

Instantly, both of us broke out into loud, hysterical, uncontrollable laughter. After a minute or two, with aching sides, our laughter began to subside.

"How did he fucking get in?" Jake asked as he got up and with his hands shaking while putting on a pair of jeans.

"That's a good question." I answered. I cinched the belt of my robe around my waist and followed him out of the dark bedroom and into the living room, my legs feeling slightly wobbly. In the pale moonlight, you could see the window next to the door, wide open and its twisted and misshapen screen below it on the linoleum floor.

His exit had been just as clumsy. Instead of unhooking the screen door, he just walked right through it! One good push and he was in, one good push and he was out. The whole episode made me realize how vulnerable we all are. If someone's gonna' get ya', someone's gonna' get ya', and that's that. The old adage that locks are to keep honest people out was true. We had just been lucky that the guy wasn't some real nut case!

❧ XV ❧

In the month or so that followed the house invasion, I had a very hard time getting to sleep at night. It was even tough for me to relax during the day while Jake was at the base. I listened to the radio most of the time while I cleaned house or did my chores, and recently the radio had been full of details about the Albert DeSalvo trial. He had been accused of being a rapist called the "Green Man", and he was also believed to be the "Boston Strangler", the murderer of eleven women.

From the coverage of the trial I had learned a disturbing detail, which combined with the "man in my bedroom" episode, made me pretty jumpy about being alone.

During the very, publicized murders, the news media as well as the rest of the world, and me, couldn't figure out why despite tons of reports and warnings, women kept letting a stranger in their house. Then during the trial it came out. DeSalvo admitted that the ploy he had used to gain access to women's homes when they were alone during the day, was to pose as a handyman and say that he had been sent by the landlord to fix a leaky pipe or do some other "Mr. Fixit" type task. Hence, the name the "Green Man", a direct result of the green handyman uniform that he wore when he intended to rape a victim, and then probably later on, as the "Strangler", to kill.

In fact, I had played out the exact scenario with a "Mr. Fixit", just a few days before hearing about

DeSalvo's clever way of fooling unsuspecting women, the knowledge of which had genuinely freaked me out.

By coincidence, a handyman had come to my door one afternoon, when I had been overdue on a phone call to the landlord about my slowly draining bathtub. With that knowledge and not wanting to be an uncooperative pain in the ass, when the man said the landlord had sent him to rod out my sewer pipe, I took a chance and I let him in. How dumb! Women were so gullible! Of course the plumber was on the up and up, and my landlord had known about the problem without any input from me because of the green grass over the sewer pipe and septic tank. But when I got to thinking about it, what was the difference between one of those murdered women and me? Luck. That's all. Just plane luck.

So, it was great to have Donna right next door. With both of us being Army wives, we had a lot in common and it didn't take long to become good friends.

This afternoon had turned out to be a scorcher. By twelve o'clock it had hit one hundred and six, and now three hours later, the heat was subsiding but it still was over the one hundred degree mark. Both of us had finished our house cleaning early, a habit that became a must considering the alternative of trying to wax a floor when the thermometer read three figures.

When the heat hit there was nothing for us to do except sit inside the house with the fans blowing, arms and legs extended, and let the sweat pour off of us. I had never experienced such heat before. I was amazed to watch droplets of perspiration form little rivers of salty water that made paths down the backs of my arms and legs, eventually dripping into pools on the linoleum floor. It was uncomfortable but tolerable for me. However, with Donna five months pregnant, I wondered how she stood it.

Sitting at the kitchen table, we were both on our third glass of lemonade and comparing notes on what we'd thought of Army life up to this point in our lives, when I thought I saw something move through the screen door, out in the backyard. I got up from the table, crept to the backdoor and peered out.

"Oh, it's only the electric guys. They're probably doing some kind of maintenance." I said.

"Boy! You sure are jumpy!" Donna said. "I told you that you've got to lighten up a bit. So you had a couple of crazy things happen since you got here, but it's like being hit by lightning. The odds are that the rest of your time here will be totally uneventful. So you can relax a bit. OK?"

"Yeah, sure."

Donna had a calming effect on me. She seemed confident and sure of herself all of the time. She didn't have the fears that I had, and she would often chide me that I was too cautious and had an overactive imagination. Life was always in her control, and being around her made me feel safe and secure.

I sat back down at the table, took a deep breath and blew it out, and then we picked up our conversation where we had left off.

"Mmmbwwop!" stopped Donna in mid sentence.

The extremely loud unfamiliar sound had filled our heads for a split second like a million humming, buzzing bees and then abruptly stopped with what sounded like a cross between a very loud snap and an ear splitting pop. The sound was so weird. My body had literally vibrated with it from the inside out. I had no idea from which direction it had come. Dumbfounded by the whole experience, I jumped up out of my chair and was about to race to the kitchen window to take a look outside.

As I pivoted around and passed the screened backdoor, a slight movement in the yard caught my eye. I stopped and stared out of the door for a second, waiting, and then I saw it again. It was a small bit of a shadow blocking the harsh sunlight and moving over the dried brown grass. It poked from behind the shadow of the house on the lawn and then quickly disappeared behind it again. Curious, I slowly walked out of the screen door into the backyard, with Donna not far behind.

There was a small ribbon of concrete that hugged the side of the house where the bathroom jutted out into the backyard, blocking the view to my left, the direction from which the shadow had come. As I walked along the small sidewalk, I looked back for a minute, distracted by the scuffling of Donna's shoes on the cement. She had come close to falling. Not watching, she had tripped on the concrete step just outside the doorway, twisted her ankle a bit, but she was OK.

"Shit!" Donna's voice was still ringing in my ears. Smiling I looked forward again. I had continued to walk passed the edge of the house, and now, got an instant view of the whole backyard and what was happening only a few yards in front of me.

A young man in his twenties was hanging upside down by a thin leather strap tangled around the ankle of one leg, from the top of the electric pole in my backyard. And his stomach was on fire.

He was a tall, lean, young man with dark hair, suspended completely lifeless by the ankle of his boot, from one of the long metal bars that stuck out the top of the thick wooden electric pole. The metal rungs started about two-thirds up the post and were used for a pole climber to place his boot on for leverage, when he was doing whatever electric guys do at the top of the pole. The metal bars were slightly bent up at the ends forming a square hook, and it was that hook which had held his leather strap tight, as he dangled below it.

The hook was about eight inches out from the wooden sides of the pole, just enough room to allow his lifeless body to hang free. He was slowly twisting back and forth in the hot, strong Texas sun, first one way then the other, the squeaking sound of leather on leather barely audible as he twisted.

I was numb and looking at him as he hung above me, arms dangling limply over his head and his free leg awkwardly bent backwards.

"Maybe he's just unconscious", I thought, and then his body turned. I could see a large black hole about the size of a football right about where his navel should be. Smoke was slowly rising from it, and a few small flames still shot out here and there from deep inside the blackness.

Standing on the ground, several feet below the hanging man, at the foot of the wooden pole, stood an older man, panicked and helpless. His arms were wrapped around his body in a grotesque bear hug as he rocked himself back and forth, tears streaming down his face. I could hear a low constant muttering.

"No, no, no..." he repeated over and over again. Each word was separately uttered in a slow low groan, painfully escaping from deep inside the man. From his attire, jeans, T-shirt, utility belt, and a construction helmet and boots, I figured that the man on the ground must be the hanging man's partner.

"Call somebody!" I screamed at him. "Get someone to help!"

I think that was the first moment the partner became aware that anyone else had been standing in the area. Disoriented with horror and grief, it took him a moment to turn in the direction of my voice, and for his eyes to focus on my face.

"I called." he said in a kind of far off voice, his eyes glassy as he distractedly gazed over my left shoulder, head cocked to the side as if he was listening to someone whispering in his ear. "But it won't make no difference. I know it won't."

And then he looked straight into my eyes as if he was seeing me for the first time and he started to sob.

"It's not safe. Can't touch him! Can't try to get him down! Can't even try to stop him from swinging!" Each sentence was chopped and came out of him in a short large spurt between heavy sobs, as if fifty pounds of air was compressed in his chest, pressurizing each sentence as it escaped his lips.

I understood and I wanted to tell him so, but my eyes were quickly drawn back to the grotesque spectacle hanging at the top of the pole.

Speechless, the three of us stood, eyes looking up at the man hanging upside down by his boot, swinging back and forth in the breeze, with his belly on fire.

It was odd. Here I was looking at one of the most god-awful sights that I would probably ever see in my life, and I didn't feel a thing! Maybe that's what shock is, not feeling a thing. I turned to Donna who was visibly trembling and looking extremely pale. Walking over to her, I took her arm and began to lead her back inside. As we walked out of the harsh blazing sunlight of the yard, into the cooler darker kitchen, the sirens started to wail.

I hadn't cared to see him taken down. That held no interest for me. We both stayed in my tiny kitchen sitting down at the table for the next hour or so. Donna had her head between her knees half the time to keep herself from hurling all over my linoleum kitchen floor, and the other half of the time she was sipping water to settle the nausea. And me, I just talked to her softly and told her that everything would be alright.

After the emergency crews were finished with their nightmarish task, Donna went home. She was feeling better and it was almost suppertime. Jake and Ray would be on their way home from the base by now. Watching her walk across the yard to her backdoor, I noticed that in the approaching twilight, with the backyard empty and as it was before, the whole thing seemed that it had never happened.

When Jake got home, I gave him a full account of the horror I had witnessed and we both listened intently that evening, when the news came on the radio. The man, who had electrocuted himself in my backyard, had been a twenty-five year old lineman survived by a wife and two very young children. He had carelessly, it was reported, bent over a high power line when doing routine maintenance on the wires, and touched the line with his stomach while still having hold of another cable on the pole. He had died on his way to the hospital with burns over 95% of his body. I didn't under-stand how that was possible since when I had seen him last the only burn mark that I could see was the gaping hole in his gut.

But Jake said, "When a person gets fucking electrocuted like that, he gets fucking fried from the inside out and it takes a long fucking while for it to show up on the fucking outside. Their mother fucking blood boils right in their veins and turns to one big hard blood clot!"

As the last of Jake's terribly graphic words fell on my ears, and the unwanted pictures that they provoked flashed one after another in my mind, it occurred to me how life is made up of a million split second decisions. We make them without blinking an eye, most without a moment's thought, like the twenty-five year old lineman did today. And then you make one tiny misjudgment which on its own has no weight. You lean too far or you open a door, and you pay the ultimate price. You pay with your life.

"One needs to be careful, really careful." I thought trying to make myself feel less uneasy "...careful and lucky!"

 XVI

I learned a lot of things in Texas. For one thing, Texas was like living on another planet. Being from Chicago, I was used to lush green globs of growing things everywhere I looked. Emerald green grass, giant green leafy trees, big thick bushes were all flourishing in everyone's front and backyards. I had subconsciously thought that everywhere else was pretty much like Chicago. Virginia, with its florae and fauna, had a few differences from my home stomping ground. But on the whole, its underlying essence of green was still the same. Texas was different.

Texas was not like any other place that I had ever been before. Its underlying essence was dirt brown. Cactus and tumbleweeds took the place of the trees and bushes that I was used to. Killeen in the summer was hot, dry and dusty, and the grass was turned to straw. The heat was something that I was not prepared for, either physically or psychologically. I demonstrated that fact to myself the Sunday after we moved into the little house.

I had decided to walk to a church located a mile away from the house for 12:00 o'clock mass. The decision hadn't taken much thought, and besides a mile walk up and back would be good for me. It had already reached one hundred and two by the time I had started out, and the air that I drew into my lungs felt like air from a blast furnace. I didn't own a hat before Texas. I had no need to, and the sun beat down mercilessly on my dark haired head. After the first block, my dress was wet from the sweat from every part of my body and I had started to feel slightly lightheaded. By the middle of the next block, my head was swimming and I thought that I was going to pass out right in the middle of the sidewalk. Turning around, I headed back home, stopping to rest at every shady spot that I could find. Once home and after lots of water, I felt OK, but I wound up with one heck of a headache and a good lesson learned. Walking anywhere in Texas in the noonday sun was a "NO-NO".

The landscape was starkly different from that of northern Illinois. The Chicago area is said to be a fairly flat place but small rolling hills here and there, left over from the glaciers of the ice age, are included in the countryside. Not so with Texas. Here you learn what flat really means. Except for a few mesas located on the way to Waco, one section of highway looks pretty much like the other, flat and naked.

Thanks to the dryness and the heat, the word bugs took on a whole new meaning when it came to Texas. If Virginia was a two on the "bug-O-meter" then Texas was a ten. Bugs, bugs, bugs! Both their numbers and sizes were beyond belief! If a bug was looking for a place to go, I'm sure it wound up in Texas.

After a few months in the Lone Star State, we had several interesting buggy experiences, which added to my intolerance of things that crawl. I found out later they were par for the course. The first was a strange encounter in a sleepy little Texas town. Jake had bought a red Honda 250 motorcycle for cheap transportation to and from the base. You could fill the tank for fifty cents and travel a hundred and fifty miles! When the evenings got hot, we would get on the bike and cruise the country roads. Even though the countryside was alien and strange to look at, it was peaceful and cool as we rode down a thin strip of black asphalt through the cactus and tumbleweeds, watching the setting sun accent the brownish-black mesas against the last bit of brilliant orange colored sky.

During one of these long lazy rides we had found ourselves riding through a small Texas town fairly late at night. The sun had gone down awhile ago and the main road was deserted. Sitting at a red traffic light talking, I had made a comment to Jake about the town being so small that it rolled up its sidewalks at ten. Laughing we waited for the light to change, and looking to the left, I noticed that the building facing the street, had an odd looking black material covering the front of it. A second later, the light turned green and Jake revved the bike and put it into gear. Instantaneously, the whole front of the building seemed to explode. Small black pieces of the front of the brick were flying everywhere. Jake immediately stopped the bike and the both of us, amazed, watched the bewildering spectacle.

"Jesus!" I shouted after a second or two, when I realized what I was seeing. "Bugs. Big black ones like the ones that JuJu eats, big black crickets!"

The swarm of crickets, once flying in a frenzy were now starting to land and collect back onto the face of the building again, covering it one by one with the odd black coating that I had noticed less than a minute ago.

These were the same shiny black bugs, of which, my cat had become a connoisseur. While JuJu was a starving stray kitten, she had developed the taste for the bugs, and now it was like an addiction. She loved Texas crickets and we had plenty of them under the house. These crickets weren't the size of Chicago crickets, a half of an inch or so, these crickets were as big as a man's thumb and just as thick around. One or two of them gulped down and her belly was full for awhile. The only problem with this particular diet was the long ugly worms that came out of her rear end several days after she would sneak off and eat a few. We kept worming her and she kept sneaking out to get a bite of her favorite delicacy.

As far as the bugs on the building, Jake and I had never seen anything like it! It was weird and fascinating at the same time. I had wondered as the motorcycle shot like a bullet down the long, flat, straight, black top road toward Killeen, how many big black crickets it took to cover the front of the building? Was it ten thousand, one hundred thousand? I had no idea. The size of the bugs was impressive but the sheer numbers of them were mind-boggling.

A month or so after we had moved into the little house, another strange bug event occurred. I had gotten up with Jake to keep him company while he showered, shaved, and dressed to go the base. After he left I decided to get my clothes on and start my housework early while it was still cool. Just before and after sunrise was the coolest part of the day. Standing next to the stove, waiting for my tea water to boil, I looked out the kitchen window into the early morning light. Preoccupied, I noticed that the grass looked awfully thick. Actually, it looked kind of puffy. I stood there a moment thinking how odd that was, and I squinted my eyes to get a clearer view in the meager light.

"What the heck is on the grass?" I wondered as I poured the boiling water into my teacup. I looked out at the grass again but I still couldn't make heads or tails of it. I decided to go out on the front porch. With the sun beginning to peak over the house's roof across the street, I could probably get a better look at whatever it was.

Teacup in hand I walked out of the kitchen, through the front room and out of the screen door. Standing on the concrete slab I intently looked at the front yard. Long thin gray globs were clearly visible on the blades of the dried grass. A quick scan of the lawn showed me that the gray globs were over every square inch of the property! They were on the lawns across the street too! Looking down the street, I realized that they were everywhere as far as I could see!

Puzzled, I knelt down on all fours at the edge of the three by three, cement square, and looked closely at a blade of grass.

"Shit! Every blade of grass is covered by some kind of worm!" I was speaking out loud as if someone was standing next to me. A habit that people with no imagination think is strange. I looked around for a little twig or something in the grassless sandy soil to my right, under the Chinaberry tree. Finding a tiny stick, I knelt down, and tried to push the tip of the twig between a worm and the blade of grass that it hung on, but it wouldn't budge. It was holding onto the shaft of grass with rows of little nubs. They began to protrude from underneath of what looked like a head at the end of its body. No, these weren't worms. These were ugly bald gray caterpillars. They looked something like the caterpillars that I had seen on tomato plants back home, only smaller and gray, and they were everywhere. After Jake came home that evening we went for a walk and saw that the caterpillars were all over the neighborhood. It was strange that no one seemed to be impressed by the situation except for us.

As suddenly as they had appeared, they were gone, and the big invasion was forgotten. A few weeks later, I was up with the sun, as usual, and had started my weekly laundry. Between the rent for the house and utilities, Jake's meager paycheck as an Army private didn't go very far, so we couldn't afford to go to the Laundromat. I did the laundry in our bathtub with an old-fashioned scrub board, hand rung it and hung it on the backyard clothesline to dry. With the heat it would dry in less than an hour.

As I swung the back screen door open I misjudged the amount of push that it needed, and it banged noisily against the wooden siding of the house.

The sound cracked through the early morning air, instantaneously filling it with a thousand fluttering pieces of what looked like white confetti, but larger. Quickly the large confetti settled down on the grass and few small scraggly tree-bushes that dotted the backyard. The grass was a light straw color and whatever it was melted easily back into the scenery.

"Wow!" I thought, as I placed my clothesbasket on the ground beside me.

Bang! I purposely slammed the wooden screen door against the side of the house. Again, I was rewarded with a spectacular display. Looking as if they had all been thrown high up into the air at precisely the same moment, countless numbers of tiny white butterflies filled my view from the early morning sky to the dry hay like grass. At first they fluttered, like tiny bits of brilliant white paper suspended by some unfelt subtle breeze against the peachy morning sky. And then like large puffy snowflakes on a still winter night, they slowly fell in unison, to the ground, blending in between the shafts of stiff grass.

"How beautiful!" I commented to myself, full of peaceful wonder at God's beauty. How neat! The plague of ugly hairless gray caterpillars had turned into lovely soft white butterflies.

"Maybe Texas isn't so bad after all."

Smiling, I thought that over. That was certainly true. There had been no drinking parties in Texas. The only people that we saw socially were Ray and Donna from next door, and neither of them drank very much. Jake had a beer now and then but most of the time it was lemonade. We were too broke for anything else. Jake was determined that we would financially make it on his check alone. No more asking the family at home for contributions to the Jake and Sue charity fund when we came to the end of the month and we were short. It was embarrassing for the both of us. So, determined to cut costs and make it on our own, we saved money whenever we could. Beer was one expensive item and so were cigarettes. We switched to Bull Durham, "roll your own", at eleven cents a pack. Boy, you really knew how addicted you were to those coffin nails when after multiple tries to successfully pack and roll a single cigarette, you would give up and smoke the damned thing with half the tobacco falling out of both ends.

It was worth it though. For the first time since Jake was drafted, we were really on our own. Without sharing the rent and house with other people like we did in Virginia, I was able to keep things the way Jake and I liked it, spotless. The linoleum in the whole house shined. I waxed all the floors once a week and after a month the floors looked like glass. I could see my face in them just like the commercial on TV had said. They were so smooth and shiny that Jake and I had to be careful not to fall on our butts if we were running around the house in our stocking feet. Jake had actually fallen on is backside while playing with JuJu one evening. Chasing the cat across the living room floor, his legs had started to slip out from under him. Feeling himself slipping, he rapidly tried a reverse running motion with his legs, looking comically like a character in a cartoon. By the time he fell to the floor he was roaring with laughter, and I was on my knees beside him trying to catch my breath in between the belly laughs.

"Yeah," I thought, "maybe Texas wasn't so bad after all!" And then I threw up.

❧ XVII ❧

I woke up the next morning with something tickling my ear. Jake had to go into the base at 2 o'clock in the morning to prepare for a very important inspection, so I let myself sleep in for once. There was that tickle again, almost like a crawling itch but now I could feel it all over the side of my cheek. I opened my eye and standing up on its haunches on the bridge of my nose was one red ant! I flew out of bed.

"Damn, ants!" I said out loud as my feet hit the floor. I must of looked peculiar as I violently shook my head from side to side and fanned my itching ear with my hand in hopes of keeping all the surprised ants from running, during the pandemonium, into the recesses of my ear.

"God, I hope if they get in there they can't eat your brain!" But on second thought I knew that it wasn't a possibility, an ear infection was probably the worst ramification of ants in the ear.

Standing still a minute I could feel one of the buggers crawling around in my hair. I ran to the old round mirror over the dresser on the bedroom wall and hunted the son-of-a-bitch out.

"Got'em!" I said in triumph, and then caught a glimpse of the four-inch wide ant trail coming through the bedroom window on the wall opposite from the bed. The trail had come in the bedroom window, the one with the Chinaberry tree directly out side of it. It had crossed the linoleum of the bedroom floor, went up the wooden leg on the foot of the bed onto the bedcovers, across the bed, the pillow and my head, and presumably up the wall and out the opposite window from where it had started. I had broken the trail but I could still see the confused and misdirected sea of ants bumping into each other in a frenzy on the white windowsill.

It was insecticide time. Once the ants stopped moving after I sprayed, I would sweep the little curled up bodies into a dustpan and be done. If I didn't wash the floor for a couple of days the ants wouldn't try to rebuild their super highway. I had gotten used to this kind of Chinese fire drill. A Chinaberry tree draws ants, and I had one just three feet from my bedroom window, so mega-ants were a fact of life.

"You would think that the damned Melee bugs would put a dent in the ant population!" I said to myself as I swept up the little turds of ant carcasses. But they didn't. I thought for a minute. I still couldn't believe that Melee bugs were real. When I was ten, my brother-in-law Mick had told me a silly story about Melee bugs who would drop out of trees, dressed in a top hat and cane, screaming, "I'll get'cha!" as they plopped on your head. I had laughed like crazy when he mimicked their voices with a falsetto ring to his own.

I'd remembered the look on my face when my Texas landlord had told me that the tiny funnel shaped holes in the sand at the base of the Chinaberry tree came from Melee bugs. I had thought that he was bullshitting me, and my face must have shown it. I was still embarrassed at the thought of how foolish I had seemed.

My tummy was slightly queasy of late. But, that didn't usually start until four or five in the evening, just about the time the hamburger place two streets over started to broil their burgers, and the aroma floated on the breeze and into my bedroom. I couldn't figure out how something that had smelled so good only a short time ago could suddenly smell so bad.

I thought that maybe the nausea was due to the diet Jake and I had been on for the last week. This month's expenses had been more than we had anticipated. For the last six weeks, the heat had been extreme. August was the hottest part of the summer, so the fans were on twenty-four hours a day, which caused the electric bill to be a lot higher than normal. And then there was the phone bill. With Momma not feeling good, there were several long distance charges that we were not accustomed to paying. Her back still hurt and the constant pain was really starting to get her down. We only had two dollars left between the two of us, and payday wasn't for five more days. In order to make it 'till then we decided to ration our food. Last week, we had cut down to one meal a day and when the hunger pains started we would chew bubble gum. After each day the bubble gum was stored in the freezer, after all, one piece was good for at least two days. Even with only eating one meal a day I had figured out that between the groceries on hand and the two bucks, we would most likely be two days short. I had no idea what we would do then, probably chew our gum and drink lots of water for forty-eight hours.

Well, maybe my bout with the upchuck demon, was because of what I was, or should I say, wasn't eating. And then again... maybe it was because I was late. Yeah, I was late, twenty-three days and counting. A smile crossed my lips as I thought about it and then recounted the missed days in my head again. Yes, I was right. I was twenty-three wonderful, glorious days late! I was almost certain that I was pregnant. Something, that after fourteen months of no birth control, I'd begun to give up hope that I would ever be.

I decided that it was time to get dressed. The ant clean up had taken longer than I had thought it would, and it was already quarter passed twelve.

"The mailman has probably already been here." I said as I pulled up my shorts and tugged at the zipper. It was getting more and more difficult everyday to get the zipper up and squeeze my belly into the space that the pants provided. I knew that the initial weight gain was probably from water and not because of the baby's size, but that knowledge didn't get my pants up any easier. When I was done I felt like, what is the saying, "Ten pounds of shit in a five pound bag"?

"God, I hope this doesn't make me throw up!" I thought. That was something I really hated! So I went out to check the mail to take my mind off of things. It didn't help much. The only thing that was going to help was to walk around with the zipper down and wear a baggy shirt over the top of my shorts, or give up and store them away until after the baby, and find something looser to wear.

"After the baby. Gee, that sounds great!" I laughed again as I walked in high spirits, through the front yard and out to the mailbox, which was nailed to a wooden four by four and sat next to the street.

There were two letters in the white roadside mailbox, one from my dad, which was highly unusual, and one from my mother-in-law, one of my least favorite people. I opened Jake's mother's letter first, saving the best for last, and when I did, an unexpected twenty slipped out of the envelope and floated quickly down to the linoleum floor.

"Wow, a twenty!" I said as I excitedly snatched the precious piece of green paper off the floor. "God, we can eat for the last two days of the month! How nice of her to send the money." Sometimes Jake's mom surprised you, but I didn't kid myself. The twenty dollars was really for Jake because in her mind I didn't exist. I was just an afterthought, a necessary evil in her son's life. That was OK with me. I didn't like her very much anyway.

It was like a miracle, a small miracle, yes, but still a miracle. I looked at the mesmerizing ticket that entitled me to a worry free week before payday. It was amazing, how one little piece of paper could change your life so much.

"Wait 'till Jake hears about this when he gets home." I said to myself as I opened up the letter from Daddy. I began to read:

My dear Susan,

Momma wanted me to write you a short letter to tell you that she's alright. She doesn't want you to worry about her. She had good news yesterday. She spent a few days at Christ hospital for some tests and the doctor gave her a clean bill of health.

The doctor thinks that muscle spasms are causing the pain in her back and that she needs to learn how to relax a little bit and learn how to handle stress a little better. She would be writing you this letter except that she's still very tired from being in the hospital and having to go through all that poking and prodding.

The weather's been pretty cool for this time of year. Usually, the end of August is pretty hot, but the last week has been in the high seventies. Maybe, it will be an early fall.

How is Jake doing? Has he found out where he might be going after Texas? How much longer do you think that you have until he's transferred to another base?

Is it still as hot where you are as you wrote it was in the last letter?

Well, time to sign off. I have to feed the dogs.

Love,
Daddy

I carefully and neatly refolded the letter and slipped it into its white envelope. It was nice to hear from my dad, but it bothered me a little because he had never written me a letter before. His handwriting was atrocious, scratchy and stiff, and often took thoughtful concentration on the reader's part, to successfully translate it. In contrast, my mother's handwriting was like looking at an example of textbook penmanship, attractive and curvy with perfectly formed letters. She was left handed but wrote with her right, a skill that was painstakingly learned at the punishing hands of a public school teacher who thought there was something improper, insolent and lazy about a left handed child. Letters had always been my mother's domain and the change in that routine made me feel slightly uneasy.

My worry slipped away as the aroma of cooking hamburgers drifted though the open bedroom window and into the front room where I was sitting when I'd opened the mail. It was after twelve and the lunch hour was in full swing. The first whiff of seared flesh had caused my stomach to roll. I knew in my heart that this was not the flu or something I had eaten the night before. I knew that this was morning sickness but mislabeled because the worst of it came in the afternoon, and I was ecstatic.

Laying down on the comfortable old bed and trying to find just the right position that would magically lessen the nausea, my face beamed with excitement as I swallowed hard, forcing the bitter taste in my mouth back down from where it had come.

It had really happened! Jake and I were finally going to have a baby. Our relationship was growing more loving every day. The strangeness of this place seemed to bond us closer together. Jake was pleased and excited about the baby, and fell asleep most nights with his hand lightly resting on top of my tummy. All the fears and worries that I had in Virginia about our future were fading away. It was happening, Jake was growing up and life would be sweet.

"However," I thought to myself accompanied by half a chuckle and half a wretch, "it may take me

SUSAN BRAUER

a very long time to be able to eat cheeseburgers again."

❦ XVIII ❧

It was difficult to believe that I was sitting next to my dad in what used to be, before Uncle Sam got a hold of him, Jake's brand new car. It was a metallic blue, 1966 Chevy "Super Sport", with four on the floor and a 396 engine that sucked up six miles to the gallon, and pinned you into the seat whenever you put the pedal to the floor. My dad had loved it! Jake had loved the car too, and we had bought it shortly after we'd gotten married. Momma took over the payments when Jake got drafted, and he grieved over the loss of it like a mother would grieve over the death of a child.

Daddy had just picked me up from the airport and we were on our way to see my mother. I was exhausted already and it was only three o'clock in the afternoon. The plane flight from Dallas to Chicago was over four hours long but flying in a jet was a relief after the hair-raising ride from the Killeen airport to Dallas. Flying in a piper cub for fifty minutes just above the trees and at the mercy of every slight bump of air turbulence was not my idea of having fun. The pilot loved it but as for me, after five roller-coaster like minutes in the air I could feel what little I had eaten for breakfast coming up for a repeat performance.

At least now I could relax for a little bit. It would take us awhile to get there. I glanced over at my dad and realized that he didn't have a pipe in his mouth. I reminded myself that he had given that up almost two years ago, along with his drinking. I'd hated the beer guzzling, but actually missed the smell of Prince Albert pipe tobacco in the air. The tiniest wisp of the aroma acted like a time machine hurling me back into the distant past and good memories of my dad and me. Even now I could envision him sitting in the driver's seat of the silver-painted '51 Chevy, his pipe clenched between his teeth and after one big long drag on his pipe, smoke streaming out of his nostrils like an old time steam engine. At night, the top of the pipe bowl would glow in the dark and if he was nursing his pipe to last as long as possible, tiny puffs of smoke would softly flow out from his lips and in slow motion, rise lazily, forming a circle around his head.

"Daddy," I asked breaking the silence, "why didn't they find it before?"

"They only had x-ray machines that took pictures directly from the front or back. So it didn't show up. This hospital is a university hospital, and it has all the latest gadgets. They have an x-ray machine that takes over eighty pictures from all angles as it rotates around the person. It was the x-rays of her side that showed the mass." Keeping his eyes on the road, I couldn't make out the expression on his face.

"I still don't understand. How could three other hospitals miss that there really was something wrong with her? Didn't she tell them how bad the pain was?" Frustrated and angry, I was also confused as to how such a misdiagnosis could have emanated from three separate sets of doctors. These guys were supposed to know it all, to take care of you when you were ill and make it better, and if need be, save your life. They were supposed to be close to infallible.

"Well, it looks like her first doctor set the stage." He began to answer.

"You mean Dr. Parks, but he's a gynecologist." I interrupted.

"Yes, I know" he said, "but we didn't have a family doctor and your mother figured that with the ache being in her back, it probably was some kind of kidney infection. After all, he is a doctor, so if it was something more, she assumed that he would at least send her to the right specialist."

Parks, I really disliked that man. He'd been my doctor too and he had always appeared to be arrogant, condescending and downright rude.

"What do you mean that he set the stage?" I asked.

"Well, he examined your mother several times over the first couple months after the pain had appeared and he never found anything, no bladder or kidney infections, nothing. So, he made the diagnosis that she was making it up, and labeled her a hypochondriac in his records. After that, when the pain didn't ease up but in fact got worse, it was one hospital after another, each one poking and prodding, looking and not finding anything, reading her records and dismissing her pain as some dreamed up tactic to get attention."

My anger boiled at this. Momma had always been strong and silent about any pain or heartache in her life. She would never give an inch to anything, not anger, tears or sickness. In all the years that I could remember there were no sick days taken, either in earnest or in folly. Life was to be faced and dealt with, and that she did every minute of every day of her life!

"But Daddy, you know Momma. Didn't you tell them that she wasn't like that! Didn't you tell them that it didn't make sense, that it wasn't a believable explanation for what was going on?" I could see that I had hit a nerve, as he visibly winced when my questions struck home.

"God, Daddy!" I thought, "You bought it hook line and sinker, didn't you? You believed them! You looked at the woman that you had lived with for thirty-six years and you believed them and not her! Jesus!" I looked at him and revulsion crept through me.

"How could he have deserted her like that?" I thought. Other people and their opinions always meant more to my dad than his own family did, and doctors yet. I guess there was no contest.

"That's what John had said when I'd called him and Carole in Pittsburgh to tell them that she had just been released from the hospital again with the diagnosis that it was all in her head. But this time they had released her on a liquid diet. Soup and flavored gelatin was all she could eat without getting sick. The pain had gotten so bad that any food at all came right up." Daddy continued, skirting around my original question, the same as he always did when he was embarrassed.

"John said that there was no way that the diagnosis fit Momma. He thought that we'd taken her to crap hospitals. That she needed to be at a university hospital where they knew what they were doing. So John called a friend and got her into the University of Chicago hospital the very next day." Daddy said.

"How long did it take them to find the tumor?" I asked trying to hide the anger that I still felt.

"Less than a day. They aren't going to wait. They're operating right away. Your mother has lost feeling in both her legs from the tumor pressing on her spinal column, so every minute counts. If they remove the pressure quickly the nerve damage may only be temporary. The faster they operate the better chances are that she will be able to walk again. It's lucky that you were on your way home already because you would have never been able to get here on time."

My dad had called me the day before yesterday and said that Momma was worse and I should probably come home to see her. He hadn't elaborated, but the few sketchy details that I was able to get out of him at the time, prompted me to get on a plane as soon as I could. I had left Jake behind, but as it was, it had turned out to be for the best. We had just gotten the news that Jake was going to Nuremberg Germany on January 1, and since it was already late October, I would have had to leave Texas within the next couple of weeks, anyway. He was getting a month leave, as was the custom, before a soldier left for overseas duty, and since it fell in December he would be home for the holidays. We had been flying high when he'd gotten the news. This meant that he would again be safe from life in a rice paddy, at least for a little while.

I was still a little irritated by the idea that my father had been less than honest with me over the last couple of months.

"Why didn't you tell me any of this before? I hadn't expected that things were this bad!" I said.

"We didn't want to get you upset, not with the baby. Momma didn't want you to worry about her." And with the last few words I could hear my dad's voice waiver, and my heart went out to him. Maybe it had been Momma's idea not to tell me, it would be so like her. And maybe he hadn't been completely at fault for believing the hypochondriac diagnosis that the other doctors had given about Momma. With her looking into a divorce before she'd gotten sick, the two of them probably hadn't been very communicative with each other over the last six months.

With my anger diffused, my attention went back to the road in front of us and I realized that the hospital building was in sight. Another couple of blocks and we would be pulling into the parking lot. It had been five months since I had seen Momma and it was comforting to know that in a very short time I would be giving her a kiss on her cheek.

"Well, here we are." My father off-handedly remarked. I thought I heard something in the tone of his voice. Sadness, apprehension, I didn't know which. It reminded me what we were here for, and a chill ran through my bones.

The university hospital may have been the best place for my mother from a medical point of view, but their interior decorator stunk! It was an old building and the hallways were done in a drab gray colored marble with faded peach walls that were dulled and dirtied with age. The privacy curtains around the beds were supposed to be a cheery matching peach, but instead were washed out, tattered and even torn in spots, and in some places unattached from the rail that was located above each bed, lending an air of overall neglect and depression to the surroundings.

Clop, clop, clop... our shoes sounded against the hard marble floors of the hallway.

"Her room is at the end of the hall on the right hand side. Hopefully, Loretta, Claudette, Carole and John have gotten here by now. They all wanted to see her before she's taken up to surgery. It looks like we've made it just in time" Daddy said as he glanced at his wristwatch. I had no response to this and we covered the remaining distance to her room in silence.

Words cannot fully describe what I saw when I turned and walked through the hospital room door. The person lying in the hospital bed could not have been my mother. The last time that I had seen Momma was five short months ago, the day that I'd gotten on a plane for Texas. I had said goodbye to a strong, vibrant, take charge human being whose determination to accomplish whatever needed to be done, was unmoved by difficulty, sickness or pain. Momma had weighed a healthy one hundred and fifty pounds, which she carried well, looking neither too fat nor too thin. She was on the verge of beginning a new life and she was excited and enthusiastic to experience what lay before her. She was on her way to living her own life after thirty-six years of living it for someone else. She had stayed in a marriage that had become a lonely empty shell of what it could have been, putting herself and her needs on hold for my sisters and me. Finally, it was her turn.

The instant feeling of recognition that we all experience when a familiar face or form enters into our field of perception was missing from the first moment that I laid eyes on the figure curled up under the sheets of the hospital bed. The sad emaciated body lying there looked as if it was that of a fugitive from a concentration camp, instead of the body of the robust fifty-one year old woman that I remembered. In only five short months, I estimated that at least sixty pounds of my mother's lifeblood had been drained away by the pain that had ravaged her body. She looked as if some hellish vampire had sunk its teeth into her healthy being, plump with life, and sucked all the essence out of her leaving only a crumpled up and collapsed container to be discarded.

No one else was in the room. The others hadn't arrived yet, and Momma hadn't noticed that Daddy and I had come in the door and were standing at the foot of her bed. She was lying on her side in a fetal position and her hands were clutched tightly around the corner of her pillow, wringing and tugging it frantically. Her upper body was rhythmically rocking side to side as long slow barely audible moans emanated from her mouth. As I was about to step forward to get closer to her and tell her that I was there, a nurse abruptly pushed passed me with an air of importance and haste.

"Mrs. Porter, here I am with your shot. We need to get you ready for surgery. Can you help me turn you on your other side?" She said speaking loudly and lightly touching my mother's shoulder trying to get her attention. My mother seemed dazed and disoriented as she tried to respond to the authoritative voice of the nurse. Her head wobbled a little as she attempted to pick it up off the pillow, and focus her attention onto the nurse and what she was saying. As her eyes swept up towards the nurses face, they stopped dead in their tracks when she caught sight of the hypodermic needle on the tray held in the nurse's hand.

A low heart wrenching moan, rising from deep within my mother's starved and tortured body, escaped from between her cracked and peeling lips, and culminated into a loud hoarse sob. Her eyes never left the hypodermic needle; her fear was so great that I could feel it filling the room. Clammy and heavy, it weighed down the breath in my chest, choking off the air in my throat.

"Oh, God! Please no!" She whimpered and begged, "I can't take any more! It's too much...no more..." This last part trailed off in a pleading, whining sob that reached down and ripped at the heart in my chest. She cried like a child and clutched the arm of the nurse as the hypodermic needle, now in the nurse's hand, was coming closer to her.

"Now, now, Mrs. Porter, stop making such a fuss. It's just a shot and it will make you feel better! Maybe we won't bother to turn you over we'll just use this side." And as she said this, in one swift movement she pulled back the thin blanket and sheet beneath it, partially exposing my mother's hip and buttocks. The official hospital issued gown that my mother was wearing was open at the back and it afforded her no privacy. As my mother feebly tried to stave off the inevitable by weakly pushing away the nurse's arm, the material slipped even further exposing more of her side and bottom.

It was grotesque! Every inch of my mother's bony skeletal hip and upper thigh was covered with bruises. Some were yellow with a slight tinge of green, the color older bruises take on as they heal, but most were deep dark purple, almost blood black, remnants of her most recent hospital stay where the bright and brilliant doctors had declared nothing was wrong with her.

"Can't find anything wrong with her. It's all in her head." I could imagine them saying. I didn't have a doctor's degree and just one look at the tragic human nightmare in front of me yelled out, "This is no head-case! This is a woman on death's door!" How could they have been so off the mark?

"No, no, no..." my mother weakly begged and protested, whimpering and sobbing as if one more drop of pain would cause a dam to burst inside of her, and an uncontrolled torrent of pain would wash away her last bit of sanity.

Inside myself I cried out to my mother, "Momma..." as I watched the nurse, in one quick sure motion peel my mother's scrawny fingers from around her wrist and drive the needle swiftly into a deep black bruise.

Instantly, the strained muscles in my mother's body started to relax. The whimpering and moaning mercifully gave way to a drug induced stupor. As the nurse stepped aside, I maneuvered my way to the head of her bed.

"You'll only have a few minutes with her to say goodbye. We need to get her up to the operating room as soon as we can. The doctors are already upstairs preparing for surgery." She reported this to us without emotion or concern, as if she was bored and this was something that she had repeated several times a day, every day, for the last twenty years. And then she left the room.

"Momma..." I said as I moved over to her bed and bent down close to her face to kiss her cheek. "Momma, I'm here. It's Susan. Momma can you hear me?" With that she sluggishly looked up at me and tried to focus her eyes the effort resulting in a disoriented frown.

"Susan? I can hear you but I can't see you very well." She said, slurring her words as if she had consumed a fifth of booze. She lifted her thin arm up a little way in a motion like she was about to pat my cheek before it plopped back down onto the bed. And then in a single moment of clarity she softly said, "I love you, my baby." As she smiled the waters of doped disorientation washed back over my mother again, and she became lost in a sea of dreams.

I stroked her head, as she seemed to slip in and out of consciousness. I noticed that her hair, which she had always kept dyed an attractive reddish honey blonde, was now snow white an inch up from the roots, ending in several inches of matted brassy orange tangles. God, she looked a million years old! Distracted, I hadn't noticed that while I was saying goodbye to my mother, my Aunt Lollie, my sisters and John had arrived. I moved away from her beside to let everyone else have their turn at goodbyes, and while I sat in the corner, I wondered, shocked and dismayed, at how bad things had gotten, in so short a time.

The nurse returned to the room with an intravenous bottle of some kind of solution in her hand, and this time my mother did not protest. After hooking up the bottle to the metal apparatus perched on the head of the bed, she matter-of-factly slipped the long needle into my mother's vein, taped her arm down to a board and started the drip. The stoic nurse clanked the bedside bars up into place, unlocked the hard rubber bed wheels and after saying, "Excuse me." pushed my mother and her bed out of the room and into the realm of the unknown.

Five hours later the doctor who performed my mother's surgery walked into the hellhole that hospitals designate as the family waiting room, where we were keeping our vigil. His face looked devoid of expression, and from the minute he opened his mouth my intuition had said that things were bad. He directed most of the conversation to my brother-in-law John, brothers under the skin you might say, a doctor-to-doctor thing. The words he spoke were unfamiliar to me and their meanings were unclear, as if he was speaking some foreign language called "doctorese", and you had to have an MD after your name to make sense of it. John nodded his head as the surgeon spoke and I listened intently trying to decipher even the tiniest bit of information about my mother's prognosis.

I heard snippets of words and phrases like, "a class five lymphoma", "crushed a vertebrae", "afford her some temporary relief", "metastasized", "will need radiation treatments", and "may regain some mobility." John countered back with some unintelligible queries as we all stood there stiff, soundless, and uncomprehending. Then during an uncomfortable silence the surgeon shook John's hand and left. I was the first to speak after the doctor left the room.

"Well John, did that mean what I think it means? It's bad isn't it?"

"I wouldn't say that. Your mother is going to have a lot less pain than she had before and it looks probable that she may regain the use of her legs." John said.

"Wait a minute," I interrupted. "I couldn't understand all of what he was saying but the gist of it sounded as if they didn't get it all out, and isn't a class five the worst type of cancer?" I asked puzzled and confused by John's interpretation of the previous conversation.

"Yes, it is the most aggressive, but lymphoma is a very rare cancer and we don't know much about it. It usually reacts very well to radiation." He said this with a matter of fact kind of tone in his voice that was very assuring. God, I really wanted to believe that what he was saying was true, that everything I thought I'd heard was wrong!

"You mean she isn't going to die?" I asked with the hint of a tiny bit of pleading in my voice, as if I was speaking to God and not to my brother-in-law.

After a slight pause, my dad suddenly spoke up, "No Susan, Momma is not going to die."

We all exchanged awkward glances between each other, but no one said a word. I chose to accept what my father had just said, but deep inside I knew something was not right, that he and John were being less than honest, but I let it be. I let it be the way that you let be the bodies of the pets that, as a child, you buried in your backyard. You have a pretty good idea of what's going on there under the dirt and grass, but the last thing that you want to do is dig it up and see exactly how right or wrong you were about the situation. I guess I chose to believe because the alternative was completely unacceptable to me.

❧ XIX ☙

The dream had come in the middle of the night, as dreams do, resurrecting hidden fear and causing excruciating pain. Pain as sharp as that of an exposed nerve in a badly cracked tooth, the first time you unsuspectingly draw your breath in and over it.

It had started out benignly enough. I was in my grandmother's old apartment, the one where Jake and I had lived, busily doing my household chores. My mother had been missing for a few days, but being a dream, I was only mildly concerned, somehow intuitively knowing that she was alright. Suddenly, there was a loud knock at the front door, which startled me. With my hands slightly shaking from the adrenaline rush, I turned the doorknob and pulled opened the door. A tall dark man stood on the front porch looking grave and somber. I instantly knew that he was a policeman even though he didn't mention it.

"Your mother is missing isn't she?" He said as he looked hauntingly into my eyes. I nodded my head slowly, fear tingling through my fingers and toes. He began again with a sense of urgency.

"We have an unidentified woman's body at the morgue and I thought that it might be your mother. You need to come with me right away and see if it's her."

And then, as dreams go, I was ushered through a nonexistent door in my front room that magically opened into the main room in the morgue, an event that seemed not to impress either one of us.

Having just stepped through the doorway, I hesitated for a moment and surveyed my surroundings. The furniture and far reaches of the room faded into shadows and blackness, despite the three lights hanging from the ceiling directly above a gurney. The lights were the kind that one sees in old-fashioned movies above a pool table. The funnel shaped metal shades above the bulb providing a bright light in only a well-defined and directed area. They served to highlight the gurney and the unidentifiable thing that lay upon it, against the black, seemingly endless rest of the room.

Staying where I was, I strained my eyes trying to make out the shape and form of the unrecognizable lump on the table. From where I was standing, it looked like a mountain of gelatinous material with some kind of clothing giving it structure, keeping it from oozing off the flat surface and dripping slime to the floor.

"This poor woman was sky diving and her chute didn't open. Sorry for the mess, but it's unbelievably disgusting what falling at that kind of speed does to a human being! It pulverizes every bone and muscle in the body leaving the unrecognizable lump before you." The stranger said from behind me in a soft sinister tone. Then I felt myself pushed firmly forward by the pressure of the dark man's hand on my back. At first I resisted, but than relief filled me as I looked more closely at the thing on the table.

"This isn't my mother!" I thought to myself. "It's not possible! What would she be doing up in a plane and besides, it doesn't even look like her!" I began to walk slowly towards the area illuminated by the shaded bright lights and the woman on the gurney within it. Finally, I found myself standing at the side of the gurney, so close that if I moved my arms my fingers would brush against what was left of the woman's jump suit.

Taking my time, I looked at every detail of the bloody, smashed mess in front of me, feeling great compassion not only for the woman, whoever she was, but also for her family who didn't know yet that she was dead. They were probably at home still feeling safe and secure, dreaming their dreams of the future, and planning their plans, all of which included her, while she laid here cold and dead, never to be a part of their future again.

My attention was drawn to what was left of the woman's face and hair. I had noticed an odd coincidence. In the harsh light a few strands of the woman's hair, which had managed to remain blood free, could be seen and they were the identical hair color as my mother's! With a macabre fascination, I looked more closely at the pulpy mass that would have been her face and followed every line trying to reconstruct her image in my mind. And then my eyes fell upon it, the only piece of bone that was left intact in her whole face, and I recognized it! My eyes were riveted to the three small inches of the lovely curve of my mother's cheekbone right below her temple on the left side of her head. Those three small inches destroyed me!

It was my dreams, my plans, and my mother that was dead! With that thought shouting in my mind, and the pain bursting in my chest, I fell on my knees and screamed, and screamed, and screamed...

It took me a minute or two after waking to realize that what I'd experienced was a dream. The feelings that it had invoked in me were real enough. The pain at the thought of my mother being dead was almost unbearable, and I knew that this nightmare was a taste of what was to come if and when she did die. I didn't think that I could stand it, and I prayed that what my father had said that night in the family waiting room had been true. In the weeks that had passed since the operation, the words and phrases that I had heard the surgeon say, had been pushed down deep into the recesses of my mind. For some reason, their meaning and the fear that they produced, were trying to surface and my nightmare brought them to the forefront of my thoughts with a hellish speed.

"Ooh!" I winced as a sharp pain in my abdomen took me by surprise. "Damn! Those cramps are coming back again!" Within seconds it had subsided and I rolled over on my side and tried to get back to sleep. I needed to slow down and relax a bit. Since the operation, I'd been visiting my mother every day. My father would drop me off at the hospital every morning before eight and my Aunt Lollie or my sister Claudette would bring me home in the early afternoon after they spent an hour or two with Momma and me. I would get home early enough to clean up the house and start supper for Daddy. Several times a week my father would go straight to the hospital from his job, eating the supper that I'd made for him when he came home, after nine o'clock at night. He and I were both dog-tired at the end of the day.

Momma was getting better and she had even started to walk a bit using a walker, but her legs were still somewhat numb. The pain in her back had all but disappeared, and it was a relief to see her start to gain some weight. A week after her operation, the doctors had started a round of radiation treatments, which had made her very nauseous and caused her to be ill for several hours after each treatment. They had continued for a couple of weeks and now, thank God, they were over. The tumor had responded well to the treatment, and what they couldn't get out with surgery, they had shrunk down to almost nothing with radiation.

The doctors had said that she could come home in a week. It was mid November and Jake wouldn't be home until the first of December so it looked like I wouldn't have much time to relax after all. I was the only one who could watch her when she came home so it would be a lot of work, but I'd find a way.

"Damn, here it comes again!" Another cramp swiftly caught hold of my belly, causing me to curl my legs up to my chest, trying to alleviate some of the pain. After it had passed, I thought to myself that it would be a good idea for me to see a doctor. With all the craziness, I hadn't been to one yet and I figured that I was most probably over four months pregnant. I could call my friend Peggy in the morning and get the name of her doctor. I sure as hell wasn't going to my old doctor, the one that had misdiagnosed my mother and labeled her a head case.

Shortly after I mused over how fast I could get an appointment, I drifted off to sleep.

I woke up to another cramp but this one was the strongest that I'd ever had. I could see out of the window that it was getting light outside. The sounds of my father gagging and choking himself as he brushed his teeth and stuck his toothbrush as far back as he could without triggering the up rush of his supper into the bathroom sink, filtered through my closed bedroom door. The sound was comforting and nauseating at the same time. I awoke to that bathroom opera every morning of my entire life and believe it or not I had kind of missed it when I was away.

The pain had reached a crescendo and then quickly passed, and shortly after, I'd realized that I needed to go pee. Daddy had left the bathroom to finish getting ready for work, and I quietly slipped inside the small maroon and pink plastic tiled room shutting the door behind me. I sat down and when I got up again what I saw in the toilet convinced me that something was drastically wrong. Blood, too much blood, filled the water in the bottom of the bowl!

I was in St. Mary's Hospital, in a room laying flat on my back in bed in less than an hour. Daddy had reacted to my medical emergency swiftly and wisely, taking me straight to the emergency room where he felt that I would get help right away.

With all of the hubbub the cramping had stopped, and there hadn't been any more bleeding.

I didn't have a doctor of my own, so I was assigned to the next obstetrician on the list. All hospitals have the list. It's for those of us who foolishly haven't taken the time to do the research to find a good doctor when we are well, so we wind up with potluck when we are sick and really need the best treatment that we can find. I hadn't seen my "luck of the draw" since I had been admitted. The nurse on duty had come into my room shortly after I had arrived and stoically asked me the usual background medical questions and without any additional conversation, started to leave.

"Pardon me." I said to her as she was getting up from the chair beside my bed. Expressionless, she turned to look at me.

"What's going to happen? Am I going to lose the baby?"

She looked at me in a matter of fact way.

"Maybe, time will tell. All you can do is sit and wait." She said, and with that she turned and walked quickly out the door.

"Boy, some angel of mercy!" I thought. "Now, what do I do?" Turning my sights to my surroundings I looked for something, anything, to keep me busy. There were some old magazines lying on the table next to the bed, so in lieu of nothing better to do, I read them for the next few hours. At lunch the only food that they brought me to eat was what was OK on a liquid diet, beef broth, Jell-O and tea. I asked the dietitian why that was, and she said when a patient is in the hospital for a possible miscarriage, the doctors want to keep the food she eats very light, just in case she goes into labor. Her comment scared me a little, but since I hadn't had any pains since I left the house I was going to keep a positive attitude.

"Don't worry Susan, everything will be alright." I said, comforting myself. "Just relax and take it easy now that you have the chance." My father called and checked to see how I was doing, and even Momma had called me, with some help from Claudette, during Claudette's afternoon visit. My room was on the maternity floor of the hospital, a place where only fathers of babies were allowed to visit during a very limited visiting schedule. Jake was still back in Texas and I was in a two-bed room without a roommate so I figured that things were going to be pretty quiet. Sometime in the late afternoon, I fell asleep with a magazine in my hand.

Dreaming that I was lying in the hospital bed in blood drenched sheets from my waist to my toes, sobbing with the realization that the baby was lost forever, I was roused back into consciousness by the pain. It was back again! I could feel the contraction twisting my muscles tighter and tighter, like a big thick rubber band on a wind up airplane. Damn, it hurt!

Then, as the pain eased, I noticed that it was evening and while I was napping they had wheeled in a woman next to me who was out like a light. The beds were close enough for me to hear her soft breathing. Laying in the darkened room and hearing my stomach growl, I realized that I must have missed supper. A sliver of light from the hallway illuminated the furniture around me and I picked my head off the pillow enough to see a food tray perched precariously at the foot of my bed on the overhanging arm of my bed-table. And then the pain gripped my insides again.

The cramping gripped me like a huge hand firmly grabbing my gut, squeezing and squeezing, tighter and tighter, until the pain came to the point of being unbearable and then it started to subside. I though to myself, "God, it can't get any worse than this!" But it did.

The time between pains got shorter and shorter, until the end of one contraction seemed to flow right into the next. The pain was no longer confined to my belly, it radiated white and hot, down my upper thighs to my knees, burning around my waist, and piercing into the small of my back. I'd never experienced such excruciating pain before in my life! As it inevitably swelled into large mountainous waves, its undertow would suck me under into a realm of torture where time was bent and had no meaning. I had no idea if I was loudly moaning or groaning. My only purpose was to do whatever I had to do to survive the peak of the wave until it slipped down into a valley where the pain had lessened. Not knowing what to do to help myself take control, I rolled back and forth from side to side chewing and pulling on the blankets until they came undone from where they had been neatly tucked beneath the foot of the mattress. The rest of the bedclothes had come off the end of the bed exposing the plastic underneath, and were bunched up under the backs of my legs, dislodged by the agitated thrashing of the heels of my feet against the sheets.

Somewhere in the smear of torturous pain an irritated nurse angrily straitened out my blankets and sheets remarking to me with disapproval on what a fuss I was making. Then answering a question, inaudible to me, from the direction of where I assumed my roommate to be, she said, "Yes, with being over four months gone, she'll go through the whole thing. The same as if she was having the baby." And then she left.

Sometime later, I have no idea if it was five minutes or fifty minutes, a little old nurse came quietly into my room. Looking at me writhing in the bed she must've felt pity for me.

"Sweetie, give yourself a break!" she said. "You aren't doing yourself any favors by getting all twisted up like a pretzel!" Gently but firmly she pulled my legs away from my chest and told me to try and relax my muscles a little bit. Then she said, "Every time you feel a pain coming, lie on your side and keep your legs straight, and pull on the bars of the bed rails of your bed, as hard as you can! That will help you not get so worked up and then the pain will lessen a bit." She smiled and patted my hip, and walked out the door. I tried what she said and it helped me to endure the rest of the nightmare.

Finally, around midnight, the pains abruptly stopped. After fifteen minutes or so I called the nurse to ask her what she thought might be happening. She commented that she didn't know, that we would have to wait and see, and then asked if I would like to sit up for a tiny bit and suck on some crushed ice. Crushed ice sounded like a wonderful delicacy and I eagerly shook my head in agreement. As she raised me up into a sitting position, I felt pressure but no pain, and as mysteriously as the baby came to be, it was no more.

She wrapped the large bloody football shaped object that had been my baby in towel, and took it away, leaving me miserable and alone. I cried all night until I was exhausted, and fell into a fitful sleep just before the sun came up. Someone had closed my privacy curtains but I could still hear the lady next to me when she was brought her baby for the morning feeding, which accentuated my feelings of loss and emptiness. I actually thought that it was really shitty to put the women having miscarriages in rooms with women whose babies had recently been born. When I asked about it the nurse had said that it was just the way that things were done.

The condescending bastard that called himself my doctor, the one who had won me in a raffle as a patient by being the next MD on the list, came into my room around nine a.m. and examined me. Afterwards, he said that I could go home. It seemed that the large blood clot that I'd passed earlier had included the placenta, embryonic sack and baby, completely intact, so I didn't need to be scraped. I'd asked him what the baby had been, a boy or a girl, but he said that it was best for me not know, and to try to forget. He also told me that I had a condition where my uterus was inverted, and its up-side-down position had slowly cut off the blood supply to the baby, probably causing some deformity and resulting in the miscarriage.

"That's why you had some difficulty getting pregnant in the first place. Don't worry. You'll be pregnant again in no time. But next time, go to the doctor sooner!" He was stiff and slightly stern in his demeanor. Then without another word got up as he flipped pages on my chart, and left.

Alone, God, I was totally alone! The "don't worry you'll be pregnant again in a little while" crap didn't do a bit of good for making me feel better. I'd lost the baby and felt empty, aching for what had been inside of me just a few short hours ago. I was so close and now I would have to start all over again, all the hoping and watching to see if it happens every month, all the disappointment when it doesn't.

God, why this, why now? Wasn't Momma enough? And then I started to cry. I muffled the sobs so that the woman in the bed next to me couldn't hear my misery. This was my private agony and I didn't want any onlookers, like those ghouls who stop at the side of the road to gleefully watch the carnage caused by cars crashing into each other. The drape was pulled so I had some privacy, and I took the time to cry.

By eleven o'clock Daddy was in my room helping me to get my things together so that I could leave and go back home. I needed all the rest I could get over the next five days. Momma was coming home on Monday, and it would be a job getting her meals and helping her to maneuver around the house. My mood had lightened a bit but the underlying feeling of emptiness remained. Maybe things would be better once Momma came home and began to get well. Thanksgiving was just around the corner, and in a week after that Jake would be home and we would be together again. I missed him and my body ached to share the loss of our baby with him.

"Just a few more weeks, and everything will be better."

❧ XX ❧

My mother's house was full of laughter again. It was Thanksgiving and we were all together, Carole and John, Claudette and Mick, Aunt Lollie, Daddy, Momma, and myself. I could hear the rumble of my nieces and nephews feet as they raced over the kitchen floor above my head and then down the linoleum covered wooden steps that led to the basement. My parents had stored our old toys down here and it was a pleasure to see the excitement and hear the laughter of the next generation as they played with the same small treasures that we had played with as children.

Many neat things were stashed in the basement. Besides our old toys, there was a bookcase full of old interesting books with beautifully intricate pictures from when my father was a boy. There were boxes full of old photos and memorabilia from before and after Momma and Daddy were married, and even my mother's salmon colored satin wedding dress and the bride and groom from the top of their cake. I'd spent hours down there as a young girl, looking through everything over and over, savoring each piece of a memory as if it was my own.

I smiled as I watched Carolyn, my sister Carole's daughter, rubbing her fingertips over the life like skin of her mother's old doll, with a look of wonder and surprise on her face. The synthetic skin and human hair on the doll had also fascinated me as a child. I could see myself standing in almost the same spot, holding the doll by its stuffed cloth torso, touching and staring, and for an instant, I felt a bond between us. It was as if the toy had become a door linking two children together, each experiencing the same curiosity and wonder, their souls touching in time.

"Deep thoughts!" I chided myself, the smile still on my face as I bent down and looked into the oven through the glass window of the pink porcelain stove that sat against the corner wall in the basement. We had a second stove down stairs for cooking in the summer to keep the house from getting too hot, and now it was keeping the extra turkey that we needed to feed our brood, warm. I was feeling pretty good. Momma had been home for the last week and she seemed to be getting stronger every day, so much for bad dreams. The cooking, cleaning, and taking care of Momma and Daddy, tired me out, but the empty unhappy feeling was gone. I was reconciled to the fact that getting pregnant again might take some time, but I had been through it before and I could do it again.

"Turkey looks good." I said aloud mostly to myself, but in response one of the laughing kids looked up and shouted, "Grrreat!"

"Johnny, you're so funny!" I heard Carole say to her son as she came down the basement steps, the comment taken by him as a compliment, and causing him great delight.

"Susan, how are things going down here?" she asked.

"Fine. I think Aunt Lollie's turkey is holding its own. It should be OK for another half-hour. I've got it on a really low setting. How are things going upstairs? Are the potatoes ready to mash?" I asked, as I turned and picked up the soapy dishrag out of the sink and started to wipe the top of the stove where someone had dripped grease while basting the turkey.

"Aunt Lollie's really helping out up there. Claudette and I don't have very much to do." Carole said this last statement in kind of an off-handed manner as if she was thinking of something else, and then she began again.

"Susan..." she hesitated and then went on. "Do you think that you could help Daddy out a little more with Momma?"

"What do you mean? Help him how?" I was puzzled by the question, so I stopped what I was doing and met her gaze.

"I talked to Grandma Porter a few days ago and she had some things to say." She hesitated again as if she was searching for the right words, but having difficulty in finding them. She looked increasingly uncomfortable as she began again.

"Susan, Grandma said... she said that she was very angry about what Daddy had told her, about how you've been handling things. I mean, helping him out. She thinks that I should talk to you so that you will do more around the house and take some of the burden off of him. It's hard for him to do so much after being at work all day and..."

"What!" I interrupted.

Carole looked into my eyes and quietly said, "Daddy told Grandma how hard it was taking care of Momma and the house, and when she asked about you, he told her that you weren't any help at all. He left her with the impression that you were loafing around all day while he cooked, cleaned, played nurse maid to Momma, and went to bed exhausted."

"DADDY!" I looked up and shouted to the basement ceiling. "DADDY! Come down here right this minute!"

I heard Aunt Lollie's muffled voice call, "Irv, Susan wants you downstairs." I could hear the light pounding of footsteps coming from the front room towards the back of the house, and the back steps leading to the basement. Carole knew right away what was going on, after all, she was her father's daughter.

"You have sold me down the river once too often! I'm so sick and tired of coming in last where other people are concerned, including yourself and your need for other people's approval and sympathy. You're pathetic, really pathetic!" I hissed at the ceiling as I listened to his footsteps, and his progress, through the house and down the stairs to me. In my rage, I'd forgotten that my sister was standing beside me. I didn't care. All I wanted to do was not let him get away with it, not this time! Daddy came down the last step as the phrase "really pathetic" rang in my ears. And then for the first time in my life, I yelled at my father, and hit him with the truth right between the eyes. I didn't wait for him to come close to me. I began confronting him with what he had done, as he walked the last few feet between the steps and where I was standing.

"How could you do this to me? How could you tell Grandma Porter that I was lazy and doing nothing to help you out around here? Over the last two months, I've broken my back with doing all the cleaning, cooking, laundry, and visiting Momma at the hospital. And now that she's home, taking care of her while you're at work... Jesus Daddy! I just lost my baby and I know that all the stress and over work didn't help things! How could you say a thing like that, when you know how it's been? You're my father, how could you do it?"

I was shouting straight into his face by the end of my tirade, and I could tell from the look on it that the dawn of recognition had come almost immediately after the first few sentences. My feelings of betrayal were glaringly harsh, and sharpened by each word as it shot out of my mouth and hit home.

When I was finished, after one agonizing moment of shock and silence, my father did the one thing that I had not expected that he would do. He started to cry. I was prepared for a denial or a screaming match, or even a slap in the face like he had done when I was sixteen and had called him a drunk, but this I was totally unprepared for. His face crumpled up like a child's as his tears fell, and my resolve crumpled with it. I'd hit my father with the truth and it had cut his legs out from under him.

"I'm sorry... I'm sorry..." he sobbed, and kept repeating it over and over.

I stared at him as he cried. I had confronted him with the truth and he couldn't deny it. He had used me to make himself look better in his mother's eyes, and he knew it. So what good would all this do? None. As the saying goes "You can't teach an old dog new tricks." and you couldn't teach my dad to care about other people over himself. In that instant, I clearly saw what he was and I knew with certainty that it was never going to change. So what do you do? There were two choices: knowingly accept him with all his deformities never expecting more than he can give, taking what you can and leaving the rest, or disown him and banish him from your life. I chose the former because the latter was unthinkable. After all, he was my father.

"I'm sorry!" he muttered one more time, and not being able to help myself, I hugged him and shushed him until he was quiet.

"It's OK Daddy, just don't do it again, huh?" He hugged me back, wiped his eyes, silently turned and went back upstairs. It was all over, just like that. Carole and I turned and looked at each other as he went, and now it was our turn to cry.

❧ XXI ❧

Standing at the front room picture window alone waiting for them to come, I gazed out into the street and watched the puffy white snowflakes, illuminated by the streetlight, gently fall to the ground. There was about an inch of new fallen snow, and it made the world look fresh and new. It was early morning, before the sun was up, and Daddy was in the bedroom with Momma. She had spiked a fever in the middle of the night and the inevitable return to the hospital couldn't be put off any longer.

Jake had left the day before yesterday for Germany and I was soon to follow. He had come home for leave just after Thanksgiving and the thirty days had flown by. Life had been in such turmoil that even though he'd only been gone forty-eight hours, I could barely remember what it was like to have him here. Momma had been my main focus and he had seemed to understand, and now he was gone.

At Thanksgiving our hopes had been high for Momma's recovery, but since then things had taken a turn for the worse. The tumor had started to grow again. The doctors decided that another round of radiation might help since the cancer had been so susceptible to the treatments the first time. My Aunt Lollie had come every day for two weeks to pick Momma up from the house and take her to the hospital for treatments, but the cancer had kept growing. As day after day had passed, I could tell that Momma was loosing the battle. At first, she had begun to lose the mobility in her legs, which she had worked so hard to gain back, and in a short time use of the walker was impossible. She was again bed ridden. On Christmas day the family had gathered at our house to celebrate the holiday. Everyone had tried to keep Momma's and their own spirits high with a pretense of the optimism and joy of the season. However, when we were out of her sight, sitting together at the kitchen table, the atmosphere among us had been that of relatives attending the wake of a loved one instead of a celebration of life.

She had tried to hide what was happening to her. I could see the fear in her eyes when she began to realize that even her own bodily functions were starting to fail her. By Christmas day I'd been pretty sure that she couldn't feel or move anything from her waist down. During the last couple of nights I could hear her muffled moans as she had tried desperately, through shear will to make her body listen to her. But will is not enough when the cancer has its way.

I saw the flashing of the red and white lights on the brick of the neighbors' houses first, before the ambulance came into view. They parked in front of our house, lights flashing but eerily silent. I watched as, with the precision of an Army drill team, they made all the preparations needed to usher my mother from the safe and loving arms of our home to the sterile cold place of gray marble and white coats.

They came up the walk and into the house in military fashion, polite but all business. The first paramedic in the door asked for directions and I replied, "Down the hallway, last bedroom on your right." in a kind of matter of fact way, sounding much more together than I was. Ten minutes later, my mother was wheeled out of her room, down the hallway and into the front room, where they stopped the gurney near to where I was standing so that Momma and I could say goodbye.

"I'll meet you at the hospital in a little while once you get settled in. OK?" I smiled as I said this, reaching for her hand, taking it and rubbing it gently. She returned my grasp and held on to me tightly as if she never wanted to let me go, tears starting to form in her eyes. She was laying on the gurney under a white blanket neatly folded and tucked in along the sides, and she was strapped in to keep her safe from a possible tumble. Her hair had been carefully wrapped close to her head in a turban made of a white towel like material, to insure that it wouldn't get caught on anything while they transported her to the hospital. The scene was all too familiar to me.

As if we were thinking each other's thoughts, Momma said to me, "This reminds me of the day that they came to take Grandma away after her last stroke." New tears welled up in the outside corners of her eyes taking the place of the ones that had overflowed the ridges of her eyelids and ran silently down her cheeks.

We were standing in almost the exact same spot in our front room where my mother had stood stroking my grandma's towel wrapped head as she had laid on an ambulance gurney, tears glistening in both their eyes.

Momma's tears had set mine in motion but I fought them down, trying to maintain a false facade of confidence in what I was about to say.

"Oh Momma, come on now, this is different. You'll be coming back home." I said lying but thinking that it was for the best. Standing in the same spot, reliving one of my mother's saddest memories as my own, how could I deny it? But I did.

"No, I won't" She said in a whisper. Her eyes met mine and I quickly turned mine away, trying to hide the fact that we both instinctively knew that it was true.

"Don't say such things! You're going to be just fine!" I scolded her, averting my eyes from her penetrating stare, as I stroked her forehead with one hand and held her thin bony fingers in the other. And then our time together was over. It was time for Momma to go...

❧ **PART 4** ❧

"GERMANY"

❧ XXII ❧

I hardly noticed the constant humming of the jet engines anymore. I only became aware of it when it came to mind and I consciously listened for the noise. I had been in the air for seven of the nine hours that the overseas flight was supposed to take and the expanse of time hadn't been half bad. The large jets that flew to Europe were so much nicer to travel in than the smaller planes that shuttled you back and forth to Texas. One rarely felt a thump or a shake due to air turbulence, making the nighttime flight fairly pleasant. The dinner on the flight had consisted of a small but tender filet mignon with all the trimmings. Following, there was a recently released movie complete with private headphones, for those who didn't care to attempt sleep in the cramped quarters of an airplane seat. After watching James Gardner in a murder mystery, I was able to get a few winks of sleep despite my fear of flying and the excitement of where I was going.

Reclining back in my seat, I was trying to get in one more mini-nap before we landed. I wanted to be fresh when Jake met me as I got off the plane. It was still dark out the porthole window next to my seat and with flying over the ocean, there was nothing to look at to catch my attention, so I started to drift off. In my semi-conscious state my thoughts drifted back to Momma, and I wondered how and what she was doing now. Almost three weeks had gone by since she had been taken back to the hospital, and in those three weeks things had gotten much worse. The daily regimen of Daddy dropping me off at the hospital early in the morning had begun. My last visit with her had been just before Daddy had driven me to the airport, and I missed her already.

Her physical deterioration, back to where she had been before the surgery, was very quick. Within a day after arriving at the hospital, she had become completely paralyzed from her chest down. Sometimes she had a difficult time breathing because the muscles in her chest weren't getting the message to move from her brain. The breathing problems always cleared up once she went for her dose of radiation, but that wasn't going to last forever. The tumor was still extremely sensitive to the treatments, and they did make it release its death grip on the nerves in her spinal column. But where in the past the tumor had slowly returned, now, it was returning with lightning speed, squeezing off the tiny conduits for messages to and from the brain within a day, and choking off her breathing or making it difficult to move her arms. The cancer was winning and there wasn't much more that could be done. There was a limit to how much radiation could be given to a patient without creating death instead of staving it off, and she was close to that limit. Radiation was a poison for the rest of the body, so as a result of the nausea that came from the treatments, she had lost all of the weight she had gained in the last two months, and her body again became the image of a Holocaust survivor.

Along with her physical changes, Momma's interaction with the outside world was changing too. Some days she would sleep all day, and not be able to be roused, and on others she would emotionlessly stare at the wall, totally unresponsive to any questions or comments that I would make. Worried, I'd asked the nurse about her behavior and she had said that it was all somehow tied to the growth of the tumor. She must have been right because Momma always bounced back after the next treatment.

She had never asked me if she was dying, but we both knew she was. In the first few weeks of her relapse, bitterness seemed to seep into her usually optimistic attitude and her patience had become short with what she thought were unnecessary hospital schedules for things like changing bed sheets and giving sponge baths. Her refusal to cooperate with such endeavors labeled her as "difficult" with the nurses who were constantly complaining to us about her behavior. She also began to vehemently refuse my father's company in her room. She made the remark to me that after thirty-six years of having to look at his face every day, she didn't want to have to look at it any longer. Defensive of Daddy, my sisters and I had chided her into rethinking her stance, and in the end she did allow him to once again sit in the hospital chair beside her bed. But her conversations with him were close to non-existent and consisted of stiff phrases like "Pass me a Kleenex". She made sure that he never touched her again, not even allowing a perfunctory kiss goodbye in the evenings when he left her bedside to go home.

Then unexpectedly, in the last few days, her mood had gotten much better. The dark brooding and bitterness seemed to pass and a kind of peace settled over her. She was Momma again, and hope rekindled in my heart that maybe the end wasn't as near as I'd thought, maybe she would bounce back. Things were looking up. And then the letter from Jake came.

Since Jake had left for Germany at the end of December, I'd gotten a letter from him almost every day. Momma had been home when Jake left and he and I both thought that I would be following him in about a week. With Momma returning to the hospital, and her health failing more every day, I'd put off our plans of being immediately reunited in Europe, and kept a vigil at her bedside.

At first the letters were the usual. They were full of words that expressed how much he missed me, and how he couldn't wait for me to join him. Despite the longing for us to be together, their mood was upbeat and positive. In my letters to him I tried to describe how quickly my mother was deteriorating in front of my eyes, how painful it was to see it, and how little hope we all had for her. I thought that he'd understood. But he hadn't. As the days passed and dragged into weeks the tone of his letters changed. He stopped making references to "when you get here" and started asking, "When

ARE you getting here?" Reading between the lines I sensed wisps of mistrust brewing in the flavor of his words, and it puzzled me. I tried to reassure him with my letters, but it didn't work.

And then it came in the mail, the poison pen letter that had changed everything, and the impetus that had forced me on this plane. Jake's handwritten words had simply and boldly stated that he no longer believed what I was telling him and that Momma was NOT on the verge of death. He felt that I was using her sickness as an excuse not to come to him in Germany, and that I was planning to abandon him there. He had gone on to say that he knew that Momma would recover ("If she really was on death's door, she would have died by now!") and my place was with him, not her. If I didn't make plans to join him, as was my duty as his wife, than he would start proceedings so that I wouldn't be his wife any longer. He would divorce me for abandonment!

"The guys around here have told me that this kind of fucking thing happens all the time. Army wives are always getting bored with fucking Army life, and they go and find some fucking civilian to hook up with. I am not going to be a fucking fool, so if you really love me you'll be on the next fucking plane!" As I finished the last few venomous lines of his "love letter", I realized that my mouth was hanging open from the shear shock of what I'd read.

Was he crazy? Why would he think that I was lying about Momma? I hadn't a clue as to where this literary nightmare had come from in his idiot male brain! What was wrong with him? Divorce!

What was he talking about, divorce? Just because I didn't want to leave my dying mother? What the hell was he talking about?

Wherever his ideas had come from, there was no doubt about it, he had meant what he'd written and now I had to figure out quickly what to do. He was my husband and he was desperately screaming out that he needed me. I had no idea what the conditions were like at his new duty station, and Jake never had been very good at expressing his inner tensions and fears. Excess tension on the job had usually resulted in groundless arguments at home, so something must be stretching him tighter than a drum and I had no way to know what it was! Boy, this was some time for him to get wacky!

Confused and torn between duty to my husband and to my mother, I confided in Momma about the situation, the day after the letter came. I had censored out the part about his accusation that I was lying about her condition, and emphasized his fear that I didn't want to be with him anymore. She counseled me in typical Momma fashion.

"Susan, your place is with your husband. You should go to him right away. He's upset and lonely and feeling abandoned, and he needs you."

So under her direction and with her blessing, I left her to get on this plane. When I said goodbye to her just a few short hours ago, I remember saying, "Momma, hurry up and get well, and before you know it I'll be seeing you again. Twenty-three months isn't such a long time." But, looking through the tears in each other's eyes, we knew that it was an eternity. And as I kissed her cheek, deep down, we both knew that it was for the last time.

"Susan," I thought to myself as I tried to find a more comfortable position in the airplane seat, "you know that there is a chance that she could make it until you come back. The doctor couldn't tell you one way or the other how long she would last, and recently, she has really been looking much better." But somehow my attempt to soothe myself sounded empty and rang hollow.

I tried to redirect my thoughts to Jake, imagining the look on his face when he would see me for the first time. I reflected on how desperately he needed me, and my mother's words about my duty lying with him and our future together. Reluctantly I had agreed, but somehow it seemed unfair. It seemed that he should've understood, and I should've had a little more time with Momma. But sometimes life's unfair, and this time was one of them.

"Would you like some breakfast?" Opening my eyes, I saw the smiling stewardess who had abruptly broken into my private thoughts.

"Sure." I said. As she walked toward the front of the plane I adjusted my seat into a sitting position and slid open the plastic shade that had covered the porthole. The clouds were turning a rosy pink color and the rising sun was just peeping up over the horizon. Smiling, I thought to myself, "It's morning and my new life with my husband is beginning."

❧ XXIII ❧

He was there! I could see him on the other side of the customs section of the airport. God, he was handsome in his uniform! I waved furiously to get his attention and it had worked. A broad smile lit up his face as he took one last drag on his cigarette before he dropped it to the floor and crushed it out under the toe of his brilliantly polished black leather dress shoe. The line seemed to move slower than molasses, but finally I was through it, and in his arms. We held each other for a long time, not saying a word, rocking back and forth, not wanting to let each other go. It was good to feel his body pressed against me in that old familiar way, smelling his after-shave, feeling his smooth, freshly shaven cheek placed against mine. Momma was right. This was where I belonged.

"Let's get going." He said as he let me go and bent down to pick up my bag. "We have to hurry up so that we can catch the fucking train to Nuremberg at 11 o'clock. If we miss it there's not another fucking train until three this afternoon." We took a taxi to the train station and made it on board just in time. The train was relatively crowded so we had to stand for a good part of the way, but I didn't mind. After sitting on the plane for nine hours it felt good to stand.

"I rented us a fucking room until we can move into the apartment that I rented on the fucking economy." The economy was another word for off base housing, that is, living amongst the natives.

Jake had been promoted, in Texas, to "Private First Class" but no special privileges came with that. A soldier had to be a sergeant in order for his wife to live in government housing on the base. Anyone below a sergeant was a peon and didn't count for much as far as the Army was concerned.

"It won't be fucking ready for us to move into until the fucking first of February. We'll have to put up with the fucking rented room until then. Don't expect too fucking much as far as the room goes. It was hard to find the fucking place, and I haven't had much time since I got here." he said as he looked out of the train window, absentmindedly watching the farmland whiz by.

"Jake, you know I don't care what the place is like. It'll be great as long as we're together in it." Boy! Did that sound corny but I meant it. Jake, expressionless, kept looking out of the window with his arm around my shoulder trying to brace the two of us against the rumble and sway of the train as it sped along the winding track.

"How do you like the new base?" I asked.

"You mean the fucking Kaserne. That's what they call it in Germany. William O'Darby Kaserne, that's my fucking new home. And I don't fix fucking trucks. The master sergeant of the base, Sergeant Ogee kind of fucking likes me so he asked me if I would like to be the company clerk instead of a fucking truck mechanic. So I said, "fucking A!" A lot more fucking truck mechanics get their nuts blown off than fucking company clerks do. I have a good chance of fucking staying here instead of getting shipped off to fucking 'Nam. And it looks like I'll get a fucking promotion to 'Spec. 4' in a month or two."

"They can't ship you off to 'Nam after they sent you here, can they?" I asked.

"Fuck, they can do whatever they god damn please! I know one poor fucking son-of-a-bitch who was shipped here and after thirty days wound up getting orders cut for 'Nam. His MOS was for a fucking tank mechanic. His wife was on a fucking plane to Frankfurt when the orders came down, so when she got here she had to fucking turn around and go back home! You would think that it was too fucking expensive for Uncle Sam to do shit like that, but when a fucking slot for your MOS opens up, you fucking go!" I could hear the anxiety and anger in his voice as he finished the last sentence.

"It's just the fucking luck of the draw. Who fucking died and who can fucking replace him! They even send fucking short-timers there if the fucking slot opens up!"

"What's a short-timer?" I asked.

"It's a fucking guy with less than ninety days to go until he's fucking discharged. Even with fucking three months left the god damn motherfuckers can send you to get your fucking head blown off!" He replied, and then continued to look sullenly out of the train window.

"There is one fucking catch though, that can slow the motherfuckers down a little. If your fucking wife and family are already here when orders come down for 'Nam, the fucking Army has to give you a month to move your family back home in addition to the fucking month's leave that you get stateside before you start killing people. It's not much but at least they can't send you back almost overnight like they did to that poor fucking US Army tank mechanic." I saw a trace of a smile flit across his normally stoic expression like the cat that had caught the canary, and realized instantly what all the fuss had been about. The letter and the divorce threats had been a ruse to get me here as soon as possible, so that he could sleep a little easier at night. My presence afforded him the tiniest amount of protection against the insatiable death monster, Vietnam. I had foolishly and perhaps arrogantly thought that the anger and anguish Jake had expressed in his letter was a direct consequence of his total inability to live without me, instead of something much more primal, the desire to survive.

The rest of the train ride was spent with very few words spoken between the two of us. Jake was not an eloquent conversationalist and I often would kid myself that living with Jake was like living alone interrupted by a few words here and there. I reflected on this as I looked out of the train window, and concluded that in some respects, I had hit the nail on the head.

❧ XXIV ❧

The rented room wasn't all that bad. It beat the hell out of staying outside overnight in the rain. It was a twelve by twelve foot room with a small sink, and leatherette chaise lounge that could barely fit two people, even if Jake and I held each other tightly as we lay down side by side, twisted together. There was no bathroom. The toilet that we were allowed to use was located down a flight of wooden stairs in a damp, dark, windowless cellar. The toilet was squeezed into a small room the size of a clothes closet, with a naked light bulb dangling on a wire from the ceiling. The door to the bathroom, if you could call it that, was made of wide wooden planks crisscrossed with inch gaps between them like the gate on a large fence. The wooden beams of the cellar and the bathroom door were loaded with spider webs. Spiders are my least favorite bugs of all. Ever since I was five and found a large hairy brown spider crawling up my bare leg in the dark in my father's '51 silver Chevy, they had grossed me out. Brushing my leg and coming up with what looked like a tarantula on the fingers of my tiny five-year old hand had caused my first moment of complete unbridled insanity. Screaming, I'd tried to smash the disgusting thing against the interior of the car door, but didn't succeed until the bastard had painfully bitten me in several places on my fingertips. God! Two weeks of peeing in this dungeon was going to be hell!

Jake and I had spent the last two days together and it had been wonderful. We'd never left the room except for the two times that Jake had gone to the corner market to get some bread and lunch meat. There was a short cement ledge outside the room's only window, which faced a brick wall. We found the ledge convenient for storing small amounts of left over food. No refrigerator and no stove meant that I would be shopping daily for food. I guess sandwiches, fruit, and milk for fourteen days wouldn't be too bad.

Jake's weekend pass was over and he'd left for the base early this morning. I'd gone back to bed when he had left, to treat myself to a few more minutes of sleep. I must've drifted off, because in what seemed like less than a minute or two, I woke up to Jake unexpectedly walking through the door. At first I was disoriented and wondered if I had somehow slept through the whole day. I've heard of jet lag but that would be ridiculous. Then taking a quick look at my watch, I realized that it was almost 10 o'clock in the morning.

"What are you doing home? I thought that you didn't get off until 3:30." I said rubbing the sleep out of my eyes and trying to focus on Jake's face. Wow! He really looked upset! His eyes were rimmed in red, as though he had been crying, something that I rarely saw Jake do.

"Honey, I don't know how to..." He choked off the next word that had been forming in his throat. After a few seconds of silence he held out a brown paper napkin towards me. "Someone on duty over the weekend took this message and it was waiting for me when I got in this morning." I plucked it out of his hand as I reluctantly got up from the couch, knowing instinctively what it would say.

"I'm sorry!" I barely noticed him mumble somewhere in the background of my mind. As I held the flimsy paper in my hand, my attention was fully focused on the partially shredded napkin with the partially illegible letters scrawled on it. I could make out something about the Red Cross and the phrase "died at 2:30 am, January 18, 1968". Then there were more indecipherable scribbles followed by, "...no need to return home. Love, Daddy."

"I...uh...thought that she had more time. I thought that she was getting well..." It was Jake again. What was wrong with him? Couldn't he see that I didn't care what he thought! All that mattered was that she was dead! And some stupid faceless insensitive idiot soldier had cared so little about the message that he had taken that he wrote it on a fucking used napkin! She was dead and there was nothing to show for it except for some crappy scribbling on a dirty fucking napkin! The screaming in my head oozed out of my mouth as a loud agonizing groan, and the remembered anguish in my dream became a harsh, cruel reality. The pain was so great that I collapsed back onto the phony leather sofa, the napkin still clutched in my fist and pulling my legs to my chest, trying a familiar but fruitless attempt at providing myself relief to the agony that was ripping though me.

Jake wordlessly lay down on the couch beside me, placing his arms tightly around my writhing body, now racked with heart wrenching sobs. He held me tight, trying to control the uncontrollable. He realized that nothing could stop the tide of tears. He hung on to me, trying to help me weather the worst emotional storm of my life. He held me for hours rocking me back and forth, not speaking a word, just holding me tight.

As early evening started to close in and the meager light dwindled from our viewless window, my tears had started to slow. The pain in my heart was still excruciating but the tears had begun to dry up. "No tears left to cry!" my Aunt Lollie had said that day in my mother's kitchen as she recounted her horror at viewing Auntie Tillie's corpse in the morgue. And so it was now.

"Momma's dead." I whispered into Jake's ear and I felt his arms hug me a little tighter in a comforting response. I took a deep breath and slowly sighed it out. The pain was still there, worse than what I had remembered from in the dream, probably because this was a reality that I could never wake up from, and I knew it. Momma was dead and I was never going to see her again. No warm coming home reunions were in our future, not even the elaborately bittersweet luxury of saying a final goodbye to the shell that once was my mother. Just a brown crumpled paper napkin and the memory of Momma in my mind. And then in God's mercy, sleep finally came.

✤ XXV ✤

Wow! The toilet seat was really cold! It was crazy that the Germans didn't heat their bathrooms! I just couldn't figure it out. Didn't their asses get cold too? Cold or not it could be a lot worse. The memory of the spider pit hadn't entirely faded from my mind. I had hated that pee place so much that I had tried to hold it during the night as long as I could. Going down into that dungeon in the middle of the night had traumatized me to the max, and I had actually wet the bed (or should I say leatherette couch) for the first time since I was a toddler. The two weeks that I'd spent in that one room hadn't done my kidneys any good.

We'd been in our fully furnished second story German economy apartment for about three months now, and it was nice. When I had first walked into the place I'd been bowled over. It was by far the best living accommodations that I had since being associated with Uncle Sam's Army. When you first walked in the front door (it was the only entrance to the place, no laws about more than one exit here!), you found yourself in a three by five vestibule/hallway, with a door on each of the three walls. All three doors had silver metal latch type handles to open them instead of doorknobs. There were no doorknobs in Germany. Doorknobs, I had come to find out, were strictly an American invention. No doorknobs was one of the tiny disorientating differences of living abroad that was a constant subtle reminder to your subconscious, that no matter how comfy you started to feel with your surroundings, you were not at home. If the terrain of Texas had caused me to feel like I was living on another planet, then the European essence in every man-made object that surrounded me, made me feel at times, that I'd slipped through Alice's looking glass.

Two of the doors in the hallway were metal and covered with an off white enamel paint. The third, the first one to your right as you entered the small hallway, was a wooden trimmed glass door, painted with the same off white enamel paint as the other two. The glass in it was thick, ribbed, and frosted, much like the front door itself and it led to a ten by twelve foot front room with two sets of European type double door windows, dressed in white lace and flowered curtains. Overall the apartment windows were the size of regular American windows, but instead of glass sections that slid up to let the breeze in, two small wooden framed glass doors stood side by side and opened out to the street.

A person's windows were considered by the Germans to be the portal of one's soul and were expected to be constantly spotless. No matter what the weather, it was a common sight to see both young and old German women hanging precariously out of a third or even fourth floor window, arduously cleaning every spec of dirt off the glass.

An old but clean maroon upholstered couch and chair sat on the front room's dark wooden floor with an Oriental rug in maroon and beige tones in the center of it. An oil space heater with a ceramic tiled front panel stood near the wall next to the door and reminded me of a smaller fancier version of the oil heater that had kept us warm on chilly country nights at my grandma's cottage in Indiana.

The kitchen was through the white door at the end of the hallway. As you entered it, a few feet to your right was the doorway to the bedroom. That door was always left open. Both of the rooms were fairly small and rectangular. The kitchen was brightly lit by a single double door window on the far wall off to your left that opened to a modest cement courtyard below. Hung outside and beneath the window were several clotheslines that were strung between two iron bars and anchored into the brick of the building. Inside the kitchen, on the wall adjacent but perpendicular to the large window, were the sink, gas cooking range, refrigerator, and coal stove. All of which looked like they belonged in a kid's playhouse, not a standard kitchen. The Germans made things as small and decorative as possible for reasons that I didn't understand. The single sink was barely wide enough to wash a dinner plate. The stove was only two feet wide, and so was the refrigerator. Both were waist high and the fridge had a six by six inch freezing compartment that was a joke by American standards. Five feet across from the row of appliances was a row of white enamel wooden cabinets that ended in a built in, three-person breakfast nook with a chair. The whole kitchen was probably eight by ten, a little cramped, but cozy.

The bedroom had the same set of two double door windows with white lace and flowered curtains that the front room had, also opening to the street, but these were spaced more closely to

one another. The room was just wide enough to fit
two German style twin beds side by side, each with
its own bulky gray enamel wooden frame including
head and footboards. A small armoire sat at the
front of the beds, in the corner. The mattresses were
not the eight inches of luxuriously stuffed padding
lying on top of a large box spring, which we were
accustomed to. German mattresses were less than
four inches thick and their support was the wooden
slatted frame beneath them.

The last remaining door in the hallway led to
the bathroom, the room that I was sitting in at this
very moment. I shivered, my bare shoulder
accidentally brushing up against the cold porcelain
corner of the sink as I got up and pulled the flush
handle of the toilet. There were only two sources of
heat in the apartment, the oil heater in the front
room and the coal-burning stove with an iron, hot
plate top in the kitchen. When the coal and oil ran
out, which was usually the case by morning, the
bedroom and the bathroom were freezing. Sleeping
under Army issued sleeping bags helped with the
former, but nothing helped with the latter.

"God this place is cold this morning!" I said to
myself as I gingerly rubbed my upper arms and
mindlessly watched the highly pressurized toilet
water clean the bowl with the same ferocity as the
water from a fire hose. German toilets were really
different from the ones in the good old USA.
Whatever one deposited in them did not wind up
directly in a pool of water. Instead the deposit
landed on a slightly cupped porcelain shelf open to
the air and in my opinion, stinking to high heaven.
When you flushed, highly pressurized water blew

the stuff off its resting place down into a hole at the front end of the toilet. I couldn't understand the German culture. Why did they tolerate not only cold asses but also toilets that maximized stink! Oh well, when in Rome... I turned to the sink to wash my hands and remembered that I would have to wait a bit for hot water after I turned the knob on the miniature hot water heater on the wall above it. There was not a "one pipe feeds all" hot water system in the building, and I'd guessed it was status quo for ninety-nine percent of the living accommodations in this country. The kitchen sink was the same and when you wanted hot water for washing dishes or your hands, a gas flame would kick on and heat up a small reservoir of water producing a tiny hot stream that would pour down into the stainless steel sink.

The hot water heater that fed the big old-fashioned claw legged bathtub, was different too. Hot water to fill the tub came from what looked like a normal sized hot water heater standing in the corner of the bathroom next to the tub, but it wasn't the good old USA type. This one had a place at the bottom of the tank for kindling and coal, where I had expected to see a gas burner. After two weeks of living in a single room with nothing more than a hand sink and a spider hell hole toilet in the cellar, I had learned very quickly how to operate the damned thing. A roaring fire stoked by two and a half round bundles of kindling wood stuffed into the tiny compartment at the bottom of the water heater, provided enough hot water for one gloriously exquisite bath. Jake, the louse, could take a shower any time that he wanted at the base, so the trips to the coal yard for kindling and the ceremonial stoking of the water heater fire was my domain. That was, if I ever wanted a bath.

By German standards, we were living in the lap of luxury. Most of the apartments that my neighbors lived in did not have bathrooms. There was a community toilet and a sits bath (a small white porcelain, three by three square foot mini tub, six inches deep with a drain) on each floor. Public bathhouses could be visited by the locals for eighty Pfennigs, approximately a quarter, a throw. A disgusting opportunity, if you asked me.

I finished washing my hands and went into the kitchen to make myself a cup of tea, but first I quietly snuck back into the bedroom to get my robe. I woke up having to take a pee so badly that I didn't realize I hadn't put my robe on until I hit the ice cold toilet seat. Jake was still sleeping soundly and would probably be dead to the world for hours. He'd drunk quite a bit last night but we still had a good time. On Friday nights we always went to the Tanz Palace, a young peoples dance club about a mile from the apartment. Jake and I thought that at one time it had been an old movie theater that had recently been converted into a nightclub. U-shaped booths placed in several semi-circle rows faced an enormous wooden stage and dance floor. A different live band played on the maroon velvet curtained stage every month, and this month it was the Batmen. Jake, who would never dance in all the years that I knew him, danced with me to the American rock and roll tunes that the German band played and sang with surprising expertise. It had taken a few weeks to coax him into it, but to my pleasant surprise, the last few times that we went to the Palace he became fucking Fred Astaire! I loved dancing and even though he was pretty stewed by the time he got up to dance, it was great fun. And even though sometimes he acted like the "Ugly American", drunkenly urinating in the street or puking in a doorway because he couldn't make it home before nature called one end or the other, it didn't put a damper on the fun that we were having. He was drinking a lot. Germany seemed to be the place for it. However, he was a happy drunk. That was one type of drunk I could put up with, if I had to.

After pouring myself some tea I lit a cigarette, took a deep drag and blew streams of smoke out of my mouth and nostrils in one long, slow sigh. I could instantly feel the tiny tingling in my finger-tips and toes and the slight wave of nausea that always accompanied my first inhaled nicotine fix of the day. I silently sat down on the yellow plastic seat of the breakfast nook in the kitchen and listened to the ticking of the alarm clock on the nightstand next to my bed. It was a comforting sound. It reminded me of the ticking of my grandma's clock at the summer cottage. I needed some comforting now. It was just starting to get light and the apartment was still full of pockets of darkness and shadows that seemed to ebb and flow around me. It was silly, me, a grown woman still afraid of the dark. I had almost gotten over it, but being in Germany had refueled the flame of fear.

It was the dreams. I couldn't say for sure, but I thought that not having any television to watch was the culprit. It was that, or the Germans were slipping hallucinogenics into the water supply to spice up their lives. I'd watched the boob tube every day of my life from the time that I was probably three years old, until now. And since I'd arrived here, I hadn't been able to watch one minute of it. I listened to Armed Forces Radio during the day while I did my housework and had gotten kind of hooked on it. They ran old radio shows like "X-1", "Inner Sanctum", and "Jack Benny", in addition to playing the "top 40" rock and roll songs of the day. To fill the void during the rest of my waking hours, I read book after book from the base library, my intellect starving for as many stories as I could fit into it. But I guessed that the radio and books weren't enough to fill the hunger because during the night my subconscious created stories of its own. It was as if my brain, which had been anesthetized at least fifty percent of every day of the last seventeen years, was coming out of a long deep sleep, and the dreams were a conduit for the enormous rush of creative energy that began to flow from my mind. At times the phenomena amused me, but there were times it scared the hell out of me. This was one of those times.

The dreams were vivid, interesting, and downright entertaining. Mysteries, situation comedies, Godzilla monster movies and the like, were nightly Technicolor extravaganzas in dreamland, complete with commercial breaks in the action. I chuckled at that as I took another sip of tea.

"Boy, we sure are brainwashed by the tube to be good consumers. I can't get away from a sell job even in my dreams!" The sex dreams were something brand new, too. If I'd ever had one before in my life, I'd never remembered it, and the ones that I was experiencing now, I couldn't forget. Erotic wasn't the word for it. For the first time in my life I knew what a wet dream was like, at least the female version of it. The dreams were great! Not only was I watching great stories, I was living them!

The only down side to this smorgasbord of fabulous fantasy was when the nightly feature, chosen by some unseen spinner of tales living in the recesses of my mind, was a horror flick in which I was the main character. When you are vividly living it, a good horror story can blow your mind. I chuckled but with very little humor, as the terror that I had felt a short time ago had begun to whisper in my ear, raising the hair on the nape of my neck. I wrapped my cold fingers around the warm sides of the teacup to ward off the approaching wave of fear and looked out the kitchen window for the first signs of the dawn. I saw a slight pink tinge beginning to appear on the horizon.

"Good. If the sun chases vampires away, I hope it works for the nightmare heebie-jeebies." Last night's nightmare had been the second of its kind and by far the worst of the two. I guess that was because when I woke up still in the dream's grip of terror I found myself in the exact same place that I had been in during the horrors of my dream. I was in my apartment, in my bed in the dark, and lying on my back. The only difference was that I was awake. It had taken me a minute or two to realize that I was safe and that the whole thing had been just a terribly bad dream.

The first dream had been on the same order as the second but not quite as traumatic. That dream, had also taken place in the apartment, but had ended with me running out of the front door of the flat chased by an unseen malevolent presence which had been haunting me throughout the duration of my excursion into dreamland. When I woke up that time, it had unnerved me to still be in the apartment that I'd been trying so desperately to escape from in the nether world. The relief that comes from the realization that it was all a dream, had come quickly when I sensed that I was tucked neatly into my bed and not standing under the glaring light located in the outside hallway. The dream had been so vivid and had felt so real that for several days after, I was uneasy in my own home. The nighttime terror that had mercilessly pursued me through every room in the apartment seemed to linger there after waking, and only diminished over the next few days as the sharpness of the dream became dulled, and faded from my conscious mind. But that dream couldn't hold a candle to the latest episode of "Susan's Subconscious Tales of the Unexpected". This one had been a lulu! I snuffed out my cigarette, took another sip of tea, and like a moth drawn to a flame, relived the nightmare again.

The dream had started where it would end, with me lying on my back in my bed. I had been roused from a deep sleep, by what I didn't know, and was mildly curious as I lazily fluttered my eyelids open. It was pitch black in the bedroom and it took a few seconds for my eyes to be able to make out even the slightest differentiation in the darkness. Blobs of black began to coalesce where I knew that familiar pieces of furniture would be. I was wondering, in drifting sleepy thought, if a bump in the night had brought me to this state of half consciousness, when the tiniest squeak hurtled me into instant full awareness. Every cell in my body screamed, "What was that?" I lay perfectly still as I listened, holding my breath and straining to hear even the slightest sound. Nothing… And subsequently I began to relax my rigid muscles when another tiny barely audible squeak came from the direction of the hallway leading from the front door. This one was closer!

"Someone's in the house!" was the terrified thought that popped into my head. "And he's walking slowly, carefully, through the hallway, towards the kitchen and my bedroom, trying not to be heard!" In my mind's eye I could see the shadowy creeping form, moving slowly and deliberately towards the back of the apartment where I lay frozen by fear unable to do anything but think. It was almost comical how slowly the intruder moved as I watched him from some previously hidden place in my imagination. He oozed forward so as not to make a sound. And just as I imagined he took his next step and touched his foot to the linoleum floor outside the doorway of my room, I heard another creak!

A thin clammy film of sweat had broken out all over my body, chilling me while my cheeks burned red hot with terror. I felt what I thought was some sort of bug or spider scurry next to my hairline and across my temple, and had an instant of relief when I realized that it was a droplet of my own sweat running down the side of my face. I lay in my bed unable to move, paralyzed with fear, listening for the next barely audible sound, a creak or a swish of clothing. I could see him in my mind's eye, looming in front of my bedroom doorway, standing perfectly still, cunningly contemplating what he would do next. Ear splitting silence seemed to last for an eternity as I agonizingly held my breath, afraid to make a sound, listening and waiting. Just as I felt that my lungs were about to burst, I heard a creak quickly followed by another. These purposeful footsteps went in the opposite direction of my bedroom, and into my kitchen.

"How odd, he's going into the kitchen." I thought as I allowed myself one slow deep breath. And then I heard it, a soft sliding sound, wood on wood, followed by a muffled "clink" of metal on metal, and then another. All at once I knew what was happening. He was rummaging through my kitchen drawer, gently pushing the forks and spoons aside until he found what he was looking for. The knives! He was looking for the knives!

I could magically see him again as I stared at the bedroom ceiling, my hands clenched in fear and the rest of my body rigid and stiff as if rigor mortis had already set in. He was taking each knife out one at a time, examining and caressing it. Holding each one delicately in his hand for a moment as if it were a tiny bird, and he needed to choose which one, if coaxed just right, would produce the sweetest, most sensual song.

And while he performed his morbid ritual, I shook with terror knowing that when he was done and he had picked just the right one, he would be coming for me. He would have to kill Jake first and then he could take his time with me. Jake's bed was closest to the door, but that wouldn't be a problem. He was fast asleep and if I moved to wake him it would only be a catalyst to the bloodbath that was surely to follow. There was nowhere to run. We were trapped! All I could do was to wait, and wait, and wait... with the sound of the clinking knives tinkling in my ears...

And then I woke up! But when I did nothing had changed! Only the clinking of the knives had stopped and I was sure that the intruder had found the one that he had wanted to do the job. He was silent and still, getting ready to jump across the few short steps to Jake's bed to slit his throat, and then on to take care of me! I squeezed my eyes tight waiting for the blows to fall, and ... nothing! I was awake and alive and scared as hell!

So here I sat, over an hour later, still trying to shake off the horror of the dream. I sat eagerly waiting for the first rays of the sun to lighten the sky and chase away the ghosts and goblins from my door, and assuring myself with another sip of tea, that there were no vengeful intruders here.

But Donna had an intruder. She and Tom had been the other Army couple in the building when Jake and I had moved in. They had lived two floors above us in a small attic apartment. I never got to know her very well. When we'd moved in Tom was "short" (less than ninety days to go) and last Saturday they had left the friendly town of Furth,

Germany, for their home in southern Indiana. There was supposed to be a new Army couple moving in next week. Jake knew the guy from the base and had given him a tip about the soon to be vacant apartment.

Donna and Tom were in their early twenties and very strict southern Baptists. She was a dowdy, kind of plump, unattractive, quiet woman, so when she came to my door about a month ago telling me her story, I'm ashamed to say that I hadn't believed her. She hadn't looked very upset, just kind of spaced out. She had an embroidered handkerchief in her hand which she was constantly twisting, but other than that she'd shown very little emotion.

She had stood in my kitchen on that sunny afternoon, wearing a simple blue cotton housedress. Her short mousy dishwater blonde hair, normally ratted and styled into a round bubble around her head had been wet and casually combed straight back away from her face. Some of the ends of her hair had still dripped water, from a recent shower, onto the fabric of her dress.

She'd stood there and told me that she had been raped. The man had been a soldier and her husband's best friend. She'd known him herself for most of the two years that she'd been with Tom in Germany. He'd knocked at her door earlier that day asking if he could look around for some personal thing that he'd misplaced. Once inside the little apartment, he'd started to make advances and when she refused, he had forced her to have sex with him, and then left. She hadn't given me many details about it and I wasn't about to ask. She'd said that she had decided not to tell her husband, because of the fuss that it would cause. They only had three weeks left and she could make it through 'till they left, and then she could forget that the whole thing had ever happened.

I'd watched her as she had told her story with tears in her eyes and no bruises on her body that I could see, and I had my doubts. Maybe she'd been having a little buyer's remorse I'd thought to myself, and then had felt a pang of guilt... and then again, maybe not.

As I sat sipping tea and smoking another cigarette, I shivered as I mulled the memory over in my mind. Either possibility was a heavy load for a woman to carry on her back for the rest of her life.

The wispy patches of darkness in the kitchen withdrew into the surrounding nooks and crannies, and were replaced by the warm glow of the rising sun that filtered through the kitchen window. The horizon above the rooftops of the old stone tenement houses turned orange and then golden as dawn unfurled itself in the April sky and my mood rose with it.

I turned my thoughts to the day ahead. It was Saturday and Jake had the whole weekend off. We'd bought an old BMW about a month ago and it gave us a ton of freedom to tool around the countryside. It had also helped eliminate Jake being spat on by little old ladies while walking home in his uniform. It was a disconcerting experience, which was an unfortunate remnant of post war sentiments if, in some people's view, you are part of the occupying army after a war.

Jake had painted the battered BMW using some yellow utility paint that the Army used for fire hydrants and the like, which he'd snatched at the right price from the base. The car got unbelievable gas mileage because the motor was built like a large grass cutter's engine. As a result of that engineering feat, whenever you put gasoline in the tank you had to also add oil to it. It made me laugh to watch Jake stand in the rear of the BMW and push up and down on the rear bumper, vigorously bouncing the backside of the car in order to mix the oil and gasoline together after a fill up.

We were planning to go for a ride into the boonies, stopping for a bite to eat wherever the spirit moved us, returning in the evening to check out the carnival that had been set up on a large vacant lot, a few miles from our place. Jake and I loved wild carnival rides and cotton candy. We had done a lot of both when we were dating, so today was going to be fun.

❧ XXVI ☙

We had been at the carnival for hours and things were not going well. The ride in the country earlier in the day had gone great. Jake and I had stumbled on a small castle about forty miles from Furth that was open to the public. On the way home we'd stopped for dinner at a small gasthaus that served delicious Wiener schnitzel. When we had gotten back to the city we'd dropped by the base and picked up both Al and Barry to join in the carnival festivities. Both were Jake's good friends. Al was the mailman for Jake's unit and Barry was the soldier whose wife was coming over in the next week or so, and had rented the attic apartment for the two of them, in our building.

In a very short time after arriving at the carnival, I'd found that there was one major difference between German carnivals and the ones back home, cheap booze and plenty of it. There weren't very many rides to speak of except for a few kiddy rides, the Tilt-A-Whirl, and the Ferris wheel. Most of the entertainment was the usual sideshow games like Ring Toss or Pitch ball, with one striking difference. The booby prizes given out when you spent a couple of Deutsche Marks (German dollars) were not innocent plastic kewpie dolls. They were cheap bottles of cognac. And Jake had won a few.

One ride on the rickety Ferris wheel with Jake after a few slugs of that shit had been enough to last me for a lifetime. He'd always been a pain in the ass when we rode it in the States, but this time he had outdone himself. Once we'd gotten into the gondola and the ride had begun, he'd started to rock it as much as he could. Visions of the car tipping over and the two of us falling out onto the ground in one big messy splat had surfaced in my imagination. Terrified, I'd begged him to stop, but the more I'd pleaded, the more he'd swung the damned thing. He'd finally got so out of control that the ride operator had shouted something from the ground that I'd been pretty sure meant that Jake should cut the crap out, and when he hadn't the German guy stopped the wheel and made us get off the ride.

"God damn it! You're no fucking fun! Because of all your crying and bitching, he made us get off the fucking ride!" and the last sentence had been emphasized by giving my shoulder a little push. Things had gone downhill from there.

I was now sitting on a small bench, trying to keep my panic under control, and watching Jake spend every last pfennig he had at the Pitch Ball game, to supposedly win me a big stuffed animal to match the four-foot princess doll that he'd already won for me. The last few hours since our fun time on the Ferris wheel were mainly spent watching Jake play Pitch Ball and drink every bottle of cheap booze that he'd received as a loser prize, as fast as he'd gotten it. Looking at him now, I knew that he was way passed the point of no return, the point at which there was no one home in his eyes. Both Al and Barry had enthusiastically started the mission with Jake to drink the carnival dry and had gleefully shared each bottle with him as it appeared, but in the last hour or so they began to slow up a lot. Not so with Jake. He was in rare form and seemed to be revving up, not slowing down.

I couldn't hear much of the recent conversation from where I sat on the wooden bench next to the beer tent area, but from the worried look on Al and Barry's faces, the irritated look on the Carney's, and the smart ass look on Jake's, I knew we were all in trouble. It was late, and probably close to closing time. The carnival midway was deserted except for a person here or there. Observing Jake's antics, my panic at the thought of what might come next began to grow. Jake started to shout at the carnival worker behind the counter, and whether he spoke English or not, didn't matter much. He easily got the drift that what Jake was saying to him, or calling him, wasn't very nice. He bellowed something in German and pointed to the parking lot undoubtedly telling all three of them to get the hell out of there. Jake responded with throwing his remaining half-full bottle of cheap cognac on the gravel, where it shattered into a million pieces splashing all over Barry and Al, and soaking the bottoms of their pant legs. Realizing that the whole situation was getting completely out of control, Barry and Al tried to calm Jake and to lead him towards the car.

In the midst of all the testosterone flying, everyone had forgotten about me, which was just fine as far as I was concerned. Jumping off the bench, I sprinted to the car taking a shorter route, over some grass and behind the now closed beer tent, to the parking lot. I had the almost life size doll tucked under my arm as I ran, and when I reached the yellow BMW before Jake and the rest, I opened the car's back door. I slid the doll into the back seat placing her in a sitting position directly behind the driver and slid in right beside her. Looking to my left passed the doll and out the driver's window I saw Jake and Al coming down the midway. Barry wasn't with them and I assumed that he must have decided to hoof it back to the Kaserne by himself, leaving Al to see to it that Jake got home safely. As they walked closer to the car I noticed that fifty feet behind them five or six young German men looked intently after the two, as they walked along the path.

After a second or two of milling around and discussing things amongst themselves, the pack of young men began to amble in Al and Jake's direction, and then quickly began to pick up speed. Alarmed by the fact that the distance between themselves and the Germans was rapidly diminishing, Al and Jake rushed the last few feet to the car. With perfect timing the two of them opened their respective car door slipped into the front seat and locked the doors behind them. There was only one problem with their extremely "cool" maneuver that they probably would have become aware of if they both hadn't been three sheets to the wind. The window on the driver's side of the BMW was open!

When Jake got into the car he didn't have enough time to roll the window up in order to hide behind the safety of the glass, before the horde of young men started to swarm around the opening like flies around road kill.

Sensing that the situation could explode in a split second into something really nasty, my survivalist mentality began to quickly evaluate a possible escape scenario. The BMW was a two-door automobile and my exit was completely blocked by Al's ass, which was sitting in the passenger's side of the front seat. I was trapped!

My thoughts of violently bashing Al up through the dashboard with the back of the car seat so I could reach the door handle and shoot out of the vehicle to freedom and safety, were interrupted when I heard a loud smacking sound. It reminded me of the sound that a raw piece of steak makes when it is flung down onto the surface of a hard Formica counter top. Turning my attention and my gaze to the direction of the first fleshy "pop", which had quickly been followed by a second, an ice cold rush of panic electrified every cell on the outermost layer of my skin. A flying fist had landed on Jake's unprotected cheek, which faced the open window.

Jake's head rocked to the side absorbing the power of the blow as he fired up the engine and slammed the car's transmission into reverse. The engine whined as the car flew back, but only a few inches, and then it stopped dead in its tracks. Another flash of flesh shot through the open window, connecting with its target making another smacking sound and again viciously bouncing Jake's head to the side. Seemingly unaffected by the blow, Jake gunned the car in reverse again, and again it slammed to a stop.

"Jesus! They must have put something behind the wheels!" Al shouted as Jake was repeatedly pummeled in the side of his head. As if he was spring loaded, Al exploded out of the vehicle throwing the car door wide open as he scrambled out to take care of whatever was keeping the BMW anchored to the same spot.

Feeling the air blow over my face as the flying door's hinges groaned in agony from the force of Al's departure, I was triggered into action. I followed him so closely, out of the door, that it was as if he and I were one person flying to freedom. The instant my feet hit the ground of the parking lot I was running. I slipped on the gravel after a couple steps but quickly regained my balance and ran as if my life had depended upon it. For all I knew, it did! Women, I was sure, had been raped for less.

Ten minutes later, my lungs burning in my chest and my hands shaking, I placed my key into the ten foot tall wooden double doors that were the guardians to the entrance of the building on 13 Lessing Strasse, and the stairwell to my apartment.

I had made it! I was home! But what about Jake and Al? Had they gotten away? I couldn't worry about that now, I needed to rest, to think. Once I got upstairs I could catch my breath and wait. Wait for the two of them to get home.

So I waited. After half an hour of pacing and nervously staring down from the front room windows at the cobblestone street below, I heard the rev of an engine and saw the beam of headlights as the BMW sharply rounded the corner, tires squealing on the red bricked street. I watched as it came to an abrupt stop directly in the front of the big wooden doors. In less than a minute, I could hear Jake and Al's shoes thumping up the stairs.

Jake drunkenly fell against the metal and glass front door and as it flew open it banged against the inside hallway wall.

"Shhh!" I hissed. "The landlord will throw us out if you're not careful!"

"Fuck 'em!" Jake retorted loudly as he stumbled through the door. Thank God for Al! Even though he was a little drunk himself he had the presence of mind to push Jake the rest of the way into the apartment and close the door behind the two of them, all the while talking softly to Jake and getting him to quiet down a bit.

Al and I tried to steady Jake as we walked across the living room floor towards the couch. With each step his legs supported him less and we supported him more, until, three quarters of the way across the room and several feet from the maroon couch, the dead weight of his body caused us to drop him to the floor.

"Maybe that's a better idea. You never know if that cheap cognac might make a reappearance." I said to Al after which we both awkwardly laughed. I took a look at the side of Jake's face that had been the punching bag for so many blows, and except for a little swelling and redness, it seemed to be OK.

"Yeah, you're probably right." Al said. "Hey, what happened to you? How'd you get out of the car?"

"When you jumped out of the front seat to find out why the car wasn't moving, I jumped out after you and ran. I know it seems like I was deserting you two but I didn't figure that I could do anything to stop what was going on and I was scared to death that after they got you guys they'd come after me!" I'd calmed down a little but my voice was still shaking. "How'd you guys get away?"

"You should've seen it!" Al began, his arms waving with the nervous excitement that was left over from the adrenaline rush supplied by the heat of the recent battle.

"When I jumped out of the car some guy was punchin' Jake in the head! I was lookin' to find the bricks, or whatever those sons-of-bitches had wedged in the back of the tires. None of the German guys were on my side. I guess they were all too busy getting a good look at Jake getting punched in the head to pay any attention to me. I saw that they had put what looked like a large cinder block behind each front and back wheel on my side of the car. I kicked the pieces of shit out of the way and barely got back into the car before Jake jammed the BMW into reverse! Gravel was flying everywhere and for a moment it looked like we weren't going to make it, when my head bounced against the windshield as the BMW flew up and over some piece of shit that must've been under one of the wheels on Jake's side." My eyes immediately went to Al's forehead where a large red "goozle" sat in the middle of it.

"Wow, you really did hit the windshield hard!" I said. Shaking his head in agreement as he rubbed his bump, he began again.

"Jake went tearing backward out of the parking lot, drove out over a curb and into the street as he screeched to a stop. He threw the BMW into first and peeled off going about eighty! All the while he's looking in his rear view mirror at the dark haired figure in the back seat and yelling things like, 'After I fucking drop you off I'm going back to get those motherfuckers!' When you didn't answer he yelled, 'Susan, are you fucking OK?' When you still didn't answer he kept yellin' stuff like, 'Why the fuck aren't you answering me?' Until after a few blocks he pulled over to the side of the road and took a good look in the back seat."

"Shit! You should've seen the look on his face when he realized that he'd been talking to that doll that he won you!" Al started to laugh and I couldn't help but to do the same. The picture of Jake yelling at a doll as he drove like a maniac up and down the cobblestone streets was just too much!

Al wiped the tears from the corners of his eyes, after his fit of laughter had subsided, and continued on with the story.

"Jake figured that you probably got snatched by the Germans before we left the parking lot, so we raced back down to the carnival but no one was there. He got crazy and began zigzagging through the streets trying to find the jags that had punched him out and maybe find you in the bargain. He started to freak me out while the car swerved as we turned up and down the side streets. I could tell how loaded he was, so I convinced him that it would be a good idea if we checked here first to see if some how you'd got home."

"God, I'm sorry I caused you guys so much trouble. I was just really scared. It looked like the whole thing was getting out of control so I took the chance when I got it to get the hell out of there!" I said.

"It's OK." But Al's voice trailed off as Jake suddenly sat up like a rocket in the middle of the living room floor.

"Hey! What the fuck is going on?" He huffed as his eyes snapped open. "Where the fuck is she?" Anger and confusion emphasized every slurred word, as he swayed back and forth, riding the ocean of too many cognacs.

"I'm here." I said, and went over to him to rub his back to try and calm him down. His face went blank and he looked at me but didn't make the connection. His zombie like stare went passed me, through me, silent as his head weaved in an unsteady circular motion. Fear tingled the back of my neck, causing my body to involuntarily shudder.

"I got to get those fuckers! They tried to beat the shit out of me!" Jake suddenly shouted his arm exploding in thrashing gestures against some unseen foe. I jumped back, fearful of what was to follow.

"Tomorrow buddy, you can get them tomorrow after you've had some sleep." Al said in a slow even voice while he got a firm hold on each erratically moving arm forcing them to Jake's sides and getting the violent movements to stop. "C'mon. Let's get you to bed."

Jake gave little resistance as Al and I helped him to his feet, his arms dangling over our shoulders. As quickly as he had been ignited into wildly agitated consciousness, Jake slipped into lifeless oblivion. His knees buckled as Al and I dragged him into the bedroom where we unceremoniously plopped him on his twin bed.

We both stared at him for a few seconds, wondering if he was going to pop up again like a maniacal Jack-in-the-Box. When he didn't, I slowly let my breath out. I must have been holding it while waiting for the next explosion.

"He'll be OK now." Al said. "He just needs some time to sleep it off." He reached over and patted Jake gently on his back and said, "You OK buddy? You need anything before I go?" Jake barely responded with a low soft groan. Al straightened up and turned to me.

"I guess I'll be on my way. 6:00 am comes pretty quick after a night like this. By the way, can I ask you a favor?"

"Sure, what is it?" I said.

"Could I borrow the car to get me back to the base? You never know if those guys are still out there lookin' for us. Besides, Jake doesn't need to have the car here if he wakes up and decides to go out looking for the bastards." Al said.

"Sounds good to me." I was relieved at the thought of not having to worry about Jake taking off in the car in the middle of the night. "Just come by and pick him up before reveille. I don't think that he will be in any condition to hoof it to the Kaserne."

I carefully searched Jake's pockets while he lay on the bed. I didn't want to disturb him just incase he wasn't all the way out. I found the car keys in his front pants pocket and with the talent of Charles Dickens' Artful Dodger, slid them out.

"Thanks." Al smiled warmly and took the keys from my hand.

"See you at 5:30 then." He said. He turned and walked down the hallway to the front door as I followed behind.

"Thanks for everything, Al." I said as he walked out of the door.

"Anytime." He smiled, gave me a salute and walked down the steps and out of sight. Smiling to myself, I closed the door.

"Thank God, that's over with." I said. Without much thought I went into the front room and curled up on the old maroon couch. My body ached from the emotional roller coaster of the last couple of hours and all I wanted to do was get some rest. Sleep had never been a problem for me so I drifted off the minute my head hit the couch pillow.

Boom! I was instantly awake, my eyes wide open and my heart pounding.

"WHERE THE FUCK ARE MY KEYS?" Jake's drunken roar broke the stillness of the night.

I sprang off the couch and into the hallway just in time to see Jake's enraged expression as he staggered out of the bedroom doorway, while solidly bumping his shoulder into the doorjamb as he tried to make the turn towards the hallway, and me.

"Shhh! Jake, the landlord will hear you!" I scolded him in a harsh whisper.

"WHAT DID YOU DO WITH MY FUCKING KEYS?" He bellowed again. Unsteady, his head turned in my direction, his eyes seeing but not seeing, locking on to where he thought I was, with that cold blank stare.

"I'm going to kill those motherfuckers! Where are my fucking keys?" He said in a raspy voice likened to what I imagined the devil himself sounded like when he was really pissed off.

"I…uh…gave them to Al. He needed to go to the base. He'll be back at…" I was in the middle of my sentence when he screamed.

"What? You gave away my fucking keys, you cunt?" And he took one terrifying step towards me, and then another. With growing uneasiness I realized that he was beginning to navigate pretty well and that in a moment or two he could be on top of me. I recognized that dark deep nothingness in his eyes. That same nothingness had unemotionally choked me close to unconsciousness, in our bed in Virginia. In a split second of sheer panic, I bolted through the door, down the stairs, and out into the street.

I hesitated for a moment on the cobblestone sidewalk. I could hear the thunder of his feet down the stairs, rolling behind me as it echoed through the stairwell of the old apartment building. Fight or flight? The decision was made. There was no question, the choice was flight and I ran. The chilly moist spring air caused my short gasps of breath to billow out of my nose and mouth in white steaming puffs. I turned back to look and he was behind me, his feet slapping on the stones of the street. For a short while it sounded as if he was gaining on me but then the slapping sound stopped. I kept running, just incase. But the next time I snatched a peek, he was gone.

I stopped and waited, still in the middle of the street, peering into the night and looking for some signs of life on the sidewalks and in the doorways. But there was none. Still, I couldn't be sure so I waited a little longer, and when there was nothing, I waited some more.

After a time, how long I didn't know, I turned and walked slowly and cautiously back up the street that I had a short time ago, ran down in terror.

"Terror of what?" I wondered. What did I think that he would have done to me if I hadn't run? Why was I so afraid? Realizing that I didn't know frightened me the most. Since the beginning of our relationship I had noticed that Jake had lacked the boundaries that normal people had inside of them. There was no point, passed which, he wouldn't go. From ripping a phone from a wall or attempting to force me to throw my engagement ring into a public mailbox, to taping our private love making for the entertainment of his friends, Jake had demonstrated that he had no bounds. I had no inner sense as to just how far he would go when he was sober, much less, when he was drunk. I reasoned that whatever sober Jake was capable of, this new "zombie" Jake could surpass. Virginia was still vivid in my mind.

Once in front of our apartment building, I tried the entryway doors but they were locked. Sitting down on the curb, I began to shake. Maybe it was the result of shock or as simple as the cool damp night air sinking into my bones. Either way, I sat and I shook, and I waited for someone to come and unlock the doors.

❧ XXVII ❧

"November 13, 1968, zero eight hundred hours, and yes, one more day of lovely German weather in the land of no sunshine. That makes the count 43 days without seeing the sun. I think that I've forgotten what it looks like. High today zero degrees centigrade. For all of you recent arrivals out there, that means 32 degrees in real speak. A little cold for this time of year but look, it could be worse, it could be raining. Stay tuned for the science fiction adventure, $X - 1$, on Armed Forces Radio."

"Zero degrees, not so bad." I said to myself as I looked out of the kitchen window, up to the cloudy sky and then down to cement and cobblestone courtyard below. Boy, another dreary day, if you weren't careful it could really get you down. I had hung Jake's fatigues outside the kitchen window on my mini-clothes lines to "freeze dry". I washed all our laundry at the base since the washing machines at the local German Laundromat only used scalding hot water and ripped your clothes to shreds.

Cleaning fatigues was a ritual. They had to be starched after being washed so I would bring them home and do so by hand. When they dried they were stiff as a board and looked like cardboard cutouts. Ironing them was always a pain but Jake liked his uniforms crisp and wrinkle free, and I aimed to please. He did look great in his uniform. I had hand tailored his fatigue pants and they fit like a glove. Jake was fanatical about his clothes.

I turned the latch on the window, opened it, and began removing the shirts and pants from the line being careful not to drop the clothespins or the laundry onto the pavement below. I didn't look down. Two stories was a long way to the ground and it made me feel queasy to look when I was half hanging out of the window. The windowsill was just below my waist so it didn't lend much to a feeling of security when you were leaning out of it. Once the stiff green uniforms were inside I got my sprinkling bottle out of the cabinet and peppered them with tiny droplets of water and rolled them up into neat damp bundles to soften them for ironing.

Placing the first shirt on the ironing board that was set up in the kitchen, I began. I liked ironing. It felt good to take something wrinkled and messy and make it flat and smooth. The process was relaxing and somehow comforting.

Jake still wasn't home. He had gone out with some friends last night after duty and I had neither seen hide nor hair of him since. I should've known that it would be like this. He was on leave this weekend and I guess he didn't want to waste any of it. Party was the name of the game in Germany for soldiers. However, I was starting to worry. He was usually home before daylight.

We had been in Germany almost a year and there were things about living here I loved and hated. The last ten months had been a learning experience full of interesting unfamiliar sights and smells. Last summer I'd experienced first hand what a Strassenbahn (trolley car) full of German citizens smelled like when it was eighty degrees with the trolley windows closed and NO air conditioning. I'd learned to really appreciate the American affinity for deodorant that day.

And while on the subject of under arms, it had come as quite a shock to me that German women did not shave theirs. Hairy legs and armpits were the European fashion statement. In my opinion, there was nothing more disgusting to see than a sexy Fraulein in a short sleeved dress, pick up her arm and have a scouring-pad of hair thicker than my husband's waving in the breeze. I guess we are all a product of our environment.

Smiling at the thought, I continued ironing and redirected my attention away from Jake and what condition he might be in when he got home, to how interesting and different living was in a European culture.

Things that I liked… Well, let's see. The people here conserved more than the people back home, and had a respect for the limited resources available to them. Nuremberg had been leveled by Allied bombing at the end of WWII, a little over twenty years ago. Now, except for a few areas that still remained here and there around the city, all the buildings had been rebuilt, and where possible, the builders had used the original stones. The streets were spotless and women washed the stone steps in front of the neighborhood buildings daily, no matter what the weather. Garbage was separated into metal and glass, and all bottles were recycled, however anything burnable was burned in your kitchen coal burner. This was a negative because burning paper added to the already heavy amounts of soot in the air from everyone heating their apartments with coal. The air quality was poor, but no one seemed to care, which was a contradiction to everything else that I'd seen. Maybe a reduction in air pollution was desired but a difficult thing to accomplish. Being a small country, landmass wise, no resource was wasted. The neighborhood farmers' sheep grazed in the fields of the city parks and wheat was grown on the small strips of land that ran along the railroad tracks.

There was plenty to do in the evenings. Every street in Nuremberg had a neighborhood gasthaus. They were nothing like American bars. They were light and airy with plenty of windows and had a family atmosphere. Ours was directly across the street from our apartment building. It's red and white-checkered curtains, light wooden tables and chairs, made it feel cozy like a cottage in the woods. Barry and Beth, our upstairs neighbors, and Jake and I spent most of our spare time there. It had a pinball machine and we all had become pinball wizards from the large spans of time that we spent popping Deutsche marks into its slot. I have come to the conclusion that pinball is an addiction.

The food at the gasthaus was great and our neighbors were friendly even though most couldn't speak English. Broken German and a few hand gestures provided us with a crude avenue of communication that allowed us to become friends. Helmut and Helga were the young couple who lived across the street in an apartment above the gasthaus. Her mother was the owner of the gasthaus and her sister was a prostitute in downtown Nuremberg, a job that her family considered a legal, respectable, and lucrative profession. There was no shame in Helga's demeanor when she had explained her sister's calling with one word "poof" (a German slang word for fuck) along with the universal hand signal for money, rubbing one's thumb and forefinger together. Helga came to us once a month with a large bag of American quarters from her sister. The money exchanges wouldn't take American coins so we were her only opportunity to change quarters to Deutsche marks. It boggled my mind when I tried to figure out where all the quarters came from. Did the bag of silver represent one soldier who broke into his piggy bank for a lay or a hundred blowjobs at a quarter apiece?

I had gotten to know our landlord and his family fairly well. They were very nice people and it surprised me to learn that he'd been a soldier in Hitler's army during World War II. When asked, he'd said that most Germans hadn't been Nazis and were privately frightened by Hitler and his cause. The existence of the concentration camps was not common knowledge during the war, but he had explained to me that once you've seen a few neighbors disappear on your block, a person goes if asked by the government to serve. People do what they need to for themselves and their families to survive, so he went to the Russian front and spent most of the last year of the war in a Russian prison with a gunshot wound in his gut. He had told me how, after the war, German money wasn't worth the paper it was printed on. A bushel of Deutsche marks couldn't buy a loaf of bread. His children had searched the streets for American soldiers' old cigarette butts, stripped them and collected the tobacco in a tin box. When the tin box was full, they would trade it with the farmer for some eggs. One man's garbage was another man's sustenance. I had a lot of respect for him and his family. They had stuck together and in twenty years had gone from scavenging in the streets to driving a new Mercedes.

Not everyone had been so lucky. The remnants of the horror of the war were scattered in the cities as well as the countryside. On the outside of most of the buildings on Lessing Strasse, painted on the dirty stones of their foundations were large yellow letters "NA". Yellow painted arrows with their shafts beginning after the "A" and ending at tiny cellar windows or at nothing at all, lined several feet of the building's first floor stone. I'd asked Helga what the markings were for.

"It's from war. After bombs come, place to go dig. Get people out." She'd said in broken English. Looking at her face, while she casually said those words, I realized, that being in her mid to late twenties, she had probably taken shelter in the bomb cellar a few yards from where we stood when she was a child. So also, had most of the people on this block, the ones that Jake and I'd spent our time with, laughing and drinking, and sharing meals. I had often wondered, if the tables had been turned would I have been as kind and gracious as these people had been to me? Occasionally a nut case might stumble into the gasthaus and start screaming, "Heil Hitler!" at the top of his lungs, while giving the Nazi salute, because he'd overheard us speaking English. That type of behavior was never tolerated. As soon as his hand had shot up in the air and the first "Heil" was out of his mouth, he had been put out the door and into the street by our neighbors with threats of the Polizei being called trailing behind. Part of the fervor to get rid of him was consideration for our feelings but the large majority of it was due to the fact that any display of pro-Nazism was against the law, and the salute was punishable by jail time. Free speech in Germany didn't count when it came to the Nazis.

Dachau, and the reaction of the German people and their postwar government to places like it, was also part of the reason for my neighbors' attitudes toward Americans. The horrible unadulterated truth about the camps and their inconceivable barbarism was not hidden. On the contrary, it was put on display for the world to see in hopes that it would never happen again. The camps were memorialized to the millions who were mercilessly slaughtered within their walls. School children were bussed in droves to view the unthinkable, impacting them forever with the horror of Germany's lowest moment in time, created by the highest point of man's inhumanity to man.

So too were Jake and I effected as we walked through the gas chambers of Dachau, and passed the ditches that were dug in the ground to catch the overflow of blood from the thousands that were shot daily in front of a firing squad wall. The number of human beings that were murdered in these human slaughterhouses was unimaginable. Black and white photographs lined the walls of the information building at the camp for people to view, whose intent was to try and drive home the enormity of the brutality that had taken place there. One photo still remained impressed into my memory that would probably never fade away. It was the picture of a large room filled to the ceiling with the shoes of the men, women, and children who had been killed at the camp during some short interval of time. A man stood in the forefront of the photo for scale. The look on his face was indiscernible and I had wondered what he'd been thinking when the picture had been taken, and where he was today.

In the front of Dachau was a large black wrought iron sculpture. A rectangle of twisted metal lying on its side, approximately sixty feet long and half again as high, mounted on top of a stone wall. Superimposed on the stone wall underneath and to the side of the black iron basket weave of long thin emaciated human bodies, were the words in five different languages and in large capital letters, "NEVER AGAIN." Those two words had said it all. They were the mantra of any and every human being who had the capacity to understand the horror of what Hitler had accomplished during World War II. They were burned into me by my "sight seeing" trip to Dachau, the same as I imagined that it was with my neighbors with whom I sat and socialized every evening at Helga's mother's place. Those words represented the shame of the past and the hope for the future, "NEVER AGAIN!"

❧ XXVIII ❧

"Ouch! Burned my hand with the damned iron!" I said to myself as I shook my hand and then instinctively put my burned finger to my mouth and gently sucked on it. I was done with the fatigue pants and had the corresponding shirts left to iron. The clock on the kitchen wall said it was half passed nine, and Jake still wasn't home. My apprehension started to build as I wondered what condition he would be in when he walked through the front door.

"Maybe it won't be so bad. Maybe he fell asleep in the car and has already slept some of last night's festivities off. God, I hate waiting!" Mechanically, when I reached for my next tightly wrapped damp bundle, rolled it out and began making wrinkled things smooth, my thoughts had free reign again to ebb and flow.

"I wonder if Beth is up yet." I thought to myself. "When I'm done, I'll call her down for a cup of tea."

Beth was my only woman friend in Germany. It worked out great that Barry was also Jake's best friend and that Beth and Barry lived upstairs on the third floor in the little attic apartment. Barry would be getting out of the service a month after Jake and we had made plans to visit them once they were back in the States in St. Anne's Ohio.

I had tried to expand my circle of friends just after Beth had gotten to Germany, but as I remembered it, things hadn't worked out so well...

I'd met a woman named Kathy at the PX while doing my laundry. She had just arrived in the land of no sun, and hadn't had time to make any friends. Jake didn't know her husband, who was stationed with another company on the other side of the Kaserne. Over the next few weeks Kathy had come over several times to my apartment in the afternoon for a cup of tea, after our housework was done. Jake seemed to be jealous of her visits. His resulting moodiness reminded me of the way he'd reacted to my friends when we'd first begun to date. When he came home in the evening on the days that she had been over to visit, he always found something around the house to nitpick. Dust on the windowsill or a fuzzy on the Oriental rug, were all excuses to pick a fight. The justification, according to Jake, was that Kathy kept me from doing my job.

Kathy's husband had to go out to the field for a few days for a military exercise, and she had asked me if it would be OK for her to stay overnight at my place. She'd confessed that she was afraid to be alone in her apartment. I thought that she would be comfortable on the front room couch, so I'd said yes, a decision that had turned out to be a big mistake.

The evening had started off on the wrong foot. Jake had stopped on the way home from the base and already had several beers under his belt before he'd walked through the door. As he silently weaved his way into the kitchen to sit down at the Formica table, I introduced him to Kathy, who was looking a bit apprehensive. I served dinner during which Jake inhaled another two beers but never touched a thing on the plate in front of him. He stared at Kathy while she and I chitchatted over our food, until we both began to feel awkward and uncomfortable.

"Jake, do you have a problem with something?" I asked after several minutes went by with him staring silently at the both of us, but mainly at Kathy.

"I was just thinking how fucking filthy this place is!" He said thickly while he continued to stare at Kathy. He was being down right rude and a little weird. I could tell that his behavior was causing Kathy distress. She had been nervously fidgeting with a piece of her hair that hung slightly in back of her ear and her gaze flitted around the room as she attempted to avert her eyes from Jake's constant stare.

"C'mon Jake. Let's not start that crap again…"

"I SAID IT IS A FUCKING MESS! WHAT WERE YOU DOING ALL DAY WASTING TIME WITH THIS CUNT?" When Jake had said the "C" word, Kathy sprang up out of her chair and headed for the door.

"I want to go home now." She said with very little emotion.

"You can't. It's dark and it will take you over an hour to walk." I said feeling helpless and inwardly cursing myself because I didn't know how to drive.

"I'll drive the bitch! The sooner that she's fucking out of my house, the better!" Jake said while he searched his uniform pockets for his keys. I couldn't believe how fast everything had degenerated in the twenty minutes since Jake had made his entrance. The whole episode was surreal.

"Are you OK to drive?" I asked. It was doubtful. He was unsteady on his feet, swaying as he continued to rummage in his pockets for his keys, trying to keep his balance.

"I said, I want to go home, NOW!" Kathy shouted as tears formed in her eyes.

"Shut up bitch, and get in the fucking car!" And to my amazement Kathy went out of the front door and down the steps. I followed her. She was determined to get home no matter what, and it didn't seem to matter that her taxi driver was three sheets to the wind. Driving with Jake when he was in this condition would certainly be an experience.

It was a couple of miles to Kathy's place, and I thought that if I rode shot gun in the seat next to Jake and talked calmly to him while I gave him directions, everything might be alright. Boy, was that a misjudgment. The main street that we had to drive down, to get to Kathy's, was under construction. It was temporarily one way and Jake had to drive on the wrong side of the street with the middle of the road to his right. The concrete median was being replaced and a large section of it was meticulously removed, leaving a deep dark chasm where the concrete had been. The gaping rectangular empty space was three to four feet across and just as deep. It traversed the last four blocks before the intersection where we needed to turn to continue on to Kathy's. I could tell that Jake was navigating by following the iridescent white line on his side of the street. That was fine by me. It was keeping the car away from the construction horses and the enormous black pit next to my door. But then, as we got within a block of the intersection where Jake needed to make a turn to the right, he began to slowly move in the direction of the deep, dark, medianless hole.

"Jake" I said calmly, trying to get his attention but purposefully not shouting. "Jake, you do know that the median is gone. It's a big hole."

"You're fucking crazy." He said as he inched the car to the right and the construction horses that lined the dark expanse of nothingness, went whizzing by. Glancing up I saw the green light of the intersection rapidly coming towards us. I knew that he was looking for a space between the construction horses large enough to slip through so that we could cross the median and turn at the corner.

"Jake! There is NO median. IT'S A HOLE!" I screamed.

"SHUT THE FUCK UP!" He screamed back, and with that he turned the steering wheel sharply to the right in order to maneuver as quickly as possible between the horses. For a millisecond we were airborne and then the BMW and the three of us inside it were brought to a dead stop. The back wheels of the car hadn't made it over the ditch. I had banged the side of my head into the windshield and I could feel a bump on it beginning to swell along with a dull ache in the back of my neck. Jake had smashed his chest into the steering column, knocking the breath out of him, causing him to rub his chest while he gasped for air. Kathy was in the back seat hysterically screaming in complete terror. I couldn't remember whether her screaming had started before or after I hit the windshield but once it had started it hadn't stopped. I remember numbly thinking, "How the hell can she breathe?"

As soon as my head cleared, I quickly got out of the front seat to let Kathy out of the car, hoping that I could calm her down and stop that god awful screaming. The minute that I pulled the back of the seat forward, she shot out of the car like a bullet, her feet hitting the pavement and she began to run. She ran without stopping, screaming with her arms waving wildly above her head, her voice echoing down the deserted German streets until she was out of sight. That was the last time that I'd seen or spoken to her. I had supposed that she was all right, physically anyway, or I would have heard something from her husband. I guess that her experience with Jake was too much for her. Once was definitely enough!

Both of the suspension bars that held the rear wheels on the car were severely twisted which made the BMW undrivable, even if we could get it out of the ditch. Jake, still rubbing his chest and now instantly sober, stood in the middle of the desolate street waiting in the hope that a tow truck would happen by, and unbelievably it did. From the way he was laughing as he towed the BMW to Lessing Strasse, the tow truck driver must've thought that our situation was one of the funniest that he'd ever seen. But as for me, I wasn't laughing.

❧ XXIX ❧

"Damn! I burned myself again. How stupid can you be?" Sucking on my two burnt fingertips, I glanced up at the clock on the wall.

"God, ten o'clock, and he's still not home." A small shiver ran through me as I became aware of the slight chill in the air. "The oil must have run out in the front room oil stove." The ten-gallon heating-oil can was full and too heavy for me to lift so Jake would have to fill the heater up when he came home. The soft patter of raindrops on the kitchen window caught my attention. Noticing that it was raining outside only made the air in the apartment feel more cold and damp. I grabbed my sweater from where it hung in the bedroom, put it on and went back to my ironing.

I was surprised that Beth hadn't been down already. She was usually down here on a Saturday morning having a cup of tea and planning what the four of us would be doing for the afternoon when the guys came home from the Kaserne. Maybe Barry had told her that Jake had a twenty-four hour pass, so she didn't want to disturb him if he was sleeping in.

Barry and Jake were very good buddies and Barry could certainly match Jake beer for beer in their mission to drink "Der Fatherland" dry. I didn't think that Barry got nasty when he drank but I couldn't be sure. Beth never talked very much about really personal things, and well, I guess I never confided in her about Jake's "bad times" either. The most we did was to complain about how we hated putting up with them when they got drunk, and they both got drunk or at least feeling good every night. Barry did have this weird habit when he was getting stewed that I had never seen anyone do before. Even though he was almost a white blonde, he had the hairiest forearms that I had ever seen in my life. The hair on his arms reminded me of sheep's wool. If he had enough beers in him, as an odd joke that he thought demonstrated how tough he was, he would rip out large tufts of hair with his hands from his arms, leaving large red marks on his skin where the hair was ripped out by the roots. He would do it with a maniacal smile on his face and never an eye flinch or twitch.

On those occasions Beth would say, "Barry, stop that!" with her impatient Ohio/Hoosier accent (St. Anne's was just across the Indiana/Ohio border). And then he, of course, would look her right in the eye, and to her disgust, rip out another curly clump of hair. It was funny and scary at the same time.

Beth was always talking about wanting to teach Barry a lesson for all the stuff that he had put her through when he drank, and last July, on her birthday she did just that...

In Germany, when it's your birthday you buy your friends drinks so that they can celebrate with you. The drink of choice was usually some kind of schnapps shot. Our gasthaus had every kind of schnapps that one could imagine: cherry schnapps, anise schnapps, chocolate schnapps, hazelnut schnapps, and on into infinitum. Beth, doing as the

Romans do, bought everyone in the gasthaus one shot of their choice for her birthday. Being early Saturday afternoon there weren't very many people in the place so the gesture wasn't too costly. Barry had ordered a beer for Beth in celebration of her special day and it was already half gone, an act out of character for her because she normally stuck to Africola. After she had downed her original birthday shot, a second round appeared at the table. It was from Helga's mother, Marta, and I was surprised to see Beth down it as soon as the shot glass hit the table. Everyone cheered and Beth laughed as she burped a little bit and politely covered her mouth with her hand.

As the afternoon progressed, more of our German friends filled the gasthaus. When they found out it was Beth's birthday they would buy her a schnapps, all the while Barry was keeping her beer glass full. In an hour or two it was obvious that Beth was feeling no pain. When she got up to go to the rest room I followed her out the door and into the garage-like entrance of the building, where the bathroom was located.

"Beth, don't you think you should slow down a bit. Aren't you mixing too many different kinds of booze together?" I asked as I held her arm, trying to help her steady herself as she stood in front of the bathroom door.

"Hell no! I've always wanted to teach Barry a lesson about his boozin' and here's my chance. This time it's his turn to take care of meee…" The "me" sounded more like "wee" and it trailed off in a tiny sing-song squeal, like that of a child being pushed high on a swing. She giggled, got her bearings and proceeded into the one-person, unisex bathroom. I went back into the gasthaus and sat down at our table.

"How is she doing?" Barry asked with some concern in a surprisingly sober voice. Hard to believe, but maybe this little escapade of Beth's was doing Barry some good. "Maybe I should try it sometime." I thought, but one look at Jake with his left eyeball cocked off to the side, a misalignment that occurred between his eyes in varying degrees as the amount of ingested alcohol varied in his system, I sardonically figured that all I would get out of it was a whopping headache.

"She's fine. She's just having a really good time." As soon as I'd finished my reassuring sentence Beth came back through the door and plopped down on her chair. Then another shot showed up at the table and she downed it in one gulp. Barry glanced at me with a "WOW" look in his eyes, and ordered her another beer.

When it had started to get dark I noticed that Beth hadn't returned to the table from her last trek to the little girls/guys room.

"Where is she?" Barry asked with a worried look on his face. "She's been gone a long time."

About a half an hour before, Beth had looked kind of green around the gills and was getting that totally wasted look that drunks get right before they pass out. I'd helped her to the bathroom because she could hardly walk. Marta had been standing with us outside the bathroom door. She'd been trying to convince Beth to put her finger down her throat so that Beth could "erp" up all the booze and food out of her tummy, so she could go and party some more. This philosophy was prevalent among the German populace. Beer tent bathrooms were always equipped with a waist high sink-type apparatus that had two handles directly above it to hold on to while you hurled. So that once you purged all the food and drink that you had previously consumed, you could start celebrating all over again.

Beth had kept shaking her head and moaning, "Uh-uh." as Marta had made what could be viewed as a comical gesture with her mouth open and her finger sticking in it.

"C'mon Beth, maybe she's right. Maybe you'll feel better if you throw up." And with that I'd helped her into the bathroom and closed the door behind her.

Now, thirty minutes later, Barry got up from the table and went outside to check on his wife. In five minutes he was back, distressed and asking Marta and I to help him open the john door. He'd been knocking on the door for a long time and had gotten no response. Marta returned with the key and all three of us rushed out and quickly unlocked the door.

You know that scene from the *Wizard of OZ* when Dorothy opens the farmhouse door, after the house has been sucked up into the twister and unceremoniously dropped on the ground, winding up who knows where? Up until that point the movie is black and white, and then the door opens. Well, that cinematographic instant in time, and Barry and I standing in front of the bathroom door as Marta swung it open, was a perfect comparison. The shift in paradigm that the audience experiences while watching the film when Dorothy goes from a boring everyday black and white world to the unexpected, unimagined Technicolor land of Oz, best describes what Barry and I experienced that day, but with a full one hundred and eighty degree twist.

Beth sat in a slump on the toilet in front of us, passed out with her head leaning on the wall next to her, and smeared across her mouth in big wide brown tracks was...shit! Shit was everywhere, on her hands, on the walls, down the side of the toilet, on the floor, on her shoes, on her clothes, and in her hair! The smell was as outrageous as the site, and Barry involuntarily slammed the door shut almost as fast as it had been opened.

"Jesus H. Christ!" he said as disgusted as any human being who had just seen his wife in that condition would be. "Holy fucking Christ! She must've puked! Ever since she was a little girl she hadn't been able to puke without it comin' out of both ends. God Damn it! She must've puked!" He repeated again.

In one instant, telepathic moment of recognition, Marta and I knew, that was exactly what she had done. A short movie clip of Marta pointing into her mouth, and me saying, "Yeah, sounds like a good idea to me." played in my head, followed by a scene of Beth with "it comin' out of both ends". It didn't take a genius to figure out how a nearly paralyzed drunk found it next to impossible, to coordinate the up and down postures necessary for getting bodily fluids in the correct receptacle, at the correct time. Once the mistiming had occurred, it was easy to imagine how wiping the spittle from your mouth after upchucking or pushing your hair out of your face, could become unintentional finger painting with excrement. No wonder Beth had been covered in shit from head to toe!

"We just can't leave her in there. Someone else will have to go sooner or later and you don't want anyone to see her like that. Do you?" I asked.

"Yeah, I suppose you're right." Barry sighed.

Jake helped with the logistics of pulling one hundred and twenty pounds of dead weight off of a toilet in a cramped space and hoisting it over Barry's shoulder, while I asked Marta for a mop and a bucket. Even with the language barrier Marta had gotten the idea of why Beth was in the mess she was in, literally, and in reparation motioned for me to go with my friends while she took care of the disaster in the bathroom.

In this situation nobody got the better end of the deal. The rhythmic rocking of Beth's body slung over Barry's shoulder, while he carried her across the cobblestone street and up the first flight of steps leading to our apartments, had taken its toll. As we reached the first landing and walked passed my apartment door, I heard a splat and realized that Beth was beginning to barf again, but this time some of it had found its way down the back of Barry's shirt.

"Jesus…" Barry groaned.

Using a damp mop from my apartment, I wiped up the mess from the linoleum floor. Barry resumed the hike up the steps to their place. With almost perfect timing, at every third step Beth would hurl, Barry's back would collect more slime and I would mop up the chunks. And so it went up three more flights of stairs to their tiny one room apartment.

Jake, who had sobered up with all the excitement and physical activity, helped Barry get Beth's clothes off, while I heated some water on the stove for a bath. Fifteen minutes later, we left Beth naked in a tub of warm water with Barry sitting beside her, trying to rinse the shit out of her hair.

Beth stayed incommunicado for two weeks after her "birthday party", totally mortified by the lesson that she had taught Barry that day.

❧ XXX ❧

"Lesson for the day kids, you lose with booze." I off-handedly remarked out loud to the kitchen walls as I hung my last shirt on a hanger. The ironing was done and I carried the neatly hung fatigue uniforms to the armoire in my bedroom. As I passed the mirror on the back of the bedroom door I noted how thin I was.

"Hooray! You look great!" I said to myself in the mirror. The eight hundred calorie a day diet was working. I'd gained over thirty pounds since arriving here. Not only was there a gasthaus on every block in Germany, but also a bakery on every corner. Inside the bakeries weren't just donuts and cookies either. They had wonders that I had never seen before, like fresh bananas on a bed of whipped cream laying on a crescent shaped vanilla cookie and dipped in a deep dark chocolate coating, or a chocolate coated chocolate-chip mousse haystack that was three inches high. The variation of extremely fattening goodies was unbelievable. It was no wonder that there were so many plump German women, and within six months I had become one of them.

Jake and I had been trying to get me pregnant since I'd arrived overseas but nothing had happened. There was an Army saying that a woman went home from Germany with one of two things, a baby or a cuckoo clock and I was trying my best for the former. I had gone to the OB/GYN clinic at the Nuremberg, US Army hospital last summer to see if there was anything physically wrong with me. Along with a clean bill of health came a thermometer with instructions on how to use it to detect my time of the month, kind of a reverse rhythm method, and surprising orders from the doctor to lose weight. He even went so far as to say that if I didn't lose twenty pounds in the next six months he wouldn't begin treating me for infertility.

"Fat pregnant mothers are risky mothers." He had said. So here I stood looking in the mirror five months later, more than twenty pounds lighter and ready for my first scheduled fertility appointment at the end of December.

With the weight off I was looking so good that while I was shopping last month at the PX, a sales woman had asked, on the spur of the moment, if I would like a job selling coats in the fur department. She'd said that they needed someone desperately, and I was just the type that they were looking for. I hadn't even known that the PX had a fur department but she had told me that fur was cheap in Europe. The officer's wives could, and usually did, buy one or two coats as personal property, taking them home duty free. The only other time that I'd worked in my life was selling kid's rubber punch balls at a local department store when I was sixteen, a summer job that I had gotten through my aunt. Jake had hated it. He'd said that it was a stupid job and after a couple of days and lots of harassment from him, I'd stopped going. The toy department job was always great ammunition for Jake during a fight. It was brought up as an example of my ineptitude and stupidity.

"What would you fucking do without me? You think that you are so fucking smart, but you're really so fucking stupid. What do you fucking think, you could support yourself being a fucking 'Punch ball sales Queen'?" He would take great delight in his little speech, and laugh in my face when he was done. Jake had radar when it came to knowing what got to me and what didn't, and I never had an answer to the question "What would I do without him?"

Now as a twenty-year-old woman, I was flattered by the new job offer and decided to take it over Jake's protests. He'd sulked every bit of the three weeks that I'd wound up working there. He'd been so difficult at home to deal with during that time, never a moment's peace without some nit-picking fight about one thing or another that I finally gave up and quit. Afterward, Jake had said that I was one of those women who should never work. We were going to have children and no wife of his was going to work! And the truth of it was that I probably wasn't very good at it anyway. In his opinion I was book smart and street stupid, with no common sense at all. And I privately thought as I listened to him that maybe he was right.

"Ke-chunk!" I heard the front door slam against the safety chain.

"C'mon and open the fucking door!" It was Jake and by the sound of his voice he hadn't slept anything off. Every drop of alcohol that he'd ingested over the last twenty-four hours was still raging in his system.

"Shit!" I thought to myself and hurried to the

door to unhook the chain. "Don't want to start him on a roll." Jake was leaning on the glass on the outside of the door in an effort to stay upright, keeping the chain so taut that I was worried that it would pop out of the wood where it was anchored to the doorframe.

"You need to move away from the door so that I can unhook it, Jake." I coaxed him.

"Shut the fuck up." He said with a knee-jerk reaction and very little emphasis. He pushed himself away from the glass, backing up a few steps, keeping one hand on the wall to steady himself, while coming close to falling over in the process. He was still standing when I opened the door and he refused any help from me as he staggered into the apartment.

"What the fuck do you have to eat? I'm fucking starvin'!" His tone was borderline belligerent and it immediately sent me the unspoken warning that I had better be careful.

"Would you like a couple sunny side up eggs? I can fix 'em up in a minute." I said. His head wobbled slowly from side to side, which I took for a yes, while he repeatedly burped up, winced, and swallowed several times like something nasty was coming up and he kept forcing it back down.

"Why don't you sit down on the sofa for a little bit, while I get those eggs?" Slowly I led him to the maroon couch where he tumbled into the seat.

"Get me somethin' for my mother fucking feet and take my fucking boots off!" He ordered. Without a word I got the footstool from the corner and gently unlaced and tugged at his boots until they were loose, placing each foot on the stool as first one, than the other boot slipped off. Sometime during the process he had fallen asleep.

"Oh, thank you God." I murmured as I tiptoed out of the front room with his boots in hand. In the kitchen I took down the ironing board and put both it and the boots away. Just as I was about to sit down for a second at the breakfast nook with a cup of tea, Jake's voice thundered from the front room.

"God damn! It's fucking freezing in here!" Jake roared back to life for a second and then silence.

"I'll get you a blanket. Just hold on a minute." I called as I reached up into the upper shelf of the armoire in the bedroom for the extra comforter that we kept there. But by the time that I had walked into the front room with the blanket Jake had gotten up, navigated across the room and was beginning to pour the ten gallons of fuel oil into the empty oil tank inside the heater. I noticed that the funnel that we routinely used to cleanly guide the fuel oil into the small hole on the top of the oil tank was on the floor next to Jake's feet. To make matters worse, his alcohol impaired aim was atrocious, and as he swayed the gurgling crystal clear stream of fuel oil was missing the hole and splashing over and down the side of the oil heater. It gave the metal an oily wet coating as the fuel oil dribbled down side into shinny puddles on the floor.

"Jake, you've got to stop! You're soaking the place with fuel oil!" I said as I pulled at his arm. He shook me off and more fuel oil splashed to the floor.

"Shut the fuck up! Heater went out. It's too fucking cold and I'm takin' care of that." He was about halfway through the ten-gallon can as he finished yelling his comment. Then he stopped pouring, placed the can on the floor in a puddle of fuel oil directly next to the heater, and began fumbling in his pockets for matches.

"Holy shit! Stop it! You'll set yourself on fire!" And with that I snatched the matches from his hand just as he had gotten them out of his pocket, and instinctively backed away from him out of his reach, closer to the front door.

"You stupid fucking bitch! Give me those fucking things!" He said as he began to move towards me. I bolted blindly out of the front room door, through the short hallway and into the kitchen, not knowing where I was going or how to keep the matches from him.

He caught me from behind as I reached the kitchen, spinning me around to face him. His two hands grabbed my upper arms like a steel vice and as he shouted, he began to shake me.

"Fucking, give them to me!" he yelled. Often, a person's thoughts in a violent situation are strangely calm and so it was with me. I couldn't understand why he wasn't prying the matches out of my hand. "He must be too drunk to figure it out." I thought as my head shook back and forth. His fingers sank into the tissue of my arms no doubt leaving dark, ugly bruises. Finally, with one large push from him my feet tangled up beneath me and I fell backward crashing to the floor, my head bumping against the gray linoleum. I had involuntarily squeezed my eyes shut before I'd fallen. Now, when I opened them as I lay on the hard kitchen floor I saw Jake with a heavy wooden chair held high above his head staring down blankly at me with those cold vacant zombie eyes.

"Shit! He is going to smash my skull in with that thing!" flashed through my mind, but the only words that I could get out of my mouth were "No! Stop! It's me!"

His blank gaze seemed to waiver with the slightest bit of recognition and then he slowly put the chair down, the legs landing with a thump, precariously close to the side of my head. The matches were still clutched tightly in my hand, and I turned my hand palm down to the ground hoping that he wouldn't see them, setting him off again. Gambling that the incident had broken his train of thought and that what he had planned to do in his alcohol sodden brain was derailed for good, I lay motionless on the floor waiting to see what he would do next.

In the gloomy daylight that filtered though the kitchen window, he stood motionless above me. He was staring off into nowhere looking as if he was communing with some unknown cosmic force, carefully listening for some alien siren's song, or maybe the staggering amounts of alcohol that he had ingested had short circuited every electrical impulse in his body leaving him brain dead. Whatever the answer, I decided to take the opportunity to get up off the floor before he decided to pick up the chair again. I had just stood up and was heading for the front door and to safety, when the devil came back to life.

"Give me them fucking matches, bitch!" the monster roared, as I glanced up and saw that I'd absentmindedly chained and locked the front door after Jake had come through it an eternity ago. In a split second change of plans, I ran into the short hallway, took a hard right and flew into the bathroom, hoping to have time to shut and lock the thick metal door behind me. But no such luck. He banged into the door when it was within an inch from being closed. After several desperate attempts to shut the metal door behind me, Jake won the battle and the door swung open wide, its handle banging hard against the wall. In two short steps he was on me. Again his fingers wrapped tightly around the soft muscle of my upper arms, digging into it with his vise like grip.

"Ouch! Jake you're hurting me! Let go!" I shouted as I pushed against him trying to peel his fingers off of my arms. My struggling seemed to make him angrier and he lifted me off my feet, slamming my buttocks down hard on the marble ledge of the bathroom windowsill. The backward momentum of my body caused my back to bang into the window glass and my heart went into my mouth when I heard the window latch pop open!

"Oh my God!" was all that I could think with each successive whap of my back against the glass as Jake banged me into the window causing the window crank to turn and the window to open a little more with each successive jolt.

Immediately I stopped struggling against his grip on my arms and began to hold on to the wall lining the window with my hands, legs, and feet. I could feel the cold air streaming in from the now partially opened window and I could visualize the wet cobblestone and concrete courtyard two stories below.

"Stop it! No!" I yelled over and over into Jake's

vacant stare while he methodically thumped me into the window, grunting and groaning after each thump as he tried to dislodge me from my hold on the wall so that he could push me through. The last thump had pushed the window open half way so I knew that the next thump and push would do the trick.

"JAKE! YOU'LL KILL ME!" I screamed into his face, leaning as close to him as I could, with my eyes riveted to his and his vacant zombie stare. Thanks to luck or God or maybe a bit of both, my screaming words had pierced the fog in his brain and I saw a fleeting moment of recognition in his eyes, and he released his grip on my arms. Without a word, he turned and left me perched on the windowsill. Frozen where I sat, I heard his footsteps shuffle down the hallway and into the bedroom followed by the screech of the wooden legs of his twin bed on the linoleum as he collapsed onto the foam rubber mattress.

Knowing that this was my chance, I exploded off the windowsill and rushed to the door, slamming it shut and locking it all in one quick motion. Collapsing against the cool white enameled metal, I slid down it onto the floor resting my back against it and the wall, wedging myself securely into the corner as far away from the window as I could.

"Safe, safe." I whispered while I rocked myself in the confines of the corner. I could still smell the fumes from the spilled fuel oil that had begun this nightmare.

"He could get up and try to light the oil heater again..." I thought with growing panic, but then I realized that somehow I still had held on to the matches! An odd laugh tinged with hysteria broke the silence, and was quickly choked away by my sobs.

I was safe now, and that was all that mattered! If the stupid, drunken fuck got up and somehow set himself on fire, that was his problem, not mine! Let the son-of-a-bitch burn!

❧ XXXI ❧

"Promises, promises… That's all I've ever gotten out of you were promises!" I said out loud as I stood in our apartment staring down at Jake lying on his back. He was passed out in the middle of the kitchen floor still wrapped in his fake fur, winter jacket despite the 65-degree mid June weather. I wondered whether it was all worth it.

I slid a chair over from the breakfast nook and sat down to contemplate the mess on the floor. He began the spitting again. He had been doing it for quite awhile, and had stopped for a few minutes, and now had begun again. I didn't understand what he thought he was doing. Eyes closed and laughing like a schoolboy he was spitting straight up into the air and letting the spittle fall back on his face and subsequently dribble down the sides of his cheeks and neck forming two pools of slime on the linoleum floor on either side of his head.

"Promises, promises…" I said again and sighed.

"Well, maybe that wasn't totally fair. After all, since the choking incident in Virginia it had been over a year and a half before you tried to throw me out the window." I said with a sarcastic smile.

I remembered that the next morning after I had been perched on the windowsill, he hadn't been able to use the excuse that I'd been "making a big deal out of nothing" like he did after the carnival and the "no median" episodes.

"It's not my fault that you fucking overreacted

and ran down the fucking street. I wouldn't have done a fucking thing to you. You fucking know that! I only lost it that one fucking time in Virginia and you never let me fucking forget it!" He had said. That was the morning after the carnival pep talk, and was followed, a few weeks later, by the explanation of the disappearing median incident.

"It was your fucking fault that I fucked up the car. I couldn't fucking concentrate on my driving with your fucking mouth going and that crazy screaming bitch in the back seat! I don't know what's wrong with you lately. I have a couple of fucking drinks and you go crazy!"

Both excuses had been followed by a conciliatory admission that he knew that he really did need to cut back on the amount of alcohol that he was drinking when he went out partying with the guys.

"I'm just getting too fucking plastered. I'm gonna' fucking stop before I'm so fucking blind. OK?" The promise was a feeble one, but at the time, it had been enough for me.

"Maybe he's right. Maybe I am too overly sensitive since Virginia." I'd thought. "I'm a high strung person. That's why I flunked the driver's test when I was a kid, and why I still don't drive. I'm too emotional. I know that. Maybe he wouldn't have hurt me if I hadn't run. Maybe I had overreacted when I ran away from him that night, and maybe I had gone out of control yelling and all, before we went over the median." And so went the conversation with myself that had made everything OK.

But after coming close to being snot on the

pavement under my bathroom window, I had known that the benefit of doubt that I'd previously given him was bullshit, and so did he. He couldn't deny the deep dark bruises on my arms and the black scuffmarks on the wall under the windowsill from the heels of my shoes.

"How can I stay here with you when you get so crazy? And we're supposed to be trying to have a baby? I'd have to be nuts to have children with you!" I had scolded him the morning after.

"I'll call my dad and see if he can send me the money to fly home." I had threatened. "I can't stay here with me being so afraid of you!" It had been a bluff. I knew that Daddy had no money. He was still paying off the hospital bills from Momma's long illness. Besides, if I had called Daddy and asked to come home, I would've had to tell him the truth about everything. Then, if Jake did stop drinking someday, things would be ruined between the two of them forever. I couldn't take that chance.

I'd been between the proverbial rock and a hard place, nowhere to go and no money to go with. Oh yes, and then there was the question of divorce. The answer to that was a no-brainer. I couldn't get one. Being Catholic was the basic identity in my persona, so divorce was never an option. To me the Church was like Jake, sometimes I disagreed with it but it was familiar and had been a part of me for a very long time. He was my husband in God's eyes and that was that. However, frustrated, confused, and afraid, I knew that I had to do something!

"It was the fucking cognac!" Jake's voice had interrupted my thoughts that morning after the bathroom scene. "That's it, the fucking cognac! In fucking Virginia I had been doin' fucking shots and yesterday I was drinkin' fucking cognac and coke! Too much hard liquor must get me fucking crazy. Fuck! That's how the fuck I got so nuts!" He'd sounded like a sinner who had just been saved. Hallelujah! His face had gone from a look of dark brooding to joyful relief in an instant. He'd found the answer to what we had both thought was an impossible situation and in the next instant he had realized the solution.

"No more fucking hard liquor for me! Honey, you fucking know that I would never fucking hurt you if I was in my right fucking mind. Some people just get fucking crazy with hard liquor." He'd said, his voice becoming soft, coaxing and seemingly sincere. "You remember Racky. You remember how he really got nuts whenever he drank whiskey." Racky had been one of Jake's childhood friends, and Jake had been right. He had been crazy. So wild and crazy that he'd wound up smashing into a ten foot cyclone fence during a joy ride in his car and had killed himself in the process.

"Fuck! It's the same with me." And then he had repeated, "Hard stuff makes me crazy." Then he came close to me, reached out, and had begun to rub my shoulders being careful not to brush against the black bruises left by him the day before.

"Honey, I wouldn't hurt you, you fucking know that. Never!" He'd said in a low soft whisper as his hands moved to my neck and rubbed it gently, rhythmically.

I had closed my eyes wanting what he was saying to be the truth.

"Please God. Make this be true!" I prayed.

"I promise never to fucking drink, not even one fucking shot of hard liquor, ever again. Never fucking ever! Please Honey, say it's fucking OK. Please." He had pleaded like a little boy who was begging his mother for forgiveness for being bad. "Pleeease…" he'd said wrapping his arms around me from behind and rocking me slowly back and forth as he breathed the word slowly into my ear.

"Maybe it will be alright." I had told myself. "Maybe he's right. It's worth a shot, after all what other choice do I have?" I'd thought, willfully convincing myself.

"OK." I had said, sounding reluctant. "But, if this happens again, I'm gone. I mean it! GONE! This is not the way that I want to live my life. Got it?" I had said this with as much conviction as I could muster. And then he'd kissed me and it was like it was before the nightmare had happened. At least for awhile.

And now it was seven months since the last set of promises that were generated by my close call with the bathroom window and the pavement below it. Over the last seven months he'd kept his promise. He'd stopped drinking hard liquor all right but he still pounded down the Bavarian beer. Sometime in early December, just a few weeks after the struggle on the bathroom windowsill, I'd gotten pregnant. By mid February I'd gone to the Army clinic and the doctor had given me a due date for the first week in September. I hadn't shown at all until I was over four months. What was weird though was that the minute the doctor confirmed that I was pregnant, Jake the sex maniac had stopped all action. When I'd asked him why, he'd said that the thought of a naked pregnant woman was revolting, and it turned him off. His feelings were troubling to me and they didn't do one heck of a lot for my ego.

"What the hell." I had thought. "It's only for six and a half months and then I'll be myself again. Other couples seem to handle the whole thing just fine, and so will we."

Coming back to the present, I took a good look at Jake on the floor. The bastard had been gone for three days and he smelled like a brothel. My eyes were drawn back to the white "snark" smeared around the zipper of his black pants and I knew that even though pregnant women weren't his forte, whores sure were! This wasn't the first time that he gave me this kind of crap since I was pregnant. I had taken his feeble excuses then, but not this time! God! How could I have been so stupid!

I remember that it had been late February and it was Fasching, the carnival season similar to Mardi Gras that the Germans celebrated several weeks before Ash Wednesday, the day that marked the beginning of Lent, a season of atonement practiced by most Catholics just before Easter. When Fasching rolled around the windows of the women's apparel shop in downtown Furth featured some very sexy lingerie accented by masks, streamers, glitter, and something that I had never seen before, a pair of crotchless underpants. I'd gotten a good chuckle from the display but I wasn't laughing the following Saturday night when one of our young married German neighbors had been sitting across from Jake and I in the gasthaus, wearing a very short skirt and possibly a pair of those same "peak-a-boo" panties, constantly giving us "beaver shots"! To be truthful I think that she had been providing Jake with a good look at everything that God had given her and I was just getting caught in the fallout. I'd been flabbergasted. I had pointed it out to Helga who thought the whole thing was pretty funny and had said in broken English, "Everything OK. Is Fasching. Poof now, und after Fasching all forgotten."

A week later, Ms. Crotchless Pants and her husband gave a Fasching party at their apartment down the block and we'd been invited. After watching Jake pound down booze for the last fourteen months, I'd lost my taste for alcohol, so I had stuck to soda all night. An hour or two had passed and between the smoke and the heavy German food that had been served for supper, I was getting a little queasy. Evening sickness had returned with the pregnancy so I wasn't surprised when I started to feel under the weather. Jake had disappeared about half an hour before while looking for another beer, even though it was obvious that he'd had more than enough. I went to look for him hoping that when I found him I could convince him that it was time to go home.

The party had overflowed into the apartment next door. I'd worked my way through the crowd and the front door, and into the hallway of the next apartment, looking into each room as I passed it. Towards the back of the apartment, just off of the kitchen was a small door that had led to what looked like a pantry. The door stood slightly ajar and I'd taken a quick glance in as I passed on my way to another short hallway, and to what looked like a bedroom beyond. The dangling naked light bulb inside the pantry had illuminated a couple located directly underneath it engaged in eagerly groping one another in the heat of passion.

"Jake!" I shouted with a mixture of disbelief, anger and pain. Showing very little surprise or guilt on his face, Jake had turned from the former beaver shot queen and flashed a large grin my way, all the while smoothly unwrapping his arms, legs, and hands from around her body.

"Fuck. I jus bin' lookin' fer you." He slurred.

"Where the fuck've you been?" He followed up, his words laced with a belligerent tone.

"Jake, I'm ready to go home now." I said, my words evenly spaced, emotionless and controlled as I stared intently at the obviously wasted woman who had giggled as she leaned back against the pantry wall barely able to keep herself upright.

"You're no fucking fun!" Jake had muttered as he stumbled out of the pantry and unsteadily began to navigate back through the apartment and out the door into the cobblestone street, with me keeping guard to make sure that he didn't get lost along the way. There had been no conversation between the two of us as I had shepherded him the hundred yards or so to our apartment building, up the stairs, through the flat, and into the bedroom where he'd fallen face down on the bed.

There really wasn't anything to say at that point, he wouldn't have remembered what I'd said anyhow. It was better to wait until morning when I could talk to him rationally. Weary and heartsick I had undressed and had gotten into bed, closing my eyes and trying not to think about the picture of Jake and that woman entwined in each other's arms.

"God damn him! How could he do that to me?" I said out loud as I squeezed my eyes more tightly shut hoping to block out the abhorrent vision of Jake and beaver woman that repeatedly flashed on my internal movie.

Later, I awoke to the sound of water splattering on... on what? I had thought for a moment.
"Is it raining?" I'd asked myself in a half conscious state as the plop-plop of water droplets continued somewhere in the background. Opening my eyes and glancing at the windowpane next to my bed to see if it was the source of the unfamiliar sound, I had noticed that the glass was bone dry. Perplexed, I lifted my head from my pillow to better locate the source of the strange sound and slowly looked around the room. Realization hit me all at once, as my eyes had become used to the darkness and began to make out some movement above Jake's bed, and simultaneously my ears honed in on the watery splattering sound.

"Shit!" I groaned. "He's pissing on his sleeping bag! Jake! Wake up! You're peeing on yourself!" I loudly pleaded. There had been no response. A steady stream of urine was shooting up like a fountain into the air above him and splattering down on the canvas of the Army issued sleeping bag that he'd been using for a blanket. What could I do? I was definitely not going to shake him awake. I knew the ramifications of that type of action.

"Fuck him. The damage is already done so I might as well leave him to finish things up. Let him lay in his piss all night. That will fix his ass!" I had said to myself, reveling in the thought of how uncomfortable it would be. I couldn't think of anyone who deserved it more. Smiling, I had drifted off to sleep contemplating the joy that I would have rubbing this one in his face. "

That was if I ever talked to him again after what he's done with Ms. Beaver Shot." I'd thought.

Of course, the next morning there had been no apology. According to Jake, beaver woman had been the aggressor and had attacked him. He'd only been fending her off when I'd come upon the scene, misinterpreting everything. And as far as the bedwetting was concerned, he hadn't thought that his wife pouring a glass of water over him while he slept, in order to get back at him for his supposed transgressions, was one bit funny. No matter how much I'd tried to convince him otherwise, he wouldn't or couldn't accept any other explanation. So I had let both issues drop. There had been no use arguing with a drunk when he couldn't remember anything, and when I'd thought about it, in the condition that he'd been in that night, he couldn't have made it with beaver lady even if he had been trying to.

"Well, there would be no getting around it this time! I may be gullible but I'm not entirely STUPID, Jake!" I shouted, but he was oblivious to the sound of my voice. Smiling, he grunted and the spit kept spurting up. I stared at him feeling disgusted and trying to answer the question that I'd asked myself when I first sat down. Was it worth it to stay with him?

In the seven months that had passed from the bathroom window violence until now, there had been some good times. We had begun to take short trips on the weekends. We'd traveled to many of the popular tourist places in Germany and because Jake was in the military we could do it on a shoestring budget. Garmisch was a lovely little town nestled in the foothills of the Alps. The stucco fronts of its ginger bread houses were painted in colorful, intricately drawn murals of the wonders of nature that surrounded them. The village was not far from the Zugspitze, the tallest mountain in Germany. Jake and I had taken a trolley car to the top, a frightening and glorious experience. Jake had been very reluctant to take the ride and once he was standing in the middle of the concrete observation deck on the top of the mountain, he'd refused to budge an inch. I'd been a little more adventurous and had forced myself to walk to the wrought iron railings at the edge of the platform so that I could experience every bit of the spectacular view.

The hotel that we had stayed at in Garmisch was leased for the military by the US government so the price of our stay was a dollar per night. The most expensive meal at the hotel was a scrumptious Châteaubriand dinner for two for the unbelievable price of five dollars! The hotel also had something that I'd never seen before, slot machines. For the first time in my life I took a quarter, placed it into a slot, pulled down the handle on the one armed bandit, and gambled my money. I'd won thirty-five dollars in less than fifteen minutes and then, in less than an hour I lost forty. In a small expanse of time I'd learned a valuable lesson. Don't gamble because it hurts too damn much to lose. The specter of how many fancy Châteaubriand dinners I could have bought if I had only quit while I was ahead tortured me for the rest of my stay.

We'd traveled to Linderhof to see crazy King Ludwig's ostentatious castle, the one that he had copied from the French castle at Versailles, the building that had broken the financial back of seventeenth century Germany. We also had gone on day trips to Berchtesgaden and saw Hitler's and Eva Braun's hideaway, the Eagle's Nest, and Neuschwanstein where we'd hiked up a mountainside to the stark, cold, stone castle whose architecture was used by Walt Disney for his corporation trademark. Mileage wise, traveling in Europe was like going from state to state back home, so going to Venice for a weekend jaunt had not been out of the question.

Last month, Jake had gotten a three-day pass and we had driven through Italy like two vagabonds, eating peaches purchased from a farm stand on the side of a country road, dining on greasy lasagna at a truck stop along a super highway, and drinking some stuff that the Italians loved that looked like cherry pop and tasted like vinegar. We had both felt like idiots when we had gotten to the suburbs around Venice and were surprised to discover that we had to park the car in a parking garage and take a ferry boat across a body of water in order to enter the city. It had taken several iterations of our going "around the block", that is, traveling in a large circle on country roads, before we had figured it out. It had never occurred to us that, as children, when we'd been told in geography class that Venice had canals instead of streets, it really had meant that there were NO STREETS.

The gondola ride had been romantic, and in the evening we'd shared the adventure of finding a rented room off the beaten tourist path. All the big hotels had been full for the night, and the concierge of one of them had given us an address. Suspicious, Jake had slept with one eye on his wallet, but the night was uneventful, and in the morning we were both grateful for what we had realized had been the hotel manager's kindness.

"Puh, puh, puh..." interrupted my thoughts, followed by a little giggle. God! He was spitting on himself again! And despite the warm scenes from our past, I couldn't get the thought of what that white gunk all over his pants implied. Standing up, I took a good look at my husband. Lovingly rubbing my tummy, I stared at him, smeared with spit and come, and evaluated it all. Tomorrow was my birthday. What a pleasant surprise.

"Fuck you Jake, you pig!" I said. "Two and a half months until this baby is born and I sure as hell don't want to spend it with you!"

❧ PART 5 ❧

"HOMECOMING"

❧ XXXII ❧

"Mmm...mmm...mmm..." I could hear the constant humming of the 747's engines in the background, however, the atmosphere of serenity that had been prevalent during my flight to Germany was not along for my airplane ride back to the States. The Army rented commercial airliners in order to fly Army wives home as inexpensively as possible. The price for this ride had been one third of what it had cost for me to travel to Germany almost twenty-three months ago. Cheap, but as the saying goes, you did get what you paid for. The trip was turning out to be a weird, twisted caricature of my previous flight.

The Army had removed all of the partitions from the inside of the airplane. There was no first class or coach section. There was only one long compartment filled with two hundred women, two-thirds of which had babies, who all looked to be under six months old. I remembered the saying that buzzed around the coffee clutches of Army wives, "You come home from Germany with either a cuckoo clock or a baby." I was coming home with

both. The clock wasn't really a cuckoo clock. I hated
those. Mine was an old handmade, wooden mini-
grandfather's clock that hung on the wall and
chimed every half-hour. Jake had bought it for me
at an antique shop on his way home from the base,
one day, and I loved it. I had shipped it home last
month along with a few other special things that I'd
wanted to bring back with me.

My baby was beautiful! We had named him
Eric. Jake liked the name ever since the first time
he'd heard it on a TV commercial for Erik cigars.
We had changed the "k" to a "c" so that it wouldn't
be too obvious to people how non-creative we had
been.

Looking down at Eric, sleeping in my lap, I
couldn't help but smile. He'd been born on time, in
early September, and now was over eight weeks
old. It still amazed me how perfect he was. Every
finger and toe was where it should be as well as
everything else that was a part of him. It really was
a miracle that the unseen lump in my belly, which
had twitched, kicked, and hiccupped for months,
was really a perfect miniature human being.

"Excuse me." The woman in the window seat
in my row said to the woman sitting between us.
"Do you think that you could hold my baby for a
minute? I'm not feeling very well and I think that I
need to use the bathroom." She said with a
distressed look on her face.

There were three of us sitting in a row and two
of us had babies. This same seating arrangement
was repeated throughout the compartment of the
plane. Each row had five seats. On the side of the
airplane with three seats, the women next to the

aisle and next to the window had infants, and the women in the middle did not. On the two-seated side, it was one lady with a baby and one without.

"Sure" the woman next to me said. "Just leave him with me and take your time." The baby exchange only took a few seconds, during which, I stood up and moved into the aisle, so that the woman heading for the bathroom could get passed my seat more easily. Standing, my stomach rolled, matching the roller-coaster motion of the plane's floor beneath my feet.

"There's such a long line. I hope that I can make it." She remarked, mainly to herself, obviously agitated as she made her way between the seats to the end of the queue for the bathroom. The line of waiting women ended not far from where we sat in the middle of the plane, and the line for the bathrooms on the opposite end of the plane was just as long.

Whatever member of the culinary department of the airline that had made the decision to serve a dinner of sauerbraten and cheap champagne to two hundred women on an overseas flight, with the possibility of bad weather on the way, was a sadist. The periodic sensation of being in an express elevator that suddenly and unexpectedly plummeted down a floor or two before it slammed to a stop, and then shot back up to where it had started, kept everyone's tummies unsettled. The storm over the Atlantic had battered the airplane with violent gusts of high winds and sheets of rain since an hour after we'd taken off from Frankfurt. The first uneventful sixty minutes in the air had given the stewardesses just enough time to serve the passengers the "lead brick" delicacy, and now everyone was paying for it.

I'd initially estimated that about two-thirds of the passengers had looked sick and it seemed that it was still the case, since both bathroom lines had remained at the same long length since the weather had begun to get rough. We all had been treated to some additional after dinner entertainment when a woman, who was one of the first to get sick, had underestimated the time it would take to get into a restroom. She'd spewed chunks all over herself, the people sitting in her proximity, and a stewardess who'd been trying to alleviate the situation by putting a sick bag to the woman's face. The stewardess hadn't been quite quick enough. The vomiting display triggered several sympathetic upchucks by women sitting closest to the incident, but they'd managed to get their sick bags out from the back of the seat in front of them, for a timely deposit. Nobody had lost it recently, but I wouldn't be too confident about remaining untouched by the situation, so to speak, if I were one of the women sitting next to those presently in line.

The weather had not let up since it had begun. The plane had been batted around by gusts of wind for the last several hours and everyone's nerves were wearing thin. This was the worst airplane ride of my life and we still had several hours to go. It was all that I could do, to keep a lid on my fear and panic, which flared up every time some turbulence would cause my derrière to be lifted a few inches off of my seat. What I was experiencing now beat the hell out of the fear that I had felt flying in a little Piper Cub from Killeen to Dallas. Even though the ride had been bumpy, it'd been a sunny day and I could see the tumbleweeds and brush below me. Now it was dark, the rain pounded against the tiny porthole, and there was nothing to see beneath me but a black void. My imagination saw the huge expanse of nothingness that was the ocean, churning and boiling thousands of feet below. Ugh… It gave me the shivers on top of my already uneasy feelings. I didn't know which flight had been the most turbulent, but I felt this one was the worst. Perception is everything.

Trying to take my mind off of the moving picture clip of the plane crashing into the dark bottomless ocean that was constantly playing and replaying in my head, I stared down at Eric, who surprisingly was sleeping like a… a… baby.

"Very funny, Susan." I said to myself accompanied by an unusually loud nervous laugh. The woman next to me never even noticed. She was busy in her own hell. She was fidgeting with her neighbor's baby and every so often, nervously turning around and trying to peer over the back of the seats, to see how far the woman from next to her had gotten in her quest for the john. It looked to me as if it was going to take some time. The line was moving at a snail's pace.

"He is beautiful!" I thought, while looking at the sleeping infant in my lap. And now that, if I thought about things in a melodramatic way, I could feel the breath of death on the back of my neck, I reviewed my decision to stay with Jake. In retrospect it had been the right one. Jake had promised again and this time he'd kept it well. He had not gotten drunk one time since his three day

binge. He had confessed his "attempt" at transgressions with some local whore at a bar, which
explained the white gunk strategically smeared all
over the zipper portion of the front part of his
pants. But considering his state of complete
inebriation, he'd admitted that the attempt had
failed. At least that is what he'd said. He'd asked
for forgiveness, and considering that he'd been
totally wasted, at the time, and without sex for
months, I'd taken pity on him and forgave him.

The day after his three-day binge had been my
twenty-first birthday and he'd done something that
day, that he'd never done before. He had bought
me a present, one dozen, long stem red roses. They
added a nice touch to his apology and promises,
and probably helped to sway my decision to stay.

I'd called my father earlier in the day, before
Jake and I had gotten things straightened out. I'd
told Daddy some of the details about what had
happened. I'd told him just enough for him to
realize that I had good reason to want to come
home, but not enough to turn him against my
husband, just incase. He'd been sympathetic but he
pointed out the reality of my situation.

"I can send you the money today, if you want.
But remember, once you come home you'll have to
stay here with Gladys and me. No going back and
forth. I can't afford it. And, you'll be having the
baby alone. Jake will be thousands of miles away."
He'd said.

God! In the middle of all the insanity I'd
forgotten that he'd remarried! From his letters she
had seemed nice enough, but to live with a stranger
day in and day out, and to have a baby all by

myself... Well, both points were pivotal in my decision to stay and, of course, the roses had sealed the deal.

The decision had been made and I hadn't regretted it since. The last five months had been OK as far as Jake's boozing was concerned. We even had a few moments that we'd shared together without the constant bickering that always seemed to happen. We'd listened to the first moon landing together and shared the historic event like two old friends. But even though Jake was sober, he'd still kept mostly to himself. I was lonely, but I had hopes for the future.

The baby hadn't changed anything either. Jake had been home when my labor had started. One of the emotional areas that Jake needs a lot of improvement in is compassion. Couple that with his inability to comfort another human being, and the "having a baby experience" had turned out to be Jake sitting in the corner staring at me from the opposite end of the room, while I laid in a heap in the bed writhing in pain.

With each contraction I'd kept thinking that it couldn't get much worse and with the next contraction it had. He stared. I writhed. So together we'd made quite a pair. Later, when I'd been admitted to the Army hospital in Nuremberg, Jake had been relieved when the nurse informed him that he couldn't go with me into the labor room. We'd kissed goodbye, and the rest of my labor was spent in a windowless six by twelve rectangular room, with nothing to look at except a large clock on the wall, and nothing to do but writhe some more. The hours had smeared by while I'd been serenaded by a Middle Eastern woman, in the dungeon next to mine, whose wailing and moaning had been non-stop. When I'd asked about the woman's constant noise making, the nurse had said that it was their custom. Damn! It had driven me crazy!

Finally someone had given me some type of drug that took the pain away and a few hours later it had been over.

For me, it wasn't true that the joy one feels when you look at your baby for the first time takes away the memory of the pain of childbirth. It was ten weeks later and I still remembered, and childbirth was something that I never wanted to do again.

My experiences after the baby hadn't been so hot either. Jake didn't know the first thing about babies and he needed his sleep in order to do his job during the day, so the whole baby caretaker thing was up to me. Having a baby without a mother or close friend who was a baby authority around to answer your questions or to stay with you for a couple of weeks so that you could get some rest and let your bottom heal, had been no picnic. I'd learned what sleep deprivation was all about in the first two weeks. Between Eric's crying and my hobbling around trying to make formula, cook meals, and clean, I'd wound up getting less than an hour sleep between feedings. I was so spaced out that I had been having weird scary dreams while I was awake, something that I didn't know a person could do. I'd even tried to sterilize several bottles of formula and had forgotten to put water in the sterilizer pot, causing one hell of an explosion.

Finally, when Eric was about six weeks old I was able to give him some rice cereal, and subsequently had gotten my first uninterrupted four hours of sleep since his birth. Things had gotten better after that. There had been one additional crisis in Eric's short time on this earth that was a direct result of my total ignorance of babies, and I could laugh about it now. At Eric's six-week checkup, the doctor had told me to begin feeding him rice cereal at meals. Because of my lack of experience, I had thought he'd meant at every meal, so I had fed Eric six bowls of cereal a day! After five days, I wound up with one very over fed and constipated baby, who in the early morning of the sixth day gave me an example of how "projectile" vomiting had gotten its name. I was, and still am, astounded that such a little baby could shoot the stuff so far. Crazy with worry, I'd rushed him into the doctor who got a good belly laugh at both Eric's and my expense.

Bright light flashing through the porthole of the plane caught my eye and my attention. I wondered how safe we really were flying in an airplane over the middle of the ocean, in one hell of a storm.

"What happens if the plane gets struck by lightening?" I asked the woman next to me. She was looking concerned that her seatmate hadn't returned from the restroom, and that the baby placed in her care was beginning to fuss.

"I don't know. You would think that it would happen all the time, so it's probably nothing." She said juggling the baby from one side of her lap to the other as he gave out the beginnings of a wail.

"Shh...Shh...Shh..." She said to the baby as she bounced him on her knees. It wouldn't have mattered much if he'd started screaming his head off. With approximately one hundred and fifty infants on board, between the weather and the nervous mothers that it caused, at least ten of the babies were crying in unison at any given moment.

"Where IS she? Can you see her? Is she still in line?" She was getting more and more worked up as the baby squawked. With the roller-coaster motion of the cabin I didn't want to take off my seatbelt. The bumps were getting worse and sometimes my belt was the only thing that was keeping me in my seat. I turned my head around, strained my neck as far as it would go, and got a glimpse of the woman walking up the aisle, making her way back to our row. Suddenly, the plane hit a large bump of turbulence and the woman disappeared in between the seats. Everyone in the plane made a collective, startled "Ohh" sound as the bump had hit, giving me the feeling that we were all connected into one organism, reacting to this maniacal carnival ride with one voice. The first bump had been the prelude to a stream of turbulence that violently shook the aircraft. I saw a stewardess make her way toward the back of the plane to where the woman had fallen. I was holding tight to Eric, trying to protect him from the jarring of the plane. And then... it stopped.

The rolling motion of the buffeted airplane still remained but the fierce jarring of the compartment had stopped. I took a quick look at my watch, trying to figure out how much time was left to endure in this nightmare. Oh my God! The ride was only half over! Panic was starting to set in and my hands began to sweat as I projected five more hours of what I had just gone through. I felt a gurgling in my gut and a wave of nausea hit me.

"I think it's my turn!" I said, undoing my seat belt and quickly getting up from my seat frantically searching the sea of faces for a stewardess to take my baby. Out of nowhere the window seat woman popped up. I noticed that she had a lump on her forehead the size of walnut as she began to slip by me to get into her seat, but seemed no worse for the wear.

"Are you OK?" I heard the lady sitting next to me say as she made a motion to curl her legs under her seat so that the mother of the baby that she was holding could get passed her.

"Sure. I just lost my balance when that big bump hit." She said as she sat down next to the window, fastened her lap belt, and reclaimed her now sleeping baby. As soon as the baby was out of her arms the woman in the middle seat looked up at me.

"Give him to me. I really don't mind. I just want to help. You all look so exhausted and frazzled." She said.

"Gee thanks. You must be a saint." We both laughed at my words, but I wasn't kidding. I made my way up the aisle and got into the lavatory within a few short minutes. Luckily, the stewardesses had forced everyone back into their seats with the last violent bump, and just a few of us had gotten up since, to brave the onslaught of the still existing turbulence.

Getting everything into the small silver bowl, that belonged there, was a real challenge. I did succeed, however, and every bit of the "gourmet" supper that had been served to us several hours before, had cleanly made its exit. Good riddance to bad rubbish! I was actually feeling much better and had hopes of making it the rest of the flight without going completely insane from the fear of crashing and burning.

"On second thought, crashing yes, burning in the sea, no." I said as I looked into the tiny mirror above the lavatory stainless steel sink. I made a face.

"God, I hope they don't have a camera behind that mirror. After all, then they would know what you've known for a long time, my dear. You are fucking nuts!" I laughed, stuck my tongue out at my reflection, turned and opened the metal door.

Closing the lavatory door was a little difficult because the roller-coaster bumps and drops had begun again. Turning to walk up the aisle to my seat I wondered why there was no line of women waiting for the john. Then a big bump of air turbulence hit the plane and lifted me slightly off my feet reminding me that the seat belt sign was probably lit.

Covering the distance from the bathroom as quickly as I could before the next big bump, I settled into my seat, fastened my seatbelt and had Eric into my arms, in less than a minute. The lady sitting in the middle of my row must have been a magician, because when she had given me back my baby, he was asleep. He stayed that way, as I held him tightly in my arms.

And then it began, a sudden elevator ride to hell. At first, it took me by surprise. So much so, that I couldn't relate to what was happening. All the other drops in altitude of the airplane had been of such short duration that they had been over before I'd become fully aware of them. But this one was different.

"Oh my God, we're falling!" The woman who was sitting in my row, next to the window, said in disbelief as my stomach took flight. Simultaneously, my attention was drawn to the actions of the stewardesses who had been located at the front of the aircraft. Both of them sprinted up the aisle from the first row of seats where they had been standing and chatting. They ran passed where I was sitting, to the tail section of the plane, hair flying, arms and legs pumping, and a grimace of fear on their faces. It was then the realization hit me that the nose of the plane was pointing down at some abnormal angle and we were going down!

For a short time there was silence. Everyone remained perfectly still, listening in unison and waiting for the sensation of falling to stop, but it didn't.

"Oh my God, I am heartily sorry for having offended…" The woman next to me began to frantically chatter, the words coming out of her like the rapid firing of a machine gun.

"Hail Mary full of grace…" The familiar prayer came from somewhere behind me, the litany periodically interrupted by hysterical and terrified sobs in the midst of a choir of infants bellowing and women crying.

"This is it." I thought to myself with surprising calm, pulling my baby close to me as he continued to sleep through the mayhem. With an odd detachment, I closed my eyes and hugged Eric, waiting for whatever was going to happen, to happen. My perception of time and reality began to warp. Awareness of the people and sounds around me became more acute, but I listened as an observer, strangely devoid of emotion and filled with a feeling of peace and total acceptance of what seemed to be inevitable. Seconds passed like minutes.

"Pray for us sinners, now and at the hour of our death…" The woman was finishing up her plea to the mother of God, and calmly I wondered how long we could drop before we would crash into the dark brooding water below.

And then… nothing.! As suddenly as it had started, it had stopped!

We had stopped falling! I couldn't believe it! Relief flooded the compartment of the plane. Cheers and shouts of joy rolled like a wave through the crowd of women. Like at the end of a revival meeting, we had been saved! It was a miracle! Praises to God and laughter filled the air.

"Thank you God!" I said out loud, overjoyed with the knowledge that I would live, and then instantly felt a pang of guilt. Over the last two years of my life in Germany, my childlike belief in the Catholic Church and the god that it had defined was beginning to wane. Questions that had once been casual inquiries about the inconsistencies of the world around me had begun to solidify into real doubts in my faith.

Sitting in my seat as the atmosphere inside the plane began to return to normal, I started to reflect on what had just occurred.

Why should God have decided that he would save Eric and me from crashing into the sea and not save my mother from the torture and death that she most definitely had not deserved? Women, children and babies were always dying all over the world from starvation and war while some priest at a catholic high school prays to Mary and Jesus so that the football team wins a game. The thought of the hypocrisy that existed in such prayers was embarrassing. What was wrong with the Church anyway, allowing that kind of arrogant behavior?

The rough weather abruptly began again, interrupting my train of thought. Eric was beginning to squirm and the peace that had enveloped me when I thought that we were about to die, instantly disappeared into the stormy bumps and thumps. My body instinctively tensed, as it kept a constant vigil, straining to perceive any slight downward movement of the plane that would signal a continuation of the terrifying elevator ride to the end of my life that I'd been on a few minutes ago.

"God, I hope our luck holds out for the rest of the flight!" I said in a worried whisper to my baby as he began to cry, and my hands shook as I got his bottle ready to feed him his supper.

Five nightmare hours later we landed in Nova Scotia, not in New York, our original destination. A stewardess explained that the constant buffeting of the airplane by the intense wind had caused the engines to use up much more fuel than was expected. It took two hours to refuel the plane after we had landed. During that time we weren't allowed to get off the plane, something to do with passports and visas, and the time dragged.

By the time we did land in New York, thirteen hours after leaving Frankfurt, the occupants of the plane looked as if they had been through some sort of survival training. One hundred and fifty babies were taking turns screaming, all in various stages of hunger, fear, or discomfort, and their mothers and the remaining passengers weren't in much better shape. The four stewardesses, once pristine with every hair sprayed in place, now stood in the doorway of the airplane wearily waving goodbye, exhausted, hair un-kept and straggling about their faces, and spots of regurgitated sour beef soiled their once clean and pressed uniforms. The soft white cotton bow that had finished off the Peter Pan collar of their uniform blouse, once tied crisp and neat under their chins framing their angel faces, now hung untied about their necks, the ties of white flapping chaotically in the chilly November wind. This had truly been a ride from hell.

"Bet that's the last time that any of them volunteer for some overtime on an Army flight!" I thought with a slightly sardonic smile, waving automatically back and surprised by my lack of sympathy. "I guess we're all tired." I whispered softly to myself and to Eric lying quietly in the baby seat that was slightly swinging at the end of my arm as I walked to the terminal. "One thing for sure, I don't ever want to fly again!" Eric looked up at me and smiled. "Yeah Eric, you're right. We have to get to Chicago and I think that a cab ride would be too damn expensive." Reminding myself that there were situations in life where the only way out was through, I braced myself for my next ride in the sky, and looked for the monitors with information on my connecting flight to home.

Walking through customs at O'Hare airport, two and one half uneventful but personally terrifying hours later, had proven not to be a problem carrying only one suitcase, a diaper bag, my purse, and Eric in his portable baby seat. Dressed in an old winter coat, a German made dime-store dress and black leather boots, makeup smeared and my long black hair in complete disarray, I must have looked like a weary refugee or "DP" as my dad would say. Whatever the case, the customs officer had taken pity on me and quickly ushered me through the line. Exhausted, I pushed my way through a pair of gray swinging doors, emerging on the other side into a large room filled with excited and expectant faces.

Bumped, bruised and on the verge of tears I scanned the crowd for my father's familiar smile and my eyes locked onto an old brown felt hat with a small red feather in its brown ribbon hatband.

"Daddy!" I called with a voice that sounded surprisingly like a lost little girl who has just caught site of her father.

"Daddy, I'm home!"

❧ XXXIII ❧

I lifted the mug of warm milk to my mouth. It was just like Momma used to whip up for us when we were kids and were suffering from a sore throat, but this was minus the melted pat of butter floating on the top. The shaking didn't stop. Waves of tremors shook my body and I had to concentrate on keeping my hand still so that I could put the cup back down on the kitchen table without spilling the white comforting liquid all over it, and possibly the worn linoleum floor. The second hand of the clock on the kitchen wall swept smoothly over its face.

"Jesus Christ! 4:45 am. Where is he?" Another wave of the shakes hit me and I was powerless to stop it. Eric would be waking up soon and I needed to try and calm down.

"He's OK. He's just sleeping it off somewhere." was my feeble attempt at trying to assure myself that there was nothing to worry about. The trembling started again. It was like someone was flipping a switch every few seconds that turned my whole body into one big vibrating machine.

"God, I've got to stop this shaking!" The more that I tried to steady my body's motion, the worse it got. Attempting to shift my attention to something else to diffuse my mounting fear, I looked out of the window at the small bit of sky, above the brick wall of the building next door, and noticed that the sky was beginning to lighten. The morning breeze had kicked in and it gently blew through the open window causing the blue and white checkered cotton curtains to rhythmically rock back and forth with each puff of air.

We had been back in the States for more than eight months. It was the end of July and the summer had seemed to be exceptionally warm compared to what my last two summers in Germany had been. The breeze through the window helped to cool the kitchen off a bit. The air-conditioning unit was busted and the temperature inside the poorly ventilated, tiny two-bedroom apartment never cooled off from the sweltering heat that built up inside of it during the hot summer afternoons. It was hot and it seemed more difficult for me to put up with than usual. Then again, maybe I was just more sensitive to the heat because I was pregnant.

Even though I was over four months gone I still had a hard time believing that it had happened. After all those years of not getting pregnant, I'd thought that the probability of having a "rhythm" baby would be zero. I'd taken my temperature every morning but not as religiously as I should have, no pun intended. Six months after Eric was born I was pregnant again. I was due on December 19, my mother's birthday, and I was terrified.

Going from married to Jake, to married to Jake with one child had not been easy. Jake was awkward with babies and having one of his own hadn't brought out any latent paternal instincts. All the responsibilities and concerns for Eric's existence and well-being were one hundred percent mine. I wasn't complaining, after all, that's the way things were. I was the caretaker and he was the breadwinner. It was just that Jake was so demanding about the way that I kept the house and myself, that the addition of the responsibility for another human being had shoved me into overload. When the probability that I might be pregnant again had occurred to me, I pleaded with God during the resulting panic that had gripped me.

"Please God, don't let it be! I won't be able to take having another baby. I'll go crazy! I can't take any more pressure. I'm not the type of woman to have more than one child. My nerves can't take it!"

So far, the pregnancy hadn't been easy. I'd spotted and cramped on and off during the course of the last four months. Rest was impossible with Jake at work all day and a six month old baby to take care of and lug around. And then last week the worst had happened, I'd fallen on the steps.

The old tattered carpet runner on one of the outside hallway steps was loose. As I had hurried down the staircase to get the mail, in one fell swoop, my legs flew forward and out from under me. My rump came slamming down on the step beneath me, and the baby and everything that belonged to it slammed down on my pelvic bone a millisecond later. Recalling the feeling of my baby smashing into the bones inside of me that were supposed to be its cradle, its safe haven, still made my skin crawl and I shivered again.

"This baby is sure one hell of a tough little booger!" I thought smiling. The doctor had examined me right after the fall and said that everything looked OK but one never knew for sure what would be happening in this type of circumstance. That was last week and the baby was still holding on. But, between my nerves and all…

"God, I've got to stop shaking!" I said again, as a new round of the tremors shook me uncontrollably.

My eyes were inadvertently drawn back to the kitchen clock, fear and anger swirling in my gut.

"Damn it! Where is he? 5:00 o'clock! He'll never make it into work today, even if he gets here now! Christ! We need that fucking money!" Still shaking I lit a cigarette, inhaled deeply and tried to get my body to settle down. Suddenly, I heard light tapping sounds traveling across the linoleum floor. Quickly honing in on the direction of the "click, click, click," I'd just enough time to catch a glimpse of my little furry friend, "the mouse", scurrying into a barely perceptible hole in the base of the cabinet under the sink.

"At least it's not a roach!" I said, feeling almost an affinity for the dirty little rodent considering what the alternative could be. "We'll be out of here soon." We were moving from the Summit apartment to another apartment in Hickory Hills in less than two weeks and it wasn't soon enough for me. Both suburbs were just south of Chicago but the one that we were moving to was in a newer and slightly more affluent area. The Hickory Hills apartment was situated in a huge complex with twelve buildings that housed fifteen apartments in each. The complex was located on several long, rolling, grassy hills. Every apartment had sliding glass doors that opened to a spacious wooden balcony overlooking a grassy common area. The apartment complex even had a pool for the use of all the tenants. It was truly going to be like heaven after living here. The rent was only thirty dollars a month more than this rattrap and we'd figured our finances out so that we could make the move. Even if we were just going to squeak by, it would be worth the sacrifice.

I didn't feel safe here anymore. After what Mick had done I'd realized how really vulnerable we were in this cheap apartment. When we had gotten home from Germany last November, we had discovered that things had gone sour between my sister, Claudette, and Mick. Not because he was a psycho pervert but because he had a girlfriend and wanted to leave my sister and the four kids. I couldn't believe it! You couldn't say that Claudette didn't take her damn obligations seriously. She had hung on to Mick a lot longer than I would have! Anyway, in my opinion, it was good for my sister to get rid of him. I was astounded that any other woman would want him with his propensity to pulling his pants down in front of old and young women alike. Maybe his newfound friend didn't know about his perversion. That would make sense, considering that I'd heard she had a young teenage daughter with whom Mick would be living, once he moved out of my sister's house and into hers. That fact conjured up all kinds of disturbing possibilities, knowing my brother-in-law as well as I did. Yuck!

Jake had been hanging around with Mick a lot lately. Jake had gotten his old material handler job back at the factory when he was released from the service, and Mick still worked there as one of the painters. They frequently bumped into each other while at work, and with the problems between

Claudette and Mick, Mick needed a shoulder to cry on and he had chosen Jake's.

Surprisingly, Jake had responded to Mick's cry for solace with sympathy and friendship. Considering Mick's affinity for not keeping his prick in his pants around me, Jake's wife, Jake's response had been a source of constant puzzlement to me. I had figured that Mick appealed to Jake on a man's man basis and that he viewed Mick like an old friend, even family. Jake was turning a blind eye to the "flashing", rationalizing it away as the action of a good guy who'd had too much to drink. But also, I'd thought that there was one underlying, captivating reason why Jake continued weekly jaunts to the bar with Mick. Way down deep Jake was afraid of him, the same as I was. We both had sensed that Mick was on the edge and have treaded lightly around him ever since that night.

Remembering back to that night, Mick had wanted Jake to go out drinking, and Jake had told him no, which evidently was not what Mick had wanted to hear. Thirty short minutes later, as Jake and I lay on our bed half asleep, Mick began to knock on our chained and locked front door, loudly calling our names.

"Be quiet!" Jake whispered. "I don't want him to know that we're here because..."

Whatever Jake's reason had been not to answer the door, I never did hear it. A loud "Boom" along with an ear splitting crack stopped him in midsentence, and catapulted us out of our bed and into the bedroom doorway, which opened to our tiny living room within full view of the front door. What we saw was shocking and fascinating at the same time. Mick stood in the naked apartment doorway, a silhouette against the glaring hallway light behind him. I could hear his rapid breathing and see the tremor of his body as he stared down at the remnants of my front door, which now lay in the middle of my living room rug. Ironically, the security chain on the door had held, but in doing so when the door went crashing in, the chain took the door jam and part of the doorframe with it. Everything lay in a splintered heap in the middle of the room, particles of wood dust still floating through the air.

"Why didn't you guys answer me?" Mick loudly whined as he started to rock from side to side, clenching and unclenching his fists. Dumbfounded, neither of us answered.

"You should've answered!" He shouted, looking up from the damage that he'd caused, right into Jake's awestruck face.

"It's all, your fault! I just wanted to talk." He started to whine again like a guilty child, his agitation growing.

Jake finally snapped out of his flabbergasted trance and spoke quickly and gently to Mick, treating the incident lightly as if Mick had just accidentally knocked over a bottle of beer while sitting next to Jake at the bar.

"Hey guy, it's OK. Don't worry about it. We can take care of the whole thing in a jiffy. Should've answered the door, but you know how it is when you're in the sack with your old lady and all." And Jake laughed in a man-to-man sort of way, walking carefully over to Mick as his swaying became more pronounced. Both of us knew that Mick was really wasted. Jake cautiously took hold of Mick's arm and led him over to the couch where he sat him down on the cushions.

"Just needed to talk to you guys." Mick babbled while Jake returned to the fallen door, hoisted it up and rested it gently in what was left of the doorframe, partially covering the gaping hole. Apprehensive of what Mick's next move might be, Jake and I sat down together on the large over stuffed chair opposite the couch, and all three of us entered the "twilight zone". Mick made small talk about his job and asked about Jake's. He casually chatted about people at work and the neighbor-hood bar, their lives and family problems. After about an hour, Mick abruptly got to his feet.

"Well, I'd better get goin'. See ya' at work on Monday." He said. Jake hopped up and gingerly moved the broken door to the side. Mick exited and Jake laid the wooden door back in front of the opening where it would stay until Jake could start hammering on it in the morning.

Since that night, I'd never felt safe in the apartment and the incident was one of the main reasons that we'd decided to move. I knew that locks were for everyday people who wanted to obey the rules and there were a whole bunch of loonies out there who didn't. We had five months left on our lease and the landlord hadn't wanted to let us out of the contract, but once I'd fallen on his loosely carpeted step, he couldn't have been more cooperative.

Jake had never refused to go out with Mick after that. As a matter of fact, that was where Jake had been last night, out with Mick. God damn him!

My anger had started me trembling, and fear quickly followed. I'd hoped that Jake would be coming home in better shape than he had the night that someone had kicked the crap out of his head, with a steel-toed cowboy boot, in a bar fight a couple of months ago. It had been during the time that we'd lived with my father and Gladys, just after Jake had gotten out of the service and a short time before we'd moved in here. He had wound up having to go to the hospital to get his eyebrow sewn back together so that the muscle that lifted his eyelid wouldn't remain severed causing his eyelid to permanently droop. I had to coax his father to come over at 4 o'clock in the morning, to help persuade Jake to take a ride to the emergency room. That was something Jake had been vehemently opposed to doing, in his still drunken state. But it was necessary, so that Jake wouldn't wind up looking like "One-eyed Pete" for the rest of his life.

"Ooosan...Op'n uhhp..." The words almost indiscernible, floated through the flimsy wooden front door into the kitchen. Startled by the unearthly sounding voice that had interrupted my thoughts, I sat completely still, all my attention riveted in the direction of the front room, alert and listening for whatever would come next. I heard heart wrenching sobs and a voice that was vaguely familiar calling to me again.

"Lee..sss...Op'n uhhp!" I barely made it out. It sounded like the low heart sick wail of an animal in pain.

Oh my God, it was Jake! Heart pounding, I rushed to the door, unhooked the chain and swung the door open wide. His face was bloated and unrecognizable, and he was so unsteady on his feet that he fell toward me as the door flew open. I partially supported his weight with my shoulder and I guided him while he limped to the overstuffed chair that we'd both sat in while we had listened to my scary brother-in-law, a few weeks before.

"What happened baby?" I asked rubbing his back and taking a close look at his swollen lips, cheeks, and eyes, which were covered with wetness, that upon hearing the next sob, I knew was tears. The area around his eyes was so swollen that the openings were reduced to slits, and the rest of his face and lips were double their normal size. I pulled him to me as if he were an injured child. Holding him and listening to his heart-wrenching sobs caused a lump to form in my throat.

"Should I call an ambulance?" I asked, hugging him and becoming alarmed for his safety, not knowing what had happened to cause him to be in this state.

"Uh-uh." He shook his head "no". "They Maced me! And it hurts like hell!" His swollen lips could hardly move and his words sounded more like "Ey aced e an if hurs ike ell".

"Maced you? Who did?"

"Hu olice." He said.

"The police?" I said and he shook his head in affirmation.

"But why?" I asked.

"Dunno." He mumbled.

"What do you mean, you don't know? The police don't just stop people and Mace them for nothing! Where's the car?" I said with my tone demanding an immediate answer. He hesitated for a moment and I could tell that he was having a hard time remembering.

"Ou fron." Thank God! We'd taken delivery of the brand new yellow and black 1970 Dodge Super Bee just a few short months ago, and all the money that we had when we got out of the service was tied up in it.

"Did you drive home like this?" I asked.

"Uh-uh. M…mick, he gah m…mee out." He said taking his time and trying to make his lips form the words so that he pronounced them more clearly, painfully wincing as he went.

"Got you out? Do you mean that he bailed you out of jail?" I asked, the tone of my voice becoming a shrill squeak by the time that I got to the word "jail". I was starting to panic. We couldn't afford to go through this kind of crap!

"I 'ot uh EeUI!"

"A DUI! Jesus Christ Jake! How could you do that? How did it happen? How did the car get parked out front? Where did they pull you over?" Confused and upset I was screaming at him an inch away from his red grossly puffed face. Another sob escaped his throat.

"Ou fron. Orgot to hutt ih' off. Fff…uckers 'ulled m…mee ou'! eeat m…mee an' 'aced m…mee un uhh f…face!" He shuttered as he finished his long painful attempt to tell me what had happened.

"They pulled you out of the car when you were parked in front of the building, then they beat you up and Maced you?" I was outraged! He shook his head "yes" to my questions but on second thought, as I looked at him it occurred to me that his story didn't entirely ring true.

"You mean that the cops Maced you for NO reason? You weren't resisting arrest or anything like that. I mean, you weren't fighting them off? Giving them a hard time?"

"Uh-uh." He shook his head "no" but I was remembering the way that he'd acted at the carnival in Germany, and how he'd said that he'd been just minding his own business when someone with steel-toed boots had kicked the shit out of him at that bar, and now this.

Moaning, he attempted to readjust his upper body and his legs, in order to get better situated in the chair so that he could curl up and sleep. He settled in and almost instantly drifted off, the air whistling through his partially open mouth. God, he smelled!

I was surprisingly calm, now that everything was over and he'd passed out. I'd get more details from him after he'd slept it off. Jesus! A DUI! What would we do if he couldn't get out of it? Where would we get the money for a lawyer? And I didn't drive! How would he get to work?

The ringing of the alarm of the Big Ben clock on the nightstand beside our bed in the next room, drilled through the stillness. I could hear Eric starting to fuss in the other bedroom.

"5:45" I noted, speaking out loud and shifting my mind from the worry that had begun to grow. "It's not too late to call in for him. Tell them that he's got the flu." My spirits raised a little as my thoughts took on a sardonic twist. "Look on the bright side Susan, we'll be out a day's pay, but at least he won't get fired!"

❧ XXXIV ❧

"Jake, let go!" He had a vise grip on my wrist and was pulling me down the hallway outside of our apartment. I was pulling back as hard as I could. My feet were planted firmly on the carpeted floor but the soles of my shoes were losing their traction and sliding over the nylon nubs of the rug under my feet. He kept pulling hard. His clothes were soaking wet, and as we struggled, a few drops of water spattered from his shirtsleeve onto the back of my hand.

"Jake, please let go!" I pleaded, twisting my wrist to try to break his hold on me, and sobbing close to hysteria.

"You gotta' fucking come with me!" He spoke loudly, unconcerned that it was 3 o'clock in the morning.

"They can't fucking find out I was driving! I'll go to fucking jail! The fucking Volkswagen still runs, so you can drive it back to my ma's house and hide it in her fucking garage, and then we can go back and find the windshield. You gotta' fucking help me find the fucking windshield so that they can't trace it back to me! My fucking vehicle sticker is still on it! What the fuck's wrong with you? Stop being a stupid bitch and come on!"

He'd stopped at some shithole bar on the way home from work and now he was drunk, desperate, and crazy! What I'd surmised from the bits and pieces of information that he'd blurted out at me since he'd burst into the apartment about ten minutes ago, was that he'd lost control of the Volkswagen on a fairly isolated stretch of Archer Avenue. He'd spun out, hitting a telephone pole, smashing the driver's side of our car which had collapsed like an accordion when the pole had hit the driver's door. Jake had gotten a large bump and gash on the side of his head as his upper body had flown partially through the open car window and into the wooden telephone pole on impact. The windshield had popped out during the crash, like a cork out of a bottle of champagne, and flew, God knows where, onto the side of the road. Jake dazed, drunk, and frantic not to be caught, had somehow maneuvered the barely drivable car away from the telephone pole, and sped away from the scene of the accident like a bat out of hell. Somewhere between there and here, it must have registered in his alcohol sodden brain, probably when he became aware of the rain pelting him in the face, that the windshield was gone and what the implications of that meant.

Jake was right. He was in big trouble if the cops found out that he was driving when he wasn't supposed to. A lot had happened over the last two and a half months. On the advice of the public defender, Jake had pleaded guilty to the DUI in exchange for the court dropping the additional resisting arrest charge. His driving privileges were revoked and he had wound up with a six month restricted driver's license, which was only good for driving to and from work. Any additional driving on Jake's part was strictly prohibited. I'd gotten my own license out of shear necessity. An accomplishment that I had found to be far less difficult than I'd imagined it to be, during all those years that I fearfully went without one. The sight of my big pregnant belly probably helped to soften up the driving examiner a little bit too. Whatever, I had done it!

We'd lost the Super Bee because of the whole thing, and also lost most of the money that we'd originally put down when we'd bought it. With the small amount of money that we had left after the sale, plus whatever else we could scrape up, we had bought a tiny tan hatchback Volkswagen. The car had a "stick shift", manual transmission, and surprisingly, I developed a knack for driving it with very little effort.

But there was no way that I was going to get my pregnant body behind the wheel of the smashed Volkswagen and drive it in the rain! There also was no way that after hiding the car, I was going to return with him to the scene of the accident and search the side of the road, in the dark, in the pouring rain, for his lousy windshield! I was almost seven months pregnant and I didn't think that my obstetrician would approve of this kind of nocturnal exercise.

"Jake, it's pouring out! There's no windshield. I won't be able to drive with the rain pelting me in the face. Don't you understand that?" I pleaded with him as I continued to try to twist my wrist free of his grasp and he continued to yank me down the hallway. My feet kept slipping on the carpet and he was gaining ground in his attempt to get me to the fire door, and the exit that led to the steps and eventually the parking lot.

"Shut the fuck up!" He roared and tugged even harder, enraged, by what he considered to be my insolent behavior. My hand and wrist were starting to get numb from the loss of circulation in them, and my upper arm felt as if he was pulling it out of my shoulder socket. I didn't care! He was not getting me into that car! I pulled back hard.

Slowly, as I pulled, his grip began to loosen. In the struggle his hand had begun to sweat and the perspiration had provided just enough lubricant to cause his hand to slip on my skin. With one quick jerk, I was free!

I had a difficult time keeping my balance, tripping over my own feet, as released from my tug of war, I flew backwards. Somehow I remained upright.

"Leave her be!" I heard as I struggled to keep my balance. The door of the apartment across the hall from ours was open and Rod stood there glaring at Jake with an "I mean business" look on his face. At six feet two inches tall, Rod was intimidating. He was over half a foot taller than Jake and outweighed him by about sixty pounds. He was all muscle over a large thick frame. Rod and his wife Betty had invited us over a few times since we had moved into the new Hickory Hills apartment, and I coffee-clutched with Betty almost everyday. After this, I thought, there was a good probability that they wouldn't be inviting us over anymore.

Jake and I were standing a few feet apart and he, ignoring Rod, made a move towards me, getting ready to take hold of my arm again.

"I said, leave her alone!" Rod commanded.

"She's my fucking wife and she's coming with me!" Jake said leaning closer to me without taking a step forward.

"She doesn't want to go with you! And I won't let you take her!" With that Rod took a menacing step into the hallway and towards Jake, putting Jake within Rod's expansive reach. Daunted by Rod's advance, Jake involuntarily moved back as Rod had moved forward, keeping what Jake thought was a safe distance between them.

"Susan! Get the fuck over here!" Jake ordered pointing to the ground next to him, his eyes burning with rage. They met mine sending the unspoken message, "You're really gonna' get yours for this!" I averted my eyes from his and stared at the brown tweed carpet under my feet. My heart pounded in my chest, my hands began to shake as bone chilling fear set into every part of my body.

"No." I whispered, slowly moving my head from side to side, still keeping my eyes on the carpet and its intricate design. The shaking of my hands progressed to full body tremors that were becoming increasingly difficult to hide. I continued to stare at the carpet in front of me, too terrified to look up and meet his eyes and see the venomous expression of hate and belief of betrayal that I was sure was in them.

"You heard the lady." Rod's voice rumbled ominously.

I could hear Jake snort in exasperation and rage.

"Fuck ya' then!" Jake bellowed. I heard the hard rubber soles of his shoes make a tiny squeak on the hallway rug as he abruptly turned and marched in the direction of the black metal fire door. The violent banging of the door as he belligerently pushed his way through it and then let it slam shut behind him, signified the end of this latest horrifying episode. And then it was silent. Now that the eminent danger was over, I became aware of my growing embarrassment. My body still trembled and my eyes continued to be riveted to the rug, reluctant to face Rod.

"Would you like to stay in our spare room?" Betty's comforting voice came from the direction of their apartment, breaking the silence. I shifted my eyes and my attention to the face of a friend. I burst into tears and she came to me, wrapping her arms around me. She held me while I cried, and after a minute or two, she led me into their apartment with Rod shutting and locking the door behind us.

"I won't take 'no' for an answer. You'll stay for the night. No use pushing your luck, just incase he comes back sooner than you think. You can settle things with him in the morning, OK? I really don't think that it would be safe for you in your apartment right now. By the way, where's the baby?"

Oh my God! I had forgotten about Eric who had been sleeping in his crib when Jake had pulled me, half asleep, off the couch and out into the hallway. Horrified at the implication of what could have happened, I frantically ran to the door, unlocked it and ran across the hall to my apartment. Thank God, that in the midst of the insanity the front door had not been locked! I rushed into Eric's room and found him sleeping peacefully. Betty was right behind me. I quickly scooped up the sleeping child in my arms and without a word Betty picked up his blanket. The two of us rushed out of my apartment, passed Rod who looked as if he was keeping guard in the hallway, and fled into Betty's front door with Rod close behind.

We all stood in their living room breathing heavy, a look of relief on our faces. Rod hadn't said a word since his altercation with Jake in the hallway, and I was grateful for that. Standing there, I began to tremble while I held Eric in my arms. Betty rubbed my back and gently directed me through her kitchenette towards her guest bedroom. She gave my arm a little squeeze when we reached the bedroom door.

"You'll be safe here for tonight. Rod won't let him in if he comes back." She said. Then she whispered, "Don't worry it will be alright." and with a reassuring smile, she turned and closed the door behind her.

I laid the baby down on the double bed and tucked him in. I sat down next to him and quietly watched his tiny chest rise and fall with each peaceful breath. I couldn't believe that he'd remained asleep through it all! How lucky! A pang of guilt tore through me. How could I have forgotten him? He was my baby. All I could feel was blind fear when I woke up as Jake had dragged me off my front room couch. The only thought in my head had been to get away from him!

It was early October and in the last two months since we had moved here, we had done a lot of socializing. There were many young couples in the complex, and with renting the apartment in August it had been easy to meet our neighbors as they sat outside in the warm summer evenings. This was truly a young married couples' paradise. There were lots of friends, lots of get-togethers and lots of booze.

Recently, I'd begun to notice that Jake was getting argumentative again when he drank, and sometimes, borderline belligerent, a nasty habit that had resurfaced. When he was sober and we'd be arguing he would menacingly move towards me, and when I was within his reach, he would roughly poke my shoulder or arm to emphasize his point, whatever it was at the time. I hadn't seen that behavior in a long time, since before the window episode. It was disturbing to see it reappear, and with its return also came that "What is Jake really capable of?" feeling again. I hated when he drank! But now my anger was being outweighed by my fear. Would he come after me again? It had been almost two years since he'd tried to push me out of the second story bathroom window. I'd thought that nothing like that would ever happen again. Had I been wrong? Would he try to hurt me if he got angry enough?

Jake had a "unique talent", one that I'd never come across before. When other people passed out from too much booze, Jake would get a second wind, or worse, would resurrect after a few minutes in a drunken stupor, as a stranger behind vacant eyes. It was that stranger who had choked me in Virginia, and in Germany, had chased me down the street the night of the Carnival, and several months later had tried to push me out of our apartment's second story bathroom window, onto the courtyard below. I hadn't seen "Mr. Hyde" pop out from behind Jake's vacant stare since that chilly afternoon when I came close to being a bloody mess on the concrete under my bathroom window, but tonight had gotten close.

But then again, tonight was different, I supposed. He'd been drunk and very upset, and in his view I was refusing to do what he was frantic to have me do. I was uncooperative and disloyal. He needed me to help him out of a desperate situation, and I'd refused. The violence wasn't aimed at me, just because I was me, it was because I wasn't going along with the plan. I imagined that much from what I supposed would be his drunken point of view.

But then again, all of the other violent episodes were a direct result of me not doing what Jake's "Mr. Hyde" had thought I should do. The only difference was that tonight when I looked into Jake's eyes he was there, and he was very, very, pissed. That terrified me. I hoped that he wouldn't come home until all the booze had worn off. If he kept drinking, the "zombie" Jake, the one whose eyes said that "Jake didn't live here anymore", would come back and bang on the door, screaming and trying to get in!

"Stop it! Stop thinking like that!" I said to myself. I pulled the covers over me, trying to stop the tremors so that I wouldn't wake up Eric. I was so cold! I just couldn't get warm. I didn't have to worry about him getting in and coming after me. Rod wouldn't let him. I knew that.

I looked at my sleeping child, and thought that it could be so perfect for the three of us, if only Jake didn't drink so much. "What was wrong with him anyhow?" I whispered to myself as a longing for the way things could be caused tears to silently flow down my cheeks. "Why?" I murmured as I softly stroked Eric's soft baby fine hair. Then feeling the new baby stir inside of me, I was reminded that pretty soon it would be the four of us, and more tears flowed.

"I could leave him." I thought. Starting to turn the possibility over in my mind, I imagined how upset he would get if I did that. Aside from the occasional coffee clutch with a few of the women in the apartment complex, and my weekly trips to the grocery store, I never went anyplace without Jake. He didn't like me being involved with anybody or anything that he didn't approve of. He was still extremely jealous, so much so, that seeing my sister, Claudette, twice in a week could cause days of arguing between us.

"If I left him, he would start drinking and then …" And then what? I remembered him laughing with several of his friends at a small get together shortly after his DUI, as he recited a parody of one of those new popular cartoons in the paper. He'd heard it at work and was repeating it for everyone to get a laugh.

"Love is: setting the one you love free like a butterfly, and if they don't come back, hunting them down and killing them!" He'd recited the saying with a smile. But as he'd said it, we'd locked eyes, and I knew, that would be just what he would do. Even though he was laughing out loud with everyone else, he was privately sending me a message. One that I fully understood, and considering, Jake's unique "ability" to turn into "Mr. Hyde", I believed. He would never let me leave him. He would hunt me down. He would find me, and then…?

My body shook with fear of the unknown. A memory, like a movie clip, of "zombie" Jake looming over me, a chair held high above his head and preparing to bash my brains in, as I lay on my kitchen floor in Germany, played in my imagination. I saw myself screaming at him as I stared into his deep dark blank eyes, "Jake, it's me!"

"…hunting them down, and killing them!" Jake's words repeated in my head. Well, whatever it would be, I knew it would not be good. I was certain of that! I wasn't going anywhere!

I had to get a hold of myself! If I kept carrying on like this, I'd wake the baby and that would be a mess. I needed to get some rest! I was safe for now. I could take care of whatever had to be taken care of in the morning.

Sniffling the sobs back, I forced myself to relax, stretching my legs from their cramped curled up position, out towards the end of the bed. The shaking began to subside.

That was better. God, I was exhausted! Then the baby inside of me abruptly did a little jig and when he was done landed on my bladder.

"Oh, shit. Pee time!" Now that I'd just gotten comfortable, I'd have to get up. And then I remembered the roaches. I remembered them because the thought of trudging into Betty's bathroom to relieve myself, conjured up the story that she'd told me last week about how nasty it felt crushing a few of them beneath her bare feet as she had rushed into her bathroom for an emergency pit-stop, in the middle of the night, in the dark.

The apartment building that we were in had fifteen apartments and all of them had roaches. The bug exterminators were sent out to our building, by the corporation that owned it, whenever the complaints became more than just a nuisance. The only problem was that the guys who came would limit their insecticide spraying to those tenants' apartments who had complained the most. This selective spraying caused a cockroach exodus to all the apartments that had not been sprayed, and in turn, yielded more complaints, and then of course, more selective spraying. It was a virtual ring-around-the-rosy for the building's bug population, which I believed, suffered very few casualties in the process.

I'd noticed my first roach when Jake and I were moving into the vacant apartment. It'd run across my kitchenette counter top, and when pursued flew across the linoleum floor onto my front room carpet! Because the bug had been light brown, unlike the big black roaches that were residents of my Virginia flat, and because it flew, also unlike my Virginian friends, I came to the totally incorrect conclusion that it was not an infamous cockroach, but some kind of benign brown beetle that had gotten in from the outside. I desperately had wanted to believe this self-told lie, because I loved the apartment, it's location in the complex, and we had just signed a one-year lease. I really hated making any kind of trouble.

Once moved in, it had become apparent that my benign brown beetles were nasty, disgusting cockroaches, and that the apartment was crawling with them. I remembered how embarrassed I'd been the first time that Daddy and Gladys had been over to visit and, while sitting on my living room couch, a big fat roach crawled up the front room wall directly behind Gladys's head! With a casual air, I'd gotten up and snatched the bug off the wall with one smooth swoop of my hand, using some lame excuse that a dust bunny had been floating up along the wall and I didn't want it to land in Gladys's neatly styled hair.

The memory of the startled look on my stepmother's face still made me giggle as I lay beside Eric in Betty's guest bedroom. Bug stories were always good for a laugh.

The baby gave me another good kick in my bladder. Well, bugs or not, I had to go or I'd make a mess of Betty's guest bed.

Sometime later, as I lay in the dark, I drifted off to sleep, finally believing that I was safe from him, at least for the rest of the night.

❧ XXXV ❧

Cauliflower. I loved it and so did Jake. I unwrapped the colored plastic, from around the large fresh head, exposing the snow-white florets and light green leaves, beneath it. It sounded silly to say it, but the sharply contrasting colors were beautiful. Jake wouldn't be home from work for an hour or so, and I was just beginning to get supper going.

It had cost us close to eight hundred dollars to straighten out the Volkswagen. The unibody design was expensive as hell to fix but it was cheaper than getting a new car, something that we couldn't afford. Jake's parents had actually coughed up most of the money to help us out, which had been really nice of them, and my dad had helped Jake find the broken windshield. The two of them had found it late the next morning after the accident, about seventy-five feet from the side of the road in some long prairie grass, evidence of the force of the impact. The cops never did find out.

Neither did either set of parents, that is, find out just how drunk and mean Jake had been that night. After leaving me in the apartment complex hallway, Jake had gotten into the car and drove it, sticking to the back streets all the way to his mom and dad's house. In the hour that it'd taken him to get there, with sheets of rain coming through the hole where the windshield had been, he had sobered up. As far as my dad was concerned, all he knew was the same story that had been told to

Jake's parents. Which was that it had been raining cats and dogs and Jake, working overtime like the good husband and provider that he was, had been forced by circumstance to drive home late at night after his driver's license curfew, and had been unlucky enough to hydroplane into a telephone pole. This small lie didn't bother me very much, considering the repercussions if everyone had found out the truth.

My dad would never forgive Jake if he knew about how drunk Jake had been when he'd hit the pole, and how mean and nasty he was when he'd come home in order to force me to do his dirty work. The truth just couldn't be told. I knew that. And I also knew that when Jake grew out of this phase he was in, it was important that by his immature actions, he hadn't caused a rift too wide to cross over between him and either side of the family.

Shifting my attention back to the cauliflower and dinner, I decided that it would be better if I kept my meals light. I wasn't hungry much anyway. I'd been experiencing cramping on and off, all day long and the pain had dampened my appetite. It had stopped for now. The doctor had dismissed it as nothing, when I'd called him this afternoon. There were seven weeks left until my due date, and even though I had lots of trouble with this pregnancy, he hadn't seemed very concerned. As a matter of fact, he'd been extremely irritated. Evidently he'd been on the golf course when he'd gotten the page for my phone call. I could tell that he'd thought that I was making a big something out of nothing. Maybe he was right, but they sure as hell had felt like mild labor pains to me. So, better to be safe than sorry, as far as the food was concerned. Labor is bad enough without throwing up all the way through it because you'd stuffed yourself just before it began.

I rolled over the large plump head of cauliflower in my hands, placed it on my wooden cutting board, and picking up a sharp butcher knife, poked the tip of the knife through the green succulent leaves to the base of the cauliflower and sliced through the large thick light green stem. The leaves and stem fell away from the snow-white bunch of cauliflower florets, all in one piece. Without thinking, I picked up the large white ball and began to examine it from the bottom, carefully inspecting each shaft in the network of stems, which led to the umbrella top of each floret. This action was an old habit still left over from my two years of Army life in Germany.

A slow warm smile worked its way up to the corners of my mouth, while I remembered the reason for the careful inspection. It was really pretty funny when you thought about it. Especially, when Jake had given me so much grief during our stay in "Der Fatherland". Even though it was a small thing, in some ways, one could say that what goes around comes around. My warm smile percolated into a few low rumbles of an exquisitely satisfying laugh as my mind replayed it all.

I'd been standing in the tiny kitchen in our apartment in Nuremberg, and had just finished fishing out six or seven large cooked cauliflower florets from a pot of boiling water, which was sitting on the top of my tiny stove. Putting them into a large bowl, I'd handed them to Jake. The rest of Jake's supper had already been served to him and he'd been anxiously waiting for his favorite dish of vegetables, hot buttered cauliflower. The instant that the bowl had reached his hands, he'd plucked a large floret from it. Then opening his mouth as wide as he could, he'd stuffed the whole umbrella top of the cauliflower into his mouth, chomped on it a few times, pushed the remainder of the stem from between his fingers, into his mouth, chomped a few times more, and swallowed. I stared at him in astonishment.

"Christ Jake! Could you fit anymore in your mouth without choking yourself?" I said.

"Fuck you, I love this shit! It's one of my fucking favorites!" He'd laughed like a little kid and I laughed with him, tickled that I'd made him so happy over such a little thing. Then staring into my eyes in defiance, he'd plucked another floret out of his bowl, popped it into his mouth in the same fashion as before, chewed, made a little "Mmm…" sound as he did so, swallowed it and rubbed his tummy.

"You're such a pig." I light-heartedly teased.

Smiling and turning my attention to the few remaining cauliflower pieces floating in the steaming water, I chose a floret, retrieved it with my fork, and placed it in my bowl. I'd been about to retrieve another when I'd notice a small irregular bump half way up the main stem of the piece of cauliflower in my bowl. It looked odd so I brought the bowl a bit closer and rolled the piece over so that I could see the bump more clearly.

I'd stared, scrutinizing the long thin white bump, trying to figure out what it could be. I could hear Jake's humming chewing sounds in the background as I'd poked at the misshapen cauliflower stem. The bump was the same color as the cauliflower but as I'd poked and prodded the thing with my fork I'd noticed that it was closely attached to the stem in several evenly spaced places. My eyes examined the irregularity from the bottom to the top, about three-quarters of an inch, and stopped at two round pinkish pinhead spots at its tip.

"Oh my God!" I said in a barely audible whisper of shock.

"What'd you say?" Jake casually asked after he swallowed the mashed vegetable in his mouth.

My eyes went to his hand and then to his bowl. Both were empty.

"Uh… nothing. Just talking to myself again." I said, after quickly reasoning that he'd long passed the point of no return.

He snorted down a mocking laugh that communicated an affirmation of how truly stupid he thought I was, and now that the cauliflower was gone, began to concentrate on finishing up the half eaten pork chop on his plate.

Quickly, I looked at the other two pieces of cauliflower in the murky water, from which the piece in my bowl, and Jake's, had come from. There was a hope that what I'd discovered was the exception, not the rule. But no such luck, at least, not for Jake. There in the pot were the last two pieces of cauliflower slowly spinning in warm water, their misshapen stems very obvious now that I knew what to look for. I reexamined the cauliflower floret in my bowl and it was full of them. On every stem under the umbrella of white vegetable, where one could fit, there was one, nestled in the available space. I also noted in horrified fascination, that what I'd thought were light green leaves here and there on some of the floret stems were actually light green ones.

I'd looked over at Jake. He sucked down the rest of his bottle of German beer, put his hand to his chest and silently squeezed out a burp. My eyes followed him as he got up and got another bottle from the tiny German refrigerator, and he met my gaze with his intimidating, "So what's your fucking problem?" expression.

"Maybe inch long, white and light green, bald, plump caterpillars were good for you." I'd silently mused as I stared back at him, and mentally calculated how many caterpillars he'd probably scarfed down.

Jake never did find out about the extra protein that he'd gotten at that meal. I'd found out later from my German neighbor that European farmers didn't use insecticide as liberally as we did in the States, so when buying any leafy vegetable, you had to soak the head first in salt water to kill the little varmints that lived in it. When they were dead they would float to the top of the water and you could scoop them out. If you cooked the vegetable first, like I'd done, the little buggers clutched onto their last meal in a death grip that made it impossible to remove them. When I'd shared my little story about Jake and the cauliflower florets with her, despite the language barrier, she'd gotten the drift, and we'd both laughed until we cried.

We'd both had a good laugh at Jake's expense, and now, three years later, I was still laughing.

❧ XXXVI ❧

"That bastard hung up on me!" I couldn't believe it!

"What am I going to do now?" It was in the middle of the night, about 12:30, and Jake was asleep in our bedroom. Thank God, Eric was a sound sleeper. I didn't think that I would be able to take care of him if he woke up fussing. The pains were getting bad.

What was wrong with that doctor anyway? Couldn't he tell that I was really in labor? He seemed extremely annoyed with me when I'd called him, but the pain was getting so bad that I couldn't put the phone call off any longer. I'd called two other times today, once in the morning but the pains had stopped, and once in the early evening after supper, when they had started up again. Both times he'd told me that I wasn't in labor. I was seven weeks from my due date, and he'd said that the pain was probably from my ligaments stretching. Like after already having had one baby, I didn't know the difference! He must of thought I was stupid or worse yet, a hypochondriac.

In this last phone conversation, when I'd argued with him and insisted that I was in labor, he'd snidely asked me if I was standing up while I was talking to him. When I'd said yes, he'd spat out into the phone "If you were really in labor you wouldn't be able to stand up!" And he'd hung up!

My anger and righteous indignation evaporated as the next pain slammed into me and I went down on the ground. I pulled my knees to my chest and rode the pain out on the linoleum floor, until it eased up allowing me to uncurl myself, and crawl over to my front room couch. My fear grew as the pain lessened. What would I do if the pains didn't stop? The doctor was right about one thing; this was way too early for the baby to be born! I knew that, but I couldn't stop it! When the pain subsided, I got up and went to the bedroom.

"Jake! Get up!" I said into the darkness as I stood in the doorway. I heard him groan.

"What do you want?" He asked with an irritated sound in his voice. "I got to fucking go to work in the morning!"

"Something's wrong! I think you're going to have to take me to the hospital." I was beginning to panic.

"Did you call the fucking doctor?" He said with growing irritation.

"Yeah, and he said the same thing that he said before. He said that it was just false labor or something. But I know it's not! I think that I might need to go into the hospital, anyway." I said with fear and indecision, not knowing exactly what to do next.

"Listen!" Jake roared at me in the darkness. "If he said that you're fucking not in labor, you're fucking NOT in labor! I'm not taking you in, in the middle of the mother fucking night just so that they can send you home, and then have to turn fucking around and go straight to work with no fucking sleep! Shut the fuck up and GO TO SLEEP!"

And that was that as far as he was concerned. Conversation over! Dumbfounded, I walked back into the living room and sat on the couch. Could they be right? Could this be false labor? It'd been about ten minutes since the last pain, maybe they were right. Maybe it would stop. Suddenly, I felt immense pressure in my bowels.

Christ! Maybe I've got food poisoning or something!" I thought as I raced for the bathroom, an enormous cramp beginning to radiate down my legs. I stood in the bathroom frantically trying to pull my nightgown up and get my underwear down despite the all-encompassing pain. Suddenly, I felt warmth spread between my legs. One quick look and I knew it was blood. I was hemorrhaging!

"JAKE!" I screamed from the bathroom. I could hear his feet hitting the bedroom floor with force and rage. I was in too much pain to be afraid.

"WHAT THE FUCK DO YOU THINK..." His shouting died away as he made the turn around the wall between the bedroom and bathroom door. I'd stripped my underwear off and thrown them in the sink and was sitting down on the toilet seat. When he caught a glimpse of the blood, the color in his face drained and I thought I saw his body sway a bit.

"It's OK! It probably looks worse than it is. Blood always does." I was saying, more to assure and calm myself than to comfort him. "You should get dressed. Even if the flow isn't as bad as it looks, I think I have to go to the hospital."

Grateful for the excuse to leave the scene, Jake turned and walked away.

Ten minutes later, I had determined that the bleeding wasn't life threatening but the flow was such that the normal means for taking care of it wasn't enough. I'd also gotten two contractions during that time, which made me aware that my pains were now less than five minutes apart. In that same ten minutes, Jake had mentally gotten a second wind of unreality, and began to repeat a warning to me from the bedroom, over and over like a mantra, while he dressed.

"If this is a fucking false alarm, I'm gonna' be very, very fucking pissed!"

I ignored him.

"Get me a pair of underwear from my drawer!" I grunted, as the last contraction began to subside. I met him in the hallway, just outside of the bathroom door, nightgown hiked up to my hips and a bath towel between my legs.

"If this is a fucking false alarm, I'm gonna' be very, very fucking…!"

"Listen, Jake!" I cut him off. "My contractions are less than five minutes apart and I'm bleeding like a sieve. I need to go to the hospital! Wake up Betty and get her over here for Eric!" He just stood there, my underwear dangling from the fingertips of his outstretched hand, mouth hanging open as if he were in shock.

"NOW!" I shouted, as I hobbled down the short hallway and over to the couch in the living room, barely making it, plopping onto the cushions while another contraction took complete control of me. I must have grabbed the underpants from Jake on the way to the couch, because when the pain eased, I managed to pull them on over the bath towel, trying to keep it in place. I hardly noticed Betty, disheveled with a bathrobe wrapped around her standing in the kitchen talking to Jake, when I passed them both on my way out the door.

"GET MY COAT!" I yelled over my shoulder. "We have to make it to the car before the next one hits!" I had to get to the hospital and I had to get there now! And no one was going to stop me! We were only ten to fifteen minutes at most from the hospital, even if Jake called an ambulance, it wouldn't get me there any faster than that.

I shuffled down the hallway as fast as I could, turned and went down a short flight of steps, in order to go out the first exit door that I came to. By the time that I was to the outside door Jake had caught up with me, coat in hand. It was the end of October, but the weather had been unseasonably warm. He slipped the coat over my shoulders without worrying about having to bundle me up, as we went through the doorway.

Both of us became aware of the problem immediately. In my haste to take the shortest route to the parking lot where our car was parked, I'd forgotten that it included cutting across several small, grassy, rolling hills. The parking lot was several hundred feet away, but as far as I was concerned it might as well have been a mile.

I began to go down onto the concrete apron in front of the door. Another contraction had started again and it hit so quickly that I instantly crumpled up on the ground where I'd stood.

"Fuck!" Jake shouted. "What the fuck should I do? The car won't make it over the fucking grass. It'll get stuck!" And then again, for emphasis "Fuck!"

He was squatting beside me while I was curled into a ball, writhing in pain.

"Do you think that you could make it back up the fucking steps?" He asked.

"Uh-uh." I managed to grunt. Then the pain began to lessen.

"How about, the minute that you can get up, we go for it! We'll fucking see if we can make it to the car before the next one hits!"

I nodded in agreement. Considering the alternatives, we could give it a shot. In less than a minute I was on my feet with Jake holding my hand and pulling me along in a slow trot. The action of my legs pumping up and down while we climbed the small rolling hills, caused the contractions to come more quickly, and I went down in the grass three times before we were able to reach the car, despite Jake's efforts to keep me up and moving.

Once inside the Volkswagen, to my surprise, when I attempted to sit down in the front seat, I found out that I couldn't. It was too uncomfortable. I knelt in the seat facing the back of the car for the ten minutes it took us to speed to the hospital emergency entrance.

I'd picked up an old pillow from the back seat of our car and used it to chew on during our car ride. It'd helped me control my body's reaction to the constant contraction that I was experiencing. There was no longer a beginning or an end to the contractions, just constant waves of rolling pain. So when I entered the emergency entrance, pillow in hand and gnawing frantically on a corner, the orderly paid attention to me when I growled, "I CAN'T!" in response to his gesture for me to take a seat in his wheelchair.

I paced round and round in a tight circle, gnawing my pillow, pain fogging my mind, as the elevator took me up to maternity. I was only slightly aware that Jake was no longer with me. When the elevator doors opened, two orderlies picked me up, placed me on a gurney and wheeled me into an operating room.

While one nurse checked me, another nurse scolded me, "Why didn't you call your doctor? You know you're lucky that he just happens to be here working late!"

My reply, that I had indeed called my doctor, and that he'd hung up on me, was lost in the frantic shouts of the other nurse. "She's crowning! No time to prep her! Let's go!"

Immediately, my night gown was pulled off over my head, a sheet hastily thrown over my chest, and from what seemed like out of nowhere, a bucket of what I assumed to be antiseptic, was dumped on my now naked bottom. While my never ending contraction continued, the two nurses grabbed me and in one swift motion plopped me onto an ice-cold, metal table. I placed the heels of my feet in a small set of stirrups at the end of the table. And when my hands searched for the same type of grips that I'd used to pull on when it came time to push, during my first delivery in Germany, I found nothing. Instead, each of the nurses was tightly buckling some kind of wide leather sleeve to my upper arms. Attached to each sleeve was a length of thick stainless steel chain that was, in turn, attached to the sides of the delivery table.

"It's for your own safety, dearie, so you don't fall off the table." One of the nurses said to me, after she must have read my reaction to being trussed up like some lunatic in an insane asylum.

In the middle of all the havoc and pain, my doctor strolled into the delivery room in his hospital gown and mask. He examined me.

"Placenta previa!" He exclaimed to the others but not to me. "Let's deliver this baby!"

And then like a miracle, the pain stopped.

"Now…" the doctor said more to himself than me, as he turned and took his position standing between my legs. "When the next pain comes I don't want you to push! I am going to have to go inside and straighten things out." I had no idea what he was talking about but he didn't seem to care. As suddenly as the agony had stopped, it seized me again. In the middle of it all, I felt his hand push inside of me against the natural action of my body, causing my agony to intensify, a feat that I didn't imagine was possible.

His action caused an involuntary motion of my body, up the surface of the cold metal table, in an instinctive effort to flee from the searing pain. When my contraction subsided, he spoke to me with obvious disdain and irritation.

"If you're not going to cooperate, this will take a long time. Now, shinny back down that table and get ready for the next contraction!"

Like a terrified child, I obeyed. And in front of God and everyone, lying flat on my back, legs spread apart, naked except for a wisp of sheet resting across my chest, I worked my bottom back down the table several inches, before it was time to visit hell again. And so it went, over and over, for I don't know how long, until finally I heard a baby cry. It was a boy! Without even a look or touch from me, he was whisked away. Seven weeks early was a long time.

My doctor didn't come to visit until the third day of my hospital stay, the day that I was to go home without my baby. Despite being so early, the baby had been over five pounds. His lungs were strong, but they still had to keep him in an incubator. I hadn't been allowed to hold him yet, only the nurses got to do that. He had to be kept in a sterile environment when he wasn't inside the clear plastic enclosure. He was having trouble digesting formula, and tubes and wires were attached to him most of the time. His little body was thin like that of a baby bird's, instead of the fat plump healthy looking body of a full term baby, and his knees were always pulled up tightly to his chest as if he was still in the womb. Overall, we'd been lucky. He'd come out perfect with all his fingers and toes. He'd only had one tiny oddity. The cartilage at the top of one of his ears, that is normally curled, wasn't. It gave him a bit of an uneven look. When Jake, standing with me outside the nursery glass, had seen the baby for the first time, he'd stood staring silently, showing no sign of emotion. And then he broke the silence.

"We gotta' get him an ear job!" He'd said, and turned and walked away.

I'd dreaded my doctor's visit. I was embarrassed by how badly I'd handled things during the birth, and felt ashamed every time the thought of seeing him came to mind. So when he made his appearance on the morning I was to be released, I averted my eyes from his stare, concentrating on my hands that were folded in my lap during most of our conversation.

"Well, you know what my six hundred dollar fee has bought you, don't you?" He said with a strange uncomfortable laugh. "Five less minutes of pushing time, and a birth in a hospital, instead of the front seat of your car!"

And that was all he had to say.

❧ XXXVII ❧

December 31, 1972.

"New Years Eve." I read to myself while contemplating the small square on the calendar hanging on the inside of the open laundry room door.

"My favorite holiday of the whole year!" I thought to myself as a deeply painful sardonic groan escaped from between my lips. "Cheer up. At least there's a party tonight."

In anticipation of the upcoming festivities, the palms of my hands began to sweat. Why did people have to drink? Why couldn't they have a good time without getting drunk and disgusting? Because I didn't drink, and was therefore, the only person at a party that saw what everyone really looked like at the end of the night, the whole party thing was a fearful enigma to me.

In the past, since Jake thought that I was "no fun" when I didn't, I'd tried to drink, but it had never turned out very well. A smile slid across my face as I remembered the very first time that Jake had tried to teach me to do shots. He and I had just begun dating, and we were home alone, in my house. Despite my protests that downing a whiskey shot would make me puke, after a short set of instructions he'd pressured me into it. You should've seen the look on his face when my recently eaten salami sandwich, along with a shot of my father's whiskey, splattered all over my mother's kitchen table and my pretty pink angora sweater sleeve, the minute the alcohol had hit the back of my throat!

When we'd first moved into the Hickory Hills apartment, I'd tried to be "sociable", but HI C orange drink and vodka, the only drink combination that we could afford at the time, didn't set very well. After an evening of cards with Betty and Rod, and one too many "poor man" screwdrivers, I'd learned one very important fact, orange drink burns like hell on the way back up!

To be honest, ever since Virginia, even ingesting one drink made me feel like hurling. I guess it was from my anticipation of what might be coming next every time I looked into Jake's eyes when he stood with a drink in his hand. With all the problems that we had when he drank and got crazy, you would think that he would lose his taste for the stuff, too.

"Yeah, right." I said out loud. Even with all the bad memories he kept pounding them down. He drank booze like water. There was never enough.

It would be one year tomorrow, New Year's Day, since we'd moved into the house. It was a little three bedroom brick ranch that we'd gotten a great deal on. The couple that had owned it before us hadn't taken care of it. There had been two junk cars in the backyard, the grass had been weedy and unkempt, and the inside of the house had been filthy. Because of the condition of the place, the house had been on the market for a long time. By the time we'd taken a look at it, the price had been reduced enough to make the payments for its purchase within our meager budget. Jake's dad had generously given us a down payment, and together with that and Jake's VA mortgage benefit, we'd become first time homeowners.

I'd hoped that having our own home would've made things better but it hadn't worked out that way. Several "bad" episodes had happened over the last year fortifying the fear that I was experiencing as I tried to cope with Jake's drinking. The "good" days were the days when we stayed at home and the amount of beer that he sucked up was limited to about four or five cans a night. On the "good" days my fear was diminished but never completely gone. It lay just under the surface of my daily routine, waiting for some small situation to spark and ignite it into its full, white-hot fury.

Sometimes the "good" days would bring anger. Not his anger, but mine. Jake's ability to push my buttons had become fine tuned over the years. We didn't discuss "things" very often when he was sober, but when we did, the discussions became circular arguments that never seemed to end. Frustration would seethe inside of me after hours of going round and round with him, trying to get him to understand or concede a point about what his drinking was doing to us. The usual culmination of these exercises in futility was Jake falling asleep on the couch with me sobbing close to hysterics in a chair across the room. Repeatedly banging my fists against a bedroom wall to diffuse my frustration and rage after these "chats" had become a common occurrence, and always left me with the hopeless, helpless feeling that I was becoming someone who was a stranger to me.

The "bad" days varied in "badness" but not in the fear that they generated inside in me. Whether we were going on a ride to do some household errands with Jake drinking while he drove, and a six pack for the road in the back seat, or at a friend's party with Jake weaving as he stood with his eighth "whiskey and soda" in his hand, the fear was overwhelming. It was white and hot in my gut and made my hands shake. It made my mind scream, "What's going to happen next?" And sometimes it made me wonder with muscles rigid and aching, "Am I going to die tonight?" I guess you could say that "bad" days had introduced me to terror, and once terror has its way with you, you are helpless to keep it from coming back, again and again.

"Bad" days were survival mode days, when it was necessary to be always watchful and careful not to be the reason for the next time that you're slammed into the wall, with Jake's vacant eyes not registering the slightest flash of emotion as your body hit the plaster board. Sometimes "bad" days, slipped out of your control no matter how careful you were, and "bad" things would happen. Like the night that he'd drank fourteen "seven-sevens" at a wedding, and drove home with that vacant look in his eyes. He'd been non-responsive to my frantic pleas to slow down, as I cowered in the front seat and we wildly swerved around the curves of a desolate, tree lined, two-way forest preserve road. That terrifying ride ended in our driveway with me on my knees, hysterically kissing the asphalt and thanking God for my life.

Or the time that, while refusing to get in the car with him, after we'd stopped for a "few drinks" at a bar, I'd wound up being pulled by my hair into the passenger's side, as he sped away from the curb, with my legs hanging halfway out of the door. He drove like that, holding on to me by my hair, the door flapping wide open, and my feet within inches of the pavement for about a mile and then abruptly stopped, the tires screeching to a halt.

"Now get in!" He'd shouted. "And bitch, don't ever fucking try that again, or next time you won't be so fucking lucky!" I'd gotten the message loud and clear.

Being aware of how many drinks he had, by vigilantly counting every one, was a good indicator as to how bad "bad" was probably going to get. The counting always fooled me into believing that I had some control over the outcome, but I didn't. And it just made me crazy with fear as the numbers climbed. I knew this all too well, but the knowledge never stopped me from counting.

"New Year's Eve is always a 'bad' day." I thought as I wiped the sweat from the palms of my hands down the front of my jeans.

An excited squeal of delight caused me to jump. It snapped me back to reality. Warren ran around the corner from the bedroom into the kitchen, toy car in hand and Bacardi, our silver German shepherd, licking his face at every opportunity provided to her. We'd gotten her as a seven month old puppy from Animal Welfare about a year ago, only a few weeks after we had moved into the house. Our old dog, Honey, the one that we'd gotten on our honeymoon, had gone to live at my mom and dad's when Jake was drafted. They'd had two old dogs of their own. But once my mother had died and my dad remarried, the three dogs got to be too much for him. My step-mother,

Gladys, wasn't crazy about dogs to begin with, and once my dad's two older dogs died, she was anxious to get rid of Honey. Supposedly she went to a farm that was owned by one of Gladys's son's friends. We were in Germany when it happened so we didn't have anything to say about it. I supposed it was for the best.

Warren squealed again, as Eric rounded the corner behind him, chasing after the toy car in Warren's hand. Warren had turned two last October, and was having a good time teasing his three year old brother, Eric. I was amazed at how big the two of them had gotten, especially Warren. Those accomplishments that marked a baby's progress from infant to toddler, sitting up, crawling and walking, were achieved at least two months later than Eric had achieved them, a result of Warren being two months premature. He'd been a baby a long time, and now he'd finally arrived, a little boy in his "terrible twos". I smiled at both of them and rubbed their heads, as first Warren and then Eric ran into me and grabbed my legs.

"How about some lunch?" I said into their upturned faces. They laughed and clapped their hands as I hiked each one up into a booster chair and pushed them close to the table. The peanut butter and jelly sandwiches were on the counter top where I'd left them before I'd thrown a load of clothes into the dryer.

Watching the two of them, I thought of how good the neighborhood would be for them as they grew. There were a lot of children on the block. My next-door neighbors had two little boys, and Kathy and Tony, who lived in the house across the street, and were having the party tonight, had a five-year-old girl. I didn't know any of the neighbors very well yet, but tonight's party would help.

"Cheer up Susan." I thought. "It might not be as 'bad' as you think."

❧ XXXVIII ❧

"Christ! Where is he?" I wondered as I reentered the carpeted basement where the majority of the people who hadn't left to go home, were congregated. The party was at its tail end and had gone from bad to worse when someone had gotten the brilliant idea to play stag movies. Tony, who was three sheets to the wind, had obliged by pulling out a movie projector and displaying his private stash of porn films on a large, portable movie screen strategically placed on the other end of the basement so that he could get the picture as large as possible.

I really hated porn movies. The women in them looked like emaciated drug addicts and the guys looked like greasy creeps who always left their black socks on as they humped away. Jake, on the other hand loved them. He had always had a private collection of "Girly" magazines and stuff like that, and the only books that I ever saw him read were plain covered sex novels that he'd gotten from who knows where. The ceiling in his bedroom at his mother's house had been covered from end to end with a collage of nude centerfolds. Why his mother or father never insisted that he take them down was always incomprehensible to me. And despite my protests he now had the back wall of our garage partially covered with nude women in the same patchwork fashion, visible to anyone who might be standing in front of the garage when the overhead door was opened. It was embarrassing.

Scanning the small crowd of people for the back of Jake's head, I was surprised not to see his greasy D.A. amongst the voyeurs. Drunk or sober, I'd expected to see him glued to the screen. He'd been hitting the booze pretty heavy this evening. I'd lost count at around seven and supposed from previous experience at gala events like this, that the count was now well into the double digits. Inwardly I sighed. Maybe it wouldn't be too bad tonight. He'd seemed to still be in a pretty good mood the last time that I'd seen him, which had been about thirty minutes ago. Maybe he would just pass out when we got back home. And maybe not... My insides flipped and an involuntary shudder caused my body to tremble as if in an instant, an ice cold wind had sucked all of the warmth out of me.

"Where is he?" I mumbled with fearful agitation, and headed through the large basement room, towards the bathroom with images of Jake, passed out clinging to Kathy's toilet bowl, dancing in my head. Keeping close to the wall in order not to ruin anyone's view of the fine work of art on display, I came closer to the large movie screen. Absent-mindedly glancing at it and the metal frame and stand that held it up as I moved closer, noticing that the whole contraption wasn't pushed tightly up against the wall. A slight movement from beneath the screen caught my eye, which drew my attention to a dark blob of something in the almost indiscernible darkness below the bottom edge of the screen.

In the same instant that I realized that the blob was two sets of legs, the conviction hit me that one set of legs was Jake's! Before I could react to what that meant, a male voice shouting "Shit!" broke the movie theatre silence of the basement, followed by the clicking sound of broken movie film slapping against the metal reel of the projector. The bright basement lights flashed on, momentarily blinding everyone, and causing me to turn my eyes away from the harsh glare and the screen. In no more than a second or two, my attention went back to the screen and what might be behind it. Like a magic act, Jake and some bitch had popped out of nowhere and were awkwardly standing next to the movie screen, their clothes crumpled and hair disheveled. His body was swaying in a small, only slightly discernable circle, with that all too familiar vacant look on his face. She looked flushed, confused and uncertain of what was going on. She slowly began to move in the direction of the bathroom.

"Jake." I called over to him. "The movie's over. How about we go home?" I said with as much of a casual tone as I could muster under the circumstances. Now or later tonight was not the time to rake him over the coals for what I thought had just happened. It was smarter and safer not to make any waves tonight. Tomorrow morning would be soon enough.

"Uh…yeah…sure." He said and blindly began to walk in my direction. He avoided a collision with the couch at the last minute before stumbling into it, like a bat flying in the dark with his sonar. When he got close to me, he gave me one of his stares where he looked right through me, and my whole body reacted with an involuntary shudder.

"Be careful, Susan." I whispered and reached out, grabbing his hand and fighting back the impulse to turn and run.

"C'mon Jake, let's go. We have to get the sitter home. It's pretty late." I said with a warm smile, hoping he couldn't sense how frightened I was of him. When he was like this, once he got wind of my fear he was like a shark that smelled blood.

One very strong steady tug on his hand and he began to move along with me, through the basement, up the stairs and out Kathy's front door. No "goodbyes" were necessary. Kathy was among the missing for over an hour now. Too many Bloody Marys had finally taken their toll.

As we walked across the street, I held Jake's hand, gently tugging and leading him like a blind man in the direction of the house. I smiled and tried to make idle chatter about how nice the party had been and what great people Kathy and Tony had turned out to be. Jake made no reply. I talked about how beautiful the house looked with the Christmas lights from my dad hung on the outside, along the edge of the roof and around the big picture window facing the street. He'd become "zombie" Jake and my skin crawled. Outwardly I rattled on, but inwardly I begged the Universe, "Don't let anything happen tonight! Please…"

Reaching the house and hoping that the sitter had fallen asleep on the couch, I hesitated on the doorstep a moment then opened the door as slowly and quietly as possible so that Bacardi wouldn't start barking. It would be nice if the sitter didn't get a look at Eric and Warren's daddy in his present condition. Luckily she was out like a light on my sofa and the dog had not made a sound. Jake followed me into the house, passed the sleeping baby sitter, and into our bedroom. The dog was still lying quietly in the corner, next to the foot of the bed. She always seemed to instinctively know when it was better to stay out of the way.

"Why don't you lie down while I walk the baby sitter back across the street?" I said while letting go of his hand and gently maneuvering him towards the bed. He didn't say anything. He just sort of stood there staring blankly off into space. He must've drunk an awful lot because the muscles in his eyes had relaxed enough to make them appear as if they were pointing in two slightly different directions. That only happened when he was really wasted.

"Jake, I'm taking the sitter home. OK?" Still no answer. Well, I would just have to leave him there and get her home. Leaving him standing silently in the bedroom, I left the room and carefully closed the door behind me.

In less than ten minutes I woke up the sitter, helped her get her things together, and walked her across the street to her house. Luckily, Jake had behaved himself and stayed put in the bedroom. Jake and his antics when he was drunk and nasty, wasn't something that I'd wanted the neighbor's daughter to see. I'd begun to relax a little as I walked through the front door, and stood listening to the silence in the house. Looking around the front room I was warmed by all the Christmas decorations. We'd picked out the largest tree that we could find and it was breathtaking with all the twinkling lights and sparkling tinsel that we had lovingly placed on its branches. Christmas cards sent from friends and loved ones lined the doorways to the bedroom and bathroom door. I'd taped each one as they had come in the mail, after reading them to the boys. It was a tradition that my mother had performed every Christmas when I was growing up, and one that I gladly repeated because it made me feel close to her. Glittering golden garland was hung on the mirror and the dark wooden wall clock that we had brought back from Germany. Everything shimmered with the warm glow of the Christmas tree lights. For a short time nothing else mattered. I breathed slowly taking it all in, and a feeling of peace settled over me.

Turning and closing the front door, I heard the bedroom doorknob rattle and the door bounce against the wall from being flung open with too much force.

"Where the fuck were you?" Jake slurred, and my body stiffened.

"Shh…Jake. You'll wake the kids." I whispered as I turned, careful to be smiling when I faced him despite my fear.

"I was just taking Marianne back across the street. You know that." I cooed as the adrenaline rush caused my heart to pump wildly, sending my blood pressure sky high, and causing a loud whooshing sound in my ears.

He was standing in the doorway of the bedroom, swaying a little and staring blankly in my direction. His belt was unbuckled, and the fly of his pants was unzipped.

"Damn!" I thought.

"Come 'ere!" He demanded and I knew what that meant. I stood, feet riveted to the floor, unable to move. I could say "no". The last thing that I wanted was to have his drunken ass on top of me! Just the thought of it made me sick. And if I did say "no", he would get very, very angry. There was no room here for me to get away, and the subsequent racket from any attempt would wake the kids. The last thing that I wanted them to see was Jake throwing me around the front room amidst the Christmas decorations.

"Shit!" I thought, with the fear making my skin clammy and my legs quiver. "Be careful. Don't make him mad!"

"I fuckin' said, COME HERE!" This time he was shouting.

"Shh…Shh! Okay, Okay." I said forcing a smile and my legs to move towards him. As soon as I was at arms length he grabbed me and pulled me roughly to him. He put his mouth on mine, and spit and slime covered my lips and chin. His breath was unbearable.

"What's fucking wrong with you? You, frigid bitch!" His voice ominously rumbled in my ear and he grabbed my arm and squeezed hard.

"Nothing. I was just thinking that we should go into the bedroom and…"

"Shut the fuck up!" And with that he pushed me to the ground. I landed next to the Christmas tree with a muffled thump. A little bell on the tree made a tiny tinkling sound when I hit the floor. "God, please don't let the kids wake up!" kept repeating in my head as he roughly rolled me on my back.

My silver satin and lace mini-dress was shoved up above my waist and my pantyhose and underwear were stripped off of me, the nylon burning and bruising my skin from the friction of the fabric being dragged across it, and being yanked down and off at an improper angle. Throwing the stockings to the side he shoved his hand between my knees spreading my legs apart and fell heavily on top of me. I could hardly breathe as he pushed and shoved trying to get inside. His misdirected attempts causing me pain.

"C'mon, c'mon…" He said ominously, with a husky impatience, as if threatening me would make things easier. Finally, after what seemed like an eternity, my fear gave way to submission and he began the ride.

Could a husband rape his wife? I wondered as the tiny bell kept tinkling above my head with every violent stroke of Jake inside of me. How long this would go on, I couldn't guess. Maybe he would pass out and maybe he wouldn't. One thing was for certain, as drunk as he was, I was going to be under this tree for a damn, long time.

"Ting, Ting, Ting…" The little green tin bell on the bottom branch rhythmically shook.

"And a very Merry Christmas, and a Happy New Year!" I thought to myself as I watched the tinsel shake and shimmer above my head.

❧ PART 6 ❧

"ENOUGH"

❧ XXXIX ❧

He stood in the archway of the dining room about four feet away from me, swaying back and forth like the tin man in the Wizard of Oz. At times, it would look as if he were just about to lose his balance and fall over, but he didn't. The face and the body were Jake's but his eyes were vacant. Jake had gone away to wherever he was at times like these and the mindless demon was in his place. Rage burned in the slurred almost indecipherable words of his speech.

"Gonna' kill that cock-suck'n, fuck'n, chick'n ssshit ass dog! Sit still you cunt!" Spit flew as he shouted out the venomous words. My complete attention was on the gun, watching it like a snake charmer while the barrel swayed and bobbed as Jake tried to follow the movement of our terrified family dog. She frantically weaved and circled her way around my legs and the legs of the children. He was holding the gun a little out in front of him at his waist, just the right height to line up perfectly with a two or three-year-old child's head. Somehow he seemed oblivious to the fact that the boys were between the gun and the target of his uncontrolled rage. Instinctively I knew that whatever I was going to say or do in the next few seconds to save my children's lives had to be controlled and deliberate. Any emotional outbursts or sudden movements could be a death sentence to one or both of my boys. Desperately, I tried to fight down the images that were exploding in my brain of what a bullet can do to a toddler's head, so that I could think clearly!

"Jake, you don't want to do this!" I said, as evenly as I could, with as much authority in my voice as I was able to muster. "Can't you see that the boys are getting in the way of the gun?" I wanted to get his attention, to redirect his efforts away from the object of his seething, blind anger, to something or someone else. There was no response.

"Jake!" I said again. "You have to put the gun down! You'll kill the boys!" No longer able to control the terror in my voice, my last sentence came from my gut, a low, guttural, heart wrenching sob, welling up from the darkest place in my soul.

Again, no response. My words couldn't pierce through the fog, which enveloped this vacant, violent stranger, to Jake who was lost and unaware of the horror that he was orchestrating. His finger still rested on the trigger of the gun. His hand still swayed as the dog danced in fear around and between us all. One sharp word, one sudden movement and my children's lives, and my world, would end.

"Jake! Please! Please, listen to me!" Standing very still, afraid to make a move, I was begging now and trying to get through.

The boys were crying, frightened by Jake's shouts and wanting to protect their dog from his anger. They were just out of my reach. They didn't understand the danger from the gun and both of them bobbed up and down in front of it, sobbing and frantically grabbing for Bacardi as she weaved in and out, and between us all.

Stan, Jake's new friend, stood open-mouthed just inside the front door, about fifteen feet from Jake, trying to comprehend the incomprehensible. It was 2:30 in the afternoon, and five minutes ago, he and Jake had staggered through the door smokin' and jokin'. I bet he never dreamed that things would end up like this when the two of them had decided to stop for a drink at 8:00 this morning, after third shift ended at the plant. He was probably wondering how things had gone from two guys coming home after six hours of boozing it up at a corner bar, to this. He should've asked me before he'd decided to go drinking with my old man. I could've told him. If he'd been drunk when he walked into my door, he wasn't now.

"Hey Jake!" He called, finally breaking out of his paralysis of disbelief and deciding to take some kind of action.

Unbelievably, Jake turned and looked at him! Giving him a blank stare, while he swayed and stood with the gun pointed in the general direction of the children and the dog.

"How's about you let me look at that neat gun you bought? I'd really like a gun like that for myself." Stan said man to man, as he cautiously moved towards Jake, holding his hand out in front of him, palm up in a gesture that showed he expected Jake to hand him the weapon. Jake, distracted from his mission to shoot the dog, let his arm droop slightly and with his body still swaying, turned towards Stan while Stan slowly and deliberately crossed the distance between them.

In that moment, while Jake's attention was diverted, I bent down, stretched out and snatched my children by their arms, pulling them to me as my legs gave way causing me to land unceremoniously on my bottom. Sitting on the floor I held them both tightly to my chest, rocked them and silently wept. The dog, which blamelessly had become the object of Jake's reign of terror, squeezed in as close as possible to the three of us huddled together on the floor, trembling uncontrollably and trying to bury her head between Eric and me as we tightly clung together.

"Wow, she's a beauty!" Stan's voice came from somewhere just above me, and then he made a low whistle of appreciation while the gun, released from Jake's grasp, slipped into his upturned hand. As the full weight of the gun landed in Stan's hand, he involuntary gave out a little chuckle that Jake, if able at the time, would've interpreted as a sign of overwhelming admiration. However, the beads of sweat glistening on Stan's forehead and upper lip told a different story.

After a few comments about how light it was and the craftsmanship of the object in his hand, Stan asked if he could borrow it to show some of his friends in the neighborhood. And then like a magician, he caused the gun to disappear, in one quick, seamless movement, into his jacket pocket. Suddenly it was gone as if it had never been there.

Stan said something about Jake getting some shut-eye after such a long day while he reached out and patted his back. Silent and expressionless, Jake turned as if on cue, wobbled passed the children and me sobbing on the dining room floor, and walked in through the bedroom doorway. A second or two later, a heavy, muffled thud emanated from somewhere in the bedroom. And then there was silence.

It was over! We were all still alive and it was over!

"Lucky, lucky, lucky…" Barely audible, I repeated as I pulled the boys even closer to me, pressing them so tight against me that I could feel their hearts beating while I rocked us all back and forth. Silently sobbing, hesitant to make a sound for fear of waking a sleeping monster, I rocked them and cried, but this time the tears were from pure joy!

"I am so sorry…so sorry! I had no idea…" Stan said, his face was drained of color and his hand shook as he reached out for me and the children, to help us get up off the floor.

"My God! Where did he get the gun?" I whispered, while slowly and awkwardly getting up from the carpeted floor. The boys still clung to me, not feeling safe and not wanting to let me go.

"He bought it from a guy in the bar. The guy was sellin' it and Jake said that he wanted one around the house for protection… y'know, with him workin' nights and all. He wanted you to have somethin' to protect yourself." Stan said.

"Yeah, right!" I said locking eyes with Stan, the irony of the situation not wasted on either of us.

"Where'd he get the money?" I asked, wondering how he could've afforded to by the gun. We were flat broke until payday. He probably had been getting drunk on credit, but it didn't seem likely that the sort of guy who sold guns in a bar let you owe him the money for its purchase until next week.

The boys were still locked tight around my legs. Their crying had stopped but they were still wide eyed with fear. Rubbing their shoulders to comfort them and smiling to assure them that everything was alright now, I glanced up at Stan and immediately knew the answer to my question.

"I'm sorry!" He blurted out, his face and eyes full of shame and regret. "He told me how scared he was to leave you and the kids alone at night. He said he needed to know that you would be OK when he left for work... I just didn't know that he would... that he was..." His voice trailed off into a small groan that got stuck in his throat.

"I'm sorry!" He said with such heart felt misery that my anger cooled a bit. I couldn't blame him. He was new to the game. He really hadn't known what he was getting into. How could he?

"Do me a favor and stay around until I get the boys' coats on and we can get out of here. He doesn't always stay down, once he's out." I said in a cold flat tone. He had made an error in judgment, a small mistake in the scheme of things, but that mistake had come very close to costing my children their lives!

"Sure." Stan eagerly shook his head, grateful for the chance to try and make up for his contribution to a situation that easily could have led to a deadly conclusion.

Lovingly, I shepherded the boys a few short feet over to the living room couch, coaxing them to stay there while I made the short trip to the bedroom door and softly shut it. Moving quickly to the front closet, I retrieved our coats and coming back to the boys stuffed them in, zippering them up in order to protect them from the rain and the cold March wind. Luckily, my purse had been hanging on the closet door and not in its usual place on the floor next to my dresser in our bedroom. All my preparations were swiftly and silently accomplished. The boys had sat on the couch without a word, watching me collect my things. I didn't want to take any chances that Jake, the monster passed out in my bedroom, might resurrect from the unconscious, so their uncharacteristic silence was welcomed. The whole process had taken no more than five minutes and we were all out the door.

Jake had left our car at the bar because, surprise...surprise, he'd been too drunk to drive! Stan, still in a penitent mood was more than happy to drive me anywhere I wanted to go. On the car ride over to the tavern where our car was parked, conversation stayed to a minimum. It mainly consisted of repetitive apologies from Stan while I stared unresponsively out the window listening to the soft drum of the rain on the windshield. How Stan did or did not feel was of no concern to me at the moment. Also, I didn't care what Stan did with the gun just as long as me and mine never saw it again. It was the one comment that I made to him in a clipped monotone voice, and he solemnly swore to me that he would take care of it. He'd done a very stupid thing. He had given a drunken man access to a loaded gun. And because today had been our lucky day, that thoughtless act hadn't ended with my children's brains on my dining room wall! It was up to him to forgive himself, and being a drunk, I was betting that after this car ride was over, he could figure out how to do that without any help from me!

⧼ XL ⧽

Arriving at my dad's house I got the kids together and made a run for it from the parked car, through the pouring rain to the front door. The storm had been brewing all morning before Jake had come home, and had settled into a steady downpour for the last few hours. After a quick ring of the doorbell, Gladys answered, and it was apparent that she had been getting ready to go out the door and do her Friday grocery shopping when she was interrupted by the sound of the bell. It was late afternoon and my dad wouldn't be home from work for several hours. I must've looked a mess, because the minute that the door opened she asked me what was wrong.

"Ma, I need someplace for the kids and I to stay for a while to think." I said, my voice strained and full of emotion, as I ushered the kids in through the front door. "Jake came home loaded today and we had a pretty big fight. The kids and I need a place to stay until he sleeps it off."

Gladys, who in her first marriage had married into a hard drinking family, was no stranger to men who drank too much and became obnoxious. She gave me an understanding nod. We had become fairly close over the years since my return from Germany. During the many times that the two of us had chatted over a cup of coffee, she'd shared some of the violent episodes from her past that had involved men and alcohol, but the evil doers in those stories were brother-in-laws or uncles, never her deceased husband. He'd been a good man who had treated her well to the last day of his life. I'd never mentioned to her how violent Jake could get. That, as always, was my secret. But I'd gotten the feeling she had a hunch that more was going on than I was telling her.

"Sure, thing. Do you want some company to talk things over? I can stay. The few things that I was going to go out for can wait." She said with a true look of concern.

"No, that's OK. I think that I'd like to be alone anyway. You know, to think and stuff." I said. Gladys responded with a knowing nod, and gathered her things together.

As Gladys left, I took the boys coats off and they immediately made their way through the front of the house, the kitchen, and to the backstairs that led to the basement. I could hear their shoes clopping down the wooden steps, the sound echoing back up the stairwell. It's odd how life repeats itself. My children were playing in the same place that I had joyfully played in when I was a child. As I moved into the kitchen and sat down at the wooden kitchen table, occasionally, a giggle or some small bit of undecipherable child chatter floated up the steps from the basement.

Now that Gladys was off doing the things that she needed to do, I was alone and grateful for the opportunity to be so. Sitting silently in my mother's kitchen I tried to feel whatever part of her might still be left there, and tried to draw some peace and comfort from it. This is where I'd sat for countless dinner times talking to my mother about a million different things that were important and unimportant to the both of us, while she'd prepared our meals. This was the place where we had talked to each other, parent to child, mother to daughter, friend to friend. This kitchen had been the heart of our home when I'd been growing up. My days of growing up had been strung together here like white pearls on an exquisite necklace, the memory of which had been made smooth and flawless by the passage of time.

This is where all the people that I loved had sat at one time or another during birthdays and holidays. This is where we had laughed and cried. This is where my mother, her hair pinned up with bobby pins on a Saturday morning while she cleaned the house, with an impish playful smile on her face, would stick her tongue out at me and tease me for some long forgotten reason as, swinging her shoulders and hips, she would dance out of my sight into the hallway. This is where my Aunt Lollie had agonized over my Auntie Tillie's death. This is where my life had happened, so it was, as it should be, that I was sitting here now.

"It had been luck, you know." I said out loud to the empty house, myself and maybe my mother. Some other people would say that it had been God who had saved my boys, but I knew if he existed at all, that was bullshit. I'd been alive long enough to realize that my children weren't more precious to the universe than a million other children on this planet. Some of those other children were the ones whose sorrowful images were continually paraded in front of my eyes on the evening news or on the cover of Time magazine. A child in Vietnam running down a dirt road his body ablaze ignited by Napalm,   the gaunt face of a small emaciated skeleton of a boy barely surviving a famine in Africa, or the charred remains of a child in the arms of an anguished fireman, were all someone's babies. Why would God save mine and not theirs? Why would any of that be His will? And if God picks and chooses between the little ones on this earth, to bestow pain and death in some godly manner, than I didn't want any part of it or Him.

It was better to believe it was luck. I remembered the lineman in Texas who wound up hanging upside down by his bootstrap from an electric pole in my backyard with his stomach on fire. Maybe a synapse in his brain had misfired or he had taken his mind off of what he had been doing for a split second, it really didn't matter. The point was that just for an instant he'd misjudged the distance between his belt buckle and the high power line. Normally when you misjudge a distance you smack your knee into a wall or thump your elbow and get a little bit of a bump, or maybe if you happen to be running you trip and fall. That's what happens to the lucky people. He had made an error in judgment, and he had died!

And it was luck that Jake had not had a brain synapse misfire while his finger was on the trigger of the gun. And it was luck that my children were now safe and sound playing in my mother's basement.

"And…" I thought, "What should I do about that?"

This time was different. This time had involved the kids. A litany from the past like, "Maybe you are making a big thing out of it. Maybe it's not such a big deal. Maybe you are being a baby about everything." which had created self-doubt and allowed life to go on as it had before, wasn't going to work, anymore. Up until today, I'd always believed that the boys had been and would be insulated from the violence. Most of the violent episodes had occurred late at night, when the boys had been asleep. But now that Jake was working the night shift, things had changed. I'd thought that I could protect them from harm, but now I knew that I'd been wrong. No one was safe.

"Divorce. Should I divorce him?" I asked myself.

The prospect of that scenario and the pain that I projected that the boys would endure because of it, made me reluctant to even entertain the thought. The boys loved him.

Even sober, I knew that he wasn't the best father in the world. In fact, he was emotionally distant from them most of the time but that was just Jake. Any attention that he did show them usually was made up of rough housing that included a lot of teasing. Teasing passed the point that I thought was good for children, always seeming to be teetering on the edge of something darker. His own father had been distant when he was a child, and still was, so I'd figured that Jake just didn't know any better. I'd believed that in a loving atmosphere, one that I could provide, both Jake and the boys would learn and grow together, and in the end, neither would be worse for the wear.

Another depressing thought was that I had no job skills. I didn't know how to type or run a cash register. Jake had always said that I was lucky to have him to support me because I was too stupid to have a job, and somewhere inside myself I'd always believed that it was true. How could I support the boys and keep the house?

Also, Jake had been the only man in my life. The thought of someone else in my bed made my stomach turn.

And then of course, there was the spoof on the little "Love Is" joke that Jake enjoyed reciting at parties. The one about hunting down and killing the one you love if you set them free and they don't come back. Remembering the look on his face as he delivered the punch-line, his eyes riveted to mine, effectively conveying the message, "Don't you ever try it!" caused me to shudder.

It was kind of ironic when you thought about it. During the last couple years, through everything that I'd been through, my faith had dwindled away to nothing. Too much anger, too many injustices in my life and the world around me, had caused me to lose my faith. And now that I didn't care about what the Pope thought about the state of my soul if I divorced Jake, I was too afraid to do it.

But I had to do something! What happened today couldn't be pushed aside. We'd been lucky, very lucky, that his finger hadn't accidentally twitched on that trigger. Maybe next time we would be just plain out of luck, like the lineman in my backyard… or like my Auntie Tillie. This was an incident that I couldn't explain away. This was an incident that drove it home. Something has to change!

I didn't know how to leave him. I hadn't seriously thought about it before. I had no idea, nothing to work with, no tools… Then I remembered. On some daily TV talk show, maybe Donahue, I'd heard about some group for people whose lives had been ruined by booze. He'd interviewed several people and they'd talked about their problems with alcohol.

Funny how bits of information casually gathered, were unconsciously stored in some back pocket of your brain, and saved there like little gold nuggets, waiting to be used to buy you a ticket that can change your life.

"Maybe these people are the guru's of this thing. Maybe they can tell me what to do." I thought, desperate to try anything that might help me to get some answers, as I dialed "0" on my father's rotary dial phone.

"Hello information? Can you give me the phone number for AA?" I said into the receiver.

"Yes, that's right. Alcoholics Anonymous."

❧ XLI ❧

Damn! It was dark in my bedroom. My body started shaking again, the tremors being reignited by another wave of fear. Almost twenty-five years old and I was still afraid of the dark.

"This had better work!" I said to myself, fear building and rebuilding, as I lay in the double bed on my back staring up at what I supposed was the ceiling. They'd said that this was a way to find out. Just this one more time and I would know what to do. I tried to relax, but it was impossible. The waves of tremors ran rhythmically through my body coinciding with the waves of fear waxing and waning while I lay here.

I contemplated what had led up to laying here in the dark, waiting for him to come home.

"Are you OK? Is he still there? Does he still have the gun?" I remembered the gentle but firm voice of the man on the other end of the AA phone line, probing me with questions. After appraising the situation and understanding that the crisis had passed, he'd said to me, "Listen. Go to an Al-Anon meeting. You're not going to get him into AA today, but you need to go for yourself. It's where you can find people to help you figure out what to do. Not to make decisions for you, but to figure it out." And then he'd commented that the danger had passed for now but assured me that the violence would happen again. "You've got to make a change in your life if you want it to stop!"

It was because of that phone call that I'd gotten into Al-Anon. The AA guy on the phone had given me an address for the closest meeting to my home. It met on Tuesday nights at the Catholic grammar school less than a mile away. Interestingly enough, it turned out that there were meetings being held within a ten minute car ride from my house, every night of the week! It seemed that there were a lot of drunks out there along with a lot of people like me.

The morning after Jake had come so close to shooting our children, while he was overwhelmed with guilt and remorse, I'd sat him down and told him that he had two choices. One was that the boys and I left him and the other was that I would go to Al-Anon. Surprisingly, he'd reacted just the way that the AA guy on the phone had said that he would, agreeing to anything that would make up for his grievous behavior, and emotionally get him off the hook.

"You've got to make a change in your life if you want it to stop!" The AA guy's words had kept running through my mind, fueling my determination to do anything that would keep my boys safe from the inevitable violent consequences of Jake's drinking. I didn't have the foggiest idea what Al-Anon was and that didn't matter. The AA guy had been right about how to get Jake to agree to me going to Al-Anon meetings so maybe he was right about everything else.

The fear and apprehension that I'd felt when walking the school halls in search of the "Teacher's Lounge", and my first meeting, were instantly dissipated by the smiling faces and the rich aroma of brewing coffee. Both of which, greeted me as I opened an oak door marked "Lounge" at the end of one of the hallways. The room wasn't very large, about the size of a small living room, and a dozen women or so were sitting or standing around a large wooden table located in the center of it. The room was filled to the brim with laughter and lively conversation.

"Hi! My name is Teresa." A thin brown haired woman with a freshly scrubbed athletic look about her, took hold of my hand and shook it gently, smiling warmly and making me feel welcome.

"I don't know if I'm at the right meeting." I said, awkwardly.

"Well, we're just about to start. Why don't you take a seat and you can figure it out for yourself." She said with a smile and some genuine good humor.

"OK everyone. Let's get started." And with that they all stood up, reached for each others hands, forming a large circle and began in unison.

"God grant me the serenity to accept the things I cannot change, the courage to change the things I can and the wisdom to know the difference."

"Hello everyone" Teresa said. "I believe that we have a new person today, so let's begin with the *Preamble to the Twelve Steps*. Who would like to read it from the Blue Book?"

"I will." Said a forty-five-ish attractive blonde with big blue eyes. She took one, long, deep drag on her newly lit cigarette and blew it slowly out as she flipped a few pages in a small hardcover book. She began to read.

"The Al-Anon Family Groups are a fellowship of relatives and friends of alcoholics who share their experience, strength, and hope in order to solve their

common problems. We believe alcoholism is a family illness and that changed attitudes can aid recovery.

Al-Anon is not allied with any sect, denomination, political entity, organization or institution; does not engage in any controversy; neither endorses nor opposes any cause. There are no dues for membership. Al-Anon is self-supporting through its own voluntary contributions.

Al-Anon has but one purpose:: to help families of alcoholics. We do this by practicing the Twelve Steps, by welcoming and giving comfort to families of alcoholics, and by giving understanding and encouragement to the alcoholic."

"Thanks Anne Marie. And now, because we have a new person, maybe we should go around the table and those of you who feel like it, can tell your stories." Everyone nodded in agreement to Teresa's suggestion.

"Patti, would you like to start?"

And so it began, the first step of many on the road to changing my life. That was almost three months ago and in that time I had begun to see the world and my place in it, in a completely different way. I was no longer alone. I was surrounded by men and women whose experiences paralleled mine. Their hard won wisdom helped to point the way for my personal growth.

Each meeting was filled with words of wisdom. I was learning to live my life "One Day at a Time". "This Too Shall Pass", "Live and Let Live", and "Let Go and Let God" were little tidbits that were the language of the program. They were tiny sayings that emphasized my need to let go of Jake's problem, and leave it to him to solve. The old mantras of fear and helplessness were replaced by these little snippets of gold helping to change my thinking, my behavior, and my life. Being able to look at myself in the mirror for the first time, and to believe that I was the owner of my destiny, to begin to be able to let him go and to let him be, was true freedom.

"You have to stop concentrating on him." Anne Marie had said to me at one of the meetings. "You've got to stop busying your thoughts with how many drinks he's had, if he will stop, if he won't stop. You've got to stop thinking that you have some control over that. You don't! You're wasting your time. You're spinning your wheels. You're repetitively clogging your brain up with futile worry, going nowhere like a hamster on a wheel in a cage, exhausting yourself and wasting your energy and serenity. You can't do anything about his drinking, but you can concentrate on doing something about yourself." As commonsense as her counsel seemed, these ideas were all brand new to me. To be the captain of my own soul, responsible for my actions alone, these concepts were opening up a whole new world. One in which I was no longer a victim. The recognition that I was powerless over his alcoholism freed me to look into myself and my future. Jake drank because he was an alcoholic, because he had a disease, not because of anything that I did or didn't do. It wasn't my bag it was his. My constant worrying about, and meddling in, his drinking, kept him from experiencing the consequences of it. No more enabling the alcoholic by making excuses to the world to soften the blow that resulted from his behavior.

"When you love someone" Teresa had chimed in, "you owe them the right to learn from their mistakes. If you are in there, always covering up, always making excuses, insulating the alcoholic from the consequences of his actions, you are taking away his God given right to grow. And because you love him, you must let go of him and give him to God. By your inaction you can indirectly give him the greatest gift that a drunk can get, the opportunity to get sober!"

"Yeah, denial is a big part of the problem. When we stop reacting, the full ramifications of their drinking fall squarely on their own shoulders, where it belongs." Anne Marie agreed. "It's a hard concept to accept but for those of us who have seen the impossible happen, their alcoholic stop drinking, we know that it works. And whether he stops drinking or not, letting go with love gets us off the merry-go-round and allows us to concentrate on what's good for our kids, ourselves, and our lives."

Detaching from the alcoholic with love and placing him in the hands of his Higher Power was indeed a difficult concept to understand and follow. It was however, vital to both our lives, because that was the only way that Jake was going to be able to learn. I'd made things too comfy for him. Why change when you don't get punished for bad behavior? Why do things differently if there is no reason not to? If you don't realize the impact of what you are doing in your life how can you change? And I owed him that. I owed him to withdraw myself as the buffer between himself and the consequences of his actions. I owed him: not to call into work for him when he was drunk or hung over so that he wouldn't lose his job, not to call a lawyer to take care of a DUI or a ticket, not to clean up the mess that he'd made in a drunken stupor or a drunken rage, and to "Let Go and Let God" and have the courage to allow Jake the opportunity to take care of all those things. I no longer needed to make excuses to family and friends if he was too drunk to keep a date. Being honest about why we couldn't make it, and better yet learning to go without him, were all exercises in breaking the cycle of denial.

In the meetings that followed I had begun to learn how to face my fears and to deal with them one by one. No matter where we went or who we were with, my anticipation of the ride home was a "biggy". At any social gathering it was all that I could do to keep from watching Jake every second for developing signs of inebriation. Counting drinks was a kind of barometer to help predict the strength of the storm that would be brewing, over getting me into the car for the terrifying car ride home. A simple yet ingenious solution was proposed to me at one of the meetings.

"Always keep ten bucks hidden in your wallet to pay for a taxi. And when he gets up tomorrow morning, by the way, mornings are the best time, you need to catch him when he's sober, tell him 'Jake if you ever get drunk again when we're out, I won't drive home with you. If you look around and I'm not there it's because I've found another way to get home without you. You'll never drive me or the kids when you are drunk again. I know that you love me and the kids, and you couldn't live with yourself if something happened to us, so because I love you, that's the way it's gonna' be.' Don't be a smart ass about it. Do it with love and he'll be able to tell that you mean business. When he gets drunk again the next time that you're out, don't even tell him that you're leaving. Just quietly ask someone else at the party for a ride home, or call a cab if you have to, and leave."

"No more trying to wrestle the keys away from him. No more arguing with him, trying to get him not to drink and drive. No more begging him to give you the keys. No more fights. You let him be responsible for Jake, and you 'Let Go and Let God'. You be responsible for the only person that you can be responsible for, yourself. Be a responsible parent too, and ensure that those children never go in a car with him drunk again, even if it does wind up that you have to call the police to do it."

Finally I had options, choices to be a victim, or not. When given choices, fear lessens. One evening while I was at a meeting I'd said to Teresa "When he starts to drink, I get so scared that I start to shake. I think about leaving the marriage but I know that if I leave he will hunt me down! I know it!"

She said to me, "What are you afraid of? Put it in God's hands and He'll see to it that things work out. Besides, the worst thing that can happen to you is that he can kill you, and then if he does, Susan, all your worries are over!"

For some weird strange reason, that piece of truth pierced through my fear and lessened it. The fog of fear that had loomed over me, perpetually pushing in on me and keeping me down, invading all of my thoughts and dominating every minute of every part of my life, began to lift.

Then Anne Marie chimed in "You know, if you want to understand the influence and impact that the active alcoholic has had on your life and your children's lives, take a look at your family dog. You can always tell an active alcoholic is present in the home by looking at the family dog. Is it a healthy dog, one that barks and warns strangers not to come in, one that is calm and wags his tail in response to your outstretched hand? Or is it a dog that at the slightest motion of a hand or raise of your voice cowers in the corner and trembles. The dog's a good indicator as to how dealing with the active alcoholic day after day, without benefit of the Program, affects you and your children. The animal mirrors the conditioning of the family."

"Listen Susan, I don't mean to make light of the possible danger to you and the kids. I would like you to try something so that we can all sleep better at night. There is a way to tell if his violence can be defused by changing the way that you react to him when he gets drunk, by not playing the game that has escalated things between you and him in the past. I know that he's been on his very best behavior since the incident that brought you here. But mark my words, he will get very drunk again sometime in the future and when he does you need to be ready."

"Sure." I said eagerly, desperate to try anything that would make me feel safer.

"Good. Once you realize that he is drinking his way to "zombie" Jake I want you to slip quietly out of the room and get into bed. If he goes out drinking I want you to be in bed before he comes in the door. Either way, once he walks into the bedroom, I want you to lie absolutely still in the bed and pretend you are sound asleep. No matter how much noise he makes or how he screams and yells for you to wake up, I don't want you to move. You see, it's sort of a litmus test. A plain old drunk will eventually give up when he gets no response, and pass out or go to bed himself."

"Yeah." Anne Marie said. "Only a real nut case will beat up a sleeping woman. And if that happens, you need to get yourself and the kids out of there as soon as you can and call the police! You can't allow yourself and your kids to be exposed to a man like that."

"If he leaves you alone, then in the morning you need to have a serious talk with him." Teresa continued. "You need to tell him how he ranted and raved when you wouldn't wake up and how you aren't going to put up with that kind of behavior ever again."

"Tell him that because you love him, and you want him to get well, if he ever gets violent again, you will put him in jail and you WILL prosecute him. Tell him that you love him and you know that he needs to learn that if he is violent with other people he will go to jail!" Anne Marie added.

"There is one catch. You really need to mean it when you say it so that he can sense that you mean business. And once you say it you MUST follow through if you want to stay with him and ensure your safety in the future as well as your kids'." Teresa reached out and gave my hand a squeeze. "Think about it. It's the only way."

"You've got nothing to lose." Anne Marie said and then took another long, deep, thoughtful drag from her cigarette.

And now I was lying in bed waiting for him to come home. He'd been building up to this night for a while. It had been over three months since the gun incident and initially his drinking had slowed down, but over the last couple of weeks he'd been drinking more and more. When he called this evening and said that he, and one of his friends had decided to stop off for a beer, it had been a good bet that he would come home as a very drunk, vacant eyed stranger.

As my eyes got used to the dark, the slow rhythmic motion of the cotton curtains on the half open bedroom window became apparent in the meager light from the street lamp located out in front of the house. It was early June and the night breezes were still soft and cool. A small inky black section of the night sky was visible from the position where I lay in bed. The street light always blanked out the view of the stars from the windows facing the street and that fact made me a little sad. I remembered the Indiana nights from my childhood visits to my Grandma's cottage, and the sky filled with a brilliant deep sea of bright stars scattered amidst glowing swirls of the Milky Way.

Jake's grotesquely blank face appeared above me in the dark as my mind flashed back to Virginia and his strangle hold on my throat. Was the sudden appearance of Jake's face in my imagination a premonition of what was to come? Waves of tremors hit again.

Then I heard it, a small jiggling sound from the direction of the front door. My body was already stiff with fright when the "Bam" reverberated through the dark silence of the house. A millisecond later a vision of the door slamming against the living room wall played in my mind. It was immediately followed by the sound of the metal slap of the screen door, as it closed behind the household intruder, my husband Jake.

It took every ounce of my strength to roll my rigid, terrified body, towards the wall, pulling the covers tight around me despite the warmth of the June night. My eyes burned as I squeezed them tight against the imaginary blows that I was sure I was about to endure.

With every sound, the slap of the heels of his shoes across the floor, the creaking of the couch springs under the weight of his body, and the two small hollow thumps echoing as he threw his shoes against the living room wall, the terror in my body multiplied.

"Where the fuck are ya'?" He said loudly from the living room, his voice thick with booze, as I lay mute and stiff as a statue with my blanket like a cocoon wrapped around me.

"Hey!" He half shouted half slurred "Where the fuck are ya'?"

"Please Lord, shut him up. Don't let him wake the kids." As if my prayer had been answered, the thumping of his feet began as he stomped across the living room floor with anger and frustration. The glasses in the china cabinet tinkled with the vibration of each thump, dancing over the glass shelf where they had been placed for safe keeping.

"Thump, thump, thump…" and he was standing at the bedroom doorway. I could feel him silently hesitating for some unknown reason and then he moved into the room bumping his lower body into the side of the dresser as he entered the darkness.

"Fuck!" He drunkenly cried in pain and the sound of the lamp sliding on the dresser's smooth wooden top mingled with the rushing of the blood in my ears. Wrapped up like a mummy and facing the wall, my body laid rigid, still, and waiting.

"Hey, wake the fuck up!" He bellowed. The vision of little droplets of his saliva spraying everywhere when he drunkenly pronounced the "f" in fuck, ran through my imagination, raising my blood pressure even higher. My hands began to sweat as they clenched the blanket more tightly than before. I didn't move.

"Hey, I said! Can't you fuckin' hear me? Get the fuck up!" Unmoving like a statue, I waited.

"Listen bitch!" And then, just above my head, I heard the lamp smash against the wall that I was facing. The light bulb popped and shattered, spraying little pieces of glass on my pillow and the headboard. The rest of the lamp crashed down between the wall and the mattress, landing on the floor in a heap. I still didn't move.

"Fuckin' stupid, lazy cunt! Fuck ya'!" And with that I heard his pants zipper unzip, followed by the soft sliding sound of material on flesh, then a few small thumps ending in one large, china cabinet shaking "boom", and then nothing… Every muscle in my body ached as my ears strained to hear even the slightest sound or movement from Jake's direction. Silence… After what seemed like an eternity, my muscles screaming from the stress of being kept taut, a barely audible rhythmic whistling emerged from behind me. My God! He was asleep. He must've passed out right on the bedroom floor in the middle of trying to get his pants off! I was elated! It was over!

Cautiously, I commanded my now cramped aching muscles to move and turn away from the wall, rolling towards the snoring lump that was laying somewhere next to the other side of the bed, on the floor. Peering over the side of the bed into the dark, a misshapen heap was barely visible on the floor a few feet from the edge of the mattress. His pants appeared to be half off and the pant legs were twisted and tangled around his feet. A nervous chuckle slipped out from between my now smiling lips.

"Sweet dreams, baby! You and I have a few things to discuss in the morning." Leaving him lay there, just as he was, I rolled onto my back and situated myself in the middle of the bed, stretching out my arms and legs in an attempt to remove the tenseness from my body. Absentmindedly staring at the ceiling, I realized that I felt an inner peace that was unfamiliar to me.

"God grant me the serenity to accept the things I cannot change, the courage to change the things I can and the wisdom to know the difference." I thought about it. Maybe, I was beginning to know the difference.

"Lookin' good!" My reflection in my dresser mirror proudly beamed back at me. The lines of the red satin halter top, A-line dress were very slimming. Impressed by the fact that the dress had actually been made with my own two hands, I lovingly ran my fingers over the fabric, gazing in the mirror and feeling the wonderfully smooth texture of the fabric. Jake was going to love me in this!

Tonight was New Year's Eve, December 31, 1973, and a lot had changed in just one year. For one thing, tonight we were going to stay home. We'd invited Marie and Jerry, Jake's sister and brother-in-law, and Peggy and Buddy, over to the house to greet in the New Year. The get-together held promise for an enjoyable evening. In the three years since Jake and I had come back from Germany, Peggy and Buddy had been our closest friends. Other couples had come and gone but through it all, Peg and Buddy had been our mainstay. We played penny ante card and board games with them at least twice a month and we always had a pretty good time. Once in a while, especially if Jake was losing or drunk, he would be rude to them, but they never seemed to care, so the relationship continued. Peggy and I talked on the phone almost every day. She'd known some of the details of the stuff that Jake and I'd gone through in the past, but not the whole ball of wax, only my friends in Al-Anon knew that. Peg and I watched the same soap operas on TV, and between her, myself and Buddy's best friend's wife, Paulette, we had quite a daily phone call "round robin" on the topic. Well, we'd had a "round robin". Paulette had died a little over a year ago from cancer. It'd been devastating to Butch, Buddy's friend. He'd been left with two boys, ages one and three, and my heart went out to him. God, it was sad! Peggy said that he was doing OK, but it goes to show you, no matter how bad you think that your life is, someone else is always getting kicked in the teeth twice as hard as you.

Things had been going well since the night that Jake threw the bedroom lamp at me. I guess one could say, that night had been a pivotal point in our relationship, or perhaps, to be more precise, the morning after had been. Sitting him down at the kitchen table I'd told him the facts as they were going to be from that day forward.

"People, who do violence to other people, go to jail. And if you are ever violent to me or the kids again, because I love you, I WILL put you in jail. I owe you the opportunity to learn that basic fact. Not only will I call the police and throw you in jail for the night, but if someone else bails you out, because I WILL NOT, I will testify against you in court when your trial comes up. It will be a very difficult thing for me to do, but there is no other choice. It is the only chance that we have to stop your violence." And my Al-Anon friends had been right, he did hear me. And because I'd meant it, and said it without anger, and with love, he'd believed me. In the six months since, the violence when he drank, and my fear of it, had ended.

Our relationship was better than it had ever been. He was still drinking, but without the constant fear of violence, it was easier to live with the situation. I'd learned to make his drinking his own business along with whatever ramifications there were from it. We were getting along better, whether he was drunk or sober. With anger and fear removed, the atmosphere was much more relaxed. It never ceased to amaze me, how once I found the courage and conviction to allow him the dignity to learn from his mistakes, how quickly the violence had stopped.

With all the ideas that I'd been learning in Al-Anon, I'd been growing. I'd actually taken up sewing! I was sewing and crocheting and being creative, now that I wasn't primarily concerned with Jake's alcoholism. Serenity seemed to be within the reach of my fingertips.

For the first time in my life I wasn't alone. All the strange weird things that had been happening between Jake and me because of his drinking, all the dirty little secrets that I'd desperately tried to hide from the outside world, that I'd assumed were only happening to us, were understood or had been experienced by the people around me. I began to laugh at myself and laugh about my situation in a way that people removed from alcoholism and the disease, don't understand. The laughter kept us from pitying or judging ourselves or others, and drove away anger, shame and fear.

Teresa had become my sponsor in the program, a mentor that I could call twenty-four hours a day if I was in trouble, needed to find a safe place to stay, or just wanted to talk. Knowing that no matter what was in store for me, in the future, I didn't have to face it alone, was a great comfort and provided me with peace of mind.

The camaraderie among all the women was incredible. I was totally accepted for who I was, and what I thought was right for me was respected. Up until the point in my life when I joined Al-Anon, when people had asked me "How are you?" It was always in an automatic reflexive way, with them not expecting or hoping to get an answer in return. The "How ARE you?" of the program was spoken with a true heart filled concern for your welfare, and was accompanied by a warm, solid, hand holding handshake that was felt by both of those connected to it, to the bottom of their souls. The connection between us, for me and all those women in Al-Anon, was so deep and so strong that it could bring tears to your eyes if dwelled upon. You know the saying "United we stand divided we fall". Absolutely true! It made me strong. It helped fill my pool of serenity so that I could face the things that I had to do in the future. It helped enable me not only to survive, but to learn courage and to grow.

Al-Anon was the place where I'd found the strength to confront Jake the "morning after" the last violence in our lives, over six months ago. It was because of the internal power that I drew from those women and the knowledge that I gained from them that I had the strength to go forward and act on that truth, and that in turn, changed our lives. Making decisions on my own wants and needs instead of Jake's probability of being drunk or sober, was difficult to learn but I was on my way.

I'd learned that Jake had a disease and both of us didn't need to suffer from it.

Studying my reflection in the mirror, I noted that the changes taking place on the inside of me were becoming obvious from the outside. My long straight black hair, the length of which had reached passed the rounded curve of my bottom, was gone. My excessively long hair which had seemed to be some kind of unspoken point of pride with Jake had recently become a pain in the neck, literally, for me. The fuss that it took to maintain it, and the pounding headaches that loomed in the evenings after a day of having a shit load of hair piled on top of my head to keep the stuff out of my face, didn't seem to be worth Jake's rooster type gratification, when compliments came my way. The thought had occurred to me after one particularly bad headache, that if Jake liked long hair so much, he could grow his own. Jake should love me for me, not for the length of my hair. So two weeks ago, I'd cut it off. My black hair was now a in a very becoming shoulder length hairdo.

"And a great decision, too!" I assured myself, pleased with how chic the shorter hair style made me look.

We were both growing.

The program had given both of us the knowledge, understanding and courage that we'd needed to try and help Jake's mother. During the two years that we'd been away and the subsequent time since our return from Germany, Jake's mother's drinking and her corresponding grip on reality, had progressively worsened. I'd learned from the AA guys that in some individuals, excessive alcohol intake can result in a syndrome called "alcoholic brain dysfunction", and we'd surmised that the paranoia and hallucinations that Jake's mother had been exhibiting could be attributed to that. Her fantasies ranged from fairly benign foolishness like her expressed belief that she was able to talk to aliens by switching her front porch light on and off in her own personally developed Morris code, to more sinister ones like her belief that the CIA was eavesdropping in on her conversations through her TV. This was a problem that she easily remedied by shooting the picture tube with the "family shotgun".

The need for the family to seek some psychiatric help for her had become obscenely apparent, when it was discovered that Jake's father had begun to barricade himself in his bedroom at night with a strategically placed heavy wooden dresser. It was in preparation for the next time God ordered her to shoot him. One occurrence of waking up and seeing her standing at the foot of his bed in the semidarkness with her "personal handgun" pointed at his head had evidently been enough. His once unyielding opposition to her commitment had softened and Jake, Marie and I seized the opportunity to place her under psychiatric observation in a state institution. Overall however, it hadn't done much good. In the hospital, without ingestion of alcohol, her paranoia and hallucinations had cleared up. And with a promise of no booze and weekly appointments with a shrink, she was released into Jake's dad's custody. In less than a month it was business as usual. Last week she was telling me, as she poured herself another beer, how she was able to make it rain by placing a big black "X" inside the numbered boxes that represented the days of the month on her calendar. Shortly after that gem of information, she began to jabber like a monkey, speaking gibberish, punctuated by a few grunts and groans, demonstrating her new found talent to speak in "tongues".

Taking in a deep breath and then exhaling with a sigh of resignation I said "You win some and you lose some, I guess."

Shrugging it off, I turned sideways and gazed at my silhouette in the mirror, to see if I looked fat in my homemade red satin dress.

"Was I showing already?" I thought. A few months ago, when the leaves had started to turn, Jake had begun to say how nice it would be to have a baby. Eric was four and Warren had just turned three when Jake had broached the subject.

"You know... wouldn't it be nice to have just one more kid?" Jake had said. Surprised by the out of character suggestion, I'd wondered at it. The boys were getting big, and not having a baby in the house was initiating a new phase in our lives. Maybe he wanted to experience what it was like to have a baby with things going well between us. And I'd thought, "Well, maybe he's right. Things are better than they have ever been. The future looks pretty rosy, so why not?" One more baby, especially under our new circumstances, I'd fantasized, would be a pleasure.

Well, you know how it goes with a thought like that, all you need to do is conceive it and you do.

Standing sideways, I took a close look in the mirror and realized that I was starting to look a little full around my middle even though I couldn't be more than six weeks gone. Jake seemed really happy about the whole thing. Our lives were finally on track.

Smoothing my hand over the red satin of my dress and my little belly underneath, I smiled, and reflected on all of the changes that had taken place in the last nine months. It was all a testament to the precept that you never knew what life had waiting for you around the corner. Just when you think you know what the future holds something totally unexpected happens, turning your life around.

"Hey honey, you look fucking great!" Jake's reflection appeared behind me in the mirror. His hand felt warm and soft as he rubbed my bare shoulder and then bent his head and lightly kissed it. In the other hand he was carrying a glass of champagne. He handed the glass to me and picked up another one from the night stand where he had placed it on the way into the bedroom. We clinked the gold rimmed German crystal together, the glasses, resonating in a low full ringing tone.

"Merry Christmas!" I invitingly whispered.

"And a Happy New Year!" Jake slyly and seductively whispered in my ear.

❧ XLIII ❧

"Clickety-clack, clickety-clack, clickety-clack…" The metal on metal sound of the train wheels on the track caused a rhythmic background noise that was very comforting. The boys had finally collapsed into a heap on the train seat directly opposite me. The need for a nap had finally won out over their unlimited energy spurred on by the excitement of the train ride back home. It had been a great week's visit with my sister Carole in Pennsylvania. She and John lived in an exclusive suburb just outside of Pittsburgh in a lovely gray cedar sided ranch house nestled on the side of a rolling hill, with several wooded acres and a small brook that ran through the front yard. Visiting my sister had replenished my soul. The six years that had elapsed since the last time that she and I had been together, seemed to melt away the minute that we'd hugged hello. Once together it seemed as if we had never been apart. Some rare relationships are like that. I gazed out of the train window at the farm fields, bushes and trees dotting the countryside, awakening to the beginning of a new spring. It was the end of March and the unseasonably warm days had caused the buds of the trees to burst into the first emerald colors of the new season. What a beautiful day, a perfect ending to a perfect trip! Well, perfect except for that dream.

"Clickety-clack, clickety-clack, clickety-clack…" Nestled back into the cushions of my seat, I sleepily glanced around the nearly vacant train car. The sun streamed in through the windows and bathed the interior of the car with a soft golden glow. Warm and comfy, my mind drifted off.

To my surprise, Jake had agreed to my suggestion that it would be a good thing for me and the boys to visit Carole. My sister, Claudette, had recently followed her new truck driver husband to Texas in search of a better job for him, and therefore, a better life for herself and her four kids. Her departure had left me feeling alone and abandoned, the solitary sibling left in the city of Chicago. The trip to Pittsburgh was a way to make me feel a little less isolated, a little more in touch with my roots, and it had done the job.

Jake's new found ability to have empathy for my emotional needs had been a pleasant surprise. Feelings of appreciation to the Program and my Higher Power, for the positive changes in his mental outlook and our relationship, which had taken place over the last year, filled my mind. I smiled.

Changes… in the not too distant past I'd been afraid of what the changes in both Jake and I might bring.

"Listen Teresa, I've been wondering about something. I can tell that I'm changing. I feel it and it's good. But what happens to me and Jake and our relationship as I change?" I'd asked with a slight amount of apprehension while sitting in Teresa's cozy kitchen sipping a warm cup of coffee on a lazy winter afternoon.

"You're right. You're changing the way you view life, Jake's drinking, and the way you react to them both. And in turn, the relationship between the two of you is changing. And that's good. That's what gives Jake a chance to sober up." Teresa had said this in her familiar, matter of fact kind of way. She was an old timer in the Program and knew a lot about the games that came with the disease. She'd also been very lucky. Her husband had sobered up and had remained so for a long time. Looking into my eyes, she leaned forward in her chair as if confiding a special secret, and comfortingly laid her hand over mine as it rested on the wooden table top.

"But Susan, you need to know that your changing may impact your relationship in a different way from what you've imagined. There are several possible scenarios that I've seen over the years, several ways that things can work out. By changing the way that you react to the alcoholic and his disease, you remove his excuses for drinking. And because he no longer has excuses to hide behind, he is forced to come face to face with his own alcoholism, and the consequences of it. When that happens, some alcoholics sober up and choose to go to AA. I was lucky, that's what Terry did. But it's been my experience that the majority continues to drink. Some of those accept the blame for their drinking but lack the ability to do anything about it. Others continue to live in the false comfort of denial, insisting on seeing the blame for their unhappiness in others, and refusing to see it in themselves. Either way, the strain on the marriage grows. Finally, when neither alcoholic nor their spouse can get what they need from the relationship, one or both walk away. There is no telling what it will be for you and Jake." Now she held my hand even tighter as she continued.

"So what you have to do is answer the question: Can you go back to the way it was because you are afraid of what might be? Can you go back to where you were, to stop changing and become the doormat that you used to be? Can you allow the merry-go-round of denial to go back into gear? If you come up with a 'no' then you have to 'Let Go and Let God', trust in your Higher Power, and have the courage to keep working on yourself and to keep changing."

It's been said that the truth shall set you free and that day I had found it to be true. Teresa had guided me through another turning point in my life. In response to her questions, I searched my soul and found the deep conviction that I could not go back. There was no choice. I had to let the chips fall where they may. This change was better for me. This change was better for my kids. And through the grace of God, this change would be better for Jake.

Still, it was probably some subconscious fear of change that must have brought about the dream. It all seemed so silly. Sure he was still drinking but the violence in our relationship had stopped. It had been defused by the tools learned in the Program. Whatever the anger and the need to feel dominance over me, whatever that was, seemed to have left the picture. With the way things were for the last year, I could live with his disease. Even if he didn't stop drinking, even if he didn't join AA, it would be OK for us. We WERE different.

"Clickety-clack, clickety-clack, clickety-clack…" I could still remember the pain of the dream. It laid there like a snake in the darkness, in the place where nightmares went when you were awake, and bit me every once in awhile when a memory of the dream would flitter through my conscious mind. Maybe it was all those unresolved feelings from Germany. Or maybe, being pregnant again had caused it. Even though getting pregnant this time had been Jake's idea, he hadn't been any different as far as sex was concerned. Shortly after New Year's Eve, I had gotten cut off. My little belly had been too much for him. So maybe that's where it came from, the dream that is. Even during the episode with Jake and the hooker in Germany, I hadn't had a dream like that.

The dream hadn't been just about Jake fooling around. I could understand the roots of that. This dream had been different. Even the feel of it had been different. It had been raw and intense and felt as if it was really happening. In it, he didn't love me anymore. He loved someone else. Until the dream, despite everything that we'd been through together, that possibility had never occurred to me.

"Jake may be a drunk, but one thing was for certain, he would never fuck me over like that for another woman." I thought to myself. And besides, there was an unspoken bond between us that we both knew from the beginning. He needed me, even more than I needed him. The stability that I infused in him, kept him afloat. That was one of the forged links between us that made it impossible for me to ever consider leaving him.

Yet the possibility must have lurked somewhere down deep inside the recesses of my subconscious. If not, where had the dream come from? The remembered look on his face as he told me that he loved someone else still caused a deep ache in my heart. And his eyes… they had been empty of feeling for me, cold and closed to all of my crying and pleading for him to say it wasn't so. In the dream, my emotional pain had been excruciating and reminiscent of the heart wrenching pain experienced during another still frequently remembered nightmare. And even though several years had passed since that one, the anguish at viewing my mother's lifeless corpse on a table in the morgue was still painfully cutting and vivid in my memory. That one had been a lulu. And this dream had run a close second to that.

A shiver from the chill of the remembered, deeply disturbing dream caused a slight involuntary shudder.

"Clickety-clack, clickety-clack, clickety-clack…" Time to think about something else. It had just been a dream, nothing more than that. Life was good and I should count my blessings. As a matter of fact, it was better than it had ever been between the two of us. We were becoming friends, now that our lives didn't revolve around his drinking. We'd just put a second floor aluminum sided addition on the top of our tiny, two bedroom brick ranch house. With the third baby on the way we wanted to ensure that there would be enough room for our expanding family. The addition was unfinished on the inside. We'd been short on money, but we figured that the two of us could take our time putting the walls and plaster board up by ourselves. It would be fun, and we were both looking forward to it.

Jake seemed more at peace with himself than I'd ever seen him. Yes, life was good, and just one short year ago I would have never guessed it could be like this. Smiling, the thought of the new baby popped into my mind.

"Maybe it's a girl. Wouldn't Jake be surprised! We could name her Beth." I mused as my eyelids got heavy.

"Just goes to show you, you never know what's coming around the corner." I said softly under my breath, as I began to drift off…

"Clickety-clack, clickety-clack, clickety-clack…"

❧ XLIV ❧

I had him cornered in the bathroom. He was taking a bath. I could hear the swirling of the water as he repositioned himself in the tub. One thing about Jake, he had impeccable hygiene. He took a bath or a shower at least two times a day. That made him a very clean, uncommunicative person. Over the last day or two, every time that I would bring up the subject, he would mumble a denial and scurry off to somewhere else in the house, saying that he had something else more important to do. With every denial the tension in my muscles grew. I was determined that this time he would talk to me, and this time I wouldn't let him out of the bathroom until he did. Jackie Gleason's voice was barely distinguishable as it emanated from the television in the background, while I stood in front of the closed bathroom door.

"The Honeymooners must be on again!" I thought to myself. God, I hated that TV show! It was one of Jake's favorites and recently, some TV station had been playing the moronic thing over and over again. Christ! With only a couple dozen episodes ever made, I could recite the dialogue from each episode in my sleep. It was yet another example of Jake's literary prowess.

Something was wrong with him. Ever since my return from my sister's last week, he'd been acting oddly. I couldn't put a finger on it but he seemed even more detached than usual, almost skulking. There also had been a few things out of place around the house and when I'd asked Jake about them, his explanations had seemed reasonable, but...

The seat cushions of my dark blue couch in the living room had become soiled with several fairly large, faint white smear spots. It'd taken quite a bit of scrubbing to get them off. Jake said that he'd been eating a bowl of cream of mushroom soup and must have slobbered some of it on the cushions. It had irritated me that he hadn't gotten it all cleaned up.

And then there were those cigarette butts in the station wagon's ashtray, Parliaments with a smudge of pink lipstick on the recessed filtered tip. I never wore lipstick. No matter what color it was when it went on, it always turned fire engine red, making me look like a Spanish dancer minus the rose in my teeth. When asked about the butts, Jake had said that the car belonging to one of the women at work, had broken down in the parking lot, and he'd given her a ride home since she lived close by. Still... she must be a chain smoker, because there were a lot of the little nasty things in my ashtray.

And then there were the phone calls. They'd started the day that I'd come back, the calls coming sometimes as often as two or three times a day. Whoever it was on the other end, the minute they heard my voice, they would hang up. Jake had said that it was probably somebody at work that he'd pissed off, and that he would put a stop to it, but it hadn't done any good.

Whatever the explanations were, things just didn't feel right. Something was wrong and I knew it. Maybe he was fooling around. I was almost five months pregnant and his track record on doing this kind of thing while I was in this condition was pretty good. The thought made my stomach ache.

"God, not again!" I thought to myself, reluctant to have to go through all that garbage one more time. But now, after a week of this crap, I was going to find out! I opened the door and walked in. Wordlessly I crossed the small distance from the door to the bathtub. Situating myself next to the wash basin at the foot of the tub, I rested my rump on the edge of the sink, and directed my gaze to my husband relaxing while completely submerged in the hot, steaming water. His eyes were closed and he gave no reaction to my entering the room.

"Jake I need to talk to you."

No reply.

"Jake, I said, I need to talk to you."

Still, no reply.

"Jake, I'm not going to leave this room until you talk to me!" I said with as much conviction as I could muster.

"So fucking talk." was his curt reply. His eyes remained closed.

"What's wrong with you?" My voice cracked, full of emotion.

"Nothing." His stoic reply matched his face, as he lay in the hot water with white swirls of steam rising from the still surface. I wasn't going to play this game any longer. I had to know what was going on. I had to know if what I suspected was true.

"Are you fooling around?" I blurted, my emotions along with the accusation, flying out of my mouth and loudly echoing in the tiny space.

Again, no response.

"Jake! Do you hear me? I want an answer to my question!" I shouted. "What's wrong with you? Do you have a girlfriend or something?"

"Yes." His lips barely moved as he hissed the word out between them while his eyes remained closed.

"What… what did you say?" I faltered, my words sticking in my throat. My brain was uncertain that it had processed what had been said, correctly.

"I said yes." This time he replied louder and with more conviction in his voice.

"A girlfriend?" I repeated more to myself than to him, trying to compute what that meant.

"Do you love her?" I pierced the smothering silence with the soft spoken question.

And for the first time since this had begun, he opened his eyes and looked at me.

"Because, if you don't. If it was a mistake, I could forgive you. We would have to work it out, but I could forgive you." My words rushed out in a tumble, unable to hide the hopeful and degrading tone in them.

Jake closed his eyes again and leaned the back of his head against the pink and maroon plastic tiled wall. The rest of his body remained perfectly still under the steaming water. A few seconds that seemed like an eternity, passed.

"Well… do you love her?" I asked again, the tone in my voice demanding an answer. Part of me was wildly impatient to hear what he had to say, and part of me was now wishing that I hadn't asked the question. Slowly, he lifted his head, opened his eyes and looked straight into mine.

"Yes." He said.

Somewhere in the background the low mumbling noise of the TV became suddenly discernable and a familiar, identifiable phrase replayed for the umpteenth time, echoing in the bathroom.

"Bang, zoom, straight to the moon!"

❧ XLV ❧

Taking a deep breath and blowing it slowly out between my lips, trying to lessen the tension in my rigid muscles as I lay on the bed, I turned my head and gazed from the darkness of the bedroom ceiling, to the soft yellow glow of the living room lamp. I always left a light on at night when I was alone in the house… and I was alone…and still afraid of the dark. There was no telling how long Jake would be gone. He hadn't come home from work tonight, and it wouldn't be the first Friday night that he would have stayed with her. I tried to relax again. I needed sleep, and even though the pain of this afternoon's chance meeting was still ripping though my chest, I had to think of the baby and get some sleep. If you thought about it, today had been the most difficult day to get through since that day in the bathroom.

I would have literally staked my life on the belief that Jake was not capable of loving someone else. Fooling around was one thing, but complete and utter betrayal, falling in love with another woman that was something totally different. I'd thought the bond between us that had been forged by mutual needs was unbreakable. I'd thought the trials and tribulations, the memories, which we had experienced over the last eleven years, had cemented us together forever. I'd thought I knew him better than I knew myself and that conviction had been rooted deep inside of me.

How could I have been so wrong? How could I have lived with another human being for all those years and been so wrong? How could I have believed that life and our relationship had finally been the best it had ever been, while the ultimate betrayal was brewing? Was my judgment that flawed? Was I that incapable of reading the signs of the world around me? How could I trust my feelings, core beliefs, and judgments about anything ever again?

It was ironic that such a small word, just three letters, Y E S, could have enough power to destroy the foundation of our relationship and blow my world right out from under me. It had the power to cut every mooring that connected me to the bedrock of my life, casting me adrift, upended in an ocean of fear and uncertainty, not knowing what to expect or how to realign and steady myself again.

The look on his face as he lay soaking in the tub avowing his love for someone else, had since become fodder for a feeding frenzy of nightmares that visited often, disturbing my sleep and leaving me exhausted in the morning. There is a saying that "The eyes are the windows of your soul." If that was the case, I'd gotten a glimpse of how cold and dead Jake's soul was in regards to me. Whatever had been there had died when I wasn't looking, and now there was a deep dark void in its place. The realization that a person, whom you have loved for what seems like forever, no longer loves you, and that no matter how hard you try, you cannot make him love you again, is what true horrors in the middle of the night are made of. It was all gone forever, and no matter how hard I tried, I couldn't make it any different. It was as if overnight, some alien species from the stars had made a replica of the man that I'd loved and left him in the bed beside me, while silently stealing away my lover, forever. The grief from my loss was overwhelming, making the remembered pain from the foreboding nightmare of my Pittsburgh visit, pale when compared to the agony of reality.

The two months since that day in the bathroom had been full of "on again" "off again" torture. At first, after the initial shock, after all of the tears and recriminations, Jake had said that even though he had feelings for another woman, he didn't want to break up our marriage.

"All of my fucking past is with you." He'd said. "I can't see my fucking life without you. If you can forgive me, I'll break it off and maybe it can be the way it used to be. It's all fucking up to you." Pregnant and desperate to make things the way they'd used to be, I'd agreed to try. However, despite his promise to break it off, all the warning signs that he hadn't, continued. It seemed that for whatever reasons, he couldn't make up his mind whether he wanted to stay or to go. Consequently, I'd been battered back and forth between the winds of an emotional storm with an excruciatingly painful game of "catch me if you can" being played.

Cigarette butts with pink lipstick on the filtered "recessed tip" continued to sporadically and mysteriously show up in the station wagon's ashtray. Jake always professed complete ignorance of the little white pieces of trash. An "I don't know how they got there." would be accompanied by a look of disdain which implied that somehow the blame lay with me. With every new found butt my hopes and dreams would go crashing into the depths of despair, and then Jake would deny and scold me for my lack of trust, leaving me to desperately try to bolster up my hopes and dreams again. It seemed so strange that those tiny pieces of "stuff" had ultimate power over me and my future.

Then there were those continuing phone calls, the hang-ups. They happened all hours of the day and night. Jake worked third shift but it didn't seem to matter whether he was at home or not, the phone calls persisted. After a while, it became apparent that there was some kind of pattern to them. During the day, Jake's impromptu visits to the grocery store for cigarettes or milk were prefaced by the calls. During the night, they were strategically timed so that getting a full night's sleep was impossible for me. The calls were from her. It was an obvious conclusion that, when confronted, Jake always denied.

Through the numerous fights, bits of information about Jake's new found love had inadvertently slipped out. Her name was Roz, she worked with Jake at the factory, and she lived near our home. The latter little tidbit of information explained Jake's new fascination with long trips to the store. Obviously, his long hours away hadn't been taken up with his inability to decide between two different brand name cans of peas!

Somewhere in the midst of all this, I'd finally put my foot down, and demanded that Jake talk to his supervisor about changing his shift at the plant back to days. If we were trying to work things out and it seemed so difficult for him to end things between them, than maybe it would be easier for him if he didn't see her at work every night. You know, "out of sight out of mind". I'd thought, after a few weeks of Jake being on days, things would be over. I was wrong.

I began to feel like Alice in Wonderland, who had just stepped through the "looking glass". Jake's explanation of what was going on was all topsy-turvy. Most of the time he would "out and out" deny that he was still seeing her. But every so often my accusations would result in an admission of guilt from him. However, along with the admission came the accusation that it was somehow all my fault. I wasn't understanding enough of the situation. He was torn because, after all, she needed him more than I did. She wasn't as strong as I was. I could make it without him, she couldn't. He had to continue to see her, to help her work things out, he owed her that much. All of which seemed like pretty crazy thinking to me, since I was the one standing in front of him pregnant with his child, mother of his two little boys, and with no other means of support besides him!

Life became a misery full of contradictions, half truths and lies. The up and down, round and round existence wore on me. Strong nausea continually plagued me and the only two things that I was able to tolerate in my mouth were warm milk and cigarettes. Not a very good diet for an expectant mother, but one does what one does, to survive.

I rolled from my side to my back, forcing my gaze from the soft warm glow filtering through the bedroom door back to the darkness of the ceiling above the bed.

"Close your eyes. Relax! Think about packaging all this shit up in a big box, tie it with a huge red bow and offer it up to your Higher Power to take care of, instead of you." I smiled and my eyes closed as I pictured the box floating up out of my hands and into the sky. Funny, I still couldn't call my Higher Power, God. The word God still had all kinds of rules, regulations, and judgments attached to it that I no longer believed. On the other hand, my Higher Power was associated only with total acceptance, love, and peace. He was my source of strength. He was what got me through the night, Him and my friends.

During all this insanity my Al-Anon friends, Teresa, Dee, and Patti had been there for me with words of wisdom and love. Teresa's take on the whole situation had been, when Jake realized he couldn't bully and control me any longer he'd thought that getting me pregnant would do the trick. And when that didn't work, he'd found someone else he could push around.

"You can bet the relationship that the sadistic son-of-a-bitch has with his new girlfriend is at best equal to what yours was with him before the program." She'd said. "And since these kinds of things usually degrade as they progress, their relationship in all likelihood, is actually much worse. So don't go concentrating on what you think that she is taking from you, or lamenting over how happy you think they are. They're not!"

Thinking back on some of the bits and pieces of information that Jake had let fly during a few really fiery discussions between us, provided a testimony to the validity of her theory. And yes, Jake was truly a sick son-of-a-bitch. Teresa had been right about that too. For the last month or so, he'd hinted, almost boastfully, that Roz had become pregnant, using the very sketchy fact to run back and forth between our two houses like a rooster running back and forth in the barnyard between two hens. Later, when I'd had enough, during one particularly ugly argument, he'd taken great sadistic pleasure in telling me that she was no longer with child and that I was somehow responsible for the abortion that he'd forced her into. He shouted that it was my lack of understanding and acceptance of their circumstance that had caused the foul deed to be done. When heartsick and tearful, I recounted his accusations to Teresa in her warm cozy kitchen, she lovingly pulled me to her, wrapping her arms around me in a big bear hug while I sobbed, and comforted me.

"This guy's a pathological liar! You can't believe a word he says. Don't you spend one minute of your time feeling guilty about anything that he says has happened between the two of them. It's their doing not yours! The only thing that you know for sure is that you are going to have a new baby in your life. Just think of it! Imagine all the joy and love that the new baby will bring to your heart and your children's hearts. You are really lucky to have such a gift at this time in your life!" Listening to her comforting words, my banged and bruised heart and my thoughts turned to the new life inside of me. And my baby began to become the focal point of my future.

My baby… Pleasant thoughts centered on what might be, swirled in my now relaxed consciousness.

As if on cue, a tiny foot or fist pushed against the inside of my belly, rolling from one side of my tummy to the other, a comforting gesture that seemed to say, "You're not alone, Mommy." And I wasn't. Despite all the crap, I had my children, my baby, and my friends. My eyes were closed now, and my breathing had become rhythmic while lying on my back, in the center of my big, comfortable bed.

Then there was Dee. Dee had been a good friend of Teresa's and when the proverbial shit hit the fan Teresa had encouraged her to share her personal and very private story with me. She was a shy and soft spoken woman whose story had been much like mine, except, as she'd put it, she'd done everything wrong when it had happened to her. Teresa convinced her that if she shared some of her painful memories it would do her good to get it out in the open, and maybe, because of it, her experiences would allow me to learn from her mistakes. Sometimes the act of sharing painful memories for the good of another can put a positive spin on some pretty horrible happenings.

Thank God for Dee! She'd saved me a couple of weeks ago, from what could have been one nasty situation. It was during the last round of, "Honey, I really love you and I promise that I will never see Roz again." Bursting through Teresa's backdoor and into her kitchen, furious about the fact that I'd just seen Jake's car up at the neighborhood bar again, I began to rave to Teresa and Dee who were sitting wide eyed at the wooden kitchen table.

"I can't believe it! He's up at the Bullmarket again! I know he's with HER! And after he just promised that it was really over this time. Does he think that I'm stupid or something? What the fuck is wrong with him?" Tears of frustration and hurt pooled in my eyes.

"Susan, calm down." Teresa said.

"Sit down, take a breath, and tell us all about it." She continued as she motioned towards a chair at the table, across from her and Dee. Furious and hardly able to contain it, I hesitated for a moment and then took her advice, plopping down in the wooden chair. Immediately, the rage began to build again.

"I should go up to the bar and surprise them! I should go there and really tell them off! Just who does he think he is, telling me that he loves me, and that things are finally over between them, and then going right out of our house to go and sit in a bar with HER?" I ended up shouting, unable to control the storm of emotion raging inside of me. Then the picture of the look of shock and shame that would be on their faces when I confronted them, as they sat on their barstools, began to feed my hunger for some kind of justice. A large wave of satisfaction, spawned from my perceived triumph, flooded my mind and provided me with a moment free from the excruciating pain of betrayal.

"That's just what I'll do!" I hissed as I relished in my imagined victory.

"Don't do it." Dee said her voice soft and full of caution. My gaze shifted to her as she spoke. Her face showed no emotion but her eyes were filled with sorrow and something else… regret?

"It won't turn out the way you think it will." She said with a cold certainty. "I know because I did it. I did just what you said. I stormed into that shithole, you know the Village, Jimmy's favorite place to meet his girlfriend, looking for the two of them. I'd seen his truck in the parking lot and figured that it was time for me to give both him and HER, a piece of my mind. They'd put me through hell and I wanted to give a little of it back. The bar reeked of booze and cigarettes and I found the two of them sloppy drunk and sitting together in a booth in the back of the place. He was slumped way low in the seat and when I got close I could see that she was giving him a hand-job right there in the booth! I couldn't believe it! The sight of the two of them drunk and her, with her hands on him, revolted me and made me crazy... righteous indignation, and all that. So I lit into him and HER, screaming and rattling off a list of everything they'd done to me and ending up with exposing the disgusting thing that they'd been doing in the booth as proof of what degenerates they were. I guess I'd thought that somehow everyone in the bar would see them for what they were, and I could shame the two of them for what they had done to me." Her voice had wavered in a few places as she had told her story, but the stony expression on her face had remained. Taking a momentary break before continuing, she took a cigarette out of her pack on the table, lit it and took a long slow drag. The pause gave her a few seconds to regroup, so that she could go on.

"For a second or two after I'd finished ranting, Jimmy just stared at me with his mouth open. Then he laughed real loud in my face. 'See I told you all that my wife was a crazy bitch and now she just proved it!' His girlfriend giggled and everyone in the bar laughed at me. Someone sitting on a barstool a few feet away shouted, 'Get the fuck out of here, you stupid fucking cunt!' Every bit of the dignity, that I thought I had, was crushed in an instant, and I ran out of there to the hoots and jeers of strangers." One small tear dripped silently onto the shiny kitchen table top. Quietly, she bent down and slipped a tissue out of her purse sitting beside her chair. She blew her nose, and began again.

"You can do what you want, but I say don't do it. You know, we have no control over the hurtful things that another human being does to us. All we can do is defend ourselves, as best we can. But the hurt that we cause ourselves, that. we have complete control over. Life is rough enough coping with what others dish out without causing ourselves unneeded pain."

So up until today I'd spared myself the pain of seeing Roz's face. Then the happenstance of today had been one of those hurtful things that had been out of my control. I'd taken Dee's advice on faith, and now was grateful that it had afforded me a few short weeks reprieve on the anguish I was feeling today. It was a complete and utter surprise to me that such a simple thing as seeing someone's face for the first time could generate such an overwhelming physical reaction. Today had been shopping day. The boys were in the shopping cart and they were babbling and laughing as we strolled down the aisle at Kmart. They'd needed some socks and underwear which were the only articles of clothing that never seemed to be handed down from one family of boys to another. Chuckling, I was thinking to myself, it was apparent that everyone's household must have a sock monster resident in their laundry room, secretly feeding on socks, when Eric suddenly shouted.

"Mommy, look! It's Roz!" Following Eric's pointing finger and simultaneously becoming aware of a cart coming towards me, just a few feet away, my gaze shifted to the woman pushing it, and by the look on her face I knew. It was HER! Without hesitation Roz made an about face leaving the cart in the aisle blocking my way, and literally ran in the direction of the door! The split second encounter had left me feeling like I'd been kicked in the chest by a mule. However, despite the agony in my chest and resulting shortness of breath, I followed, pushing two small children in a shopping cart through the store as quickly as I could, but it wasn't fast enough. Standing in the parking lot, I'd given up hope of catching up with HER, when as luck would have it, a silver car backed out of the parking space in the row directly in front of me and when it did, I got a glimpse of HER license plate.

Shit! The nausea was coming back. Just the thought of seeing her this afternoon was twisting my stomach in knots and my chest still ached. I couldn't lie on my back any longer. The baby was too heavy. Thoughts began to churn and boil in my head.

"That bastard's been spending time with her while he's had the kids with him and making them a part of his dirty little game. They even know her name! Well, I know her license plate number now! We'll see what my cousin Tom can dig up!"

Tom was a Chicago cop and I'd given him the number earlier this evening. He'd been off duty, so any digging would have to wait until tomorrow. That was OK with me. I could wait until tomorrow. After all, patience was a virtue, and tomorrow my questions about her would finally be answered.

Still angry despite my rationalizations, I roughly rolled over on my side and packed the comforter around my belly and legs attempting to find a comfortable position. The nausea and chest ache persisted. Questions ran round and round in my head. Where was Jake anyway? I bet the bastard was with her, comforting her after her terrible KMart experience! My blood started to boil.

"Stop it!" I said to myself. I was working myself up again. It wasn't a good idea to do that. The baby and I needed some rest. I'd have to start all over again with mentally wrapping my box of emotional garbage in a big red bow and offering it up.

"Or... I could think of that poem "Footsteps", the one where your Higher Power carries you when you're too tired and weary to go on." Immediately thoughts of how it would feel to be picked up and carried by Someone safe and strong, held in His arms, comforted and shielded from all pain and sorrow, radiated warmth through my tense and aching body. Teresa had been right. He could help me get through this. Her words still echoed in my head.

"Because of freewill, your Higher Power can't do much about the evil things that Jake and the world can do to you, but He sure can help to get you through it, and to figure things out. All you have to do is ask." So, I asked and my racing thoughts began to slow down as I began to think things over.

"Considering everything, it's probably a good bet that I'll need a lawyer." I softly spoke into the darkness with peaceful resignation. "And because of Jake's regular disappearing trick, a new car is probably on the horizon, though God only knows where I'll get the money…" Listening to my spoken words break the silence of my room, I realized the true meaning of what I'd casually said. "Well… I guess I'll put it in Your hands… After all… You really are the only One Who knows." I thought with a silent, silly, little, mental chuckle. Then my thoughts sleepily moved on to the happenings of the day.

"What's it going to matter who she is… and where she is? It doesn't change anything." I was drifting now. "She was pretty damned old and ugly too! She looked like a barfly. You would have thought that after me he would have had better taste!" This time a smile softly relaxed my almost sleeping face. "Maybe she can be his new butterfly."

As I finally drifted off to sleep, Teresa's words from today slipped though my weary mind like a soft, smooth, silky blue ribbon.

"You need to look at it this way… maybe, just maybe, when your ready, she could be your key to freedom."

❧ XLVI ❧

Thank God it was over! Every time was the same, nine months of cold sweats when my thoughts would turn to just how bad this time would be. That old saying "Once you see your baby, all the memory of the pain is forgotten." was bull. I always remembered, and very graphically too.

Matthew was beautiful and definitely worth it, but it still had hurt like hell. Thank God, he'd been on the small side, and that I'd gone to Lamaze classes with Teresa as my coach. She'd taken the classes herself with her last baby and had strongly encouraged me to do the same. With the way that things had turned out I'd needed the advantage. My labor had progressed slowly at first, and kind of stalled out after several hours, so drugs for the pain were not on the agenda. Then, suddenly Matthew appeared, demanding to be born, and caught everyone by surprise including the doctor. Delivering a baby without the complimentary episiotomy had turned out to be quite an experience. The description that I'd previously heard somewhere at some coffee-clutch was true. It did feel as if your bottom had been doused with gasoline and set on fire.

As grotesquely painful as the whole thing sounded, and was, it did have its positive side, reminding me of another old saying "Pay me now or pay me later". Here it was less than twenty-four hours since the birth and I was comfortably sitting in the maternity floor waiting-room. Sunshine was streaming through the tenth floor hospital windows, reflecting off of everything that was smooth and shiny and giving the meticulously clean room a magical glow. And my bottom wasn't sore! Halleluiah!

Sitting fairly close to the shiny metal elevator doors, my eyes caught a glimpse of an unfamiliar reflection in them. It was still hard to get used to, hard to recognize that the stranger in the reflection was me. The closely cropped brown hair, my newest haircut, was barely an inch all over my head, quite a striking difference from the last eight years of long black hair. The black hair had disappeared along with my wedding ring. Looking at my naked left ring finger, I smiled. Recalling that it, along with the absence of a husband and a woman Lamaze coach in his place, had lead the kind nuns of St. Mary's Hospital, who'd taken care of me, to assume that I was an unwed mother.

Looking more closely at myself in the elevator doors, I assessed my new image. The woman who looked back at me was thin, almost too thin. With all the stress and insanity, I'd only gained five pounds during my pregnancy, and this morning, when I got on the scale it had read "114 pounds".

"Was that too thin?" I wondered. From somewhere the saying; "A woman can't have too much money or be too thin." came to mind so I guessed 114 pounds on my 5'6" frame was OK.

The short brown hair was really me. The color was really mine. It was just as Sister Joseph Mary had preached to our high school class years ago. "God knows what he's doing. The color of your eyes, your skin, everything was planned to match.

Any other color looks so… unnatural." She'd said the word "unnatural" as if she had something that really tasted bad in her mouth and wanted to spit it out. I'd thought at the time that she was an incredibly old fuddy-duddy, but now, much to my amazement, I believed that she'd been right.

The long black hair and the wedding ring had gone out the door along with Jake. He'd made his decision shortly after the impromptu K-Mart meeting between me and his mistress. He'd decided that his future lay with Roz and not with me. Thinking back on it, it seemed strange that the only reaction that I'd had at the time, after eleven years of my life had been spent with the son-of-a-bitch who was deserting me, was one of complete and utter elation. The front screen door hadn't slammed shut behind him when the triumphant thought, "I will never again be forced to watch another mindless episode of the Honeymooners!" shouted freedom in my heart. I'd done everything that I could do to make my wedding vows of eight years work. I'd left no stone unturned no task undone, and now I was free!

Since that glorious day about four weeks ago, Jake had only sporadically come back to the house for some clothes or a few personal things. Most of his stuff was still in the house. The impact on the kids had been far less than I'd thought it would be. Over the last five months he'd been gone most of the time, so for them nothing much had changed. He'd never told me where he was staying. That was the reason that he probably still didn't know that Matthew had been born. I'd always supposed that he was staying with Roz or a friend and had never pressed him for that information. If there was an emergency, something where he would be needed, he could always be tracked down through work. But that would probably never happen. I'd always handled everything without him anyhow.

We were using the same lawyer since the divorce was uncontested, and doing so saved us both a bundle of money. We'd already agreed to how things would be split up once the divorce was final. All that Jake would be responsible for was eighty dollars a week child support. In exchange for not paying any additional support or alimony, he'd sign over his half of the equity in the house to me, which came to approximately fifteen hundred dollars. The agreement sounded like I was getting the shaft, however, realistically we both needed to be able to afford to live after the divorce, and there was also a big unspoken bonus in it for me. Jake would have no claims on the house. It would be all mine, free and clear of any future interference from him. That would be at least one tie to him that would be completely severed. My instincts told me, the fewer things that he had control over in my life, the better.

When the nurse had come by today to ask information for Matthew's birth certificate, the thought had occurred to me that it would be so easy to sever another tie with Jake. "Unknown" could be placed in the box labeled "Father" and would keep his meddling interference out of that arena too. But my unwavering belief in truth above all things, won out and his name was grudgingly written in its rightful place. At least, the only material thing that I would have to count on him for, in the future, was his lousy eighty bucks a week. In the meantime, he was to continue to give me the majority of his weekly check. So far, he'd shown up a few times with money for the bills and food, but I knew that wouldn't last much longer. We'd had a bit of a cushion in our bank account but that was dwindling down to nothing. Teresa had said that she knew a woman manager at a neighborhood bank, who'd agreed to interview me for a job, as soon as I was able. With the no stitches birth, maybe I would be able sooner than I'd planned.

A soft "Ting" of a bell drew my attention to the brightly lit, plastic number ten above the shiny elevator doors. The doors slid smoothly open and through the slowly widening slit I recognized a familiar figure, my sister Carole. She and her husband John had coincidentally been in town at some surgical conference when I'd had the baby. It was good to see her face.

My leg muscles ached a bit as I got up off the plastic cushioned waiting room chair to greet my sister, lingering evidence of the extreme physical exertion of bringing Matthew into the world. Carole stepped quickly off the elevator and easily crossed the distance between us, meeting me with a big bear hug.

"How are you doing?" She said with a look of true concern in her eyes, her arm still around my shoulder as we walked the short distance to the couch.

"I'm OK." I said as we both sat down side by side on the plastic cushion. A silence settled between us as I searched my thoughts for a place to start, a way to tell her where I was at in my life, and why.

"I just got done talking to Daddy and Gladys. They're worried about you." Carole broke the silence first. "Are you sure you're doing the right thing? I mean, are you being realistic about all of this? You've just had a baby. How are you going to take care of yourself and the kids? Even if things are bad between you and Jake, can't you stick it out a little while longer? At least you won't be facing things alone. You've made it this long, in another year or two you'll be in a much better position to think about going on your own. Are you sure you've thought this through?" Her voice was soft and caring, but the questions came out one after another, as if their rapid succession would bring me to some kind of reason in the midst of the impossible choices that she'd believed I'd made.

"I don't have a choice, Jake wants out. He wants his girlfriend, and a divorce is the best thing for the both of us." I was saying the words but at the same time realizing how difficult it would be to make Carole understand.

"Maybe if you give him some time, he'll see that he's being a fool. It's all so quick. Things haven't had time to settle down. The prospect of a new baby, additional responsibility, can make some men act crazy for a little while. If you just hold on he'll probably come to his senses. He's been a pretty good husband and father up to this point. This is all probably just a phase. He'll probably snap out of it and you can see if you can work things out." She said, keeping her voice low so that the other new mothers who had just recently hobbled into the waiting room couldn't overhear our conversation.

I couldn't blame her for not understanding. I hadn't told Carole, or anyone else in my family, the whole story. Now that I no longer needed to protect his reputation for a future with my family, how could I begin to explain? How could I explain that Roz was only the end, not the beginning, of what was wrong between Jake and me? How could I make her understand that because of Jake's infidelity, I'd finally found the courage to do what I should've done a long time ago, for myself and my children. In Jake's betrayal I'd found my freedom. I would put myself and my children in God's hands and we would be just fine. There was no need for anyone to worry. Somehow I needed to get that across to this person who loved me and cared for me. I owed her to try. But this was not the time or the place to do it.

"I know that it looks as if I've rushed into this decision, but there's been a lot going on that I need to talk to you about. It's too complicated for here." I said quietly as the bell "tinged" again and the elevator doors slipped open. Several people got out and strolled over to the other patients who were now sitting fairly close to Carole and me.

"Trust me." I said, the tone of my voice low yet emphatic. Then with my hand touching her arm in a reassuring manor, I added. "It's the only thing left to do." And then changing the subject, I said in a conversational tone "Have you seen the baby? He really is beautiful!"

Reluctant to shelve our discussion on my problems 'till later, Carole hesitated a moment before she replied. Slowly, she searched my eyes with hers, looking for some reassurance that it would be alright to let go, and seeing the resolve in mine responded with a warm trusting touch of her hand on my arm.

A slight stiffness had settled into my lower muscles while we'd sat talking, causing me to get up from the fake leather couch with a bit of a wobble.

"Are you sure you're OK?" Carole asked again, grabbing a hold of my arm and steadying the both of us.

"Yeah… just fine." I said as we began the short walk down to the nursery.

Later, after saying my goodbyes to my sister, I walked back to my room, immediately removed my robe, slipped into the bed, and snuggled under the covers, glad for the opportunity to get some rest. As luck would have it, the bed in my two person hospital room was vacant so I was free from the unwanted intrusions of a stranger. Thinking about it, it was true what Carole had said. I was alone. There weren't any flowers or cards laying about my room, tokens of undying love from a devoted husband. But that was the way things were, and… It was wonderful! It sounded crazy! And someone not knowing all the details, contemplating my plight, would believe I was crazy for feeling this way. But I knew it would all work out, everything would be alright. I just knew it.

I wasn't really alone. My kids and, of course, my friends in Al-Anon were always there. They were my real family. They never gave me "advice" or judged my decisions. I was free to choose whatever path that I thought was good for me and my kids, and they were always there to support me in those choices. Their never ending love and concern provided a space for me to grow. We were in the trenches together, fighting our lives' battles together, and they always had my back. Through my whole emotional nightmare Teresa had been my rock, my tether to reality, and Patti had been my friend. Teresa's knowledge and humor about the disease and those who suffer from it, helped to guide me through the fear, anger, and uncertainty of the last two years of my life. How we both laughed over a cup of coffee, when I told her about the look on the lawyer's face, when Jake had said that he actually wanted a clause in the divorce papers, that if in the future, he changed his mind about the divorce, it would become null and void.

And then there was Patti. Her husband was a drunk who was still attempting to drink the world dry, and most of my time over the last few nightmare months, was spent with her. The two of us were quite a pair. Her with a husband in the deepest throws of his alcoholism and me with Jake, his booze, and his girlfriend. The both of us worked very hard at living the slogan, "Let Go and Let God". It allows a person to become an observer instead of an emotional participant in the insanity of the disease. It enabled us not only to survive, but also it cultivated within us a perverse sense of humor which replaced fear and anger with laughter. One Sunday afternoon, after a particularly awful scene with Jake, I'd showed up unannounced at Patti's front door needing a friendly shoulder to cry on.

"Is Dean home? I know that it's Sunday afternoon and all, but…" I'd reluctantly asked as I stood in the doorway, worried that my knock on Patti's door had caused an intrusion on her and her husband's time.

"Home? That drunkin' motherfucker!" She responded in her usually colorful and expressive way. "He's out driving around in his tow truck with my car up on the tow hook. That stupid fucker thinks that him driven' drunk around the neighborhood, with my car towed behind, is good advertisement for the tow business. Suzie, ya' know that I got to let go and leave him to God. Who else would want the sorry motherfucker?" With that we both laughed until tears ran down our cheeks. Anyone from the regular world, i.e. "earth people", would have thought that we had gone insane.

The two of us were like the three musketeers minus one. Together we presented a brave face to the world and to our problems. Patti appeared to be unafraid of life and the things it had to offer. Just being with her, seemed to bolster my courage and ability to meet difficult situations head on. My first experience with the daunting task of changing a flat tire had happened while we were together. Immediately after the tire had gone flat while driving up a large, long hill, we'd pulled off on to the shoulder of the busy city street, in the middle of rush hour traffic. Without hesitation Patti jumped out of her car and popped the trunk. Beside her, while she pulled out all kinds of paraphernalia with which to change the tire, I stood in amazement.

"Aren't you gonna' call Dean to come and change it for you?" I'd asked. Her husband was a car mechanic and considering that we had four preschoolers in the backseat, and me being very much with child, the thought had never occurred to me that she would attempt to do anything else.

"Fuck no!" She laughed. "Besides, the bastard's at work. I don't need him to get fuckin' fired. We can change it ourselves. It's only a fuckin' tire. Here, hold this shit, while I change it." So there I stood along the side of the road. The traffic going up Cicero Avenue hill whizzing by me, with Patti's keys and purse in my hand, and fascinated with the idea that we weren't powerless and could actually do this "man thing". There was one hitch however, one thing that neither of us had thought about. Patti had gotten the bumper jack out of the trunk, placed it under the back bumper on the right side of the car, and standing in back of the bumper, pumped the handle a time or two. The back end of the car had begun to rise up ever so slightly. And then the driver of a bus sitting next to our car, in traffic, and waiting for the light at the intersection on the other side of the hill to turn green, opened the bus doors and tried to get our attention. The noise of the traffic was almost deafening and part of what he was saying was lost.

"Hey! Ladies... Hey!"

Patti raised her head and peered over her shoulder at the bus, evaluating the look on the bus driver's face. The fact that he'd judged us as two stupid broads, and was having a gay old time belly laughing about it, was written all over his face. She'd assumed that his remarks had been some wise ass comment, and flipped him the finger in retaliation, after which, she pushed the jack handle down for one more pump. At that, the driver's smiling expression slipped away and, what I thought to be anger, took its place. He shouted this time much louder, trying to get his voice to carry over the din of traffic. We only heard part of what he was saying.

"Stop! You're on a … You better…" His face was turning red as he strained his voice to be heard.

Patti raised her head again and shouted back.

"Fuck you, you sick son-of-a-bitch! Leave us alone!" Again, emphasizing her words with a raised finger, she started to bend down in order to resume pumping on the handle of the jack.

Realizing her intent, the bus driver began to frantically blow his horn, his face revealing agitation, frustration and fear. The bus was holding up traffic and the horns of the cars stuck in back of the bus were adding to the pandemonium of deafening noise. Up until this point, the kids had been pretty good in the back seat, despite the circumstances and the summer heat. But with the windows rolled down, the confusion and the loud blaring horns became too much for them, and all four began to cry. I quickly moved from in back of the car, to the open window, to try and comfort our wailing brood. At the same time, Patti stood up straight as an arrow, and with determination to end this nonsense once and for all, stomped passed the back of the car, and over to the open bus doors. I wasn't able to hear the exchange of words, but when Patti came back her whole demeanor had changed.

"Thank God for that pushy, know it all, son-of-a-bitch!" She said with an ashen gray face, as she slowly and carefully jacked the car back down one notch at time, until it rested safely on the ground. Then by incredible, unbelievable luck, or by the grace of God, whichever one is inclined to believe, Dean happened by in his tow truck on his way home from work, and the rest was history.

I'd learned two valuable lessons that day. One was that you can't change a back tire with a bumper jack on a rear-wheel drive car, on a hill, without having the car roll back on top of you and at best case, breaking both your legs.

The second was that Patti was good for me. Despite our brush with a grave mishap, she'd taken action. She'd done something, instead of wringing her hands and waiting to be saved. She'd faced the situation and the people in it without fear, a mode of operation for a woman that I hadn't remembered seeing before, at least not to the degree that made it worth remembering.

"Mrs. Burke!" The candy striper abruptly blurted out as she stuck her head into my hospital room doorway, giving me quite a start. "Would you like a magazine or a book to read?" She gestured towards her cart which was still in the hallway.

"No thanks." I replied, after which she popped out as quickly as she'd popped in. Sitting up and fluffing my pillows, I resituated myself trying to find a more comfortable position in the uncomfortable hospital bed. It was important for me to get as much rest as possible because when I went home, there would be no rest. And besides, lying here relaxing and thinking things over was actually very pleasant. It was cathartic, like being on a retreat.

So all in all, Carole had been mistaken. I was definitely not alone. And maybe... just maybe... there were other possibilities in the future. Patti, Teresa, and Peggy had all told me that they knew somebody who, when the divorce crap was over, they'd thought, I should meet. Teresa had confided in me a couple of months ago that her husband's cousin, who'd been widowed and left with two little boys, was a really nice guy.

"I'm not pushing you into anything. I just want you to know that there are "normal" men out there. And... Well, when things settle down, you may want to consider being introduced to him." She'd said. In response I'd said that after Jake, I didn't want to look at another man for the rest of my life, thank you, and we both laughed.

"Seriously," She'd said. "You never know what could be around the corner. Just remember what I've said, when you think that you're ready."

Then there was Patti and Dean. Dean worked with a guy, a fellow mechanic, who coincidentally also was a widower with a couple of kids. I remembered thinking when Patti told me about it, that widowers must be hanging around the south suburbs of Chicago like low hanging fruit, just waiting to be plucked off the vine. I was more than a little reluctant to meet him considering he was a good friend of Dean's. Bird's of a feather and all that...

And then there was Butch. Paulette had been dead for almost two years. Both Peggy and Buddy had thought that Butch might be interested in being re-introduced to me, so to speak. The two of us only casually knew each other, and the last time that I'd seen him had been nine years ago at Peggy and Buddy's wedding. Butch had been the "best man". As a teenager, he'd been a good looking guy with a blonde curly pompadour hair style, a "greaser" like Jake. When Peggy had mentioned the possibility to me, I'd figured that when I was ready to meet someone, he'd probably be the safest man to meet. The other two were unknowns. Butch had been Buddy's best friend since Buddy had moved in next door to him over twenty years ago. There would be less of a question as to who he was, and if he had any monsters hidden down deep inside, away from public view. I didn't need another "crazy". One had been more than enough. Through the insanity with Jake, Peggy and I had remained close, and she was the only person "outside" of Al-Anon, who knew some of the gory details. She would have told me if Butch seemed the slightest bit strange in some way. Besides, she had been best friends with Paulette, Butch's wife, so there was a good possibility that Peg would have had visibility to any dirty laundry, if there'd been any.

The whole thing was pretty humorous when you thought about it, everyone trying to set up a pregnant woman with "Prince Charming". But sometimes things are just meant to be.

The situation between Jake and me had been exceptionally difficult just before the fourth of July. Spending time in Patti's kitchen had been a must. It kept my spirits up and filled the long periods of alone time while Jake was off with HER. Dean was hooked up with a fireworks manufacturer near

Chicago, and had a side-job shooting off fireworks for the company at July 4th celebrations around the city and suburbs. Patti had the idea that it would be good for me, if the boys and I would join Dean, Patti and their kids for the two fireworks shows that he was shooting on the 3rd and 4th. The idea sounded great to me. The boys would love it. After the arrangements were made, Patti ended our conversation with a surprising comment.

"This will give you a chance to meet that friend of Dean's. You know, the guy he works with, the widower with the kids? He shoots the shows with Dean. His kids will be there too. We can get there early and have a picnic while the guys set the fireworks up in the field across from the park." My reluctance to meet him must've shown all over my face, because she immediately followed up with, "Suzie, Art's a good guy. You'll see."

"Yeah, right. He's gonna' love the way I waddle around! Pregnant women are soooo... sexy." We both laughed as I made an over exaggerated gesture of rubbing my tummy with my hands.

In the morning, on the 3rd of July, Patti had driven over to my house and picked us up. All four of our children, my two and Patti's two, were in the backseat and their shouts and squeals of excited anticipation were deafening. Patti had said that we'd needed to get an early start because it took a long time for Dean and Art to set up the fireworks. Both of them were already at the park, where the show was scheduled to begin at 9:00 o'clock, that evening.

The morning was still pleasantly cool as we pulled the car into the large grassy field, located next to the railroad tracks, and tucked behind and over to the side, of a fairly large suburban park. The open land was located on the far south side of the city, smack dab in the middle of some high density housing. Even though it was quiet and peaceful at the moment, with the number of people living within a radius of a mile or two, it was a very good bet that the area would be swarming with people, as the evening settled in, and the show was about to begin.

According to the weatherman, the day was supposed to get hot, so we'd strategically set up a blanket on the ground in the shade of a large cottonwood tree, placing the plastic coolers filled with food on its corners to secure the blanket against the warm summer breeze. We could see two men across the field near the tracks, digging with shovels, and I'd surmised that the one next to Dean was Art. In the distance, his silhouette looked tall and slim. His long hair hung loosely around his face, brushing against his shoulders as he worked. Two little blonde haired boys were off to his right, running towards a baseball diamond that marked the official beginning of the park. Our kids, who had been helping to unpack the car, noticed Art's boys running around the ball field and began to wail and moan, pleading to join them in their pursuit to make as much dust as possible in the infield.

Suddenly, as if through an ESP connection, Dean's attention shifted from his digging, to the tree, and to Patti, and me. A few short words to the man beside him and Dean ambled over to the blanket and the coolers.

"Anything cold to drink inside those fucking things?" He'd asked, looking at Patti.

"Yeah. There's some cola in the blue one." She'd said, as she pointed to one of the plastic coolers that we'd filled before we left with ice and cans of soda. Dean opened the top of the chest and pulled out two cans of pop.

"Butch says hello." Dean said as he'd slammed the cooler lid shut and began to walk back across the field. We looked in the other man's direction and he waved. Patti and I waved back. Despite the long hair, something about the other man looked familiar.

"Patti, Dean called him Butch. I thought that his name was Art?" I'd said.

"His name is Art but he's a junior, so his nickname is Butch." She'd said, settling down on the blanket in a comfortable position.

"Oh my God!" I'd thought to myself, "Could it possibly be…?"

As it had turned out, it had been an incredible coincidence. Dean's good friend Art, the one he worked with every day, the "good guy" that Patti wanted to set me up with, was Paulette's husband, and Buddy's childhood friend, Butch!

We barely said a word to each other that first day. He didn't even recognize me. I'd guessed that no makeup and closely cropped brown hair, being pregnant and fifteen pounds lighter, had changed my look since the last time we'd met. Later that evening, when the fireworks show was over and all the hordes of people had left, we both sat quietly on the benches next to the baseball diamond, watching our four boys running round and round the bases on the field. We were both taking a rest while Patti and Dean continued to pack things up for our ride home.

"So…" I'd said, breaking the silence, my eyes locked on the kids as they continued to run large circles, passed all the bases to home plate and then around again . "What do you prefer to be called, Art or Butch?"

"I guess, Art is best." He'd said. His eyes also locked on the boys and their never ending pursuit of the next base, and the next, and the next.

"Butch… I mean Art, don't you recognize me? Don't you know who I am?" I smiled and looked at him. He looked at me, really looked at me, searching his memory. He hesitated a moment and a faint wisp of recognition came into his eyes, but I could tell that he couldn't quite place me.

"It's me. It's Suzie." I'd said a little embarrassed at his inability to recognize me. Then some memory of me, registered in his eyes.

"Suzie! Hi, how are you doing?" He'd said and smiled a big broad smile.

"Fine." I'd replied the expected words. "So, which do you want to be called, Butch or Art?"

"Both are fine, but I'm getting a little old for Butch." He'd said.

"OK than Art it is. And I'm getting a little old for Suzie too. My family calls me Susan."

He'd smiled and I'd smiled and that was that. It was time to go home. For the next day, the 4th of July, there had been another show at another park, and things had gone pretty much the same way.

We'd spoken very little to one another. I was busy with the kids and he was busy with the fireworks. But then, during lunch, he'd come over to my picnic blanket where I was kneeling and getting peanut butter and jelly sandwiches out of the cooler for the boys.

"So, how's Jake doing?" Art asked in order to make conversation.

"How the hell should I know?" was my curt stoic reply. I'd assumed that Patti and Dean had told him all about me. However, noting the surprised look on his face and his speechless reaction to my comment, I could tell that he hadn't had a clue. His smile had faltered a bit as he'd wordlessly walked away.

Within a few days after the 4th, Patti had mentioned to Art that I desperately needed a cheap but reliable car. Between work and his girlfriend, Jake was gone eighty percent of the time, and so was the family station wagon. Dean and Art both worked at Art's Auto Repair, Art's dad's shop, and sometimes they had the opportunity to find a good deal. Art obliged a week later, by digging up a twelve year old "beater" Chevy, for a hundred and fifty bucks! Art had been very distant during the transaction, no chit-chat between us, just business. The car ran OK but it had one occasional problem. Every so often, the stick shift would lock up while shifting down from third to first gear. The kids and I must have been quite a picture with the Chevy sitting at a light, the two of them in the back seat praying that the car would be healed. And me, running around the back of the Chevy with my big baby belly, giving the car a push so that it would roll forward an inch or two. Then getting back into the driver's seat and driving us all away when the light turned green. Crazy as it sounds that's the only way to get that car moving again. I didn't care what people thought, it was a small price to pay. The car had been cheap and despite that one little flaw, it runs.

Patti and I had been amazed when we realized that "her Art" had been "my Butch", Buddy's best friend. But both of us, along with Teresa, were totally blown away when we found out he was also Teresa's husband's cousin, the "nice widower guy" Teresa wanted me to meet when I was ready! Coincidence or fate?

Peggy had also been amazed, and then went one step further. She'd said that she and Buddy invited Butch and his boys over every weekend to the house to swim in her backyard pool. Subsequently, she offered some advice.

"Why don't you stop by, and if you bump into him, the two of you can talk and get to know each other without any pressure. You know, just a couple of people in the backyard, on a warm summer afternoon shooting the breeze. At least that way you'll get some idea if you like each other, and once things settle down after the divorce, you never know..."

I'd taken her advice and before Matthew was born, had enjoyed several weekends full of interesting conversation with Peggy and Buddy, their neighbors, and of course Art, as we all sat in Peggy's backyard watching everyone's kids play in the pool. We'd even gotten into the pool ourselves a few times when the late July, early August afternoons got hot and sticky. The visits had been a respite from the constant upheaval caused by Jake and the divorce, and they left me wondering if there were possibilities of "something" happening between Art and me, once all the crap was over, and I was skinny and legally single again.

"Mrs. Burke, time for your baby." The nurse said as she carried Matthew through the hospital room door. Readjusting myself and the pillows and blankets in my bed, she came over to me and gently laid him in my arms. "You can have him for an hour but then he goes back to the nursery." She said in an official manner. I replied with a silent nod.

He was beautiful and truly my bundle of joy. It was wonderful to have this gift all to myself during a time that could have been one of the darkest in my life. Thoughts of the baby had often supplanted those of pain or fear during the hell that I'd been going through over the last few months. And now, the prospect of raising this baby without my mind being focused on the fear and anger that had always surrounded Jake, and his drinking, was a promise of a new beginning. My mind would be clear to see the wondrous things that were there to see, as all my children grew. Yes, I was lucky indeed.

"Mrs. Burke" A nurse's voice came from the direction of the door. "There is a man at the nurse's station who says he's your husband. Do you want me to let him in?" She asked with a concerned look on her face. Jake had been conspicuously missing until this point, so I couldn't blame her for her hesitation.

"Sure." I said.

Less than thirty seconds later he walked through the door. He came over to the bed and stared wordlessly at Matt.

"He's beautiful, isn't he?" I said breaking the silence.

"Why didn't you tell me?" He said with irritation in his voice. He kept his eyes on the baby, avoiding mine.

"Jake, you haven't been home since Friday. I had no idea where you were all weekend, or how to get in touch with you." His silence implied a reluctant acceptance of my answer. He offered no explanations or excuses, he remained silent, his eyes fixed on the baby. Unable to tell whether he felt shame or irritation, I changed the subject.

"Would you like to hold him?" I asked. He nodded. "I think it would be easier if you pulled up a chair and sat down." With that he retrieved a chair from the corner of the room and pulled it over to the bed. I handed him Matthew and Jake slowly sat down.

Jake sat quietly, smiling a little and murmuring "Hi buddy." to the baby in his arms, while coaxing Matthew's little baby fist to open and then close over Jake's much larger index finger. Watching Jake with the baby caused an overwhelming feeling of sadness and loss inside of me. And then I realized that Jake hadn't even asked the baby's name.

"His name is Matthew." I said.

The moment that I said the name, I could tell by the look on Jake's face, that one, he hadn't known about it, and two, he didn't like it.

"It means 'Gift of the Lord'" I said smiling warmly, thinking of how wonderfully true it was.

"More of that fucking Program crap!" He said almost to himself with a disgusted look, as he still kept his eyes on the baby.

Who was Jake, really? Did the person that I'd thought he was ever actually exist at all? Did I want him so badly to be the person that I'd wished him to be, that I only saw what I wanted to see? The pain of loss was still there and at times it felt as if my heart would break in two. I knew that I was grieving for "my Jake", the one I'd thought had been my husband, my lover, and for all the hopes and dreams that I'd planned for us. Looking at him again, not understanding anything about him, I asked myself, "Who was he?"

For that matter, who was anyone? How could you tell? Art seemed like a nice guy… but it'd been my experience that everyone I knew had some kind of monster hidden down deep inside. Well, not everyone, just every man that I'd ever known.

After fifteen minutes or so, he began to nervously look at his watch.

"Got to get going." He said after another minute or two. Then without another word he gently handed me our son and walked out my hospital room door.

✎ XLVII ✍

"Brrrrrrring… Brrrrrrring… Brrrrrrring…"
Tripping over the dog who was laying in the
middle of the kitchen floor in my rush to answer
the phone, I began to fall head first into the brown
Formica and aluminum kitchen table. Luckily, my
hand caught hold of the orange flowered, vinyl
back of a kitchen chair, breaking my fall and
enabling me to wind up on the floor, on my knees,
instead of banging my head on the edge of the
table, and saving me from quite a nasty bump on
the head. The kids AND the baby, an extra bonus,
had fallen asleep early tonight and the last thing
that I'd wanted was for any of them to wake up
screaming, ruining up my plans to get some rest.

"Brrrrrrring… Brrrrrrring… Brrrrrrring…"
Getting up off my knees and crossing the short
distance to the wall in a rush, I lifted the receiver off
the rotary dial wall-phone.

"Hello!" I panted in the phone.

"Hi Honey."

"Jake?" I said, not being able to mask my
surprise. He hadn't been making very many phone
calls to me lately, and during those that he did
make, he sure as hell wasn't addressing me as
"Honey".

"I need to come over. I have something
important to talk to you about." He said.

"Well… The kids are asleep… I really don't
want to wake them…"

"No!" He interrupted. "Don't fucking wake them up. I only want to talk to you, ya' know, about something really fucking important."

"How about in an hour?" I said, surprised by the urgent tone in his voice.

"Yeah, sure. Sounds good." He said and hung up.

I wondered what was so important to talk about. It couldn't be what Teresa said would happen, could it? The hit rate on Teresa's predictions was disturbing. So far, she seemed to be batting a thousand. But this prediction had been one that I'd insisted was not even in the realm of possibility.

"You'd better get ready and figure out what you're going to do when he tells you that he wants to come back." She'd said. I'd laughed at the absurdity of the prospect.

"That will never happen!" I'd said emphatically.

"Sure it will. They always do, just wait and see. Make sure that you've already decided what to do, when he does." She'd prophesied.

Could she have been right? Is that what was so important for us to talk about?

A lot of things had happened in a very short time over the last six weeks. At the end of August, two and a half weeks after Matthew had been born, Jake had officially moved out of the house, and into his own apartment. One would have expected that a woman in my situation would have had feelings of great sadness and fear at seeing her partner walk out the front door, leaving her with two little boys and an infant and no adequate means of support.

But that was not the case for me. His walking out the door had marked a beginning not an end. It had been the beginning of a new life, a rebirth, a renaissance. The timeline of my life had been redefined by that one simple action. This was the beginning of year one, A.J., after Jake.

However, freedom has a price. With his own place to maintain, Jake could no longer afford to give me the majority of his check. When he'd moved out we'd decided that he should start paying me the eighty dollars a week child support payment that we'd agreed upon in the divorce papers. Both of us would try to make do with that arrangement. So... the Monday after Jake moved out, three weeks after Matthew's birth, I'd started a job at a neighborhood bank. Teresa's friend had hired me into the accounting department and I was learning how to run the "proof" machine that processed and routed various deposited checks into customer bank accounts. The job paid two dollars and fifteen cents per hour, fifteen cents above minimum wage. Consequently, my take home pay was approximately seventy-five bucks.

That was almost three weeks ago, and it was beginning to become apparent that one hundred and fifty dollars a week might not be enough for the house, the bills, and food. Of course, things needed to financially settle down a bit first, before I jumped to that conclusion. The bank had held back my first bi-weekly paycheck. Today was Friday, and thank God, my first check had been handed to me this afternoon. Meeting the bills over the previous three weeks on just eighty bucks a week had been pretty rough. Patti, God love her, had been my savior. She'd dropped over unexpectedly last Wednesday evening, with a carton of cigarettes, a box of laundry detergent, and a crisp five dollar bill. I'd been sitting at the kitchen table desperately trying to figure out what to do. The realization had just hit me that there wasn't enough money left to buy baby formula for Matt and bread and milk for the boys to last until payday, when I'd heard her knock on my front door, through the din of the kids playing in the front room.

"Hey, I thought that it was about time I paid back all the fuckin' cigarettes and money that I've bummed off of ya' over the last year" She'd said with a wide smile. To some people, ten bucks worth of stuff would've been no big deal, but for me it was the same as if it was a hundred bucks. And, I also knew, that it was the same for Patti too.

"I can't take this Patti. I know how bad things are for you lately…"

"Shut up." She said softly. "You need it more than I do right now, to feed that baby. Don't worry, "Let Go and Let God" and all that stuff. Right?"

"Yeah." I said, fighting back the tears. "Thanks."

"No problem." She'd said nonchalantly and immediately changed the subject. "I got time for one cup of coffee and then I got to beat it. Dean's home with the kids and I promised the bastard that I wouldn't be gone long. How ARE you?" She'd asked, her eyes searching mine with genuine concern. And with that we'd settled in for a few minutes of conversation full of warmth and comfort.

As I walked through the hallway, picking up yet another Match Box car off the floor, I glanced into the slit of darkness where the boys' bedroom door stood slightly ajar. The sound of heavy, steady breathing emanated from the dark crack. I softly closed the door.

"Good!" I said out loud to the quiet house. "Those babies have put up with enough, lately." My thoughts went to my twenty dollar a week, fifteen year old, pregnant and unwed, baby sitter, Barbara. She knew nothing about raising children and even less about babies. The only reason she'd taken the job was to get some experience with handling an infant and Matthew was her training tool. A pang of guilt stung my heart, but reality caused me to harden myself against it.

There had been no choice. The only other option had been my dad and step-mother, Gladys, and when asked by me if they could manage to watch the kids even for as little as one day a week, they'd replied that their lives were much too busy for that sort of responsibility. So things were as they had to be. We would all have to make do.

Barbara didn't clean. I guess I was lucky that she could manage to watch Eric and Warren all day, feed them lunch, and take care of the baby. She always looked exhausted and half crazy when I came home from work, which made me reluctant to criticize her housekeeping abilities. After work, my evenings were spent getting supper on, the kids fed and ready for bed, and straightening out the daily unsupervised demolition of my house that had taken place under the not so watchful eye of Barbara. I'd even come home one evening to my drapes and their corresponding curtain rod lying on my living room floor. It seems that they'd been ripped out of my front room wall by my children, because, as Barbara had put it, "The boys had been especially rambunctious…" that day.

My dad blamed me for the divorce. After many years of covering up, now that it'd become necessary for me to tell my father about all of Jake's ugly deeds, my father had chosen not to believe me. My dad had believed that Jake had been the son he'd never had, so the reality about Jake was too bitter of a pill for him to swallow. He'd never out and out said to me, "You're a liar!" but I could see it in his eyes whenever the subject came up.

"What the hell does Jake want?" I said a little too loudly, as I roughly stuffed the toys that I'd been picking up from around the house, into the small red plastic toy box next to the front room couch. It took all the composure that I could muster, not to slam the lid. The court date for the divorce was one week from today. Divorce court was always scheduled for Friday mornings in Cook County. The legal profession in the state of Illinois must have thought that it was the most logical day of the week for such proceedings. It was good for future business. After all, one could get rid of one pain in the ass in the morning, and celebrate with another that same night. Off with the old and on with the new. That sounded kind of heartless, but wasn't that what I was doing? I was going out with Art, and Peggy and Buddy, next Friday to celebrate my divorce. Art didn't seem like a pain in the ass. He actually seemed pretty nice, but one never really knows, does one?

The aluminum storm door, which was always locked now that I was living alone, began to rattle loudly on the other side of my large wooden front door. Sneaking a peek through the peephole, I recognized a few strands of Jake's greasy blonde hair bobbing back and forth in my small field of vision, as the rattle continued.

"Jake, shhh…! You'll wake the boys!" I said in a harsh whisper, as I opened the big wooden door and unlocked the storm door.

"What the fuck do you have it locked for? You knew I was on my way!" There was an undertow of anger in his words as he walked through the door.

"I have to lock the door all the time, now that you're not here. It's safer that way." I said. My thoughts went back to last week when Mick had tried to pay me a night time visit! He had gotten wind of the pending divorce through the grapevine at the plant and thought that he might be able to come over and keep me "company". The lock on the aluminum storm door had kept him out that night. To my relief, when I'd told him to go home, that I was not going to let him in, he actually did!

"Yeah, if it makes you feel fucking better." Jake said, his momentary irritation waning as a small smile began to spread across his face. "You know, you may not have to fucking worry about that ever again!" The smile broadened and he reached out and grabbed my arm.

"Come on over and sit on the fucking couch. I have some things I wanna' say to you." Keeping hold of my arm he directed me to the blue cloth couch, the one we'd bought for our wedding and the one that he and his girlfriend had their first real wild weekend fuck party on. The momentum with which he pushed me toward the couch, caused me to sit down with a plop on the cushion when my feet caught on the carpet and my legs lightly bumped into the wooden couch frame

"Now sit there and don't say a fucking word until I'm finished! You need to hear the whole thing." He said as he knelt down in front of me, while I sat awkwardly in the middle of the couch.

"Christ!" I thought. "Here it comes!"

And he began. He told me that he'd made the biggest mistake of his life! He told me that his days with HER were empty. He told me that I was the one that his memories were made of! He told me that I'd been there from the beginning, and now realized that I should be there with him at the end! He told me everything that in the past I'd prayed for him to tell me, after this thing had begun! He said it all and more! And I cried.

The tears had started slowly, one small bit of moisture at a time, pooling in the corner of my eyes. Then, as his revelations continued the small bits of moisture welled up and turned into tears that began to track down the sides of my cheeks. As much as I tried to fight them back, the tears continued to flow.

"I realize that if you take me back, you'll have to do all the fucking work. I know that you are the one that has been hurt and will have to forgive me for everything that I've done to you. And I know that won't be fucking easy for you. You'll be the one that will have to forget so that we can make things the way they were before this all fucking happened. But just think about it. You won't have to work anymore and I won't need the apartment. It's all up to you, but I know that if you want to, you can make it work." Noticing for the first time that I was crying, a look of concern flitted across his face for a moment and then was quickly replaced by a knowing smile.

"Wow, I can't believe that what I've just said has made you so fucking happy that you're cryin'!" With that he actually touched one of my cheeks and wiped the tear streak off of it with his thumb in one of the tenderest moments of our eleven years together.

"I don't want you to say yes right away. I want you to be sure. After all, it is all fucking up to you." He said and let go of my face. "I'll call you tomorrow and we can talk it over again before we call the lawyer and cancel the fucking court date. Don't fucking get up, I'll just leave and you can think things over." And with another broad smile he patted my leg, got up off his knees and walked quietly and confidently out the front door.

A deep sob erupted from my throat, and tears streamed down my cheeks in a response to the agony that I felt. With crystal clarity I'd seen him for who he was not for who I'd desperately wanted him to be. Once you've lifted Santa's beard and seen your daddy underneath, you can never believe in the jolly old elf again. I could read between the lines of the things that he'd spoken, and see the sadness, anger, and fear, that lay there for the children and me. I ached for the days when I was not able to see, and could forgive him one more time in the false hope that this time things would be different, but I knew that there was no going back. My grief was overwhelming. The feeling of loss for all of my familiar hopes and dreams was complete. Though I now realized that "my Jake" had been in my imagination, I was mourning his death the same as if he'd just collapsed unmoving at my feet. I lay down on the couch and cried at innocence lost, until there were no tears left.

Several hours later, exhausted and empty, I turned onto my back and looked up at the ceiling from my position on the couch, contemplating how things would be tomorrow when I told him that I was not taking him back. Surprisingly, any discomfort at the thought of what his reaction would be was squelched by the truths that I'd learned tonight. Sometimes there is no way out but through. And in some things there is no choice, and this was one of them.

❧ PART 7 ❧

"HAPPILY EVER AFTER?"

❧ XLVIII ❧

"You know that there is no shame in calling things off." Teresa said. "This is your last chance. If you're not sure or have any doubts, this is the time to stop things before they go too far." We were both sitting in her brand new blue 1975 Chevy in the parking lot of the Church of the Nazarene, and I was seriously thinking over what she was proposing. Teresa had been right in everything that she'd ever counseled me on, so what she was now saying deserved my full consideration.

Her "soothsayer" wisdom had always been eerily correct and had often saved me untold amounts of pain and suffering. She'd been the first person that I'd called after Jake had left me sitting on the couch with tears, of what he'd thought were happiness, streaming down my face. God, he'd been so sure of himself that night as he'd walked out of the door. That had been less than six months ago, such a short time, but so much had happened since then that it seemed like it'd been an eternity.

"I'll bet that he's had a fight with his girlfriend and now he's back trying to make things up with you because he doesn't want to be alone." had been her pearls of wisdom about Jake's sudden change of heart that evening six months ago. "When he calls in the morning, ask him about it and see what he says."

And I'd done just that. To my surprise and relief, her borderline psychic prediction had been true. Just a little bit of sympathy and encouragement from me had sent him off on his merry way back into HER arms and thankfully, out of my mine.

"Susan, do you love him?" Teresa asked gently, breaking the silence and bringing me back to the present. I shifted in the front seat of the car and thought.

Art was the only man I'd ever met who I could respect. He didn't have some ugly side or some perversion that it was necessary for me to learn how to tolerate, at least not that I'd discovered so far. He was a good and kind man, and the feelings that had been growing inside of me since we'd begun to get to know each other, had their roots in my deep abiding admiration for him. He'd walked the floor all night with a colicky, screaming Matthew just a few days after our first date, so that I could get some desperately needed rest, before the both of us had to go to work the next morning. Shortly after, he'd taken care of me when I'd come down with a high fever from the flu, staying with me until the fever had broken, and checking up every few hours after that, to make sure that the boys and I were alright. He'd also found a more reliable replacement car for the old Chevy that I had, and when asked about the additional cost, told me that he'd stumbled on an incredible deal and the car switch was an even trade. A lucky circumstance that I'd highly doubted. He'd insisted on giving a large, lush, green Christmas tree as a present to the boys and me while we were Christmas tree shopping, after he'd noticed that I was wearing a pair of sandals in the snow. Money was scarce and they were the only shoes that I'd had at the time, and without them I would have literally gone barefooted. And when working fifty hours a week and taking care of three little ones by myself was pushing me to the limits of exhaustion, forcing me to make a choice between continuing to see him and trying to get some rest, he'd lovingly said, "That's OK. I'll wait for you until you're ready. No matter how long it takes, I'll be waiting. Take all the time you need."

We had been lovers from the start. It had been difficult at first being a one man woman so to speak. But Art was an attractive man with a warm caring manner, and that, together with the natural desire of a healthy twenty-six year old woman who'd been starved for the touch of a man for almost a year, had easily overcame any inhibitions or misgivings that I might have had. It was the 70's after all, and with the advent of the "pill" attitudes and mores about that sort of thing had radically changed since I'd been involved in the dating scene. Casual sex without any emotional strings attached was supposed to be the norm. However, despite my attempt at "new thinking" it only took a few weeks to figure out that for me, any intimate relationship had to be exclusive. I'd guessed that the saying about "teaching an old dog new tricks" was true.

Being a swinging single was not my forte, and Art seemed more than happy to accommodate my prudishness. Whatever I'd wanted was OK with him. There were no arguments between the two of us. We'd each gone through our own private hell so day to day differences of opinion didn't matter much. Once you've watched the love of your life whither and die, or watched him walk out the door, the cap being left off of the toothpaste tube, is the least of your worries.

Did I love him? What was love? The feeling that I'd had for Jake, the one that I'd mistakenly thought was love, the compulsive need to "take care if him" that still tugged at my gut like an addict's need for a fix, didn't exist in my relationship with Art. What I felt for Art was completely different. It was warm and peaceful and good. It had no rough edges, no sharp places to prick your feelings or your heart. I didn't know what this emotion was. I'd never felt anything like it before. All I knew for sure was that I'd wanted to keep it deep in my heart for the rest of my life.

"Yes!" I said looking directly into Teresa's deeply serious eyes. "It's the way it's supposed to be."

She held my gaze, her hands holding mine tightly as they lay in my lap, and with an intense look that penetrated into my soul, she searched my eyes for confirmation of the certainty that I'd just expressed. Then she took a deep breath followed by a long, slow sigh.

"OK. Then let's get you married."

Getting out of the warm car into the chilly February air, we walked together in our full length powder blue dresses, "bride" and "matron of honor", hand in hand with the late afternoon sun dancing through the leafless trees. We crossed the parking lot and entered the little church.

The vestibule was silent and looking through the inner doorway that opened into the main room, I could see a small gathering of our close friends and family loosely scattered amongst the dark walnut pews. Large white bows with long flowing pieces of ribbon cascaded down the end of each pew, lining the aisle with a brilliant contrast of white on dark warm wood that added a simple but elegant beauty to the surroundings. Two white flower arrangements were nestled on each side of the altar, and beside each basket of flowers stood a tall plain brushed gold set of candelabras. The bows and flowers had been an unexpected addition, thoughtfully saved from some recent church doing, and placed there by the minister's wife. Both Dean and Keith, Art's two little boys, had at one time or another since Paulette's death, been attending the Day Care Center at the church, so the minister's wife was very familiar with the circumstances that had brought Art and I together. The kindness that both she and her husband had always shown to Art and the boys had made their small church the perfect place in which to declare our love.

Art and all the boys were standing in the front of the church near the altar and each of them was fidgeting in one way or the other. Art was busy putting the finishing touches on uncombed hair, untucked shirttails, and untied shoelaces, while the baby fussed in the baby carrier next to his feet. Watching the almost comical mayhem, my heart melted. In a short time, we would become a family and these six human beings, Dean, Eric, Warren, Keith, Matthew, and of course Art, would become a part of my life until the day that I would draw my last breath on this earth. How could I be so lucky?

The organ music began to play and Art herded the boys into the first pew, next to my dad and Gladys. With a little luck, the two of them plus stern looks from Art and me, might keep the boys somewhat under control until we'd said our "I do's".

All at once, I became aware of Teresa standing behind me as she lightly touched my shoulder with one hand and pointed at something near the entrance to the church with the other. On a waist high, two foot square wooden table top, sitting next to the doorway, lay a single white rose with a white ribbon bow tied around the long green stem.

"It's time." She said. "Are you ready?"

"Yes." I said as I picked up the white rose and held it lovingly in my hands. "As ready as I will ever be." Suddenly out of nowhere, Art's "best man", Buddy, appeared at Teresa's side and they both walked through the doorway and down the aisle together. And then, without another thought or hesitation, so did I.

❧ XLIX ❧

Teresa's house was lovely! She'd offered it as the place for us to hold a small cake and champagne reception after the ceremony, and had decorated the entire downstairs with white crepe paper wedding decorations. Snow white wedding bells, hearts and love birds, were hanging in every available nook and cranny of her kitchen and living room, and white streamers hung around the doorways like garland. Her kitchen table was set with good silverware and fine china cake plates, strategically placed around a modest but beautiful, two layer wedding cake.

Sitting with Matthew on my lap and rocking him to and fro, trying to get him to doze off for a short nap, I looked around at our friends and people that loved us. Everyone who'd been at the wedding had come back to Teresa's. Dean and Patti, Peggy and Buddy, Daddy and Gladys, were busy eating cake and sipping champagne.

Carole and Claudette couldn't make it to the wedding, that's the kind of price you pay when your family lives far apart. I hadn't seen Carole since that day in the hospital when I'd had Matthew. But I'd been lucky enough to see Claudette last month, during a brief visit when she had accompanied her truck driving husband on a cross country run from Texas to Chicago. She had stayed at my house for less than twenty-four hours, during which time we'd stayed up all night and chatted like two school girls. I'd shared with her all the gory details about Jake, all the things that I'd hid for so long, and then after baring my soul, I'd asked her the question that I'd been dying to ask her for the last twelve years. And to my amazement, her answer to "How did you stay with Mick after you found out that he'd flashed, me, Momma, and Tina?" was beyond my wildest imagination. It seems that while Momma and I had been watching the kids so that Mick could tell Claudette about his "dirty deeds", he had done no such thing! He'd told her instead, a very believable lie. He'd told her that Momma had found out that he'd been cheating on my sister and had demanded that he "come clean" and beg my sister's forgiveness. Which, of course, she did. All those years that I couldn't figure out why she put up with him being the family pervert, and now I had found out that she never even knew!

Matthew squirmed in my lap as I continued to rock him. His little eyelids were getting heavy and in a minute or two he would be drifting off to sleep. Glancing through the doorway and into the kitchen I could see Art's two sisters standing next to the back door, huddled together in an intense conversation about something. I'd always had the feeling that Art's family had thought that he was a little crazy for going out with me, and a lot crazy for marrying me. Art's grandmother had actually hinted to Art that she'd suspected that Matthew was his illegitimate child, because, after all, why else would he be interested in me? Looking at Matthew's half asleep little face I couldn't help but laugh.

What did I care what people thought? Grandma's supposition was certainly mild compared to stories that I'd learned that Jake had told about me in the past. I'd always known that he lied about things, but the size of the lies that he was capable of, was more than a little disturbing. By another incredible coincidence it had turned out that Art's first wife's father had worked at the same factory as my mother. He was well acquainted with her, also knew Jake, and had been a manager at the plant during the time that the Jake and Roz saga had occurred. Art had gotten very close to Mom and Dad Moore after Paulette's death, and over the last six months, our frequent visits with the boys to their home had allowed the three of us to get to know each other. One evening while we were all commenting on life's coincidences, Dad Moore confided in me the story Jake had given to management as the reason why he had been desperate to change shifts, from working nights to working days. He'd told them, all those people who had known my mother and respected her, that I was such a whore that he had to stay home at night to watch me and keep the men out of his bed! He'd said that the situation was so bad that he had no idea if Matthew was really his! Well, so much for my reputation!

But, considering the new revelation from Peggy, I guessed that as far as the guys at the plant were concerned, my reputation had been tarnished a long time ago. The whole circumstance reminded me of a twist to the old joke, where the one guy says rudely to the other, "Hey buddy, do you have naked pictures of your wife?" And indignant, the other guy says, "Why, of course not!" Then the first guy says, "Well then, how would you like to buy a couple?" It seems that those pictures that Jake had coerced me into posing for, shortly after we'd gotten married, and just before he went into the service… the ones that were for "his eyes only" and represented a deep commitment to trust… THOSE were the pictures that Buddy's friend Ralph had been disturbed about Jake showing around work all those years ago. It wasn't the picture of me in my little white dress. It was THOSE pictures that had been passed around. The big revelation about THOSE pictures had occurred last week while Peggy and I were talking on the phone. We were both commenting on how sad it was that Ralph had died from leukemia at such a young age and what a great guy he'd been. When Peggy had said, "Remember how angry Ralph got over Jake showing those naked pictures of you to the guys at work?" Then followed a litany of "Why didn't you tell me?" and "I did but evidently, you weren't listening!" It had taken eight years for the ugly facts to finally sink into my thick skull. I was shocked and mortified, and the whole thing still made me ill whenever it crossed my mind. How could I have been so stupid? How could I have been so blind?

It was hard to believe that Jake had been such a complete scum from the very beginning, and I'd kept my blinders on. I hadn't been able to even conceive that he was capable of such a betrayal, but now I knew, didn't I? He was one sick son-of-a-bitch!

Well, he wasn't going to ruin this day for me! No matter what kind of a piece of crap he was!

From somewhere off to my right and down the hallway, Eric's muffled laughter broke through the constant drone of friendly conversations that buzzed around me. His laugh reminded me of what was really important. The boys were happy. Divorce is supposed to be devastating to children, or so I'd envisioned for all those years, but my children were flourishing under the attention of their new role model, a man who gave them unconditional love. Art seemed not to notice a difference between his children and mine. Kids were kids to him and he loved them all. I felt the same, and from the first time that I'd met Dean and Keith they had stolen my heart. The boys followed Art around like the "Pied Piper", and the stories that he told them in the evenings before bed, were so captivating that they would repeatedly beg him to tell them "just one more". Piggy back rides, wrestling and lots of laughing and love filled their days. We had told the boys that today was a special day. Today we would become one family bonded together by love. Art and I had vowed that from this day forward there would be no "yours" and "mine" where the children were concerned. They were all our babies now, and the thought made me smile.

Jake hadn't been taking the news about my remarriage very well.

"What do you mean that you're fucking getting married? You fucking promised me that you'd never get married again!" He'd shouted at me after I'd told him the news.

"No Jake. What I'd said was that after being married to you, I didn't even want to look at another man much less marry one!" I remembered telling him this tidbit with more than just a little satisfaction. On the day that he'd come over to get the rest of his things from the garage, I could tell, by the way he was roughly shoving stuff into his station wagon, that he was very upset. Oh well Jake, live and learn!

Over to the left of where I was sitting on the couch with Matthew in my arms, Art, and his friend Dean, Patti's husband, were engaged in an animated conversation full of riotous laughter. I took a good long look at my new husband as he laughed and joked with Dean. "He was a great guy!" I thought. He was tall, six foot four, blonde hair with gorgeous crystal blue eyes. The kind of eyes my mother used to call "bedroom eyes", and very apropos if I did say so myself. Also, by another coincidence, he was a Libra like Jake and his initials were exactly the same as Jake's, AJB. "You won't have to change your fucking monogrammed towels." Patti had said when we both had realized that the letters were the same.

Remembering Patti's face as she'd teased me, still made me smile. Then a small pang of guilt dampened my spirits. He didn't really understand what he was getting into. I'd tried to warn him that I came with a lot of baggage, tried to explain things to him but... he really didn't understand what dealing with Jake was like. The only drunk that Art could relate to was his harmless little old Uncle Fred, and drunk or sober, Fred had always stayed within the bounds of normal. You just can't explain what "crazy" really is to another person, unless they've experienced it for themselves. Art still thought that he and Jake would be able to get along, especially in matters where the kids were involved. He would appeal to Jake's love and concern for the boys and that alone should be enough to make things between the three of us run smoothly. But somehow I had an uneasy feeling that things that involved dealing with Jake would never run smoothly. Appealing to his better nature had never worked for me, maybe because he didn't have one. But explaining that to Art...

Looking in my lap, I realized that Matthew was finally asleep.

"Susan, let me take him for awhile." Gladys said as she came over to the couch where I'd been sitting. "You need to spend some time with your friends." She reached her arms out and we lovingly, transferred my sweet small bundle of joy into her care.

"Mrs. Brauer, how the fuck are you doing?" Patti said, smiling as she placed her hand on my shoulder.

"Great! Just great!" I beamed, as Art's full gentle laugh came from somewhere behind me.

❧ **L** ❧

"Push!"

The doctor's voice was coming from somewhere between my legs. I wasn't able to see his face from my position on the delivery table, only the top of his green surgical hat. The pushing contraction had started a second or two ago and the doctor's order was being echoed by Art's encouraging voice from slightly in back and to the right of the operating table, insisting that I keep it up, while he nervously rubbed my shoulder.

"C'mon baby, push! We're almost there!" He coached. Art hadn't seen Dean or Keith born so this was all new to him. It was his first time coaching and my first time having a coach in the delivery room. We were both doing great. The Lamaze class that we'd taken had been a refresher for me and a brand new experience for Art, preparing us both for the birth. It was a good thing too because I'd been through this several times so the whole process wasn't taking very long, and I hadn't been given any anesthetic since arriving at the hospital. Things had progressed too quickly.

"You can take a rest now." My obstetrician said as the feeling of having to push quickly ebbed away. "I can see a small patch of dark hair at the opening, about the size of a quarter. The baby's right there! Art, take a look in the mirror over there. It's really something!"

"One more good push when it starts up again and I think we'll have a baby." The doctor said to me as I closed my eyes and tried to relax.

"One more good push... God, I hope he's right." I thought, my legs trembling slightly and the rest of my muscles sore and aching. "This is my last chance for a girl. I wonder if..." Suddenly the compulsion to push started up again.

"Push! C'mon... C'mon... push!" I didn't know who was saying it but I was obliging with every bit of energy that was left in my body. And all that I could think about was getting the baby out!

"Here comes the head! Here it comes..." The doctor said coaxing one last long push out of me as he spoke the words.

"...and... you have a baby...boy!"

"That's just what I wanted!" I cried in response, my voice breaking up with emotion. From out of nowhere Art's face was next to mine the wetness on his cheek cool against my flushed skin. He lightly kissed my brow and the two of us sobbed like babies from the pure joy and magic of the moment, as the doctor placed our screaming son on my chest for both of us to see.

"He's beautiful!" I sobbed again as they took him away to clean him up and do the things they had to do to ensure that he'd be alright.

"God knows what He's doing, ya' know." I whispered to Art. "Boys are what we do best!" He kissed me again on the cheek. Art and I had planned this baby. We had both wanted the experience of having one child, together. For me, sharing every day, the joy of my pregnancy with another human being had been wonderful and unique. Art loved the idea of my body changing with the growth of his child inside of me. The more pregnant I became, the sexier he thought my body was! God, I loved him!

In half an hour after the birth, they'd stitched me up and wheeled me into the recovery room. The damned bed they put me in was really uncomfortable! Well, it wasn't the bed, it was the damned afterbirth contractions. They were really bad! I'd expected that I'd get a few but these were worse than my labor! It'd started about fifteen minutes ago, right after they'd wheeled me into the room. And now the pain was so bad I was hanging half in and half out of the bed, with my one leg over the guard rail, trying to find a position where the pain would lessen.

"Art. Call the nurse. Tell her this is bad!" I was panting tying to get control of the pain. He nervously pushed the nurse's button, worry and fear causing large creases of skin to furrow his forehead. Hugging the railing with my leg and trying to control the pain by concentrating on my heavy breathing, I was turned partially over on my tummy when the nurse walked through the door. Forcing me to roll onto my back, the nurse made no effort to conceal her contempt for the way that she thought I was handling the pain.

"Surely Mrs. Brauer, you've had afterbirth contractions before!" She admonished me as if I was a naughty child, while she forcefully poked and prodded my stomach with her fingers, checking for what, I did not know. It took everything I had not to slap her in the face when she touched me. The pain was overwhelming as she pushed against my abdomen.

"Well, you seem fine. The cramping should subside in a few minutes." She said stone faced, and then stared at me as I began to involuntarily rock side to side.

"Please try and get a hold of yourself, Mrs. Brauer!" She said in an exasperated tone. "You're not doing yourself any good."

"Don't you think that I would if I could?" I snapped back. "I've just made it through labor without drugs and made barely a sound. This is different! Something's wrong!" I shouted, rocking even more as the cramp in my belly reached a crescendo.

"Really, Mrs. Brauer! You'll be fine." She said stoically and walked out of the room.

All at once, the pain stopped! Then I felt it, a gush from between my legs that seemed as if a garden hose had been turned on full force.

"Art call the nurse! I'm hemorrhaging!" I said with a cold unfeeling certainty, locking Art's eyes with mine. Looking at me in disbelief Art pulled back the covers and let out an audible gasp. In a few seconds, I'd been covered in my own blood from my waist down to my toes, and bright red patches were pooling around the heels of my feet. Art screamed for the nurse, and I closed my eyes.

After that, time and happenings began to become disjointed, almost like a dream. A light flashing in my eye, along with an official female hospital voice saying, "Code Blue in Recovery…Code Blue in Recovery…" brought me back to an awareness of the people and things around me.

"What's your name?" A soft male voice asked as my eyes tried to focus.

"Susan" I said trying to keep my eyes open.

"How old are you?"

"Uh… twenty-eight?" I said closing my eyes and thinking that this whole thing was silly.

"Could someone please tell my husband…uh, I'm OK? See his first wife… died… and…" The room started to go fuzzy again, and a squeezing sensation on my arm was followed by a loud male voice saying, "Sixty over forty! Her veins have collapsed! Let's get her elevated!"

"Please tell my husband… I'm OK…" I began to drift as I felt the foot of my bed rise up and my brain sluggishly registered the sharp stick of a needle, as IVs were attached through the veins in my ankles.

The fog cleared to lots of activity around me. People were standing on either side of my bed with their hands under my bottom, lifting me up, while a third person, a young doctor, was pushing his hands inside of me.

"Can't reach it like this! We'll have to try and pack her, slow down the bleeding, and operate as soon as we can stabilize her." Then everything and everyone was gone again.

My eyes opened and focused on some big lights on the ceiling above me.

"Hi." A woman's voice said. "You've had quite a time of it. Do you remember anything?" She asked.

"Sure but it doesn't make much sense." I said and moved my eyes to look at the woman who was standing beside me while I lay on the gurney. She was dressed in a green operating gown, cap, and face mask. The way her skin was crinkling around her eyes I could tell she was smiling under the green gauze mask.

"You lost a lot of blood and we have to go in and try and stop the bleeding." She said. "Don't worry, you'll be alright. Just rest. You'll go to sleep soon and then it will all be over." She said and patted my shoulder reassuringly.

"All be over..." I thought to myself, as my heavy eyelids closed. I was so unbelievably tired. "What does she mean?" I thought. "I guess she means I'll be OK, but... maybe not. Maybe I could... die..." and I thought about that for a moment, weighing everything in my mind. "Well... I guess that would be fair. Since Art, life's been better than I'd ever imagined it could be." The image of Art and me standing in the middle of a deserted intersection in downtown Chicago, at three o'clock in the morning, floated to the surface of my thoughts. Art was holding me in his arms and kissing me, the way that the handsome leading man kisses the leading lady in the movies. It had been his crazy idea, dragging me into the middle of the street to kiss me. It was the most romantic thing I'd ever done!

Yes, every day with Art and the kids has been a gift, a bonus.

"So God, thanks. I've had it all... if this is it, it's more than fair."

"You're going to go to sleep now." She said breaking my train of thought. "Start counting back for me from one hundred."

"One hundred…" I said, at peace with myself and my God, as I began to drift off. "Ninety-nine… ninety…eight… nine…"

✤ LI ✤

It was hard to breathe. It felt as if an elephant was sitting on my chest. Wearily opening my eyes for a second or two, I realized that the room was dark. "My labor pains had started about six this morning and Joseph, that was what we were going to call him, had been born at about noon, and now it was… what…? sometime in the middle of the night… How many hours had passed…? Joseph… I loved that name… it was my grandfather's name… strong… loving… kind…" Fragments of thoughts floated in and out as I lay in a pleasant dreamlike state, until it was time to breathe again.

The struggle to pull air into my lungs, my chest muscles laboring to do what normally was done without so much as a conscious thought, forced me into full awareness. A loud wheezing sound came out of my open mouth, kind of like a long slow gasp. It scared the hell out of me, and evidently did the same for the nurse on duty. In an instant she was there by my bedside.

"Hey, take it easy. You're OK, you're OK." She said as she checked the IV bottle hanging above the head of my bed.

"What's happening?" I asked in a barely audible whisper, the beginning of panic showing in my eyes.

"You lost a lot of blood before and during the surgery, so your oxygen exchange isn't so hot. They didn't want to give you any blood during surgery. The doc was worried about a blood reaction.

There's less risk with a total transfusion but you didn't bleed out enough for that. It will be hard for you to breathe for awhile. Don't let it scare you, just take it slow and you'll be fine. You should get a pint or two before you go home. That will make things better." She said offhandedly while still fiddling with stuff over my bed.

"We're going to keep you here for another couple of hours and then you'll go up to your room, so try and get some rest. It'll make the time pass quicker." Just as quickly as she'd appeared, she was gone. I closed my eyes and tried to relax, but the effort that it took to breathe kept me awake despite the anesthetic hangover that was making me groggy.

So, I'd made it through the operation. Now that I had time to think about it all, it was a very good thing, indeed. The scenario of Art taking care of six kids by himself would not have been the best. There was also one tiny problem that I'd forgotten about when I was philosophically thinking things over, and that was Jake. Jake would never allow Art to raise Eric, Warren and Matt, if something ever happened to me. The prospect of the boys living with Jake, without me there to watch over them, was more than I could bear to think about. Everyday it was becoming more and more clear that Jake was not a fit father.

In the two years since my marriage to Art, Jake had seemed to be having a slow melt down. It'd started a month or two after our wedding. Jake asked the courts for a reduction in child support. He had presented the case that the addition of Art's income, as an auto mechanic, changed the basis for the original determination of eighty dollars a week support for the three boys. It'd been necessary for me to quit my job shortly after Art and I had been married. Child care for five little boys under five was twice as expensive as my take home pay from the bank. However, it was true that Art did make a lot more money than I had, so we all agreed that fifty dollars a week was more equitable. Despite the reduction, Jake had stopped paying child support a few months later, and we were now in the second round of a court battle over non-payment. The first had resulted in a three hundred dollar back payment from Jake, after which he'd promptly stopped sending checks again. He was now over one thousand dollars in arrears and there was a court date set for a month from now. Of course, through all of this, we'd been reminded by our lawyer that payment of child support had nothing to do with whether or not a divorced parent can exercise their visitation rights. Jake picked up Eric and Warren every other weekend. Matthew was too young for out of the home visitation and didn't have to go with Jake until he was three. We'd offered for him to come and visit Matt anytime, but Jake had declined. Since my remarriage, he'd refused to step one foot inside the house, consequently Jake hadn't seen Matthew for almost two years, and he didn't seem to care. He never mentioned it and neither did we. Considering Jake's bad behavior over the last two years, it was a Godsend.

Most of the time, after a weekend with Jake, the boys came home in a foul mood, bickering and picking on one another. Their depression would linger a day or two into the next week, enough so, that the boys' teachers had made inquiries about the reason for the obvious change in their normally happy-go-lucky dispositions. When Art or I would ask the boys how their weekend had gone, an "It was OK." response was all that we could get out of them. At first we'd chalked it up to a separation anxiety, but now I was gathering strong evidence that it wasn't so.

Art's relationship with Jake had gone down hill fast. He'd had high hopes that he and Jake could come to terms on the basis of what was best for the kids. Having children himself he'd thought that they could deal with each other on that common ground. Art's supposition would have worked if Jake had been a "normal" guy. As it was, Art had begun to get an education on what "not" being normal meant.

Jake had made it rudely clear to Art from the start that in matters where Eric and Warren were concerned, I was to be the only conduit of communication. Consequently, to keep things on a more amicable basis, my smiling face was the only one that Jake saw when he pulled in our driveway every other weekend. Even so, Jake was getting more difficult to work with.

Over the last two years Jake's list of bad behaviors had continued to grow. It had begun with his continual inability to pick up or drop off the boys on time. It may sound like a little thing but it had resulted in long hours of waiting and frustration for the boys, and the same for Art and me, when the time came for the boys to be brought home. Jake's blatant disregard for Eric and

Warren's feelings was a constant irritation, and when several times, he'd been a "no show" without out so much as a phone call, it had added fuel to the already brightly burning fire of contention between him and us.

The whole thing had come to a head last summer. Jake was supposed to have brought the boys home one Sunday about six in the evening. He'd finally pulled into the driveway at about 11:30 at night. The waiting and worrying had driven Art to the breaking point. At the flash of Jake's car lights through the living room window, Art was off the couch, out the screen door, and standing on the concrete porch. Following close behind, I peeked through the doorway just in time to see Jake staggering out from behind the open, driver's car door, on his way to the boys in the backseat. After fumbling with the handle of the rear door, he opened it, and clumsily removed the first sleeping child, placing him on the concrete step just below the front porch landing, a few feet from where Art was standing. Jake wobbled as he turned around and proceeded to retrieve the second sleeping child from the vehicle. By the time Warren had been placed on the concrete step, Eric had already been placed inside on the living room couch. I was halfway to the couch with Warren when I heard Art's voice.

"You're late!" Art said.

"Yeah. Shit happens." Jake said. He'd turned and stood facing Art only a few feet from the porch, directly between it and the front of his car.

"You're drunk aren't you? I can smell the booze from here!" Art growled, his hands clenched at his side.

"What the fuck is it to you!" Jake slurred, the "f" in fuck lasting way too long.

By the time that I'd deposited Warren next to his brother on the couch and returned to the porch Jake was laying belly up arms stretched out and unmoving, on the hood of his car with Art bent over him, his large hands around Jake's neck and both their eyes riveted to each other's.

"Get this, and get it straight, you drunken son-of-a-bitch! You will never, and I mean never, bring those boys home in this condition again, or I'll break your neck!" Art shouted in Jake's face.

"Do you understand me?" Art shouted again, emphasizing every word with a sharp shake that propagated through Jake's upper body. With that, Art suddenly let go, releasing his grip and backing off away from the car by a few feet, his body rigid and visibly trembling, and breathing heavy as if he had just run the hundred yard dash.

"Now get the fuck out of my driveway!"

We had both tried to laugh about it later, but the experience had shaken Art to the core.

"I'd wanted to kill him, to wipe him away from our lives and the kids' lives forever." Art had confessed. "The only thing that'd kept me from breaking his neck was the kids and what it would've done to them. God, I've never felt that way before!" He'd said full of guilt and fear.

"Hey, don't feel so bad." I'd said rubbing his back and giving him a big hug. "Jake has the knack for bringing out the best in people. It's his job." And with that I'd gotten Art to smile.

I'd tried to warn Art about what he was getting into by getting involved with me, and now, after two years of watching Jake do his little dance from a front row seat, Art had learned what I'd meant, all too well. After the incident Jake had stopped paying child support again, but continued to pick the boys up on his appointed weekends. He still wasn't very punctual, but he'd never, never, dropped them off again, when it was obvious that he'd had one too many. That was something! As far as the back child support went, he would probably be made to cough it up when we went back to court next month, at least that's what the lawyer had said.

"Mrs. Brauer. It's time to take you to your room. Did you get some rest, since I saw you last? Is your breathing any better?" The nurse had appeared again, from wherever she'd been.

I thought about the question for a moment as I painfully pulled in another breath.

"No, but I guess that I've already gotten used to it."

✎ LII ✎

God, I hated sitting and waiting to see Mr. Reagan. Sitting here always made me feel like some kind of misfit or lowlife. The last two years had been exhausting when it came to dealing with the court, but both Art and I knew that it was necessary pain so that the boys could be safe. Hopefully, today all the misconceptions would be cleared up and the court sponsored "Family Reconciliation Service", of which Mr. Reagan was a court appointed counselor, would be set straight on what was really going on here.

"Wednesday, January 17, 1979." My eyes glanced over today's date written on the calendar, hanging on the wall opposite from where Art and I were sitting. Had it only been two years since Joseph had been born? It seemed like it had been a lifetime of dealing with lawyers and the court system. Once both are put in motion the wheels of justice grind very slowly, indeed. Those who have never been entangled by the system assume that justice is fairly and swiftly doled out by it, but neither is usually the case.

Looking back on it all, I would have to say that things had gotten progressively worse, shortly after Joseph was born. Up until that time, except for the encounter with Art on the hood of his car, Jake's greatest sins had been his inability to pay child support and to be on time, and then came Joe.

Shortly after that, about a month to be precise, on the day that the courts had decreed that Jake pay us the fourteen hundred dollars in back child support that he'd owed, we woke up to quite a surprise. Our neighbor across the street, an early riser who had been walking her dog, had phoned just as the sun was coming up and suggested that we go outside and take a look in our driveway. Standing outside in the warm, late April sunshine, light dew still coating our two cars parked next to the house, Art and I stared in disbelief. Someone had taken an ice pick to each tire flattening all eight of them, making both cars undrivable. Later, after Dean had come over in his tow truck with an air compressor on board, and a box full of tire plugs, the three of us contemplated the message that "someone" had left for us.

"Christ! There had to be at least fifty-three punctures in one fucking tire alone!" Dean had said in amazement. "The tire with the least still had maybe fourteen or fifteen. Boy, that son-of-a-bitch really hates your fucking guts!" Dean said with a curt laugh. The picture of Jake sitting in the middle of the night cross legged on the black asphalt in my driveway, and slowly and methodically ice picking each tire, sent shivers down my back.

"Thank God for the alarm system!" I'd thought. We'd installed it in the house last summer, after "someone" had tried to break into the kids' first floor bedroom window, in the middle of the night with them sleeping inside. Somehow, the alarm sitting on top of the roof made the vision of Jake puncturing my tires a little less terrifying, but just a little.

He'd sent us a message and it had been crystal clear. It had boldly said, "I don't have to follow the

rules! I can do what I want and you can't stop me!"
Coincidentally, the cost of the damage that had
been done could easily have come to the amount of
money owed in child support, if automobiles had
not been Art's bread and butter. Yeah, he'd given
us our fourteen hundred bucks back, and right on
time.

The next Monday, we'd called the lawyer and
told him everything. There was no proof that it'd
been Jake who'd punctured our tires, but we all
thought that the courts could still force him to pay
the child support, that had been due last Friday.

"He quit his job!" Our attorney was
flabbergasted when he reported this tidbit of
information. It was hard for him to believe, that any
man would quit his job in order to stop paying the
money that would help support his children. Well,
he didn't know Jake!

Things had gone down hill fast after that. Patti
had called me up one day and told me a pretty ugly
thing. Jake had punched Roz square in the face, in
front of God and everyone, at a drink and dance
place just down the street. He'd actually knocked
her out during a loud argument, right on the dance
floor! Well, now I knew the answer to the question
about what would've happened to me if I hadn't
gotten away from "zombie" Jake for all those years.
Roz was stupid, she obviously tried to stand her
ground and that was a "no-no", at least while
"zombie" Jake was around.

Then the worst began to happen, Eric and
Warren were dropping hints that visiting "Daddy
Jake" wasn't all that it was cracked up to be. The
boys would never come right out and say that

going with Jake was sometimes a nightmare. Being as young as they both were, saying so was probably thought by them to be some sort of betrayal. They did however, drop hints that would slip out in everyday conversations during the days after their time with Jake. Comments about "Daddy Jake" driving real fast, would lead to a story of an insane car chase between Roz and Jake after an argument between the two of them, while the terrified boys would be curled up on the floor in the backseat of Jake's car. Stories about being left alone all weekend with Jake's crazy mother at her house near Lake Michigan, while Roz and Jake went to the bars, would slip out in response, when the boys were asked how they'd liked being at the beach. But the most disturbing story was the one that we'd coaxed out of Warren when he'd come home from another Michigan trip. He'd had a very large scab forming on his shoulder, from, what Art and I both conjectured, was being left out in the sun too long. When I'd asked Warren about it he'd said, with Eric vigorously nodding his head in support, that Jake had left him alone on the beach while he'd taken Eric onto a friend's boat anchored near the shore. Eric had also volunteered the information that Jake had swam out to the boat with Eric on his back.

"We almost drowned! I guess I was holdin' onto his neck too tight or somethin'. It was real scary." My seven-year old confided, with his big green eyes still mirroring the fear.

That had been it! That had been the moment when Art and I had decided to do something to protect the boys from Jake. We'd needed a new lawyer. Our old one, who also had become a good friend of ours, had quit. In his own opinion, he'd become too emotionally involved in our case to be effective. After all of Jake's unpunished attempts at intimidation, and the futile battles over unpaid child support, James had thrown in the towel.

"When a lawyer wants to help a client find someone to break the legs of the opposition, it's time to call it quits." James had said. "He's like Teflon, nothing sticks to him. It's so frustrating. He does what he damn well pleases, and never seems to be held accountable!"

My Aunt Lollie had been remarried to a nice guy named Frank. He was a Sicilian from the city and his brother's son was supposed to be a "hot shot", go after the jugular, downtown attorney.

"He'll put Jake in his place!" Frank had said. So we hired him in late June of '77. I didn't like him. Gerald Dimone was an arrogant dick. But then maybe, we'd thought, it took a dick to catch a dick.

Gerald had gotten immediate action as far as the courts are concerned. Within two weeks after we'd retained him, he'd gotten a court order for "supervised" visitation, which was supposed to last until the courts could make an evaluation of Jake and the situation. Other than the fact that Jake was still jobless and continued to be in arrears for child support, all of the complaints against him were hearsay.

"Supervised" visitation didn't last long. Jake and Roz abruptly got married. Despite the fact that the court ordered counseling evaluation hadn't begun, after three short months, Jake no longer was required to visit with the boys in the presence of his sister. Jake's lawyer had pointed out that the boys would now be visiting with Jake in Roz's house, together with Roz's children. He'd argued that Roz was an upstanding individual who was providing a safe environment for her own children, and therefore, would do the same with mine. We'd agreed to the arrangement on Gerald's advice.

"You'll lose if you fight this. The court will think that it's a reasonable request. They don't like curtailing a father's rights with his children unless there is adequate proof of abuse." Gerald had said. But we'd also insisted on the stipulation that Jake was not to take the children out of state without the court's permission, which had included Jake's mother's house in Michigan. Surprisingly, Jake had agreed. That was a victory, as far as Art and I were concerned. Even though the house where Jake's mother now lived and drank herself to oblivion was Jake's childhood home, it had been the pivotal point around which most of the boys' nightmare experiences had occurred.

Gerald had also suggested, since we were no longer dropping Eric and Warren off at Jake's sister's house, that it would be a good idea to have a person of impeccable credentials to witness Jake's behavior, when the boy's were being picked up. Gerald believed that doing so would curtail any possibilities for confrontations between Jake, Art or me. It was a good idea and it had worked. We'd asked Sister Armedea, a nun from the catholic school where all the boys went to catechism class, to help out. With her presence, the long agonizing periods of waiting for a father who was late or, without notice, didn't show up at all, had ended.

Shortly after Jake and Roz were married, and "every other week" visitation had become more or less routine, Jake had asked that Matthew begin coming with Eric and Warren. During the three years since Matt was born, Jake had showed no interest in seeing him, so, to Matt, Jake was a stranger. Jake's request had been unexpected, however, the law was clear on his right to have Matt visit. So late in October in '77, I was forced to put another of my angels into Jake and Roz's hands.

Matthew and Jake did not like each other from the minute they'd met. Being three, Matt took constant maintenance in everything he did, from going to the bathroom to cutting his meat at the dinner table. It only took three weekends of Matt's dirty fingerprints on Roz's walls, for both Roz and Jake to realize how a three year old severely dampens one's life style. During the last tear-filled weekend, Matthew's favorite bedtime companion, a stuffed, cloth Raggedy Andy doll, had his red string hair ripped off by Roz's family dog. The tragedy had been made worse by Jake unceremoniously throwing Matt's bedtime buddy in the garbage. Matthew, traumatized by Jake's complete lack of empathy and his adamant refusal to retrieve Andy from the garbage pile, had snuck the damaged doll from garbage heap in the middle of the night, and hid it in his overnight bag for a safe trip home. After returning, Matthew only wanted two things. One was to have Andy's hair fixed, and two, to never go to "Daddy Jake's" again. A little glue helped with Matt's first request and the second, with the grace of God, took care of itself. The next day Jake called and said that he and Roz had decided Matthew was still too young for weekend visits. They'd come to the conclusion that it would be best if things were put on hold until he was five. Ecstatic, I'd agreed and hung up the phone taking comfort in knowing that, for the time being, Matthew would be out of harms way.

From just after Jake and Roz's marriage in late September of '77 until now, an approximately eighteen month odyssey of court appointed counseling had occurred. Once you get into the system there is no getting out. The court decides when enough is enough. It had been a costly and time consuming process but from our point of view, the whole court mess had been worth it. Overall, Jake had behaved himself since all of the court ordered counseling had begun, and overt hostilities between the three of us had begun to lessen. Thank God, there were no more "wild rides" to or from Michigan and no more terrifying overnights for the kids, alone with his mother in the Michigan house. However, a certain amount of underlying turmoil still remained. Constant irritation as to whether or not Jake would drop the kids at their catechism class, little league game, or latest extracurricular activity, when one of them fell on his weekend, was a crap shoot. It was a continuous stress on the kids. Jake didn't seem to think that any of those things were important and the courts felt that he was entitled to his view of child rearing.

Initial psychological evaluations of all concerned had started in late October of '77 with three trips to a court appointed, private family counselor in downtown Chicago. After that it had taken an additional seven months for sessions to be scheduled with the court sponsored "Family Reconciliation Services". Those sessions had sporadically continued until today.

Through the whole counseling experience it had been my contention that Jake was an active alcoholic, who when drunk, had demonstrated a capability for violence, and therefore, his visitation with the boys should be kept under the strict supervision of the court. Jake had a different explanation.

Because my contentions had no "concrete" evidence attached to them, no police records or medical records, I'd found out last month at our last session with Mr. Reagan, that he was leaning to Jake's interpretation of the situation! I couldn't believe it! He had believed Jake and not me!

"Some counselor this guy is." I'd thought when I'd found out. "He can't even tell a lying drunk when he sees one! You'd think that he'd seen a million of them in his years with the court."

You had to hand it to Jake. His side of the story made me fit the classic profile of a spurned woman. He had an uncanny ability to perceive the things that a person would believe, and say them, to get his way in order to survive. And within the male dominated power structure of the court system, a vindictive ex-wife who was overly sensitive to alcohol use because of a childhood with an alcoholic father, and who was trying to extol revenge at the price of her children and the court system, was a believable personality profile for Mr. Reagan.

Well, now I had the proof in my hand, who was the liar here. Five more minutes and Mr. Reagan would get a big surprise! I had our "old" friend and lawyer, James, to thank for that. Just before last Christmas, after our last appointment with the reconciliation service, Art and I were beginning to get the idea that Reagan was siding with Jake. We had asked James if he could get someone to run a report on Jake, to see if he had been a "good boy" over the last two years, and we had hit paydirt! There were two notable arrests. One was for carrying an unlicensed hand gun in his car in the state of Michigan, and the other was a report on a domestic dispute. The former was bad enough, but the latter was really distressing.

It seems that just after Roz and Jake had gotten married, the local police were summoned by two children to an apartment, where the kids had said that their mother was being beaten by some guy in a drunken rage. When the cops broke down the door, there was Jake and Roz, both naked as jaybirds on the front room floor. He was mounted on top of her, beating the hell out of her in between thrusts. The animal was raping his own wife! It had taken awhile to get the copies of the report but now I had it, and the police report had all the gory details.

"Hello Mr. and Mrs. Brauer. How are things going today?" Mr. Reagan offhandedly inquired, as he opened the door to his office, and we both stepped inside. "Please take a seat."

"Mr. Reagan," I said as Art and I sat down. "I have something to show you, something that will set things straight, as far as what has been going on in this office for the last year and half."

Slipping the paper over the highly polished surface of Reagan's desk, he picked it up and began to read. I took great pleasure in seeing his smug expression transform into a look of surprise, astonishment, and then fear, as he finally grasped the true situation.

"He fooled me! I can't believe it... He fooled me! This means he's a pathological liar... And he's a good one too! Why the implications of this... You've been telling the truth all along! Oh my God, he could be a real sociopath! Do you know what that means, what a danger he could be to you or the kids?"

"No kidding!" was all that I could say.

❧ LIII ❧

This time would be different. This time he wouldn't get away with it. This time he was charged by the state with assault and the state's attorney's office was prosecuting him in criminal court. It wasn't just a civil case. It wasn't like the fiasco last January with Mr. Reagan from the court reconciliation service. Even after he had the evidence of how sick Jake was and how violent he could be, in his hands, it hadn't really made a difference. It turned out that nothing which was said or produced during the counseling sessions could be used by either party in the court room. All that was able to be submitted to the court record was a letter from Reagan, stating that, he'd recommended Jake's visitation should be overseen by a person established by the court as suitable. Roz was still considered to be an upstanding wife and mother, and her presence during the visitation was enough for the letter of the law to be satisfied.

James, our lawyer friend, had explained things to me on the day that, in frustration I'd commented about it being better for the boys if Jake would just shoot me. I'd thought, that would surely stop his bi-monthly weekends.

"No, you don't understand. Art would still have to take them to the jail so that Jake could see them." James said with a sardonic smile. "You see, Jake's record only establishes his violent behavior towards women, not children. In the eyes of the law, because he's never physically abused the kids, his rights as a father cannot be curtailed. In its quest to be just, the law isn't always fair."

In the long run, however, we'd been lucky. After the court counselors were done, things had remained quiet. Then had followed a year of on again, off again, weekend visitation. If the boys had some sports or school activity that they'd wanted to go to, Jake would rather cancel the weekend than drop them off at school or show up for a game. I'd guessed that he'd thought he was in some way punishing them, or that supporting the kids in their endeavors was too much of an inconvenience. Either way, over the last year, his attitude had cut the number of weekends that the boys were forced to go with him, in half. By the spring of 1980, the Little League season had started up again and the boys hadn't seen Jake since Christmas. He'd cancelled all his visits with one excuse or the other, and Eric and Warren, eager not to go with Jake, were enjoying the freedom of living normal lives without him.

As the boys had gotten older and farther removed from Jake's influence, more detailed accounts of the violent, drunken brawls that they'd witnessed between Roz and Jake, on their weekends of "fun", had begun to come to light. Upsetting stories of punishments doled out by Jake to Roz's boys that bordered on abuse, while Eric and Warren watched, were distressing. The realization, that these stories were probably just the tip of the iceberg, deeply troubled me. The boys still had some misplaced loyalty towards Jake. I knew that as his hold on them lessened, the unadulterated truth would eventually be revealed, and then we would all have to face the pain, they'd been made to endure, in the name of a father's rights.

Then, out of the clear blue sky, it had happened. One wonderfully warm and breezy spring day last May, Eric and Warren had been walking home from school. Dean and Keith, anxious to get home to change their clothes and get to the park for baseball practice, had run ahead of the other two boys, and were already inside our house, which was about a block and a half further up the street. Out of nowhere, Jake had appeared in a beat up old pickup truck, and had pulled it close to the sidewalk, where the boys were now standing still, in surprise.

"Hey Eric, get inside. I want to take you for a fucking ride." He'd said and pushed open the passenger door. As the door swung wide, a current of alcohol sodden air whooshed passed the ten-year- old's face.

"No thanks, Dad. Warren and me have to hurry up and get home for practice." Eric had politely answered as he slowly shook his head and backed away from the vehicle.

"C'mon." Jake slurred. "I only want to fucking talk to you." In response, Eric had backed up further from the truck. Jake, infuriated by Eric's refusal, shouted at him, "Get in the fucking truck!"

Warren, who to this point had stood motionless, now began to move towards the truck and Jake. Eric quickly grabbed hold of the back of Warren's shirt and pulled him in the opposite direction.

"No, don't go with him!" Eric said in a harsh whisper, trying to keep his voice low so that Jake couldn't hear him over the noise from the engine. "He's really drunk!" Warren pulled against Eric's hold on his shirt, trying to get out of his grasp. Jake noticed Warren's effort to get free and a look of disgust passed over his face.

"No! I don't fucking want you! I want him!" He bellowed and pointed at Eric.

Instantly wounded by Jake's overt rejection and frightened by his sudden rage, one last tug on Warren's shirt from his brother was enough to set his legs in motion. The two of them sprinted away from the pickup and down the street towards the neighbor's house, leaving Jake alone, and parked awkwardly in the road with his truck door hanging open.

A few frantic bangs on my neighbor Jean's door and a hurried explanation were all that Jean had needed to rush the boys into her house for safe keeping. Within seconds, Jake had pulled into her gravel driveway. When she'd refused to hand over the boys, he'd made quite a scene, spinning his wheels in the stones and spraying them all over her lawn. Then he proceeded to squeal his tires, as he sped off like a maniac down the middle of the street.

The dust from the gravel hadn't settled yet, when I'd driven up to the house with Matthew, Joseph, and a load of groceries in my station wagon. I'd gotten stuck in the checkout line at the grocery store five minutes longer than I'd planned, and as a result, had missed the whole thing.

When I'd pulled up to our house, Dean and Keith shot out of our front screen door, and Eric and Warren came running out of Jean's house from just across the street. Between my children and my neighbor, I'd been quickly brought up to speed.

Fearful that Jake would return, the decision was made not to let any of boys out of my sight for the rest of the day. While they were changing for baseball practice and the groceries were being put away, the phone rang. It was Art. Jake, furious that his plan hadn't panned out, had shown up at the car dealership where Art worked. On his knees in the middle of the cement floor of the shop, overhauling a transmission and engrossed in his thoughts, Art had suddenly become aware of someone standing directly in front of him. He'd looked up to see Jake standing above him.

"I want to fuckin' talk to you outside!" Jake had ordered. Then he'd attempted a quick about face, losing his balance and coming close to falling flat on his butt. Taking a second or two to regain his balance, he'd stalked out through the large overhead door of the service department.

When Art hadn't followed him out through door, but instead had stood looking and laughing at Jake as he'd staggered to his pickup, Jake got into his truck and began to wildly drive around the parking lot, revving his engine, smoking and screeching his tires. It didn't take long for his crazy antics to take their toll on his tired pickup, and there in front of a shit-load of laughing mechanics, he'd dropped his drive shaft in the middle of the asphalt parking lot!

After comparing notes on Jake's sudden whacky behavior, Art and I had agreed that after all the mayhem Jake was probably exhausted, so it was safe to assume that we'd seen the last of him for awhile. However, we were more than a little surprised when, while sitting down with the boys at the table for supper that evening, we'd heard a pounding on the front screen door. Art sprang out of his seat and ran towards the door as the banging continued. It sounded as if the glass louvers in the aluminum door would shatter or the door itself would come off its hinges. Not far behind, I'd peeked out of the front room window while rounding the turn in the living room, going towards the door, and saw Jake's brother-in-law, Billy, pacing uncomfortably out in front of my house. As Art had stuck his head out of the partially opened aluminum door, a choking sound began to emanate from the opening. When I got closer to the doorway I saw that Jake's hands were clenched around Art's neck!

"Call the police!" Art had managed, as he pushed through the door taking the whole scene out to the front porch while Jake continued to attempt to throttle him. Herding our frantic children, who'd followed us from the supper table, back into the kitchen, I'd dialed the police to the tune of Jake's brother-in-law shouting, "Jake! What the fuck are you doing?" floating through the open windows on the early evening breeze.

Commanding that no one leave the boundaries of the kitchen, I'd rushed back to the front door in time to see Art take Jake to the ground. Jake's hands were still clenched around Art's neck, but now,

Art's hands were reciprocated the action, choking Jake as they hit the ground. Both men were red faced and grunting, as Jake had tried in vain to roll Art to his back. Art had wound up sitting on Jake, pinning him to the ground with both of them still clutching each other's throats, as the screaming of sirens rose in the background.

When the cop had rushed out of his squad car, seeing a large man sitting on top of a much smaller one, he'd mistakenly assumed that Art had been the aggressor. He'd pulled out his billy club and raised it, threatening Art with a blow.

"Get off of him!" His voice boomed as two more squads had pulled up in the street, sirens wailing.

Art had instantly complied with the policeman's order by letting go of Jake's neck, thrusting his hands high in the air, and attempting to stand. As Art had stood partially upright with his knees still slightly bent and muscles straining against the effort, Jake's body rose from the gravel driveway and hung like a pendulum, attached by Jake's hands which had remained clamped tightly around Art's neck.

The first policeman now joined by a second, had reacted swiftly, swooping down on Jake as he'd hung suspended beneath Art, prying Jake's hands from Art's bruised and chaffed throat. If Jake had not been in a drunken rage when he'd first jumped on Art, he was certainly in one when they'd pulled him off. He'd wailed, snarled and spit like an animal, while he wrestled with the two cops on the blacktop driveway. It didn't take long for the cops to overpower him and slap a set of cuffs on his wrists. I'd gotten a glimpse of his eyes as he was drug passed me, fighting every inch of the way to the squad car, and no surprise, nobody was home. "Zombie" Jake was in rare form as he tried to bite the cop that pushed him into the back of the cop car.

Now, three months later, Art and I were sitting in the court room waiting for Jake's trial for assault to begin. He was represented by a public defender and had chosen a judge instead of a jury trial.

Stan, one of the cops from the neighborhood, and our friend, came over to where Art and I were sitting with his jaw set and a look of anger and total disbelief on his face.

"The judge ruled that all of that asshole's behavior back at the jail is inadmissible, because it happened after the alleged assault. None of us can testify! I can't believe it! We can't even tell the court what an insane bastard that son-of-a-bitch is!" Stan and two of the cops, who'd arrested Jake and taken him to the jailhouse after the incident in front of our home, had desperately wanted to make sure that Jake got put away. They'd thought that Jake was crazy and dangerous and wanted him to do time. When Jake had been put into a cell at the police station the evening of the assault, he'd screamed for hours that he was going to kill each one of them, calling them by name and threatening them and their families. After an hour or two of shouting and screaming, he'd quieted down and when they went back to see if he was OK, the picture that they saw was beyond belief! Jake had ripped the acoustic tiles down from the ceiling and had stuffed them into the toilet causing the water to overflow and flood the entire backroom of the police station. Furious, the cops had handcuffed Jake to the bars of the cell door. Jake had then proceeded to howl and throw his body into the cell bars like a caged animal, while slicing up the skin around his wrists from all of his wild thrashing against the restraint of the metal cuffs. He'd carried on like that for hours, until he finally passed out. Stan had told us, after witnessing Jake's entire violent display, that in his professional opinion, Jake was one exceptionally crazy mother fucker, who was capable of doing real damage to anyone who got in his way. Something that Art and I already knew, but it was nice that someone else supported our "non-professional" opinion.

"Well that's par for the course!" I said with disgust to Art and Stan as everyone stood up for the entrance of the judge into the courtroom.

Roz and Jake were sitting on the other side of the room, expressionless as the charges were read. Sitting and watching them, every part of me yearned for justice. Finally, I'd thought, he was going to get what he'd deserved after all these years! He'd been so sure that he could get away with anything, that he'd thought he could just walk onto my property and assault my husband without any repercussions. Well, finally he would be taught a lesson!

"Mr. Burke, please rise and approach the bench." The judge began as Jake left his seat and made his way to the front of the room. "It is your contention Mr. Burke, that Mr. and Mrs. Brauer had lured you over to their Chicago Ridge home on the evening in question, on the pretext that there was something that urgently needed to be discussed in regards to your two children, Eric and Warren Burke. Is this true?" Jake nodded in response to the judge's inquiry.

"It is your honor." Jake said.

"And that after you had arrived on the premises, Mrs. Brauer encouraged you to come to the front door of her home where her husband Mr. Brauer was waiting, unseen by you, behind the aluminum storm door. And that when you were sufficiently close to the door, Mr. Brauer reached out and grabbed you by the neck as he yelled for Mrs. Brauer to call the police. And that any physical action on your part that had transpired after Mr. Brauer's initial attack was only made in self defense. Is that also correct?"

"Yes, your honor, it is." Jake said.

I sat frozen in my seat. I couldn't believe my ears. Jake was trying to weasel out of everything and he was doing a damn good job! Couldn't the judge tell it was all bullshit, I thought as I stared at the back of that lousy lying bastard's head.

"Pray tell me Mr. Burke." The judge began again. "Why would Mr. and Mrs. Brauer do such a thing?"

"It was because I wouldn't sign over my kids to them, your honor. Ya' know, so that Mr. Brauer could adopt 'em. A couple of months ago they tried to get me to do it. When I said no way they got real mad and said that they'd get me in trouble if I didn't, and I'd be sorry."

"Do you have any proof that what you are saying is true?" The judge looked up from his notes and stared at Jake.

"Yeah. My ex-wife called me a couple of months ago. That's when she tried to get me to sign the kids over. She didn't know it, but my wife, Roz, was on the extension and heard every word." Jake said staring directly back into the judges eyes.

"Is this so, Mrs. Burke?"

"Yes, your honor. I heard the whole thing." Roz said as sweet as pie from her seat in the front of the courtroom.

"Mrs. Brauer." The judge called my name. "Please come up to the bench."

Stunned by the false testimony, unashamedly sworn to as the truth in open court, I stood speechless in front of the judge.

"Mrs. Brauer, is what your ex-husband and his wife, have testified to in this court, what you believe to be the truth? Did you, indeed, try to blackmail him so that your husband could adopt the children?" The judge's eyes drilled into mine as he asked the question.

"No, your honor. It's all a lie." was all that I could manage to say.

"Do you have anything else that you would like to add?" He asked his eyes still riveted to mine.

I slowly shook my head side to side unable to say another word, looking, I imagined much like a deer in the headlights just before the fatal impact.

"Are there any witnesses to the first blow?" The judge asked the district attorney.

"No, your honor." The district attorney responded for the first and only time, with a tone of disappointment and defeat in his voice.

"Well, as I see it, it is your word against Mr. Burke's, Mrs. Brauer. I have no other choice but to rule that this case is dismissed."

"Oh my God, he got away… got away with it! He lied and he got away with it!" I said to myself in disbelief, as the rap of the gavel signaled the end of the trial and the people standing around me began to file out of the courtroom. Without a hesitation, I walked straight over to Roz who was sitting a few feet from where I'd been standing, with an uncertain smile on her face.

"You wanted him and now you've got him!" I said standing in front of her as she looked up at me. Immediately, the court bailiff appeared out of nowhere, caught hold of my arm and pulled me away and escorted me towards the door. But my message had been clear, and by the look that I saw in her eyes, it had hit home. She had taken my place in hell.

In less than five minutes, Art and I were in the car, driving out of the municipal parking lot and onto the open road, with the windows conspicuously rolled up on a hot August day, and me screaming in the front passenger seat. As the minutes went by, I screamed because he'd perjured himself in court and publicly defamed my good name, and there was nothing that I could do about it. I screamed because he'd walked onto my property, choked my husband and got away with it, like he'd gotten away with every other rotten thing that he'd ever done. And mainly I screamed because life was just not fucking fair! And then I screamed until I could not scream anymore.

Through it all Art drove. Peacefully and lovingly, he just drove.

"Dear God, when is it ever going to be over?" I whimpered like a child as I sat in an exhausted heap in the front seat. I'd thought that I'd become impervious to his crap, but once again Jake had mounted a surprise attack puncturing through my carefully crafted armor, and piercing another deeper, more vital area of my soul.

It was incredulous that one decision made as an eighteen year old kid, had put the wheels of heartache and pain in motion, negatively impacting my life and the lives of everyone connected to me, forever. The ramifications of my foolish teenage decision to marry Jake, was going to fuck everyone's life up until the day we died!

With that thought, a brand new torrent of tears came. Art silently continued to drive, but placed a hand on my knee for a second or two, just to remind me that he was there.

"Damn it! Damn it! Damn it!" In exasperation, I murmured the litany.

"You sound like a victim again. Stop it Susan, just stop it" I rubbed my temples as I thought the whole situation over. "He can't get in unless you let him in! He can't destroy you unless you give him the weapon! Christ! What did it all matter anyway? Does it really make a difference what anyone thinks of you? It doesn't change who you are, not really."

"Sticks and stones can break my bones, but names can never hurt me." I'd reflexively thought, and then laughed through my tears. Who would have ever thought that childhood playground poetry would turn into genuine words of wisdom?

Looking over at Art, knowing how hard he was trying to be there for me, to do whatever I needed him to do, to help make things alright, I smiled. He glanced my way and smiled back. He loved me so much, beyond my wildest hopes and dreams. What incredible luck to have found him! And then there were the boys, my babies. The six of them were our whole lives. Over the last six years we had made a family bonded through love, not blood, which would withstand any onslaught from the outside, a union that would stand for all time. I needed to get myself together, to look at the things that had come my way that were more than fair, and revel in good things instead of despair.

I'd learned a lot over the last few years using the tools from the Program. But the most important lesson learned was that you have a choice in life. Either you allow the fear and disappointment to beat you to the ground becoming life's punching bag, or you change what you can, and deal with the rest. The only way to win is to just keep dancing. Life was like a marathon of will. As long as you're alive and able to see the love and beauty that exists, you're not losing the battle. There were no promises in life. There was no "fair". Just being alive is the gift and it was up to us to realize it.

"Hey baby, are you alright?" Art asked, noticing that my tears had finally subsided.

"Yeah. I think that it's time to go home." I said.

"Yeah." I smiled and thought to myself. "When the shit hits the fan, you just keep dancing!"

❧ LIV ❧

The sheets fluttered in the warm early September breeze and shone a shockingly iridescent white against the deep blue sky. Whenever I hung the bed sheets out on a beautiful day like today, and watched them billow in the wind, pleasant thoughts of Momma would fill up my mind. The sight of the brilliant white against the crystal blue sky, the fresh smell of the bleach, and the popping of the corners of the sheets as they flapped in the tiny puffs of air, were snippets of life that when taken all together, propelled me back in time, to see Momma's smiling face and hear her gentle laugh. "How long had it been since we had to say our sad goodbyes? She had died on January 18, 1968 and... what was today? Well... today is Saturday, so that means it must be the 8th of September. And sixty-eight from eighty-four is sixteen years, last January. That's a long time." I thought, involuntarily letting out a big sigh.

The only time that I hung laundry, anymore, was on a beautiful day like today, and that was mainly as a treat for Art and the boys, to make their sheets smell fresh and clean. Art had hung a couple of lines for me in the backyard and I had a bag full of old clothes pins. I didn't even mind hanging some of the other clothes while I was at it. It was kind of cathartic. Besides, sheets out of the dryer never smelled like the ones hung outside on the line. With the summer coming close to an end, this might be one of my last opportunities to sleep on great smelling sheets.

After hanging the first sheet, I stuck my hand into my old clothespin bag, and looking at the fabric, was amazed at how long it had lasted. I'd gotten this bag and the clothespins inside of it for a shower gift, for my wedding to Jake. It seemed kind of ironic that an inexpensive piece of cloth filled with wood should still be around, when my mother wasn't… and neither was Jake. Boy, life never turns out the way that you think that it will.

Eric and Warren had refused to go with Jake for visitation, immediately after he'd tried to snatch them from school and strangle Art in the driveway. As it turned out, Jake had never tried to contact the boys after the incident and nothing had changed after the assault charges were dismissed in court. It seemed that we'd reached some kind of a truce. Jake didn't try to contact the kids and we didn't try to sue him for back child support. As far as we knew, he'd remained unemployed. Even if he was working, Art and I would rather have the boys safe than take his lousy money.

We'd heard rumors, from time to time, over the last four years. Some of the stories had been pretty bizarre and led us to believe that Jake's disease and his capacity for violence while drunk or high, was escalating. Everything from shooting the windows out of his station wagon with a shotgun from the roof of Roz's house, to burning a neighborhood business down to the ground when he and the owner had a falling out, were topics of discussion from one reliable source or another. We'd even gotten some frightening warnings from our friends in the Program. During the year or so before Jake and Roz had separated, Jake had become severely depressed and he'd continually fantasized that the solution to all his problems was doing away with Art, Dean, Keith, and Joseph, so that he and I could live happily ever after! And so the story goes, that one night he'd actually left Roz's house with a loaded rifle, to travel the five minutes to my house to accomplish his dream. Roz had called one of my friends in Al-Anon to warn us of the impending doom, but as luck would have it, the boys, and Art and I, were at the drive-in movies at the time. We never did find out whether or not Jake had actually made the trip to our house. But after that night, Art and I had repositioned our bed so that if Jake did happen to get the bright idea to try the whole thing, one more time, we'd have a better chance of survival if he pointed a gun through our bedroom window.

As crazy as it seems, there was no protection available to us under the law. All the rumors that we'd heard had been just that, and as far as the prospect of Roz helping us to prove that Jake was dangerous, that was just plain out of the question. She was even more afraid of him than I'd been, so the only choice for us was to be careful, and put our lives in God's hands. I guess that after having to cope with the specter of Jake for so long, we'd developed a thick skin when it came to worrying about things that might be.

Despite the occasional wacky Jake, horror story, life had settled down. Our two oldest boys, Dean and Eric were sophomores in high school, and Warren had just spent his first week as a freshmen.

Keith was in eighth, Matthew was in fifth, and Joseph, our baby, was already in second grade. Everyone was doing well in school and each child was engaged in one sport activity or another. Jake had been out of all our lives for over four years, and life was good.

I'd gone back to school and had done very well. I was within a couple of classes from completing my Associate in Science from the local community college. With a straight "A" average, I even had dreams of becoming an electrical engineer! That was another thing, about which, Jake had been completely wrong. I was not stupid!

A little over a year ago, we'd heard that Jake had left Roz. He'd moved to the house in Michigan to take care of his mother while his father had continued to work in Chicago. The arrangement had conjured up all kinds of strange images, since both he and his mother suffered from the same addiction. Maybe Jake's dad was hoping that if Jake lived in Michigan for awhile, he'd shake off his depression and get his life back together again. It certainly had been good news for all of us. Oh well...

Placing another sheet on the clothes line, I thought how odd it was that after such a long time of Jake being out of sight and out of mind, he'd been on my mind a lot this morning. From inside the house, I heard the muffled ring of the kitchen phone.

"Mom, phone for you! It sounds like Aunt Marie." Eric called out through the open back screen door.

"Tell her I'll be there in a minute." I called back.

"Gee, haven't talked to her in quite awhile." I commented to myself as I finished hanging the last sheet that had been left in the white plastic laundry basket. Despite everything that had happened, Jake's sister and I were still relatively close. "God, I hope it's not Jake's mother acting up again!"

The contrast of walking from the bright, sunshine filled backyard, through the back door and into the subdued kitchen light, resulted in an instant dampening of my rather pleasant mood. And the prospect of having to deal with Jake's family's problems didn't help much either.

"Hi, Marie. What's up?" I asked, trying to keep the tone in my voice friendly and cheerful.

"Susan, Jake's dead!"

❧ LV ❧

Sitting in the Funeral Home in Ann Harbor Michigan, I still couldn't believe it was all real. Jake was dead. When we'd first heard the news Art hadn't believed it. In our judgment, Jake had demonstrated that he'd degenerated into a "super" bad guy, and one really sick son-of-a-bitch. His crazy escapades in violence and cruelty had so often, far exceeded our imaginings about what he would or could do, that Art was ready to believe anything was possible when it came to Jake. The prospect that Jake had faked his own death had crossed Art's mind. It would be one way for Jake to assume that he could enact his plan to murder the kids and Art, without any ramifications. Considering we'd heard through the grapevine that he'd been fantasizing about the plan for years, Art's idea hadn't seemed so farfetched.

As it turned out, we didn't have to worry about having doubts because Marie had insisted on an open casket, in spite of the way he'd died. Consequently, it had taken the funeral director an a day to prepare the body for "viewing" during services. Jake had not gone quietly into the

Saturday, September 8, 1984, at 4:00 in the Jake, who for some unknown reason, had g on the pavement in the middle of U.S. 30, just outside of South Bend ddenly stood up. A man driving a late scort had seen him at the last second, popping up out of nowhere, and unable to react in time, had hit him going about seventy miles an hour. Jake's body had totaled his car. It had bounced from the bumper, to the hood, to the roof, and onto the pavement again, winding up in a broken mangled heap on the asphalt behind the vehicle. According to the coroner, Jake had died instantly, and drunk. The injuries to his face and head had been extensive, hence the reluctance of the funeral director to have an open casket for the memorial service.

The body in the casket didn't look at all like Jake, even though the mortician had done his best. But I knew it was him. It was his hands. Evidently they, or at least the one that was showing, had escaped the carnage of the accident. One look at his hands as they lay peacefully folded on the body, had told me that the lifeless corpse in the royal blue, paisley print, economy model coffin in front of me, was Jake.

Jake's body had been waked for one day. One day had been more than enough. I would have been very surprised if the sum total of the people, who had come to pay their respects to Jake and his family yesterday, had numbered more than half a dozen. There had been a few, long time neighbors from the Michigan house that had come by, along with the last two people, that we knew of, who had seen Jake alive. The motorcycle couple had been sitting with Jake in a local biker bar for the better part of a day. They had been watching Jake chug down, in their estimation, over a fifth of booze when two unsavory characters had walked into the bar. According to the couple, after a few minu animated conversation, Jake had left with the "strangers" and of course, the rest was history. No one had any idea how or why Jake had wound up twelve hours later, over fifty miles away, laying in the middle of the highway. That would probably remain a mystery for the rest of our lives.

Jake's "wife", Roz, and his stepchildren hadn't shown up. She had sent a small basket of daisies, and they were placed beside the casket along with the floral displays from his parents, sister, and us. Other than that, the chapel was bare.

It was understandable why Roz hadn't made an appearance. After all, her court date for her divorce from Jake had been scheduled for this Friday. Marie and Roz had not turned out to be friends once she had become Jake's new wife. So when Marie had called on the day that Jake had died, I'd understood completely her refusal to contact "that woman" to tell her the shocking news. It was obvious that someone had to do it, and because I had Roz's phone number, I'd volunteered.

I'll never forget the dead silence on the other end of the phone line after Roz had heard the news, and then the torrent of emotion that had followed.

"Thank God! Thank God he is dead!" She'd cried.

"I can't believe it's true! No more being afraid! I was so afraid... for myself... for my kids. We're finally safe!" She's said these short, clipped words punctuated by bursts of, close to hysterical sobbing.

For a fleeting instant, I'd felt some kinship with the woman who had been my enemy. She had been his new butterfly, and now she'd been set free.

The burial was to be this morning, after a short nondenominational memorial service was conducted by the funeral director. Even though the funeral parlor room where Jake was being waked was small, it looked conspicuously empty of mourners, sad but a testament to the impact that Jake had made on other people's lives. Jake's mother had not attended any part of the service. Marie had remarked that her mother hadn't coped with the whole thing very well, and that it was best for her to stay at home. Jake's dad, Marie and Jerry, Art and I, and the six boys sat silent and alone, waiting for the service to begin. In an unspoken agreement, we'd grouped together in the back of the room, as far away from the open casket as possible.

The funeral director stepped into the room. He solemnly walked up to the front and stood a few feet in front of the coffin and began to deliver his canned eulogy, which I was sure, was written for just this type of situation. While he droned on about death and sorrow, I shifted my attention to my children.

I looked at the four older boys who were sitting in front of Art and me, and thought of the two littlest ones, who were sitting at our sides, and wondered how Jake being in all their lives had and would influence each one. For those who had not experienced Jake firsthand, it had been a sure thing that they had gotten caught in the emotional fallout of the family turmoil, caused by the threat of Jake and his actions. And for those, who had known Jake all too well, Art and I knew that despite all our efforts, there had been damage done. For all, I prayed that with love, good example, strong family ties, and time, the import of bad "things" that had happened in the past, would fade away.

In the nine and a half years that we had been a family, I had seen my four oldest sons grow into young men. Their strength, kindness, and ability to love each other, were a direct result of the tools for living and growth that I'd learned in the Program, and Art's nurturing guidance and unconditional love.

Taking comfort in our closeness as we all sat together, brought me to the realization that the threat of Jake had cemented our family together, instead of pulling us apart.

"Even out of the worst of things, good can come." I thought.

In the silence, I reflected on my life with Jake, the few good times and the bad, and I questioned if it was fair. I stared at his body and couldn't help but wonder.

"Jake, how did you get to this?"

I guess you could say all the old platitudes seemed to reaffirm that it was fair… Live by the sword and die by the sword… What goes around comes around… You reap what you sow.

I had to admit that I felt just like Roz, I was glad that "me and mine" would never have to be afraid of "zombie" Jake, again. By the grace of God, the saga of pain and suffering, both ours and Jake's, was over.

Then another old platitude came to mind. Whatever doesn't kill you makes you stronger… And I concluded that it was so. I had survived Jake, we all had, and in order to do that I had to stop being a victim and learn how to take control of my life. I had to stop wailing about the things that I couldn't change and do something about the things that I could. Because of Jake, I had been forced to view the world differently, and in doing so, I had opened myself up to its beauty. The day that he had left me and the kids, he had given us our lives back on a silver platter. Surviving him had made it possible for me to be ready to learn what love really meant, and share it with my soul mate, Art. Jake had also taught me the most important lesson of all. No matter what life has to offer, it NEVER gets the best of you, as long as you just keep dancing.

Refocusing my attention from Jake's body in the casket to the funeral director, I realized that the service was coming to an end. He was leading us in the "Lord's Prayer".

"…And lead us not into temptation, but deliver us from evil. For Thine is the kingdom, and the power, and the glory, for ever and ever. Amen." We all finished.

"And now…" the funeral director continued "could I have the pallbearers please rise."

I watched as Jerry, slowly stood up and began to walk to the center aisle. Then, my four sons, Dean, Eric, Warren and Keith, silently stood up in unison and followed by their father, my husband Art, made their way to the front of the room and stood next to the coffin, ready to take on and share their heavy load…

"What doesn't kill you makes you stronger." I thought as they lifted the casket between the six of them and carried Jake out the side door to the waiting hearse.

"I guess…" I softly said to myself. "Sometimes, there is justice in this world."

NOTES

NOTES (Continued)

The Honeymooners:
Staring Jackie Gleason
CBS 1955 - 1956

The Prisoner:
Staring Patrick McGoohan
Copyright 1961 ITC Entertainment Ltd (now
PolyGramTelevision Ltd)

The Phil Donahue:
Staring Phil Donahue
1969 - 1974

The Wizard of Oz:
MGM 1939
Turner Entertainment Co. ©1998

(You're My) Soul & Inspiration:
Recorded by The Righteous Brothers 1966 (Mann-
Weil)

X Minus One:
1955-1958
By Ray Bradbury and Earl Hamner, Jr
Produced and Directed by
 Danny Sutter, Ed King, Fred Weihe